THE *Five* LOVE LANGUAGES OF YOUR FAMILY

TWO BESTSELLERS IN ONE VOLUME

GARY CHAPMAN

with ROSS CAMPBELL *(The Five Love Languages of Children)*

NORTHFIELD PUBLISHING
CHICAGO

This Special International Edition
© 2009

This is a combination of
Five Love Languages of Children
© 1997, 2005, 2012 by
GARY CHAPMAN and
ROSS CAMPBELL
and
Five Love Languages of Teenagers
© 2000, 2005, 2010 by
GARY CHAPMAN

All Scripture quotations, unless otherwise indicated, are taken from the *Holy Bible, New International Version®*. NIV®. Copyright © 1973, 1978, 1984 by International Bible Society. Used by permission of Zondervan. All rights reserved.

Scripture quotations marked NKJV are taken from the *New King James Version.* Copyright © 1982 by Thomas Nelson, Inc. Used by permission. All rights reserved.

Editors: Randall J. Pagleitner and Elizabeth Cody Newenhuyse
Interior and Cover Design: Smartt Guys design
Cover and Author photos: See each book's copyright page

The 5 Love Languages® is a registered trademark of The Moody Bible Institute of Chicago.

ISBN: 978-0-8024-1333-8

We hope you enjoy this book from Northfield Publishing. Our goal is to provide high-quality, thought-provoking books and products that connect truth to your real needs and challenges. For more information on other books and products written and produced from a biblical perspective, go to www.moodypublishers.com or write to:

Northfield Publishing
820 N. LaSalle Boulevard
Chicago, IL 60610

3 5 7 9 10 8 6 4

Printed in the United States of America

The 5 Love Languages of Children

The 5 Love Languages of Children

GARY CHAPMAN, PhD
ROSS CAMPBELL, MD

NORTHFIELD PUBLISHING

CHICAGO

Library of Congress Cataloging-in-Publication Data

Chapman, Gary D.
  The 5 love languages of children / Gary Chapman & Ross Campbell.
    p. cm.
  Includes bibliographical references.
  ISBN 978-0-8024-0347-6
  1. Child rearing. 2. Parenting--Psychological aspects. 3. Love.
  I. Campbell, Ross II. Title. III. Title: Five love languages of children.
  HQ769.C395 2012
  649'.1—dc23

                                              2011036535

Edited by Elizabeth Cody Newenhuyse

Cover and interior design: Smartt Guys design
Gary Chapman photo: Mike Apple
Ross Campbell photo: Boyce Shore and Associates
Cover photo: boots: Ivonne Wierink / 123RF
                    flowers: Norman Kin Hang Chan / 123RF

We hope you enjoy this book from Northfield Publishing.
Our goal is to provide high-quality, thought-provoking books and
products that connect truth to your real needs and challenges.
For more information on other books and products written and produced
from a biblical perspective, go to moodypublishers.com or write to:

Northfield Publishing
820 N. LaSalle Boulevard
Chicago, IL 60610

contents

THE 5 LOVE LANGUAGES OF CHILDREN

physical touch

words of affirmation

quality time

gifts

acts of service

speaking your child's love language

"LOL." "Sweet!" "BFF." Our children at times speak a language we may not, at first, fully understand. And they don't always understand what we say. But of all the ways we misunderstand one another, perhaps the most harmful is to not properly communicate love to our children. Can you speak—and do you speak—your child's love language?

Every child has a primary language of love, a way in which he or she understands a parent's love best. This book will show you how to recognize and speak your child's primary love language as well as the four other love languages that can help your child know you love him or her. As we will see, your child needs to *know* he is loved in order to grow into a giving, loving, responsible adult.

The 5 Love Languages of Children will introduce you to all five love languages of children and help you determine the primary languages in which your child hears your love. Be careful to read all five chapters (2–6) that describe the love languages, as your child will benefit from all five ways of receiving love. Yes, we believe your child perceives your love best from one of the five languages, but the other four ways of showing your love also will benefit him. Besides, over time, your child's primary love language may change.

For these reasons, each chapter on the love languages will begin by pointing out the importance of that specific love language for your child. Even though that chapter may not describe your child's primary love language, learn to speak that language as well. Practice all five love languages and you can be sure your child will sense your love. To help you do this, each of these chapters ends with practical ideas for helping you speak that love language with your children.

In this book we will emphasize the importance of love in rearing your child. The ultimate goal is to rear your child (or children) to become a mature adult. All aspects of a child's development require a foundation of love. As a book about learning to better love your child, *The 5 Love Languages of Children* includes suggestions throughout for good parenting. As you work on those areas that are most important, you will find that your family relationships will be stronger and also more relaxed and enjoyable. For instance, in our discussion of discipline (chapter 8), you will learn that two key words to keep foremost in your mind are *kind* and *firm*. Just as love covers a multitude of sins, so being kind but firm will cover a multitude of parenting challenges.

But how can you figure out your child's love language? Chapter 7 has many ideas. And to help you get to know your child even better—and have some fun with them along the way—look for the "Love Language Mystery Game" at the back of the book on page 218.

And now, some personal words from each of us as you begin this "language course" to improve the way you speak love to your children.

a word from *Gary*

The success of *The 5 Love Languages: The Secret to Love That Lasts* has been gratifying. Millions of couples have not only read the book, but have practiced its principles. My files are filled with letters from couples all over the world expressing gratitude for the difference the love languages have made in their marriages. Most tell me that learning the primary love language of their spouse has made a radical change in the emotional climate of their home, and some have credited the book with actually saving their marriage.

This book grew out of the many requests I received to "write a book on the five love languages of children." Because my professional career has focused on marriage counseling and enrichment, I was reluctant at first to write about children, even though I received hundreds of reports from parents who applied the concept of the love languages to their children.

When Northfield Publishing talked with me about doing such a book, I contacted my friend of many years, Ross Campbell, to ask him to coauthor the book with me. To my delight, Ross agreed. Ross has spent many years in psychiatric medicine, with a focus on the needs of children and adolescents. I have long admired the quality of his work, have profited from his writing, and have appreciated our personal contact through the years.

Just as the original book on love languages has helped so many people in their marriages, so now I hope and pray that this book will aid countless parents, teachers, and others who love and work with children to become more effective in meeting the emotional need children have for love.

Gary Chapman, PhD
Winston-Salem, North Carolina

a word from Ross

Gary Chapman and I have both devoted our careers to writing and speaking about love. Gary has been helping thousands of couples find deeper meaning in their relationships, while I have been writing and leading seminars for parents in their critically vital but wonderfully rewarding tasks of rearing their children. Even though I have known Gary for decades, I had not realized that our messages were so similar. I discovered this positive fact when I read his meaningful book *The 5 Love Languages*. The parallels to my books, *How to Really Love Your Child* and *How to Really Love Your Teenager,* were supportive and encouraging.

The emphasis I particularly liked in Gary's book was that each of us has a primary love language. If we identify this particular love language in our spouse and also in ourselves, we can use this priceless knowledge to enhance our marriage. There are wonderful applications of this for children, because each child has his or her own way of giving and receiving love. As Gary became aware of this, the present book was a natural outcome of the similarities in our work.

I am grateful for the privilege of working with Gary on this critically important book. I sincerely believe it will help parents and others who care about children to fill the deepest needs of the children they love. Please join us on this journey as we explore the five love languages of children.

Ross Campbell, MD
Signal Mountain, Tennessee

love is the foundation

Brad and Emily couldn't figure out what was wrong with Caleb, their eight-year-old son. He had been an above-average learner and still did his homework, but this year he was struggling in school. He would go to the teacher after she had given an exercise and ask her to explain it again. He'd visit her desk up to eight times a day, asking for further instructions. Was it poor hearing or a comprehension problem? Brad and Emily had Caleb's hearing tested, and a school counselor gave him a comprehension test. His hearing was normal and his understanding typical for a third-grader.

Other things about their son puzzled them. At times, Caleb's behavior seemed almost antisocial. The teacher would take turns eating with her third-grade students during lunch, but Caleb would sometimes push other children aside so he could be near her. During recess, he would leave other children whenever the teacher appeared on the playground, running to her to ask an insignificant question and escape the others. If the teacher participated in a game during recess, Caleb would try to hold the teacher's hand during the game.

His parents had met with the teacher three times already, and neither they nor the teacher could find the problem. Independent and happy in grades one and two, Caleb now seemed to show "clinging behavior" that made no sense. He also was fighting much more with his older sister Hannah, although Emily and Brad assumed that was just a stage he was passing through.

When this couple came to my "The Marriage You've Always Wanted" seminar and told me about Caleb, they were worried, wondering if they had a budding rebel on their hands. "Dr. Chapman, we know this is a marriage seminar and maybe our question is out of place," Emily said, "but Brad and I thought that perhaps you could give us some guidance." Then she described her son's worrisome behavior.

I asked these parents whether their own lifestyle had changed this year. Brad said he was a salesman, out on calls two nights a week, but home between 6:00 and 7:30 p.m. on the other weeknights. Those nights were spent catching up on emails and texts and watching a little TV. On weekends, he used to go to football games, often taking Caleb. But he hadn't done that in a year. "It's just too much of a hassle. I'd rather watch the games on TV."

"How about you, Emily?" I asked. "Have there been any changes in your lifestyle over the last few months?"

"Definitely," she said. "I've been working part-time at the college for the last three years since Caleb entered kindergarten. But this year I took a full-time job there, so I get home later than usual. Actually my mom picks him up at school, and Caleb stays with her for about an hour and a half until I pick him up. On the evenings that Brad is out of town, Caleb and I usually have dinner with my folks and then come home."

It was almost time for the seminar session to begin, yet I sensed I was beginning to understand what was going on inside of Caleb. So I made a suggestion. "I'm going to be talking about marriage, but I want each of you to be thinking about how the principles I am sharing might apply to your relationship with Caleb. At the end of the seminar, I'd like to know what conclusions you have drawn." They seemed a little surprised that I was ending our conversation without making any suggestions, but they both were willing to go along with my request.

At the end of the day, as other participants at our seminar were filing out, Brad and Emily hurried up to me with that look of fresh discovery. "Dr. Chapman, I think we have just gained some insight into what's going on with Caleb," Emily said. "When you were discussing the five love languages, we both agreed that Caleb's primary love language is *quality time*. Looking back over the last four or five months, we realized that we have given him less quality time than we had before.

"When I was working part-time, I'd pick him up from school every day, and we would usually do something together on the way home, maybe run an errand or stop by the park or get ice cream together. When we got home, Caleb would play games for a while. Then after dinner, I would often help him with his homework or we'd watch something on TV, especially on the nights Brad was away. All that has changed since I started my new job, and I realize I'm spending less time with Caleb."

I glanced at Brad, and he said, "For my part, I realize I used to take Caleb with me to football games, but since I stopped going, I haven't replaced that father-son time with anything. He and I haven't really spent a great deal of time together the last few months."

"I think you may have discovered some real insight into Caleb's emotional need," I told them. "If you can meet his need for love, I think there is a good chance you will see a change in his behavior." I suggested some key ways to express love through quality time and challenged Brad to build time with Caleb into his schedule. I encouraged Emily to look for ways she and Caleb could once more do some of the things they did before she started her full-time job. They both seemed eager to translate their insight into action.

"There may be other factors involved," I said, "but if you will give your son large doses of quality time and then sprinkle in the other four love languages, I think you will see a radical change in his behavior."

We said good-bye. I never heard from Emily and Brad, and to be honest, I forgot about them. But about two years later I returned to Wisconsin for another seminar, and they walked in and reminded me of our conversation. They were all smiles; we hugged each other, and they introduced me to friends they had invited to the seminar.

"Tell me about Caleb," I said.

They both smiled and said, "He's doing great. We meant to write you many times but never got around to it. We went home and did what you suggested. We consciously gave Caleb lots of quality time over the next few months. Within two or three weeks, really, we saw a dramatic change in his behavior at school. In fact, the teacher asked us to come in again, and we were worried. But this time, she wanted to ask what we had done that had brought about such a change in Caleb."

The teacher told them that Caleb's inappropriate behavior had stopped: no more pushing other children away from her in the lunchroom; no more coming to her desk to ask question after question. Then Emily explained that her husband and she had begun to speak Caleb's "love language" after attending a seminar. "We told her how we had started giving him overdoses of quality time," said Emily.

This couple had learned to speak their son's love language, to say

"I love you" in a way that Caleb could understand. His story encouraged me to write this book.

Speaking your child's primary love language does not mean he or she will not rebel later. It does mean your child will know you love him, and that can bring him security and hope; it can help you to rear your child to responsible adulthood. Love is the foundation.

> You may **truly love** your child, but unless she **feels it**— she will not feel **loved.**

In raising children, everything depends on the love relationship between the parent and child. Nothing works well if a child's love needs are not met. Only the child who *feels* genuinely loved and cared for can do her best. You may truly love your child, but unless she feels it—unless you speak the love language that communicates to her your love—she will not feel loved.

Filling the Emotional Tank

By speaking your child's own love language, you can fill his "emotional tank" with love. When your child feels loved, he is much easier to discipline and train than when his "emotional tank" is running near empty.

Every child has an emotional tank, a place of emotional strength that can fuel him through the challenging days of childhood and adolescence. Just as cars are powered by reserves in the gas tank, our children are fueled from their emotional tanks. We must fill our children's emotional tanks for them to operate as they should and reach their potential.

But with what do we fill these tanks? Love, of course, but love of a particular kind that will enable our children to grow and function properly.

We need to fill our children's emotional tanks with unconditional love, because real love is always unconditional. Unconditional love is a full love that accepts and affirms a child for who he is, not for what he does. No matter what he does (or does not do), the parent still loves him. Sadly, some parents display a love that is conditional; it depends on something other than their children just being. Conditional love is based on performance and is often associated with training techniques that offer gifts, rewards, and privileges to children who behave or perform in desired ways.

Of course, it is necessary to train and discipline our children—but only after their emotional tanks have been filled (and refilled—they can deplete regularly). Only unconditional love can prevent problems such as resentment, feelings of being unloved, guilt, fear, and insecurity. Only as we give our children unconditional love will we be able to deeply understand them and deal with their behaviors, whether good or bad.

Molly remembers growing up in a home of modest financial resources. Her father was employed nearby and her mother was a homemaker, except for a small part-time job. Both parents were hardworking people who took pride in their house and family. Molly's dad cooked the evening meal, and he and Molly cleaned up the kitchen together. Saturday was a day for weekly chores, and Saturday nights they enjoyed hot dogs or burgers together. On Sunday mornings, the family went to church and that evening they would spend time with relatives.

When Molly and her brother were younger, their parents read to them almost every day. Now that they were in school, Mom and Dad encouraged them in their studies. They wanted both children to attend college, even though they did not have this opportunity themselves.

In junior high, one of Molly's friends at school was Stephanie. The two had most classes together and often shared lunch. But the girls didn't visit each other at home. If they had, they would have seen vast differences. Stephanie's father was a successful execu-tive who was able to provide generously for the family. He was also away from home most of the time. Stephanie's mother was a nurse. Her brother was away at a private school. Stephanie had also been sent to a boarding school for three years until she begged to attend the local public school. With her father out of town and her mother working so much, the family often went out for meals.

Molly and Stephanie were good friends until the ninth grade, when Stephanie went off to a college-prep school near her grandpar-ents. The first year, the girls exchanged letters; after that, Stephanie began dating and the letters became less frequent and then stopped. Molly formed other friendships and then started dating a guy who transferred to her school. After Stephanie's family moved away, Molly never heard from her again.

If she had, she would have been sad to know that after marrying and having one child, Stephanie was arrested as a drug dealer and spent several years in prison, during which time her husband left her. In contrast, Molly was happily married with two children.

What made the difference in the outcome of two childhood friends? Although there is no one answer, we can see part of the rea-son in what Stephanie once told her therapist: "I never felt loved by my parents. I first got involved in drugs because I wanted my friends to like me." In saying this, she wasn't trying to lay blame on her par-ents as much as she was trying to understand herself.

Did you notice what Stephanie said? It wasn't that her parents didn't love her, but that she did not feel loved. Most parents love their children and also want their children to feel loved, but few know *how* to adequately convey that feeling. It is only as they learn how to love unconditionally that they will let their children know how much they are truly loved.

A Word of Hope

Raising emotionally healthy children is an increasingly difficult task these days. The influence of media, the cultural push for kids to grow up quickly, the violence and drugs that plague some communities—not to mention the fact that many parents are struggling economically—challenge families daily.

It is into such stark reality that we speak a word of hope to parents. We want you to enjoy a loving relationship with your children. Our focus in this book is on one exceedingly important aspect of parenting—meeting your children's need for love. We have written this book to help you give your children a greater experience of the love you have for them. This will happen as you speak the love languages they understand and can respond to.

Every child has a special way of perceiving love. There are five ways children (indeed, all people) speak and understand emotional love. They are *physical touch*, *words of affirmation*, *quality time*, *gifts*, and *acts of service*. If you have several children in your family, chances are they speak different languages, for just as children often have different personalities, they may hear in different love languages. Typically, two children need to be loved in different ways.

Whatever love language your child understands best, he needs it expressed in one way—unconditionally. Unconditional love is a guiding light, illuminating the darkness and enabling us as parents to know where we are and what we need to do as we raise our child. Without this kind of love, parenting is bewildering and confusing. Before we explore the five love languages, let's consider the nature and importance of unconditional love.

We can best define unconditional love by showing what it does. Unconditional love shows love to a child *no matter what*. We love regardless of what the child looks like; regardless of her assets, liabilities, or handicaps; regardless of what we expect her to be; and, most difficult of all, regardless of how she acts. This does not mean that we like all of her behavior. It does mean that we give and show love to our child all the time, even when her behavior is poor.

Does this sound like permissiveness? It is not. Rather, it is doing first things first. A child with a full love tank can respond to parental guidance without resentment.

Some people fear that this may lead to "spoiling" a child, but that is a misconception. No child can receive too much appropriate unconditional love. A child may be "spoiled" by a lack of training or by inappropriate love that gives or trains incorrectly. True unconditional love will never spoil a child because it is impossible for parents to give too much of it.

> No child can receive too much appropriate unconditional love.

These principles may be difficult for you because they go against what you have previously thought to be true. If that is the case, you may not find it easy to offer unconditional love to your children. However, as you practice it and then see the benefits, you will find it easier to do. Please hang in there and do what is best for your children, knowing that your love will make the difference between children who are well-adjusted and happy and those who are insecure, angry, inaccessible, and immature.

If you have not loved your children in this way, you may find it difficult at first. But as you practice unconditional love, you will find it has a wonderful effect, as you become a more giving and loving person in all your relationships. No one is perfect, of course, and you cannot expect yourself to love unconditionally all of the time. But as you move toward that goal, you will find that you are more consistent in your ability to love, no matter what.

You may find it helpful to frequently remind yourself of some rather obvious things about your children:

1. They are children.
2. They will tend to act like children.
3. Much childish behavior is unpleasant.
4. If I do my part as a parent and love them, despite their childish behavior, they will mature and give up their childish ways.
5. If I love them only when they please me (conditional love), and if I express my love to them only at those times, they will not feel genuinely loved. This will damage their self-image, make them feel insecure, and actually prevent them from moving into better self-control and more mature behavior. Therefore, their development and behavior is as much my responsibility as it is theirs.
6. If I love them only when they meet my requirements or expectations, they will feel incompetent and will believe it is pointless to do their best, since it is never enough. They will always be plagued by insecurity, anxiety, low self-esteem, and anger. To guard against this, I need to often remind myself of my responsibility for their total growth. (For more on this, you will want to read *How to Really Love Your Child* by Ross Campbell.)
7. If I love them unconditionally, they will feel comfortable about themselves and will be able to control their anxiety and their behavior as they grow to adulthood.

Of course, there are age-appropriate behaviors with our sons and daughters. Teens act differently than little children, and a thirteen-year-old will respond differently than a seven-year-old. But we must remember they are still minors, not mature adults, so we can expect them to fail at times. Show patience with them as they learn to grow.

What Your Child Needs from You

This book focuses primarily on our children's need for love and how to provide it. That's because it is their greatest emotional need and greatly affects our relationship with them. Other needs, especially physical needs, are easier to recognize and usually easier to fulfill, but they are not as satisfying or life-changing. Yes, we need to provide our children shelter, food, and clothing. But we are also responsible to foster the mental and emotional growth and health of our children.

> A child needs to develop **relational skills** so that she will treat **all persons** as having **equal value.**

Volumes have been written on a child's need for *healthy self-esteem* or an appropriate sense of self-worth. The child with an embellished sense of self will see himself as superior to others—as God's gift to the world and deserving of whatever he wants. Studies show this inflated sense of self-esteem is rampant among the young today. Psychology professor Jean Twenge notes that measures of self-esteem have risen consistently since the 1980s among children of all ages—and "what starts off as healthy self-esteem can quickly morph into an inflated view of oneself."[1]

But equally damaging, the child who underestimates his worth will struggle with thoughts such as, "I am not as smart, athletic, or beautiful as others." "I can't" is his theme song, and "I didn't" is his reality. It is worthy of our best efforts as parents to see that our children develop appropriate self-esteem so that they will view themselves as important members of society with special talents and abilities and will feel a desire to be productive.

Children also have a universal need for *security and safety*. In our world of uncertainties, at home and "out there," it is increasingly difficult for parents to provide this sense of security. More and more parents hear the painful question of children who ask, "Are you going to leave me?" The sad fact is that many of their friends' parents *have* left. If one parent is already gone, a child may fear that the other will also leave.

A child needs to develop relational skills so that she will treat all persons as having equal value and will be able to build friendships through a balanced flow of giving and receiving. Without these skills, a child is in danger of becoming withdrawn and remaining that way into adulthood. A child lacking essential relational skills might also become a controlling bully who lacks empathy and treats others cruelly. Finally, a child must learn to relate properly to authority. Without this, no other abilities will mean very much.

Parents need to help their children develop their special gifts and talents so that the children will feel the inner satisfaction and sense of accomplishment that come from using one's innate abilities. Conscientious parents must maintain the delicate balance between pushing and encouraging.

Love As Children Grow

All these and more are legitimate needs of children, and yet, in this book, we are focusing on love. We believe a child's need for love is basic to all other needs. Receiving love and learning to give love is the soil out of which all positive endeavors grow.

During the Early Years

During infancy, a child does not distinguish between milk and tenderness, between solid food and love. Without food, a child will starve. Without love, a child will starve emotionally and can become impaired for life. A great deal of research indicates that the emotional foundation of life is laid in the first eighteen months of life, particularly in the mother/child relationship. The "food" for future emotional health is physical touch, kind words, and tender care.

As toddlers gain a greater sense of identity, they begin to separate themselves from their love objects. Although before this time the mother may have removed herself from the child's vision, now the child has the ability to remove himself from persons he depends on. As he becomes more outgoing, he learns to love more actively. No longer a passive receiver of love, he now has the capacity to respond. However, this capacity is more one of possessing the loved one than of self-giving. During the next several years, the child's ability to express love increases, and if he continues to receive love, he will increasingly give love.

The foundation of love laid in the early years affects a child's ability to learn and largely determines when she is able to grasp new information. Many children go to school ill-prepared to learn because they are not emotionally ready to learn. Children need to reach appropriate emotional levels of maturity before they are able to learn effectively at their age level. Simply sending a child to a better school or changing teachers is not the answer. We must make sure our children are emotionally ready to learn. (See chapter 9 for more on the relationship between love and learning.)

> Children need to reach appropriate emotional levels of maturity before they are able to learn effectively at their age level.

During Adolescence

Meeting a child's need for love is not as simple as it may sound, and that's especially true when adolescence begins. The dangers of adolescence are threatening enough in themselves, but a child entering this time with an empty emotional tank is particularly vulnerable to the problems of the teenage years.

Children raised with conditional love learn how to love that way. By the time they reach adolescence, they often will manipulate and control their parents. When they are pleased, they please their parents. When they are not pleased, they frustrate their parents. This leaves the parents paralyzed because they are waiting for their teens to please them, but these teenagers don't know how to love uncon-ditionally. This vicious cycle usually turns into anger, resentment, and acting out by the teenagers.

Love and Our Children's Feelings

Children are primarily emotional beings and their first understand-ings of the world are emotional. Several studies have shown that the mother's emotional state even affects the baby in the womb. The unborn child responds to the mother's anger or happiness. And as children grow, they are extremely sensitive to the emotional state of their parents.

In the Campbell family, many times our children were more aware of their father's feelings than of their own. Often, for instance, one of them would identify how I was feeling when I wasn't aware of it. My daughter would say something like, "What are you so an-gry about, Dad?" Even if I wasn't aware of my anger, I would stop and think and realize that, yes, I was still upset about something that had happened during the day.

Other times, one of my children would say, "What are you so happy about, Daddy?"

"How did you know I was so up?" I would ask, wanting to know if I had given some clue. Once our daughter Carey said, "Because you were whistling a happy tune." I didn't even realize I was whistling.

Aren't kids great? They are so sensitive to our feelings. That is why they are so keenly aware of our displays of love to them. And that is also why they are afraid of our anger. We will talk more about this later.

We must communicate love in a language our children under-stand. The teenage runaway is a child who is convinced that no one loves him or her. Many of the parents of these runaways would protest that they do love their children, and that may be. But they have not successfully communicated that love. The parents have cooked meals, washed clothes, provided transportation, and given educational and recreational opportunities. All of these are valid expressions of love if the unconditional love is in place first. But they are never a substitute for this most crucial kind of love, and children know the difference. They know if they are receiving what they most deeply crave.

Does Your Child Feel Your Love?

Nearly all parents deeply love their children, yet not all children feel that unconditional love and care. Why this contradiction? Often, parents assume that their kids just "know" they love them, or that saying "I love you" will be enough. But children are behaviorally motivated. They respond to actions—what you *do* with them. So to reach them, you must love them on their terms.

There are advantages to this approach for parents. For example, if you have had a hard day and you're down and discouraged when you return home, you don't feel especially loving. But you can behave in a loving way, because behavior is simple. You can give your love to your children, even when you don't feel loving.

> Your children will sense **how you feel** about them by **how you behave** toward them.

You may wonder if that is being honest and if your children can see right through you. In a way they can, because they are exquisitely sensitive emotionally. They know when you don't feel loving, and yet they experience your love behaviorally. Don't you think they are even more grateful and appreciative when you're able to be loving, no matter how you feel inside?

Your children will sense how you feel about them by how you behave toward them. It was the apostle John who wrote, "Dear children, let us not love with words or tongue but with actions and in truth."[2] If you began to list all the behavioral ways to love a child, I doubt that you could fill more than one page. There just aren't that many ways, and that is fine, because you want to keep it simple. What matters is to keep your children's love tanks full. You can simply remember that behavioral expressions of love can be divided into physical touch, quality time, gifts, acts of service, and words of affirmation.

Beginning with chapter two, we will help you uncover your child's primary love language. A word of caution, though. If your child is under age five, don't expect to figure out his primary love language. You can't. The child may give you clues, but his love language is rarely clearly seen. Just speak all five languages. Tender touch, supporting words, quality time, gifts, and acts of service all converge to meet your child's need for love. If that need is met and your child genuinely feels loved, it will be far easier for him to learn and respond in other areas. This love interfaces with all other needs a child has. Speak all five languages when your child is older, too, for he needs all five to grow, even though he craves one more than the others.

A second caution: When you discover your child's love language and thus she receives the love she needs, don't assume everything in her life will be problem-free. There will still be setbacks and misunderstandings. But your child, like a flower, will benefit from your love. When the water of love is given, your child will bloom and bless the world with beauty. Without that love, she will become a wilted flower, begging for water.

Because you want your children to grow into full maturity, you will want to show them love in all the languages and then teach them how to use these for themselves. The value is not only for your children, but for the people with whom they will live and associate. One mark of a mature adult is the ability to give and receive appreciation through all the love languages—physical touch, quality time, words of affirmation, gifts, and acts of service. Few adults are able to do this; most of them give or receive love in one or two ways.

If this is not something you have done in the past, you may find that you too are changing and growing in understanding and in the quality of your relationships. In time, you will have a truly multi-lingual family.

THE 5 LOVE LANGUAGES OF CHILDREN

physical touch

words of affirmation

quality time

gifts

acts of service

2

physical *touch*

Samantha is a fifth-grader whose family recently moved to a new community. "It's been hard this year, moving and having to make new friends. Back at my old school, I knew everybody and they knew me." When we asked if she ever felt as if her parents didn't love her because they took her away from her old school and town, Samantha said, "Oh, no, I never felt they did this on purpose. I know they love me, because they always give me lots of extra hugs and kisses. I wish we hadn't had to move, but I know Daddy's job is important."

Samantha's love language is physical touch; those touches tell her Mom and Dad love her. Hugs and kisses are the most common way of speaking this love language, but there are other ways, too. A dad tosses his year-old son in the air. He spins his seven-year-old daughter round and round, and she laughs wildly. A mom reads a story with her three-year-old on her lap.

Such touching activities happen between parents and children, but not as often as you may think. Studies indicate that many parents touch their children only when it is necessary: when they are dressing or undressing them, putting them in the car, or carrying them to bed. It seems that many parents are unaware of how much their children need to be touched and how easily they can use this means to keep their children's emotional tanks filled with unconditional love.

Physical touch is the easiest love language to use unconditionally, because parents need no special occasion or excuse to make physical contact. They have almost constant opportunity to transfer love to the heart of a child with touch. The language of touch is not confined to a hug or a kiss but includes any kind of physical contact. Even when they are busy, parents can often gently touch a child on the back, arm, or shoulder.

Though some parents are quite demonstrative, others almost try to avoid touching their children. Often this limited physical touching occurs because parents simply do not realize their pattern or do not know how to change it. Many are glad to learn how they can show love in this most basic way.

Chris was worried about his relationship with his four-year-old daughter, Audrey, because she was pulling away from him and seemed to avoid being with him. Chris had a big heart, but he was very reserved and usually kept his feelings to himself. He had always felt uncomfortable in expressing his emotions through physical touch. Because he wanted so much to be close to Audrey, he was willing to make some changes, and began showing love to her with a light touch on her arm, back, or shoulders. Gradually he increased his use of this love language and eventually could hug and kiss his precious daughter without feeling uncomfortable.

This change wasn't easy for Chris, but as he became more demonstrative, he discovered that Audrey needed extraordinary amounts of paternal affection. If she didn't receive it, she would become angry and upset. Chris came to understand how a lack of affection on his part could distort Audrey's relationships with all males later on.

A Young Child's Need for Touch

Chris found out the power of this particular love language. In recent years, many research studies have come to the same conclusion: Babies who are held, caressed, and kissed develop a healthier emotional life than those who are left for long periods of time without physical contact.

Physical touch is one of love's strongest voices. It shouts, "I love you!" The importance of touching children is not a modern notion. In the first century AD, the Hebrews living in Palestine brought their children to Jesus "to have Him touch them." The writer Mark reported that the disciples of Jesus rebuked the parents, thinking their teacher was too busy with "important" matters to spend time on children. But Jesus was indignant with His disciples. "'Let the little children come to me, and do not hinder them, for the kingdom of God belongs to such as these. I tell you the truth, anyone who will not receive the kingdom of God like a little child will never enter it.' And he took the children in his arms, put his hands on them and blessed them."[1]

You will learn to spot your child's primary language in chapter 7. It may not be physical touch—but that does not matter. All children need to be touched, and wise parents in many cultures recognize the importance of touching their children. They also recognize the need to have their children receive the tender touch of other significant adults, such as grandparents.

Touch through the Growing Years

Infants and Toddlers

Our children need plenty of touches during their first few years. Fortunately, to hold and cuddle an infant seems almost instinctual for mothers, and in most cultures fathers also actively participate in giving affection.

But in busy America, parents sometimes do not touch children as much as they should. They work long hours and often come home tired. If a mother works, she should be sure the caregiver is free and able to touch. Will the child be lovingly touched throughout the day or left to lie in a crib alone, unattended, and unloved? In child care, a baby deserves loving and gentle touches whether in changing diapers or during feeding or carrying. Even an infant is able to tell the difference between gentle and harsh or irritating touches. Parents should make every effort to ensure the loving treatment of their children during the hours they are apart.

As a baby grows and becomes more active, the need for touch does not lessen. Hugs and kisses, wrestling on the floor, riding piggyback, and other playful loving touches are vital to the child's emotional development. Children need many meaningful touches every day, and parents should make every effort to provide these expressions of love. If you are not naturally a "hugger," you may feel that you're consciously going against your natural tendency. But you can learn. When we come to understand the importance of lovingly touching our children, we are motivated to change.

Boys and girls alike need physical affection, yet young boys often receive less than young girls. There are many reasons for this, but the most common is that some parents feel that physical affection will somehow feminize a boy. Of course, this is not true. The fact is that the more parents keep the emotional tank full, the healthier the child's self-esteem and sexual identity will be.

School-age Children

When your child begins school, he still has a strong need for physical touch. A hug given as he leaves each morning may be the difference between emotional security and insecurity throughout the day. A hug when the child returns home may determine whether your child has a quiet evening of positive mental and physical activity or makes a rambunctious effort to get your attention. Why is this? Children are facing new experiences at school each day and they feel both positive and negative emotions toward teachers and peers. Therefore, home should be a haven, the place where love is secure. Remember, physical touch is one of love's strong languages. As it is spoken in a natural and comfortable way, your child becomes more comfortable and has an easier time communicating with other people.

But I have a couple of boys, and as they grow older, they have less need for affection and especially for physical touch, some may argue. Not so! *All* children need physical contact throughout their childhood and adolescence. Many boys from age seven to nine go through a stage when they are resistant to affectionate touch, and yet they still need physical contact. They tend to be responsive to more vigorous contact such as wrestling, jostling, playful hitting, bear hugs, high fives, and the like. Girls also enjoy this type of physical touch, but they do not resist the softer touches as well, for unlike boys, they do not go through the affection-resistant stage as boys do.

Much physical touch at this stage in a child's life will come through playing games. Basketball, football, and soccer are all contact sports. When you are playing games together in the backyard, you are combining both quality time and physical touch. But touch should not be limited to such play. Running your hand through your child's hair, touching him

> Much **physical touch** at this stage in a child's life will come through **playing games.**

on the shoulder or arm, patting him on the back or leg, along with some encouraging words, are all meaningful expressions of love to a growing child.

A favorite kind of physical touch for many parents is to hold a small child while reading a story. This enables parents to maintain the touch for longer periods of time, something deeply meaningful to the child that becomes a lifelong memory.

Other times when physical touch is important are when a child is sick, hurt physically or emotionally, tired, or when something funny or sad has taken place. Parents need to make sure that they treat boys in the same way they do girls at such times. Most boys tend to consider physical affection as "feminine" in some periods of their development; when they are resistant, it is easier for parents to keep more distance from them. Also, some adults regard boys as less appealing during certain stages. If parents experience such feelings, it is important to resist them; go ahead and give boys the physical touch they need, even if they act as if they don't want it.

From Tweens to Teens

During your child's grade school years, it is essential to remember that you are preparing him or her for the most difficult part of childhood—adolescence. When a child is small, it is comparatively easy to fill the emotional tank. Of course, it becomes empty very fast and must be replenished. As the child grows, the emotional love tank also grows and keeping it full becomes more difficult. Eventually that boy will be bigger than you, and stronger and smarter—just ask him! And your daughter will become a wonderful adult-like person who is brighter and smarter than you are!

Continue to fuel their tanks with love, even when they may not give you signs of their needs. While boys approaching adolescence may pull back from touch, fearing it's too feminine, girls may find their fathers pulling back. If you want to properly prepare your pre-adolescent daughter for the future, don't hold back with the touches. Here's why.

During the preadolescent stage, girls have a particular need for expressions of love from their fathers. Unlike boys, the importance of being assured of unconditional love increases for girls and seems to reach a zenith around the age of eleven. One reason for this special need is that mothers generally provide more physical affection at this stage than fathers do.

If you could watch a group of sixth-grade girls at school, you would see the difference between those who are prepared for adolescence and those who are struggling. As a girl nears this delicate stage in her life, she intuitively knows that she needs to feel good about herself. She also unconsciously knows that she needs to have a good sexual identity in order to weather the years ahead. It is crucial that she feel valuable as a female.

As you watch the girls, you will see that some have a difficult time relating to the opposite sex. They are either shy or withdrawn around boys, or they may be flirtatious and even seductive. While boys may enjoy the flirtations of an attractive girl, they do not hold her in high regard and usually ridicule her in private. But the real agony for this girl is not just her reputation but her ongoing relationships with other girls. They tend to resent her because of her behavior with boys. At this age, having normal and supportive friendships with other girls is far more important than getting along with boys. These friendships also set a lifelong pattern.

Some of those girls you observe do not resort to awkward behavior with boys. They can simply be themselves because of their healthy self-esteem and sexual identity. Their behavioral patterns are consistent and stable, whether they are interacting with the star quarterback or a shy, hesitant boy. You also notice that the boys hold them in high esteem. But best of all, they have close, supportive, meaningful relationships with other girls.

Girls with strong and healthy self-esteem and sexual identity can better stand against negative peer pressure. They are more able to hold on to the moral standards they were taught at home, and are better equipped to think for themselves.

What makes the difference in these girls? Some have such problems with their peer relationships and others are doing beautifully. You guessed it—the emotional love tank. Most of those who are doing well have fathers who take their part in keeping the emotional tank full. But if a girl does not have a father present in the home, all is not lost. She may find a good father substitute in a grandfather or uncle. Many fatherless girls grow to be healthy women in every way.

Your Teenager and Touch

When your child reaches the teen years, it is important that you show your love in positive ways and also at the right times and places. Mothers should never hug a son in the presence of his peers. He is seeking to develop his own independent identity, and such behavior embarrasses him; it will also likely make him the brunt of jokes later on. However, at the end of the day, in the privacy of the home after the son has had a grueling football practice, his mother's hug may indeed be received as an expression of love.

Some fathers withdraw from hugging and kissing their teenage daughters, feeling that it is inappropriate at this stage. In fact, just the opposite is true. A teenage girl needs the hugs and kisses of her father; and if he withdraws, she will likely seek physical touch from another male and often in an unwholesome manner. But here again, time and place are important. Unless a girl initiates a hug in public, it is well to refrain. But at home, you can take the initiative.

Teenagers find hugs and other forms of loving touch especially helpful when they are going through a difficult time or struggling with an impossible project at school. And don't forget, physical touch from the same-sex parent is also important. Fathers hugging sons and mothers hugging daughters are appropriate at every stage of our children's development. A son needs his father's loving touch as well as his mother's, and a daughter needs an adequate supply of loving expression from her mother as well as from her father.

If you look for ways to show loving touch to your teenage children, you will find them. For instance, when they come home sore after a practice in their favorite sport, you can offer to rub the stiffness out of their muscles. Or, after they have been intensely studying for some hours, you might massage their sore necks and offer some relaxation as well as a loving touch. And many children like to have their backs scratched, even after they are grown and living away from home.

However, you don't want to force physical touch on a teenager. If he pulls away from your embrace or jumps back when you touch his shoulder, don't pursue it. For some reason your child doesn't wish to be touched at this time. The reason might have nothing to do with you or might be related to another aspect of your relationship. Teenagers are filled with emotions, thoughts, and desires, and sometimes they just don't want to be touched. You need to honor their feelings, whether they are expressed in words or by actions. However, if they consistently refuse your touch, you then need to make a time to talk with them about the reasons for this.

> You don't want to force physical touch on a teenager.

Remember, you are a role model for your children; they will be watching the way you practice physical touch. One way you can tell if they are following your example is to watch their use of physical touch. It is wonderful to see your children using this love language effectively in relating to others.

When Your Child's Primary Love Language
Is Touch

Is your child's primary love language touch? Be sure to read chapter 7 to determine for sure. However, here are some clues. For children who understand this love language, physical touch will communicate love more deeply than will the words "I love you," or giving a present, fixing a bicycle, or spending time with them. Of course, they receive love in all the languages, but for them the one with the clearest and loudest voice is physical touch. Without hugs, kisses, pats on the back, and other physical expressions of love, their love tanks will remain less than full.

When you use physical touch with these children, your message of love will come through loud and clear. A tender hug communicates love to any child, but it shouts love to these children. Conversely, if you use physical touch as an expression of anger or hostility, you will hurt these children very deeply. A slap in the face is detrimental to any child, but it is devastating to children whose primary love language is touch.

Michelle didn't learn about the five love languages until her son Jaden was twelve years old. At the end of a love languages seminar, she turned to a friend and said, "Now I finally understand Jaden. For years he has annoyed me by constantly picking at me. When I'm working at the computer, he walks up behind me, puts his hands around my face and covers my eyes. If I walk past him, he reaches out and pinches my arm. If I walk through the room when he's lying on the floor, he grabs my leg. Sometimes he pulls my arms behind me. He used to run his hands through my hair when I was sitting on the couch, although he doesn't anymore since I told him to keep his hands out of my hair. He does the same thing to his father, and the two of them usually end up in a wrestling match on the floor.

"Now I realize that Jaden's primary love language is physical touch. All these years, he has been touching me because he wants to *be* touched. I admit that I'm not much of a toucher—my parents were not hugging people. I now realize that my husband has been loving Jaden with his wrestling, while I have been drawing back from his efforts to get love from me. How could I have missed it all this time—it seems so simple now."

That night Michelle talked with her husband about the seminar. William was somewhat surprised by what he heard. "I hadn't thought of the wrestling as love, but that makes a lot of sense," he told his wife. "I was just doing what came naturally for me. And you know, physical touch is my primary love language too."

When Michelle heard this, another light went on. No wonder William was always wanting to hug and kiss! Even when he wasn't interested in sex, he was the "touchiest" person she had ever met. That night Michelle felt as if she had almost too many new things to think about, and yet she determined to learn to speak the love language of physical touch. She would start by simply responding to their touches.

The next time Jaden came by where she was sitting at the computer and put his hands over her eyes, she rose, turned, and gave him a bear hug. Jaden was surprised, but he laughed. And the next time William put his arms around her, she responded the way she did when they were dating. He smiled and said, "I'm going to send you to more seminars. This stuff really works!"

Michelle persisted in her efforts to learn a new love language and, in due time, touching began to feel more comfortable for her. But long before she felt fully comfortable, William and Jaden were reaping the benefits of her physical touches and were responding to her by speaking her primary love language, acts of service. Jaden was picking up after himself and William was vacuuming, and Michelle thought she'd gone to heaven.

What the Children Say

For many children, physical touch speaks louder than words, gifts, quality time, or acts of service. Without it, their love tank will never be overflowing. Look at what these children had to say about the power of physical touch.

Sophia, age seven: "I know my mommy loves me because she hugs me."

Jeremy, a junior in college, told us how he knew his parents loved him: "They showed it all the time. Every time I left the house as long as I can remember, I always got a hug and kiss from my mom and a hug from my dad, if he was home. And every time I came home, it was a repeat performance. It's still that way. Some of my friends can't believe my parents, because they didn't grow up in touching families, but I like it. I still look forward to their hugs. It gives me warm feelings inside."

Eleven-year-old Hunter was asked, "On a zero-to-ten scale, how much do your parents love you?" Without batting an eye he answered, "Ten." When we asked why he felt this so strongly, he said, "Well, for one thing because they tell me, but even more from the way they treat me. Dad is always bumping me when he walks by, and we wrestle on the floor. He's a lot of fun. And Mom's always hugging me, although she has stopped doing it in front of my friends."

Jessica, twelve, lives with her mother most of the time and visits with her father every other weekend. She said that she feels especially loved by her father. When we asked why, she said, "Because every time I go to see him, he hugs and kisses me and tells me how glad he is to see me. When I leave, he hugs me for a long time and tells me he misses me. I know my mom loves me too—she does lots of things for me—but I wish she would hug me and act as excited about being with me as Daddy does."

If physical touch is your child's primary love language and you are not by nature a toucher and yet want to learn your child's love language, it may help if you begin by touching yourself. Yes, we're serious. First, take your hand and touch your arm, beginning at the wrist and working slowly up to your shoulder. Give yourself a shoulder rub. Now take the other hand and do the same thing on the other side. Run both hands through your hair, massaging your scalp as you work from front to back. Sit up straight with both feet on the floor and pat your legs—with rhythm if you want. Place one hand on your stomach. Then lean over and touch your feet and massage your ankles. Sit up and say, "There, I did it. I touched myself and I can touch my child!"

For those who have never been touched and find touching uncomfortable, this exercise can be a first step in breaking down barriers to physical touch. If you are one of these people, you may want to repeat this exercise once a day until you have enough courage to initiate a touch to your child or spouse. Once you get started, set a goal and consciously touch your child every day. Later, you can work up to several touches a day. Anyone can learn the language of physical touch, and if it is your child's primary love language, it is worth your best efforts.

physical touch...

Here are a few more ideas especially for parents. Pick and choose among them to try something new you think your child will appreciate.

- When you greet or say good-bye to your young child, gather them into your arms and hold them. Kneel down for small children.

- Let your child hold or cuddle a soft item, such as a blanket to soothe them.

- Hug and kiss your child every day when they leave and return from school, as well as when you tuck them in at night for younger children.

- Stroke your child's hair or rub their back when they tell you about a difficult day or are upset.

- Shortly after disciplining your child, take a moment to give them a hug to show them the discipline was based on the consequences of their wrongful choices but that you still love and cherish them as your child.

- Snuggle closely together on the couch when watching television together.

- Give each other a high five or similar congratulations whenever you catch your child doing something positive.

- Purchase a gift for your child that is touch-oriented, such as a soft pillow, blanket, or sweater.

- Occasionally yell out a "group hug" for your entire family, regardless of how small or large the family size. To add more fun, include family pets such as the dog or cat.

- Play games or sports together that require physical touch. This will allow both shared time together and touch that is meaningful without appearing forced.

- Sing action songs together with your children that require touching and action, such as clapping hands, spinning, or jumping. Many of today's children's DVDs make this even easier.

- Have "tickle fights" with your children, being careful not to allow it to become a stressful activity for your child.

- With younger children, read stories together with your child on your lap.

- When your child is sick or gets hurt, spend extra time providing comfort, like wiping her face with a cool cloth.

- Hold hands during family prayers.

THE 5 LOVE LANGUAGES OF CHILDREN

physical touch

words of affirmation

quality time

gifts

acts of service

words of affirmation

"Does my father love me? Yes, because when I play ball, he always cheers, and after the game he tells me, 'Thanks for playing hard.' He says that the main thing is not to win but to do my best."

Sam, age fourteen, continued. "Sometimes I make mistakes, but he tells me not to worry. He says I'll do better if I keep on doing my best."

In communicating love, words are powerful. Words of affection and endearment, words of praise and encouragement, words that give positive guidance all say, "I care about you." Such words are like a gentle, warm rain falling on the soul; they nurture the child's inner sense of worth and security. Even though such words are quickly said, they are not soon forgotten. A child reaps the benefits of affirming words for a lifetime.

Conversely, cutting words, spoken out of short-lived frustration, can hurt a child's self-esteem and cast doubts about his abilities. Children think we deeply believe what we say. The ancient Hebrew proverb did not overstate the reality: "The tongue has the power of life and death."[1]

The second love language is *words of affirmation*. Some children feel their greatest sense of love in expressions that affirm them. These expressions need not be the words "I love you," as we will see.

Understanding "I Love You"

Long before they can understand the meanings of words, children receive emotional messages. The tone of voice, the gentleness of mood, the sense of caring all communicate emotional warmth and love. All parents talk to their infants, and what the babies understand is the look on the face and the affectionate sounds, combined with physical closeness.

Because young children grow gradually in their ability to use words and concepts, they will not always know what we mean by our words, even when we say, "I love you." Love is an abstract concept. They can't see love as they can see a toy or a book. Because children tend to think concretely, we need to help them understand what we mean when we express our love. The words "I love you" take on greater meaning when the child can associate them with your affectionate feelings, and often this means physical closeness. For instance, when you are reading to a child at bedtime, holding your little one close, at a point in the story where the child's feelings are warm and loving, you can softly say, "I love you, Honey."

> Because **children tend to think concretely,** we need to **help them understand what we mean** when we express our love.

Once your child begins to understand what your "I love you" means, you can use these words in different ways and times, so that they become connected to regular events, such as sending a child off to play or to school. Also, you can combine your words of love with genuine praise for something about your child. Kathleen, now a mother of two, says, "I remember how my mother used to talk about my beautiful red hair. Her positive comments as she combed my hair before school have been a constant part of my self-perception. Years later when I discovered that we redheads are in the minority, I never had negative feelings about my red hair. I'm sure my mother's loving comments had a lot to do with that."

The Right Kind of Praise

Praise and affection are often combined in the messages we give to a child. We need to distinguish the two. Affection and love mean *expressing appreciation for the very being of a child,* for those characteristics and abilities that are part of the total package of the person. In contrast, we express *praise for what the child does,* either in achievements or behavior or conscious attitudes. Praise, as we are using it here, is for something over which the child has a degree of control.

Because you want words of praise to be genuinely meaningful to your child, you need to be careful about what you say. If you use praise too frequently, your words will have little positive effect. For example, you may say something like, "You are a good girl." Those are wonderful words, but you need to be wise in using them. It is more effective to say this when the child has done something for which she feels good and would expect a compliment. This is especially true with specific compliments such as, "Great catch!" when it was just an average catch. Children know when praise is given for justified reasons and when it is given simply to make them feel good, and they may interpret the latter as insincere.

If you use praise too frequently, your words will have little positive effect.

Frequent random praise is risky for another reason. Some children become so accustomed to this type of praise that they assume it is natural and they come to expect it. When they are in situations where such praise is not given, they assume something is wrong with them and they become anxious. When they see other children who do not receive such bolstering, they can wonder why they feel such excessive need of praise.

Of course, we want to praise children we care about, but we want to make sure that the praise is both true and justified. Otherwise they may regard it as flattery, which they can equate with lying.

The Power of Encouragement

The word *encourage* means "to instill courage." We are seeking to give children the courage to attempt more. To a young child, almost every experience is new. Learning to walk, to talk, or to ride a bicycle requires constant courage. By our words, we either encourage or discourage the child's efforts.

Speech pathologists say that children learn to speak by mimicking adults, but that the process is enhanced if the adults not only pronounce the words clearly but also give verbal encouragement to the child's struggling attempts to say them correctly. Statements such as, "That's close, that's good, yes, great, you've got it," encourage the child not only in learning the words at hand but also in developing future vocabulary.

The same principle is true in the child's learning of social skills. "I saw how you shared your toys with Madison. I like that—life is much easier when we share." Words such as these give a child that added inner motivation to go against what might be a natural desire to hoard. Or consider a parent who says to a sixth-grader, "Danny, I noticed that tonight after the game you were listening closely to Scott as he shared his feelings about his game. I was so proud of you for giving him your undivided attention, even though others were slapping you on the back as they walked by. Listening to people is one of the greatest gifts you can give them." This parent is instilling in Danny the courage to develop the art of listening, one of the most important arts in the field of human relationships.

Maybe you find it difficult to use encouraging words. Keep in mind that one aspect of feeling encouraged is feeling good physically. Exuberance and vitality require energy; this means as parents we need to be in the best possible health physically, mentally, emotionally, and spiritually. When we feel encouraged, we are better able to encourage our children. In two-parent households, the parents should encourage one another; if you're a single parent, have trusted friends or relatives who will bolster your spirits and energy.

The greatest enemy of encouraging our children is anger. The more anger the parent harbors, the more anger the parent will dump on the children. The result will be children who are both antiauthority and anti-parent. This naturally means that a thoughtful parent will do all in his or her power to assuage anger—to keep it to a minimum and to handle it maturely.

The writer of Proverbs is wise indeed: "A gentle answer turns away wrath."[2] The volume of a parent's voice has great influence over a child's reaction to what the parent says. It takes practice to speak softly, but we can all learn how to do it. Also, when we are feeling tense with our children, we can learn to speak calmly, asking questions whenever possible, rather than issuing commands. For example, which of these statements would best encourage a child or teenager? "Take out the garbage now!" or "Would you take out the garbage for me, please?" When we try to encourage our children in a particular matter, they will more likely respond favorably rather than reject our ideas.

Years ago a middle-school teacher in Minnesota did a remarkable thing. She asked her students to list the names of all the other students in the class, leaving a space between names. Then she told

> The volume of a parent's voice has a great influence over a child's reaction to what the parent says.

them to think of the nicest thing they could say about each of their classmates and write it down. At the end of the period she collected these sheets and over the weekend, she wrote the name of each student on a separate sheet and listed what everyone had said about that person. On Monday, she gave each student his or her list.

As they began reading, they started whispering to each other, "I never knew that meant anything to anyone" or, "I didn't know others liked me so much." The papers were never discussed in class, but the teacher knew the exercise was a success because it gave her students such a positive feeling about themselves.

Several years later, one of those students was killed in Vietnam. After his body was returned to Minnesota, most of his classmates, along with the math teacher, attended the funeral. At the luncheon after the service, the father of the young man said to the teacher, "I want to show you something," and took a wallet out of his pocket. "They found this on Mark when he was killed. We thought you might recognize it." Opening the billfold, he removed two worn sheets of notebook paper which had been taped, folded, and refolded many times. It was the list of good things Mark's classmates had written about him.

"Thank you so much for doing that," Mark's mother told the teacher. "As you can see, our son treasured it." One by one, Mark's classmates began to reveal that each of them still had their sheet and that they read it often. Some carried it in a billfold; one had even put it in his wedding album. One man said, "I think we all saved our list."[3]

Right Message, Wrong Manner

Encouraging words are most effective when they are focused on a specific effort your child has made. The goal is to catch your child doing something good and then commend him for it. Yes, this takes far more effort than catching your child doing something wrong and then condemning him for it, but the end result is worth it: direction that guides your child in his moral and ethical development.

Children need guidance. They learn to speak by being exposed to a particular language. They learn how to behave by living in a certain kind of society. In most cultures, parents have the primary responsibility for socializing children. This involves not only the social dos and don'ts but also their ethical and moral development.

All children are guided by someone. If you as their parents are not their primary guides, then other influences and individuals assume that role—school, media, the culture, other adults, or peers who are getting their guidance from someone else. Ask yourself this question: *Are my children receiving positive and loving guidance?* Loving guidance always has a child's best interests in mind. Its purpose is not to make parents and other adults look good; its purpose is to help the child develop the qualities that will serve him well in the future. The fourth type of affirming words offers your child guidance for the future. It's a powerful element of the second love language.

Too often parents give the right message but in the wrong manner. They tell their children to stay away from drinking, but their harsh and cruel manner may in fact drive the children to alcohol. Words of guidance must be given in a positive way. A positive message delivered in a negative manner will always reap negative results. As one child said, "My parents are yelling and screaming at me, telling me not to yell and scream. They expect me to do something they have not learned to do. It's unfair."

One child said, "My parents are yelling and screaming at me, telling me not to yell and scream."

Another difficulty is that many parents view parental guidance as an exercise in prohibition. "Don't lie." "Don't hit your sister." "Don't cross the street." "Don't eat too much candy." Then, later: "Don't drink and drive." "Don't get pregnant." "Don't smoke." "Don't experiment with drugs." "Don't go to that concert." These are all good warnings but hardly enough direction to build a meaningful life. To be sure, prohibition is part of parental guidance, but it should never be the predominant element. In the biblical account of the Garden of Eden, God gave Adam and Eve only one negative; all other guidance was

positive. He gave them meaningful work to fill their lives with productive activity. Much later, when the children of Israel came to Sinai, they were given the Ten Commandments, five of which are positive and five negative. In Jesus' Sermon on the Mount, His guidance is overwhelmingly positive.

> Many parents view parental guidance as an exercise in prohibition.

The negative is necessary, but only as a part of the guidance we give our children. The supreme law is the law of love, and it is loving, positive guidance that our children so desperately need. If we can guide them into positive, meaningful pursuits, they are less likely to fall prey to the perils we want them to avoid.

Parents who offer words of loving guidance will be looking closely at the interests and abilities of their children and giving positive verbal reinforcement of those interests. From academic pursuits to simple rules of etiquette to the complex art of personal relationships, parents need to be expressing emotional love in the positive verbal guidance they give their children.

When your son or daughter is a teen, rather than condemning your child's friends who are making poor choices, it is far better to take a loving approach that expresses concern for them. You might show your child accounts of accidents and deaths that involve drugs and alcohol and share how painful it is for you to think about such devastation in the lives of these young people and their families. When your child hears your loving expressions of concern for other young people, he is far more likely to identify with you than when he hears you condemning people who do such things.

When Your Child's Primary Love Language Is Words of Affirmation

The words "I love you" should always stand alone in reality or by implication. To say, "I love you . . . will you please do this for me?" dilutes the theme of love. To say, "I love you, but I'll tell you right now . . ." cancels itself out. The words "I love you" should never be diluted with conditional statements. This is true for all children, but especially for those whose primary love language is words.

To his parents, ten-year-old Cole seemed very lethargic. They had tried all sorts of things to help him be more interested in life— from sports to a dog—and they were at their wits' end. They often complained to Cole about his attitude, telling him that he should be thankful to have parents who cared about him and also that he needed to find an interest he could develop. They even threatened to take him to a counselor if he didn't get more excited about life.

After Steve and Jen attended a seminar about the love languages, they wondered immediately if Cole's primary love language might be words of affirmation. They realized that this was the one thing they had not given him. Instead, they had showered him with gifts, hugged him daily, and provided quality time and acts of service. But their actual words to their son sent another message—one of criticism.

So they developed a plan. Jen and Steve began to make a conscious effort to give Cole words of affirmation, starting with comments about what they liked about him. As they prepared for this experiment, they decided that for one month they would concentrate on making their words communicate the message, "We care about you, we love you, we like you."

Cole was a physically attractive child, and so they would begin by commenting on his appearance. They would not tie their words of affirmation to a suggestion such as, "You're strong—you should be playing football." Rather they would talk about his athletic build

Parenting is not just a matter of **doing what comes naturally.**

and leave it at that. They also began to watch for things in Cole's behavior that pleased them and then made positive statements. If he fed their dog Lucy, they expressed appreciation rather than saying, "It's about time." When they had to give guidance, they would try to keep it positive.

A month later Steve and Jen reported, "We can't believe the change in Cole. He's a different kid . . . maybe because we're different parents. His attitude toward life is much more positive. He's sharing jokes with us and laughing. He is feeding Lucy and was recently out playing football with some kids. We think we're on the right track."

Steve and Jen's discovery changed them as well as Cole. They learned that parenting is not just a matter of doing what comes naturally. Because every child is different, it is essential to communicate love to that child in his or her primary language. Jen and Steve's story shows that it is possible to use a child's love language wrongly, bringing hurt and frustration to the child. Cole's language was words of affirmation—and they were giving him words of condemnation. Such words are harmful to any child, but they are extremely destructive to a child whose primary language is words of affirmation.

If you think this is your child's language, and yet you have a hard time saying affirming things, we suggest that you keep a notebook titled "Words of Affirmation." When you hear other parents giving affirmation to their children, write their statements in your notebook. When you read an article on childrearing, record the positive words you find. Look for books on parent-child relationships and record all the words of affirmation you discover. Then practice saying those words in front of a mirror. The more often you say them, the more they will become your own. Then consciously look for opportunities to say these affirming things to your child, at least three times a day.

If you find that you fall back into old patterns of condemnation or negativism, tell your child that you are sorry, that you realize the words are hurtful, and this is not how you feel about him. Ask him to forgive you. Tell him that you are trying to become a better parent and that you love him very deeply and want to communicate that love more effectively. In due time, you will be able to break the old habits and establish new patterns. The best reward of all is that you will see the effect on the face of your child, especially in his eyes, and you will feel it in your heart. And the chances are good that you will begin to receive words of affirmation from him; the more he feels loved by you, the more he is likely to reciprocate.

What the Children Say

The following four children share words of affirmation as their primary love language.

Melissa, eight, said, "I love my mother because she loves me. Every day she tells me that she loves me. I think my father does too, but he never tells me so."

Taylor, age twelve, broke her arm this year. "I know that my parents love me because while I was having such a hard time keeping up with my schoolwork, they encouraged me. They never forced me to do homework when I wasn't feeling well, but told me I could do it later. They said how proud they were that I was trying so hard and that they knew I would be able to keep up."

David is an active, outspoken five-year-old, confident that his parents love him. "My mommy loves me and my daddy loves me. Every day they say, 'I love you.'"

John, ten, has been in foster homes since he was three. For the past eight months he has lived with Doug and Betsy, his fourth set of foster parents. When he was asked if they genuinely loved him, he said they did. We asked why he said that so quickly. "Because they don't yell and scream at me. My last foster parents yelled and screamed all the time. They treated me like trash. Doug and Betsy treat me like a person. I know I have lots of problems, but I also know that they love me."

For children whose primary love language is words of affirmation, nothing is more important to their sense of being loved than to hear parents and other adults verbally affirm them. But the reverse is also true—words of condemnation will hurt them very deeply. Harsh and critical words are detrimental to all children, but to those whose primary language is words of affirmation, such negative words are devastating. And they can play those words in their minds for many years.

Thus, it is essential for parents and other significant adults in the child's life to quickly apologize for negative, critical, or harsh remarks. While the words can't be erased by an apology, their effect can be minimized. If you realize that you have a negative communication pattern with your child, you might encourage your spouse to record some of your episodes so that you can hear yourself. This can be very sobering, but it can also be a step in breaking negative patterns of speaking. Because positive communication is so important to every successful parent-child relationship, it is worth the effort to break old patterns and establish new ones. The benefit to your child will be enormous, and the sense of satisfaction you gain will be very rewarding.

IF YOUR CHILD'S LOVE LANGUAGE IS

words of affirmation ...

Here are a few more ideas especially for parents. Pick and choose among them to try something new you think your child will appreciate.

- Put a Post-it note in their lunchbox with some encouraging words.

- Make a habit of mentioning something specific you've observed that highlights your child's accomplishments. Examples include: "I really appreciated how you showed kindness to that other child," or "I liked the positive attitude you had during the game."

- Ask what your child wants to do or be when they grow up. Then encourage them in ways that help them pursue these dreams. If your daughter says, "I want to be a veterinarian when I grow up," say things like, "I think you'd be a good vet."

- Send your older child a text message telling them how much they mean to you. Even better, make this a habit for when you have to go out of town or on a special holiday such as a birthday.

- If you are artistic, create a painting or drawing that shows how much you love your child.

- Take a picture or other creation your child has made and frame it with a note of why it means so much to you.

- Call your child at home whenever you think of them just to say, "I love you."

- Create a special name of affection for your child that is only used between the two of you.

- When you have to be out of town for work or other reasons, leave a series of short notes for your child, one for each day you are apart.

- Make it a habit to say, "I love you" whenever you tuck in your child or leave one another.

- Place their artwork in areas they recognize as important to you such as the refrigerator, the office, or special scrapbook.

- When your child is feeling down, share five reasons why you are proud of them.

- Leave a note on a cereal box, bathroom mirror, or other place you know your child will look. A simple "Daddy loves you," or "Mommy loves you," in a unique location can be very powerful.

- Get a picture key chain and put photos of your children in it. Talk about the photos with family or friends when your children are present.

- Create an encouragement jar that you and your child can use to drop in notes of praise and read together on a regular basis.

- Draw a large picture or words of encouragement using sidewalk chalk on your driveway, either together or as a surprise for them to see later.

- When a child makes a mistake trying to do something helpful, first use words to recognize that you knew of their good intentions.

THE 5 LOVE LANGUAGES OF CHILDREN

physical touch

words of affirmation

quality time

gifts

acts of service

quality *time*

Four-year-old Ella is pulling on her mother's leg. "Mommy, Mommy, let's go play!"

"I can't play right now," Kate says. "I have to finish paying bills. I'll play with you after that. Go play by yourself for a few minutes and then we'll do something together."

In five minutes, Ella is back, begging to play. Kate responds, "Ellie, I told you that I have to do this one important thing first. Now run along and I'll be there in a few minutes." Ella leaves the room but in four minutes she is back. Eventually the bills are paid and the two have their playtime together. But Kate knows that the scenario will be repeated tomorrow.

What can we learn from Kate and Ella? The chances are good that little Ellie is revealing her primary love language—*quality time*. What really makes her feel loved is her mother's undivided attention. This is so important to her that she returns again and again. But Kate often sees these repeated requests as intrusions. If they persist long enough, she may even "lose it" with her daughter and send her to her room for an isolated time-out—just the opposite of what Ella needs.

What's the answer? Kate wonders. *Is it possible to love a child and still get my own work done?* The answer is a resounding yes. Learning a child's primary love language is one key to reaching that objective. If Kate had given Ella fifteen minutes of quality time *before* she started paying bills, she probably could have done her work in peace. When a child's love tank is empty and attention is the only thing that will fill it, that child will go to almost any length to get what she needs.

> Even negative attention seems better than no attention to the child.

Even if your child's primary love language is not quality time, many children crave the undivided attention of parents. Indeed, much childhood misbehavior is an attempt to get more time with Mom or Dad. Even negative attention seems better than no attention to the child.

For years we have heard people talking about the need to give children "quality time," especially amidst the busyness of today's culture. And yet, while more people are talking about quality time, many children are starving for it.

Quality time is focused, undivided attention. Most infants receive plenty of quality time—feeding and changing alone offer that kind of attention, not only from mothers but fathers and perhaps extended family as well.

As a child grows, the giving of quality time becomes more difficult, because it requires real sacrifice on the part of parents. It's easier to give physical touch and words of affirmation than quality time. Few of us have enough hours in the day to get everything done as it is; giving a child quality time may mean that we have to give up something else. As children grow toward adolescence, they often need our attention just when we parents are exhausted, rushed, or emotionally out of sorts.

Quality time is a parent's gift of presence to a child. It conveys this message: "You are important. I like being with you." It makes the child feel that he is the most important person in the world to the parent. He feels truly loved because he has his parent all to himself.

When you spend quality time with children, you need to go to their physical/emotional level of development. When they are learning to crawl, for instance, you can sit on the floor with them. As they take their first steps, you should be nearby, urging them on. As they progress to sandboxes and learning to throw and kick a ball, you are there. When their world widens to include school, lessons of various sorts, sports, church, and community activities, you are all the while keeping up with them. The older a child is, the harder this may be, especially as you try to make private time for each child while staying involved in their more public activities.

"He Does Things with Me"

The most important factor in quality time is not the event itself but that you are doing something together, being together. When seven-year-old Nathan was asked how he knew his father loved him, he said, "Because he does things with me. Things like shooting baskets and playing games on the computer. And going to the pet store together."

Quality time does not require that you go somewhere special. You can provide focused attention almost anywhere, and your most nurturing quality times will often be at home, when you are alone with a child. Finding time to be alone with each child is not easy, and yet it is essential. In a society where people are increasingly spectators rather than participants, focused attention from parents is all the more critical.

In many homes, children would miss their computers and other electronic toys more than they would miss their fathers. Children are more and more influenced by forces outside the family and they need the strengthening influence of personal time with their parents. It takes real effort to carve out this kind of time in your schedule, and yet making the effort is rather like an investment in the future— of your children and your family.

If you have several children, you need to look for times when you can be alone with each one. This isn't easy, but it can be done. Consider Susanna Wesley, who raised ten children in eighteenth-century England. She scheduled an hour a week with each one alone. Her three sons, Sam, John, and Charles Wesley, became poets, writers, and preachers; Charles penned thousands of hymns, many of which remain classics in the Christian church. In addition to helping her children learn the alphabet, writing, and math, she taught them politeness and good manners, moral values, and frugal living.

In an era when women had little opportunity to advance, she prepared her daughters with a full education. The wise mother once told her daughter Emilia, "Society offers no opportunity for the intelligence of its women."[1] Emilia later became a teacher. While we don't necessarily advocate all of her ideas about raising children, we can admire the way Susanna set her priorities and then carried them through. The key to quality time is found in the values and priorities you as parents determine to cherish and implement in your home.

Positive Eye Contact

Quality time should include loving eye contact. Looking in your child's eyes with care is a powerful way to convey love from your heart to the heart of your child. Studies have shown that most parents use eye contact in primarily negative ways, either while reprimanding a child or giving very explicit instructions.

If you give loving looks only when your child is pleasing you, you are falling into the trap of conditional love. That can damage your child's personal growth. You want to give enough unconditional love to keep your child's emotional tank full, and a key way to do this is through proper use of eye contact.

Sometimes family members refuse to look at one another as a means of punishment. This is destructive to both adults and children. Kids especially interpret withdrawal of eye contact as disapproval, and this further erodes their self-esteem. Don't let your demonstration of love to a child be controlled by whether the child is pleasing you at the moment.

Sharing Thoughts and Feelings

Quality time not only means *doing* things together, but it is a means for *knowing* your child better. As you spend time with your children, you will find that a natural result often is good conversation about everything related to your lives. Phil Briggs, longtime professor of education at a California seminary, loves the dividends of golfing with his son. "My son wasn't much of a talker until we started golfing together regularly." The Briggs' father-son twosome often talk about their game—the swing and other golf nuances—as they walk the fairways, but soon they get around to discussing other areas of life. When a parent shows a child how to throw a football or make pasta, he or she often creates an environment in which the parent and child can talk about more important issues.

Quality Conversations

This is when a father can reveal something of his own history, perhaps tell his child of his dating relationship with the boy's mother, and discuss moral and spiritual issues. This kind of "real" conversation communicates deeply to a child on an emotional level. It says, "My father trusts me. He cares. My father sees me as an important person and he loves me." A mother can mention her own fears about her appearance growing up as she helps her daughter shop for her first pair of glasses or a special dress for the prom. The conversation draws them together and helps the daughter understand that her value is not based on appearance.

Children never outgrow a need for quality conversation with parents and other adults. Such sharing of thoughts and feelings is the fabric of which life is made. Learning how to communicate on this level will serve them well in their own future relationships, including marriage. It will teach them how to build friendships and relate to work associates. It will show them how to process their own thoughts and to communicate in a positive, caring manner that respects the ideas of others. It will provide an example of how to disagree without being disagreeable.

> Children never outgrow a need for **quality conversation** with **parents** and **other adults.**

Because your children will learn more from talking with you than you will probably ever realize, it is crucial that you spend time in healthy conversation with them, no matter what their age. If you limit your talking with them to correction, your children may never learn the value of positive, focused attention. Negative attention alone cannot meet their need for love.

With younger children, one of the most effective times to initiate conversation is at bedtime, when they are especially attentive. This may be because there are fewer distractions then or because the children want to delay going to bed. Whatever the reason, they are listening well and this makes meaningful conversation much easier.

"Read Me a Story"

All children love stories. Reading to them is a great way to begin your bedtime ritual—and do make it a ritual, because this will help to keep communications open when they become teenagers. During or after a story, you can pause to let a child identify his feelings about the events or characters and then talk about them. As you are reading a story about someone who experiences disappointment, for example, you may talk with your child about feelings of disappointment she has had, along with the accompanying sadness, anger, or whatever is appropriate.

We strongly recommend these times of conversation. Sadly, many young people today do not understand how to handle their feelings, especially anger. Many years of warm and close bedtime talks, which include gentle, relaxed sharing of feelings, can help prevent some of life's deepest problems down the road.

Bedtime rituals that are warm and close, gentle and relaxed, sound just the opposite of the busy world in which many parents live. Don't be a victim of the urgent. In the long run, much of what seems so pressing right now won't even matter. What you do with your children will matter forever.

Planning for Quality Time

During the first eight years of a child's life, you can assume a fairly sane schedule, as the child's life centers primarily around the home. But as your child grows and becomes more involved in activities outside the home, you need to spend more time and effort preparing for family quality time. Otherwise it just won't happen. Here are several ideas.

First, mealtimes are natural events around which to plan. Over the years, a regular family dinner hour together can be one of the most bonding experiences that you will have. We all hear about families that just set out a pot of food and let everyone eat whenever they arrive home. To those who know the warmth and strength of a regular dinnertime together, year after year, this sounds chaotic. Parents are the only ones who can set the schedule for the family and decide when and if certain events will interrupt that schedule. Some families are able to have breakfast together. And, you may be able to meet a child for lunch once a month.

Second, consider overnight trips. Burney and his son, Jeff, do an overnighter every three months. They usually travel only an hour from home and camp out in their tent for a day and a half of uninterrupted time together. Allyson takes a walk two nights a week with her twelve-year-old daughter, Brittany. On those nights, her husband and son do the dishes and get some father/son time.

Third, simply riding along in the car as Mom or Dad runs errands or drives to a soccer game can result in quality conversation. There is something about sitting in a car that seems to bring out the desire to talk—and listen. Parents should be alert for those times when children seem to need to talk.

Those are just a few ideas. Remember, planning for your times together need not stifle spontaneity. You can always change your plans if you want to, but without making plans, you may find that you have little quality time with your children. You schedule other people into your calendars—why not your children? They will appreciate the fact that you value your time with them so much that you are willing to say no to other activities. And one by-product of planning is that you teach your children how to schedule their own time.

One of the most difficult times in a family's day can be when everyone returns from work and school, hungry and tired. So planning for time together also means preparing yourself. If you come home from a pressured workday, you need to release the stress of the day, clear your mind of things at work, and then focus on your home. Some people do this by playing their favorite music on the way home. Some friends we know stop the car near home and take a few minutes to pray. Find what will help you to feel relaxed and upbeat, so that you have the energy you need to give to your child.

If you cannot prepare yourself prior to arriving home, you and your spouse can work out a time for you to have to yourself, before you begin interacting with your children. You may need simply to change into comfortable clothes, open a Coke, and stroll in the backyard before settling in with the family. The more refreshed you are, the more you will be able to give to your family.

When Your Child's Primary Love Language Is Quality Time

If quality time is your child's primary love language, you can be sure of this: Without a sufficient supply of quality time and focused attention, your child will experience a gnawing uneasiness that his parents do not really love him.

Gerry was a firefighter who worked forty-eight hours on and twenty-four hours off. During his "on days" he stayed at the firehouse; when he was off, he and a fellow fireman often painted houses to make extra money. Meanwhile, his wife, Maggie, worked nights as a nurse and slept days. When both were working nights, their children, Jonathan, age eight, and Grace, six, had their grandmother stay with them.

Gerry and Maggie became concerned about Jonathan, who over time seemed remote. Maggie later told a friend, "When we try to talk to him, he's very withdrawn-seeming. But when he was younger he talked all the time.

"Before he started school and I was still home all the time, he and I would go to the park almost every afternoon. Now he's so different that it makes me wonder if something's wrong. Gerry doesn't notice it as much as I do, because he hasn't spent as much time with Jonathan, but I can see a big difference."

Maggie's friend Rosie had just been reading *The 5 Love Languages* and remembered the one chapter on how the love languages relate to children. So Rosie gave Maggie a copy and suggested that it might help her with Jonathan. Two weeks later Maggie told her friend, "I read the book and I think I know Jonathan's primary love language.

Looking back and remembering how much he enjoyed our times together, and how talkative and excited he was, and then realizing that all that changed when he started school and I began work, I think the last two years he may have been almost starved for love. I've been meeting his physical needs, but haven't been meeting his emotional needs very well."

The two women talked about how Maggie could work quality time with Jonathan into her schedule. Because her flexible time was afternoons and early evenings, she had been using that time for housework, shopping, an occasional night out with the girls, and a rare night out with Gerry. She also supervised Jonathan's homework. Maggie decided that if she tried, she could carve out an hour twice a week to spend concentrated time with Jonathan.

Three weeks later, Maggie told her friend, "It's working. Jonathan and I have had our hour twice a week since we last talked, and I'm seeing real change in his response to me. We decided to take our dog to the park one afternoon a week and out for tacos the other. Jonathan is beginning to talk more, and I can tell that he's responding emotionally to our time together."

"By the way, I've asked Gerry to read the book," Maggie added. "I think we need to learn to speak each other's love language. I know he's not speaking mine, and I don't think I'm speaking his either. Also, Gerry might see the importance of spending more time with Jonathan."

What the Children Say

Here is how four children clearly reveal their primary love language to be quality time.

Eight-year-old Bethany has a twinkle in her eye most of the time. "I know my folks love me because they do things with me. Sometimes we all do stuff together, even with my little brother, but both of them do things just with me." When asked what sorts of things, she responded, "My daddy took me fishing last week. I don't know if I like fishing, but I like being with Daddy. Mom and I went to the zoo the day after my birthday. My favorite place was the monkey house. We watched one eat a banana. It was fun."

Jared is twelve. "I know my dad loves me because he spends time with me. We do lots of things together. He has season tickets to the Wake Forest football games and we never miss a game. I know my mom loves me too, but we don't spend much time together because she often doesn't feel well."

Ten-year-old Brandon said, "My mom loves me. She comes to my soccer games and we go out to eat afterward. I don't know if my dad loves me. He said he did, but he left us. I don't ever see him."

Haley, sixteen, said, "How do I know my parents love me? Mainly because they are always there for me. I can discuss anything with them. I know that they will be understanding and try to help me make good decisions. I'm going to miss them when I go to college in a couple of years, but I know they'll still be there for me."

For those children who crave time with their parents, and for all the others as well, a parent's gift of focused attention is an essential element in ensuring that they feel loved. When you spend time with your children, you are creating memories that will last a lifetime. You want your children to be blessed by the memories they carry from the years they spend in your home. They will have healthy and uplifting memories when their emotional tanks are kept full. As parents, you can give such healthy and uplifting memories and help assure your children's balance, stability, and happiness for the rest of their lives.

IF YOUR CHILD'S LOVE LANGUAGE IS
quality time...

Here are a few more ideas especially for parents. Pick and choose among them to try something new you think your child will appreciate.

- Instead of waiting until all your chores are done before spending time with your child, include them in your daily activities such as laundry, grocery shopping, or yardwork. Though it may take longer, the time together will make up for the inconvenience.
- Stop what you are doing to make eye contact with your child as they tell you something important.
- Fix a healthy snack together, such as a plate of cut-up fruit.
- Find silly things to laugh about and laugh a lot about them.
- Give older children single-use cameras to record meaningful occasions.
- Turn off your television show to watch your child's favorite show with them.
- Go to the toy store and play with some fun toys with no intention of buying anything.
- Ask very specific questions about your child's day that do not have a yes or no answer.
- When taking your younger children to a park or playground, spend the time actually playing with them instead of watching from the park bench. Pushing your daughter on the swing or riding the slide with your son creates lifelong memories and communicates love.
- Instead of screen time, focus on arts such as singing together or fingerpainting.
- Schedule a specific "date time" with each of your children individually. Put it in your calendar and don't allow other priorities to take its place.

- Surprise your child with tickets or a trip to a special place. A camping trip, big-league baseball game, or day in the city can build lifelong memories. Add pictures of the event to further strengthen this surprise.

- If possible, take your child to your workplace one day. Introduce your child to your coworkers and take your child to lunch with you.

- Set aside a special place in the house where you go to play. A walk-in closet can serve as a "castle," while a place in the garage can serve as your "workshop."

- Involve older children in vacation planning, researching the Internet together.

- Have a campout together, even if it is simply a tent in your yard. Include flashlights and special camp foods to make the event complete.

- Occasionally take family walks or bike rides together. Seek opportunities to spend time together that also include exercise.

- Share more meals together as a family. Make dinnertime a special occasion with lots of talk about the day. Family prayer can also strengthen this time.

- Spend a few extra minutes putting your child to bed at night. Bedtime stories, talking about the day, or praying together at night can each be part of your everyday pattern.

- For older children, spend time doing "homework" together— they with their schoolwork and you with any work projects. Tell them what you're working on.

- Plant something together. For those with outdoor-oriented children, time together in a flower garden, planting summer vegetables, or landscaping the yard can create lifelong positive memories.

- Make photo albums together on your computer. Talk together about the memories you shared in the process.

- On a rainy day, sit in the same room and read quietly, each of you with your own book or magazine.

THE 5 LOVE LANGUAGES OF CHILDREN

physical touch
words of affirmation
quality time
gifts
acts of service

5

gifts

When we asked ten-year-old Rachel why she was so sure that her parents loved her, she said, "Come to my room and I'll show you." Once in her room, she pointed to a large teddy bear. "They brought me this from California." And then touching a fluffy stuffed clown, she said, "They bought me this when I went to first grade. And this silly monkey was from their trip to Hawaii for their anniversary." She continued around the room, pointing out more than a dozen gifts she had received from her parents over the past few years. All of them were in a special place, displaying her parents' love.

The giving and receiving of gifts can be a powerful expression of love, at the time they are given and often extending into later years. The most meaningful gifts become symbols of love, and those that truly convey love are part of a love language. Yet for parents to truly speak love language number four—gifts—the child must feel that his parents genuinely care. For this reason, the other love languages must be given along with a gift. The child's emotional love tank needs to be kept filled in order for the gift to express heartfelt love. This means that parents will use a combination of physical touch, words of affirmation, quality time, and service to keep the love tank full.

Julie told how the love languages were helping her to better understand her two daughters—Mallory, six, and Meredith, eight. "My husband and I often go on business trips and the girls stay with their grandmother. While we are away, I buy something for the girls. Meredith is always much more excited about the gifts than Mallory is, talking about them as soon as we get home. She jumps up and down in excitement as we take out the presents and oohs and aahs as she opens her gift. Then she finds a special nook in her room for it and wants us to see where she put it. When her friends come over, she always shows them her latest gift."

In contrast, while Mallory is polite and appreciates the gifts from her parents, she is more excited to learn about the trip. Mallory "comes to us to hear every detail of our trip," Julie reported. "She talks with us separately and then together, and seems to drink up everything we tell her. Meredith, on the other hand, asks few questions about where we have been and what we have seen."

When someone asked Julie what she was going to do with her insight, she said, "Well, I'm going to keep on buying gifts for the girls, because I want to. But now I don't feel hurt when Mallory doesn't act as excited as Meredith. It used to bother me because I thought Mallory wasn't being appreciative. Now I understand that our conversation means to Mallory what the gift means to Meredith. Both my husband and I are making more effort to give Mallory more quality time after a trip and all the rest of the year as well. And we want to teach Mallory the language of gifts just as we hope to teach Meredith to speak the language of quality time."

The Grace of Giving

Giving and receiving gifts as a way to express love is a universal phenomenon. The English word *gift* comes from the Greek word *charis,* which means "grace, or an undeserved gift." The idea behind this is that if the gift is deserved, then it is payment. A true gift is not payment for services rendered; rather, it is an expression of love for the individual and is freely given by the donor. In our society, not all giving is so sincere. Especially in the business world, much of it is payback for doing business with a certain company, or a bribe in hope that someone will do business in the future. The item is not given simply for the benefit of the receiver, but is more a way of saying thank you for making a financial contribution or a request for a further contribution.

The same distinction needs to be made in parental giving to children. When a parent offers a gift if the child will clean his room, this is not a true gift but a payment for services rendered. When a parent promises an ice cream cone to a child if he will watch TV for the next half hour, the cone is not a gift but a bribe designed to manipulate the child's behavior. While the child may not know the words payback or bribe, he understands the concept.

At times parents who have every intention of offering a true gift may be sending confused messages if they ignore the child's deep emotional need for love. In fact, a child who doesn't feel truly loved can easily misinterpret a gift, thinking it is conditionally given. One mother, under great stress and at odds with her son, gave him a new baseball. Later, she found it in the toilet.

"Jason, what's your ball doing here? Don't you like it?"

"Sorry," was Jason's only reply.

The next day she found the ball in the garbage can. Again she talked with him, and he just looked down and said, "I'm sorry."

Later Mom learned to concentrate on keeping Jason's emotional tank full, especially at bedtime. Soon she began to notice a change. In a few weeks, she gave him a baseball bat, and this time he hugged her and said with a smile, "Thanks, Mom!"

Jason is typical of compliant children who have empty emotional tanks. These children seldom show their pain and their needs openly, but display their feelings in indirect ways. The disposing or ignoring of gifts is a classic example of this type of child needing a fill-up.

Make the Most of Giving

The grace of giving has little to do with the size and cost of the gift. It has everything to do with love. Maybe you remember a grandparent who told you about receiving an orange plus a necessary item of clothing on one harsh Christmas during the Depression. Today we parents don't always think of necessities as gifts but as items we must supply for our children. And yet, we often give these items with loving hearts for the sincere benefit of our children. Let's celebrate such gifts. If we do not present gifts as expressions of love, children may learn to receive them as "what is to be expected" and not recognize the love behind the gifts.

> If we do not present gifts as expressions of love, children may learn to receive them as "what is to be expected."

Here's a suggestion to help a common gift become an expression of love. Take time to wrap up the new school clothes and then present them when the family is gathered around the dinner table. Unwrapping a present provides an emotional thrill for a child, and you can demonstrate that every gift, whether a necessity or a luxury, is an expression of your love. Such celebration of all kinds of gifts will also teach your children how to respond to others who give them presents. As you give to them with grace, you want them to respond with grace, whether a gift is large or small.

One warning in buying your children toys as gifts. In the toy department, you need real wisdom. The sheer volume of items available means that you must be very selective. This volume is compounded by television ads that parade the latest toys before the eyes of children, thus creating desires that did not exist sixty seconds before and may be gone by the next day. But in the meantime, many children are sure they must have the toy they just saw on the screen.

Do not let advertisers determine what you buy for your children. Examine toys closely, asking yourself questions such as, "What message does this toy communicate to my child? Is it a message with which I am comfortable? What might my child learn from playing with this toy? Will its overall effect tend to be positive or negative? How durable is the toy? What is its normal life span? Does it have limited appeal or will my child turn to it again and again? Is this a toy we can afford?" Never buy a nonessential toy if you can't afford it.

> Never buy a nonessential toy if you can't afford it.

Not every toy needs to be educational, but they should all serve some positive purpose in the life of your children. Beware of buying high-tech computerized toys that may expose your children to value systems far removed from those of your family. They will get enough of this on television, from the neighbors, and from friends at school.

When Giving Is Abused

Be careful. It's often tempting to shower children with gifts as substitutes for the other love languages. For many reasons, parents sometimes resort to presents rather than being truly present to their children. For some who grew up in unhealthy families, a gift seems easier to give than emotional involvement. Others may not have the time, patience, or knowledge to know how to give their children what they genuinely need. They truly love their children, but seem unaware of how to provide the emotional security and sense of self-worth that they need.

Abuse of gift-giving can occur when a child is living with a custodial parent following a separation or divorce. The noncustodial parent is often tempted to shower a child with gifts, perhaps from the pain of separation or feelings of guilt over leaving the family. When these gifts are overly expensive, ill-chosen, and used as a comparison with what the custodial parent can provide, they are really a form of bribery, an attempt to buy the child's love. They may also be a subconscious way of getting back at the custodial parent.

Children receiving such ill-advised gifts may eventually see them for what they are, but in the meantime they are learning that at least one parent regards gifts as a substitute for genuine love. This can make children materialistic and manipulative, as they learn to manage people's feelings and behavior by the improper use of gifts. This kind of substitution can have tragic consequences for the children's character and integrity.

We think of Susan, who is raising three children alone. Susan had been divorced for three years from Charles, who now lives with his second wife in a luxurious lifestyle. Susan and the children were just getting by financially, and the children were eager to visit Dad. Lisa, Charley, and Annie, ages fifteen, twelve, and ten, saw their dad two weekends a month. On these visits he would take them on expensive outings such as skiing and boating. No wonder they wanted to visit—that's where the fun was—and they increasingly complained about being bored at home. They often returned with lavish gifts, and they displayed increasing amounts of anger at Susan, especially for the few days following a visit with their father. Charles was turning their feelings against Susan, as he tried to earn affection for himself. He didn't realize that as the children grew older, they would come to despise him for manipulating them.

Fortunately, Susan was able to persuade Charles to receive counseling with her and to seek healthy ways to handle their children. Initially, this meant setting aside past differences and anger so that they could work together to meet the emotional needs of their children. During the counseling, they both became expert love tank filler-uppers. When Charles used all five love languages to relate to his children, and learned to use gift-giving as a love language instead of a manipulating device, the children responded beautifully. While it is still uncommon for divorced people to work together in this way for the good of their children, more parents are attempting to do so.

Other parents (and grandparents) may choose to shower their kids with so many presents that their rooms look like disorganized toy stores. With such excess, the gifts lose their specialness; the child has more toys than he can possibly experience. Eventually none of the gifts has any meaning, and the child becomes emotionally dead to receiving gifts. The toys seem a burden to him, because his parents expect him to keep the toys in some semblance of order.

Lavishing too many gifts is like taking a child into the toy department and saying, "All of this belongs to you." The child may be excited at first, but after a while is running in all directions and playing with nothing.

Appropriate toys should help a child learn how to focus his attention with enjoyment. For this to happen, parents and grandparents may need to give less rather than more, carefully choosing gifts that will be meaningful rather than impressive.

> Parents and grandparents may need to give less rather than more, carefully choosing gifts that will be meaningful.

Guidelines for Giving

As you give to your children, you need to keep some guidelines in mind. Gifts should be genuine expressions of love. If they are payment for services rendered, or bribery, you should not call them gifts but should acknowledge them for what they are. This way, the true gifts selected for the benefit of your children and as an expression of love can be enjoyed for what they are.

Except for Christmas and birthdays, many gifts should be chosen by both you and your children. This is particularly true as your children grow and have more opinions about their clothes, shoes, backpacks, etc. Your children also have desires about their nonessential toys, and while you can't give them everything they want, you will want to consider their preferences. This involves discerning whether the desire is momentary or lasting, healthy or unhealthy, and whether the toy will have a positive or negative effect. Whenever you can, it is wise to select a gift that a child truly wants.

And remember, not all gifts come from a store. You may find a special gift as you walk down a winding road or even across a parking lot. Wildflowers, unusual stones, even driftwood can qualify as gifts when wrapped or presented in a creative manner. Gifts can also be made out of household items. Young children have no concept of money, and whether a gift is made or purchased is of little consequence. If the present stimulates their creativity, it can be meaningful and can bind you more closely to your children in love.

Amy's Ring

Earlier we said that some children who do not respond with great enthusiasm when they receive a gift may in later years come to value it much more. Ted found that out years after his daughter rejected his present. While traveling abroad, Ted bought a ring for his twelve-year-old daughter Amy and gave it to her when he returned home. She showed little interest in it and put it away in a dresser drawer.

Ted was disappointed but eventually forgot about the ring. In her teen years, Amy gave her parents great amounts of grief with her adolescent behavior, to the point that Ted despaired about her future. Even when Amy made a dramatic recovery in her attitudes and behavior, her father was still not convinced that she was all right. He questioned her sincerity and this made it very difficult for either of them to move toward the close relationship they craved.

Then one day Ted noticed that Amy was wearing the ring he had given her so long ago, before her problems began. Tears came to his eyes as he realized what his daughter was trying to tell him—that she was in control of herself and could now be trusted.

When Ted asked Amy if this is what she meant, she acknowledged that was all she wanted—to be trusted as she developed and changed. The two cried together. Amy continues to do well.

This story shows how symbolically important a gift can be. Amy probably would have never had the deep problems she experienced if her caring parents had been able to keep her emotional tank full. Her emotional needs had to be met before she had the capacity to receive or appreciate a gift in the same spirit in which it was given.

When Your Child's Primary Love Language Is Receiving Gifts

Most children respond positively to gifts, but for some, receiving gifts is their primary love language. You might be inclined to think that this is so for all children, judging from the way they beg for things. It is true that all children—and adults—want to have more and more. But those whose language of love is receiving gifts will respond differently when they get their gift.

Children whose primary love language is the receiving of gifts will always make much of receiving the gift. They will want the present to be wrapped or at least given in a unique and creative way. This is all part of the love expression. They will look at the paper, maybe talk about the bow. Often they will ooh and aah as they open the gift. It will seem a big deal to them—and it is. They are feeling very special as they open the present, and they want your undivided attention as they do so. Remember, for them this is love's loudest voice. They see the gift as an extension of you and your love, and they want to share this moment with you. Once they have opened the gift, they will hug you or thank you profusely.

These children will also make a special place in their room for the new gift so that they can display it proudly. They will share it with their friends and will show it to you again and again in the next few days. They will say how much they like it. The gift holds a special place in their hearts because it is in fact an expression of your love. Seeing the gift reminds them that they are loved. It doesn't matter to them if the gift was made, found, or purchased; whether it was something they had desired or not. What matters is that you thought about them.

What the Children Say

The comments from the following children reveal that, for them, receiving gifts is the language that best communicates love.

Marco, five, was talking to his grandmother after his second day in kindergarten. "My teacher loves me, Nana. Look what she gave me." He held up a bright blue ruler with large numbers printed across it, the evidence of his teacher's love.

Elizabeth, six, asked us: "Have you ever met the love man? He is right over there," she said, pointing to an older gentleman. "He gives all the children gum." For Elizabeth, he was the love man because he gave gifts.

Courtney, fifteen, was asked how she knew her parents loved her. Without hesitation she pointed to her jeans, top, and shoes. Then she said, "Everything I have, they gave me. In my mind, that's love. They have given me not only the essentials but far more than I need. In fact, I share things with my friends whose parents can't afford them."

Josh, eighteen, was leaving for college in a few weeks. When we asked how strongly he felt loved by his parents, on a zero-to-ten scale, he immediately said, "Ten." Why ten? "See this car?" he asked, pointing to a red Honda. "My folks gave it to me. I didn't really deserve it because I didn't do my best in high school, but they told me they wanted me to know that they were proud of me. This car was an expression of their love. All I have to do is be responsible for changing the oil and doing other maintenance.

"My parents have always been like that. They have given me everything I have ever needed—all my sports equipment in high school, all my clothes, everything. They are the most generous people I know. I have tried not to take advantage of their generosity, but I'm sure that they love me. Now that I'm going off to college, I know that I will miss them."

For such a child, gifts are more than material objects. They are tangible expressions of love that speak deeply. That is why it is especially traumatic if the gifts are destroyed or misplaced. And, if the parent who gave the gift moves or damages it, or, in a fit of rage says, "I'm sorry I gave that to you," the child may be emotionally devastated.

Remember, your children may not now realize how much you are giving, even as you continue to fill their emotional tanks. But as they grow older, they may look back and realize that your love and presence has been the best gift of all.

IF YOUR CHILD'S LOVE LANGUAGE IS

gifts...

Here are a few more ideas especially for parents. Pick and choose among them to try something new you think your child will appreciate.

- Keep a small collection of inexpensive gifts packed away for your child. Then give them one at a time as you sense there is a need.

- Select presents that fit the interests of your child.

- Carry snacks or small candies you can give out as a "treat" when away from home.

- Make a meal you know your child likes, go to a special restaurant, or make their favorite dessert.

- Start a collection of unique gift boxes and wrapping papers that can be used to package even the most simple of presents.

- When away from home, mail a small package to your child with their name on it.

- Give personally made coupons for your child good for some of their favorites, such as a free spaghetti dinner, an extra-half hour of time with you before bedtime, or a small gift next time you are shopping together.

- Keep a "gift bag" of small, inexpensive gifts your child can choose from as a reward for doing something positive.

- Make after-school snacks memorable by serving them on a special plate.

- Be on the lookout for personalized gifts with your child's name on them. Save them for a rainy or difficult day as an encouraging surprise.

- Give your child a "song," either one you make up or a special song you select that reminds you of them.

- Create a treasure hunt for a gift that includes a map and clues along the way to the main surprise.

- Hide a small gift in your child's lunchbox.

- If you are away from your child a few days, leave a small package for each day with a special gift and note reminding how much you love them.

- Instead of spending money on a larger gift for a birthday, host a birthday party at a special event location.

- Consider a gift that lasts, such as a tree you can plant together or a computer game you can play together in the future.

- Buy or make your child a special ring or necklace to wear that is just from you.

- For young children, find "nature gifts" such as wildflowers or interesting stones wrapped in a special paper or box.

- For a birthday or Christmas, shop with your child for a special gift—asking her opinion. This personal involvement will make the gift more meaningful.

- Keep a chart and some fun stickers to keep a record of accomplishments. Reward your child with a gift after a set number of stickers are earned.

- Create a "secret drawer" where your child can keep her small "treasures"—anything from a bird feather to a pack of gum.

THE 5 LOVE LANGUAGES OF CHILDREN

physical touch

words of affirmation

quality time

gifts

acts of service

6

acts of service

Jacob has just started his first full-time job and is thinking about getting married next summer. He also is remembering his childhood: "I think the thing that made me feel most loved was the way my parents worked so hard to help me with everything. I remember how they'd get up early on Saturdays to take me to my games, or stay up late helping me with a homework project."

The twenty-four-year-old continues to reminisce. "The little things and big things—they did so much to help me, even though they were both busy. I realize it now more than I did then, but even at the time I knew they were working hard to help me, and I always appreciated it. I hope I can do the same for my children someday."

Some people speak acts of service as their primary love language. Even if your child does not, know this: Parenting is a service-oriented vocation. The day you found out that you would have a child, you enrolled for full-time service. Your contract called for a minimum of eighteen years of service with an understanding that you would be

The day you found out that you would have a child, you enrolled for full-time service.

on "active reserve" for several years after that.

As a parent who must serve, you probably have discovered another truth about this love language: Acts of service are physically and emotionally demanding. Therefore, we parents must give attention to our own physical and emotional health. For physical health, we need balanced patterns of sleeping, eating, and exercising. For emotional health, self-understanding and a mutually supportive marital relationship are crucial.

As we consider acts of service, we must ask ourselves, "Who do I serve?" It is not just your children. If you are married, you serve your spouse, doing things that will please him or her in order to express your love. You want to keep your partner's love tank full by your acts of service. Because children need a mother and father who give them a balanced model for life, making time for your marital relationship is an essential part of good parenting. If you are a single parent, it is even more important to keep yourself physically and emotionally healthy—see "Speaking the Love Languages in Single-Parent Families" on page 179 for some ideas.

What's Best?

As parents, we serve our children—but our primary motivation is not to please them. Our chief purpose is to do what is best. What would most please your children at the moment is likely not the best way to express your love. Put three candy bars in your child's lunch and she will cheer, but you won't be giving her what's best. In serving your children, the main motive—doing what's best—means you are trying to fill their love tanks. And to supply that need for love, you should use your acts of service in conjunction with the other languages of love.

A caution as we explore the final love language: Don't view acts of service as a way to manipulate your children. This is easy to do, because when they are young, children desire gifts and services more than anything else. But if we parents give in to desires or even demands for too many gifts and too much service, our children can remain childishly self-centered and become selfish. However, this caution should not keep parents from using the language of service and gifts in appropriate ways.

Acts of service can become a model for your child's service and responsibility. You may wonder how your children will develop their own independence and competence if you serve them. But as you express your love by acts of service to your children, doing things they may not yet be able to do for themselves, you are setting a model. This will help them escape their self-centered focus and help others; that's our ultimate goal as parents (see the section "The Ultimate Purpose of Service").

> What would most please your children at the moment is likely not the best way to express your love.

What a Child Should Do When

Children with full love tanks are far more likely to pick up on that loving model of service than children who are uncertain of their parents' love. Such acts of service must be age appropriate. You should do for your children what they cannot do for themselves. Obviously, you are not still feeding them when they are six. Making beds for four-year-olds is an act of service, but eight-year-olds are capable of doing this themselves. Children don't need to wait until they get to college to learn how to run a washer and dryer—colleges don't offer courses in this! Parents who are too busy to teach children how to do laundry, or too perfectionistic to let them do it, are not loving those children but crippling them.

Thus, acts of service has an intermediate step. We serve our chil-

> We serve our children, but as they are ready, we teach them how to serve themselves and then others.

dren, but as they are ready, we teach them how to serve themselves and then others. Of course, that is not always a convenient or quick process. It takes more time to teach a child to prepare a meal than to fix the meal yourself. If your only objective is to get the food on the table, you might as well prepare all the meals. But if your objective is to love your children—looking out for their best interests—you will want to teach them how to cook. But before and during that time, the best motivator for your children is to see your genuine acts of love for the family as you serve them over many years.

Remember, too, that some acts of service you will perform for your children come from highly developed skills you have that they may never acquire. We all have different aptitudes, and within a family we can serve one another with our unique abilities. As parents we must be careful not to force children to be replicas of us or, even worse, fulfill the dreams we never accomplished for ourselves. Rather, we want to help them develop their own skills, follow their own interests, and become the best they can be using their endowments from God.

Shootin' Straight

Some parents, wanting their children to develop their skills and independence, lean too far in the direction of letting their children figure things out for themselves. Will and Kathy from Colorado were like that. They embodied a pioneer spirit of rugged independence and self-reliance and wanted to raise their two boys to be the same way. Western to the core, they seemed as if they had just swung off a stagecoach.

After Will and Kathy attended my (Gary's) marriage seminar and heard about the five love languages, they concluded that service could not be one of the languages of love. Will told me, "I don't believe parents should do things for children that they can do for themselves. How are you gonna teach them to be independent if you keep on doing things for them? They've got to learn to rope their own steer."

"Do the boys cook their own meals?" I asked.

"That's my job. But they do everything else," Kathy said.

"They cook when they are out on the trail and do a great job," Will added. These two were obviously proud of their sons.

"As you listened to the love languages, do you have any idea what your boys' primary love languages might be?"

"Don't know," Will said.

"Do you think your boys really feel loved?"

"Suppose so. They should."

"Do you have the courage to ask them?" I probed.

"What do you mean?"

"I mean, get each of them alone and say, 'Son, I want to ask you a question that I've never asked you, but it is important for me to know. Do you feel that I love you? Shoot straight. I really want to know how you feel.'"

Will was silent for a long moment. "That'll be hard. Don't know that it's necessary."

"It's not necessary," I responded, "but you won't ever know their language if you don't ask."

Will went home with my words ringing in his head, "You won't ever know if you don't ask." So he started with his younger son, Buck, out behind the barn when they were alone. He asked the question I had suggested and Buck answered.

"Sure, Dad, I know you love me. You spend time with me. When you go into town, you always take me along. On the trail, you make sure we get some time to talk. I've always thought it was pretty spe-

cial to get to spend so much time with you, as busy as you are."
When Will choked up, Buck asked, "Is something wrong? You ain't
gonna die or something, are ya?"

"Naw, I ain't gonna die. I just wanted to make sure you know I
love you."

This was such an emotional experience that it took Will a week
to work up the courage to talk with seventeen-year-old Jake. One
night when they were alone together after supper, he turned to his
son and said, "Jake, I want to ask you a question that I've never
asked before, but it's important for me to know. It might be hard for
you, but I want you to shoot straight, because I really need to know
how you feel. Do you really feel that I love you?"

After a long silence, Jake said, "I don't know how to say this exactly, Pa. I guess I know you love me, but sometimes I don't feel it.
Sometimes I feel that you don't love me at all."

"When's that, Son?"

"When I need you and you don't help me. Like the time the fire
started on the lower forty and I sent word by Buck that I needed
your help. He came back and told me that you said you knew I could
do it by myself. Buck and I got it out all right, but I kept wondering
why you didn't come. I kept telling myself that it was 'cause you
were trying to make me independent, but I kept feeling you didn't
love me.

"That time when I was ten and having a hard time with my math,
I asked you to help," Jake continued. "You told me I could do it myself 'cause I was smart. I knew you knew how to do it, and you could
have helped me if you would have just explained it. I felt let down.
Or that time the wagon got stuck and I asked you to help me get it
out. You said I got it stuck and I could figure out how to get it out. I
knew I could get it out, but I wanted you to help me.

"Them's the times I felt you didn't care. Like I said, I know you do love me, but I don't always feel that you do."

It was enough to make a cowboy cry. "Jake, I'm sorry," Will said. "I just didn't know how you felt. I should've asked you sooner. I wanted you to be independent and self-reliant—and you are. I'm proud of you, but I want you to know that I love you. The next time you need my help, I'll be there for you. I hope you give me another chance." The two men hugged in the quiet kitchen.

Will got his chance about seven months later when a wagon was stuck in the creek. The boys worked more than two hours and couldn't loosen it. Finally, Jake sent Buck for their dad. Buck couldn't believe his father's response when he immediately saddled up and rode back with Buck to the creek. Once the wagon was out, Buck thought it strange that his dad hugged Jake and then told Jake, "Thanks, man. I appreciate it." The healing that started in the kitchen was consummated at the creek. A tough rancher had learned a tender lesson.

Service or Slavery?

Because service to a child is constant for so many years, and takes place in and around so many other obligations, parents can forget that the daily and mundane acts they perform are expressions of love with long-term effects. At times they can even feel more like slaves than loving servants, put upon by spouse, children, and others. However, if they assume this attitude, it will communicate itself emotionally to the child, who will feel that he is receiving little love from the acts of service.

Loving service is not slavery, as some fear. Slavery is imposed from the outside and is done with reluctance. Loving service is an internally motivated desire to give one's energy to others. Loving service is a gift, not a necessity, and is done freely, not under coercion. When parents serve their children with a spirit of resentment and bitterness, a child's physical needs may be met, but his emotional development will be greatly hampered.

Because service is so daily, even the best parents need to stop for an attitude check now and then, to be sure that their acts of service are communicating love.

The Ultimate Purpose of Service

The ultimate purpose for acts of service to children is to help them emerge as mature adults who are able to give love to others through acts of service. This includes not only being helpful to cherished loved ones, but also serving persons who are in no way able to return or repay the kindnesses. As children live with the example of parents who serve the family and those beyond the walls of their home, they too will learn to serve.

The Bible suggests that sacrificial service is one way we please God. While dining in the home of a prominent religious leader, Jesus told His host:

When you give a luncheon or dinner, do not invite your friends, your brothers or relatives, or your rich neighbors; if you do, they may invite you back and so you will be repaid. But when you give a banquet, invite the poor, the crippled, the lame, the blind, and you will be blessed. . . .[1]

What powerful words! This is what we want for our children—to be able to perform acts of service with compassion and genuine love. But our children are immature. They are naturally self-centered and cannot be expected to serve others with selfless motivation. They want to be rewarded for their good behavior. It takes a long time for them to be able to give love through selfless acts of service.

How do we move toward this ultimate goal? First, we make sure that our children feel genuinely loved and cared for. We keep their emotional tanks full. Also, we are role models for them. By our example, they first experience loving acts of service. As they grow older and are able to show appreciation, we can gradually move from commands to requests. Requests do not demand. It is difficult for children to feel good about expressing appreciation when they are commanded to do so. It is the difference between "Say thank you to your father," or "Would you say thank you to your father?" Making requests is more soothing, forestalls anger, and helps us be positive and pleasant.

> It is difficult for children to feel good about expressing appreciation when they are commanded to do so.

As children mature, they increasingly notice what is being done for them and are also aware of what has been done in the past. Of course, they don't remember anyone changing their diapers or feeding them. But they see other parents caring for their infants in this way and know that they enjoyed the same acts of service. With an assurance of being genuinely loved, they are able to appreciate when food is prepared and served. They will become more aware of story times and family play, of parents teaching them to ride a bicycle, helping them with homework, caring for them when they are ill, comforting their feelings when they are hurt, taking them to special places, and buying treats and gifts.

Eventually these children will notice that their parents do things for others. They will learn how to wait on a sick person or to give money to the less fortunate. They will want to participate in work projects that help other people, especially those adventures which take them out of their familiar routine. They don't have to travel far to find the less fortunate. In most towns of any size, there are people in need. Your family, either alone or with a community or church group, can take a day or a week to offer your services to a mission, a camp for underprivileged children, a food pantry or soup kitchen, a mission, or a nursing home. When parents and their children work together in such acts of service, the activity becomes a powerful lesson in the joys of helping others.

And, of course, there are those occasional more exotic service opportunities overseas through work or private organizations. One year I (Ross) volunteered as a doctor with a Christian mission agency —Wycliffe Bible Translators—in Bolivia. The whole Campbell family came and helped. I remember treating a three-year-old Indian boy with a badly broken leg in our clinic. For six weeks he was in traction and unable to be moved. Many missionary children there performed acts of service for the little boy. I was thrilled at Christmas, when our Carey, then eight years old, gave the boy's sister her most treasured Christmas gift, a new doll.

Teaching by Example

The heart of social and missionary service is a desire to help others with acts of service. Yet parents can get off track and actually prevent their children from being able to give of themselves unselfishly. We must be careful in our acts of service to never show conditional love. When parents give of themselves to their children only when they are pleased by their behavior, such acts of service are conditional. Our watching children will learn that a person should help others only if there is something in it for him.

"What's in it for me?" is a predominant attitude in our society. And yet, it is exactly opposite to the love language of acts of service (and contrary to the heart of Christian social and missionary service). You may be one of the children raised in this self-involved mind-set. Now you want your own children to develop into people of integrity. You want them to be kind and generous to others, particularly to the less fortunate, without expecting anything in return. And you may wonder if that is possible in our society.

It certainly is possible, but it depends very much on you. Your children need to see in you the traits you want them to develop. They need to experience your acts of service to them and be involved in your caring for other people. You can teach them by example to show concern for others.

"Do-Good Projects"

One of the finest ways to do this is by hosting others in your home. Family hospitality is a great treasure, for in this act of service people truly get to know each other and to form strong friendships. As you open your home to others, your children learn this meaningful way of sharing love with friends and family.

Interestingly, people increasingly are hosting gatherings in restaurants instead of their homes. But the warmth and intimacy of a home is special. It is important to foster good relationships with other people, and that happens at a deeper level in a home.

In the Chapman family, we had an open house every Friday night for college students during the early '70s. The students came from nearby schools, including Wake Forest University, and we'd pack in from twenty to sixty students. Our format was simple. From 8 to 10 p.m. we had a discussion about a relational, moral, or social issue, drawn from a Bible passage. Next came refreshments followed by informal conversations. At midnight we kicked them out.

Our children, Shelley and Derek, were young during those years and wandered in and out of the meetings. It was not unusual to find one of them sleeping in a student's lap by the fireplace, or engaging someone in conversation. The students were our extended family, and the children looked forward to Friday evenings.

Often on Saturday mornings some of the students returned for what we came to call "Do-Good Projects." We would load up in the van and distribute them around the community to rake leaves for the elderly or clean gutters or other jobs that needed to be done.

> We are convinced that **sharing our home** with others and involving the family in **service projects** had a profound and **positive effect** on **our children.**

Shelley and Derek always went along on these service projects. And yes, they insisted on having their own rakes, although their greatest joy was to jump in the leaves after they were raked.

As adults, Shelley and Derek look back on this involvement with students as a significant part of their childhood. Shelley, who is now an OB/GYN physician, acknowledges that talking with the students from Bowman Gray Medical School made a strong impression on her choice of vocation. Both she and Derek are very people-oriented. Derek has been known to invite street people into his apartment during the winter (did we really teach him this?). We are convinced that sharing our home with others and involving the family in service projects had a profound and positive effect on our children.

Make it your goal that your children will learn to be comfortable in serving others. Your children won't pick this up by accident. Rather, they will learn it as they watch you serving them and other people. They will also learn as you give them small levels of responsibility for helping you serve. As they grow, you can increase what they do.

When Your Child's Primary Love Language Is Service

Acts of service that are genuine expressions of love will communicate on an emotional level to most children. However, if service is your child's primary love language, your acts of service will communicate most deeply that you love Johnny or Julie. When that child asks you to fix a bicycle or mend a doll's dress, he or she does not merely want to get a task done; your child is crying for emotional love. That's what Jake was really asking his dad, Will, to do.

When we parents recognize and respond to these requests and give the help with a loving and positive attitude, the child will go away with a full love tank, as Jake did. But when parents refuse to respond to the needs, or do so with harsh or critical words, the child may ride off on a repaired bike, but do so with a discouraged spirit.

If your child's primary love language is acts of service, this does not mean that you must jump at every request. It does mean that you should be extremely sensitive to those requests and recognize that your response will either help fill the child's love tank or else puncture the tank. Each request calls for a thoughtful, loving response.

What the Children Say

Look at what the following children say about their primary love language.

Krystal, age seven, has had numerous health problems during the past three years. "I know Mommy loves me 'cause when I need help with my homework, she helps me. When I have to go to the doctor, she gets off from work and takes me. When I am really sick, she fixes my favorite soup."

Bradley, twelve, lives with his mother and younger brother. His father left when Bradley was six. "I know my mom loves me because she sews the buttons on my shirt when they fall off and also helps me with my homework every night. She works hard in an office so we can have food and clothes. I think my dad loves me, but he doesn't do much to help."

Jodi, fourteen, attends a special education class at the public school. She lives with her mother. "I know Mom loves me because she helps me make my bed and wash my clothes. At night, she helps me do my homework, especially my art."

Melanie, also fourteen, is the oldest of four children. "I know my parents love me because they do so many things for me. Mom made my costume for the school drama; in fact, she made costumes for two other people too. That made me really proud of her. Dad has always helped me with my homework, and this year he has really put in some time on my algebra. I couldn't believe he could remember all that stuff."

For these children, their parents' acts of service came through as emotional love. Parents whose children speak this primary love language learn that serving is loving. Serve your child—and others—and they will know you love them.

IF YOUR CHILD'S LOVE LANGUAGE IS
acts of service ...

Here are a few more ideas especially for parents. Pick and choose among them to try something new you think your child will appreciate.

- Help your child practice for their sports team, such as pitch and catch for baseball or shooting free throws for children participating in basketball.

- Sit down and help your child if they're having computer problems.

- Instead of just telling your younger children to go to bed, pick them up and gently carry them and tuck them in their blankets.

- For school-age children, help them select their outfit for the day as they are waking up in the morning.

- Occasionally wake up a half hour earlier to make a special surprise breakfast for your children.

- Begin teaching your child the importance of serving others through regular involvement together in a local community group or church ministry.

- For younger children, set up your child's favorite toys while they are taking a nap or are at school so they can immediately play with them (with you!).

- When running late to an appointment or meeting, help your child quickly finish what they are doing so you can both be ready faster instead of just telling them to hurry.

- During a time when your child is sick, go the extra step by setting up their favorite movie, reading them stories, or buying them a book in one of their favorite series.

- Connect your child with one of your friends or family members who can help them in an area of interest such as computer technology, soccer, piano playing, or scouting.

- Choose one area in which you determine to always serve your child above and beyond normal expectations. Examples could include making sure there are always marshmallows in your child's hot chocolate, making sure their favorite teddy bear is in their bed at bedtime, or having all of the paint supplies ready when they are ready to paint.

- Start a "birthday dinner" tradition where you make your child any meal they want on their birthday.

- Make a list of several of your child's favorite things they do with you. Then periodically do one of their favorites when they least expect it.

- Create flash cards for your child's upcoming test or quiz. Work together with your child until they feel confident with the material.

- Assist your child in fixing a favorite broken toy or bicycle. Simply taking the time to repair it communicates love to a child whose love language is acts of service.

THE 5 LOVE LANGUAGES OF CHILDREN

physical touch

words of affirmation

quality time

gifts

acts of service

7

how to discover your child's
primary love language

We have introduced you to each of the five love languages, and you have heard the children describe
how a certain love language really speaks to them. Yet you may still
wonder, *What's my child's primary love language? I'm not sure I
know.* Spotting your child's primary language of love may take time,
but there are clues all around. This is our detective chapter, in which
we help you discover your child's primary love language.

Before you begin to uncover those clues, however, let's consider
one other crucial reason it's worth the search. We have mentioned
that speaking your child's primary love language helps her feel
loved. When your child feels loved, when her emotional tank is full,
she will be more responsive to parental guidance in all areas of her
life. She will listen without resentment. But there is an equally grand
reason to learn your child's love language—and to speak the other
four languages as well. As we speak love in the five languages, all the
while specializing in her language of love, we show her how to love

others and her own need to learn to speak others' love languages.

The Way of Unselfishness

The ability to give love and nurture in all the languages will make your children more balanced persons who can function well in society. As they do this, they can speak the love languages to meet their own needs and to be of help to others.

All children are selfish, so they are often unaware of the importance of communicating in ways that are not familiar or comfortable. For example, one child may have a problem sharing—and thus in giving gifts. Another may tend to be a loner and find it difficult to understand the need of gregarious people for quality time. A third child may be so behaviorally oriented that he has difficulty communicating verbally. Very quiet children are often this way. Helping such a child to be more verbal, affirmative, and outgoing is a significant expression of love on the part of the parents. He will be learning the important language of affirming words.

> When we as parents learn to speak our children's love language, even though it differs from our own, we are showing them the way of unselfishness.

When we as parents learn to speak our children's love language, even though it differs from our own, we are showing them the way of unselfishness, the way of serving others. We are guiding them into an important part of becoming an adult—giving and caring for others. Imagine, for instance, if all our children learned to appreciate love language #5, acts of service. Community associations that go begging for volunteers in city cleanup campaigns would have most streets cared for on the big day; they'd have lots of volunteers for the "welcome neighbor" program. Churches would have a waiting list of people wanting to help with committee work and serve behind the scenes.

It Takes Time

Knowing this, we should agree that speaking the five love languages with our children is important, and learning our children's primary language is crucial. How do we learn their language?

It takes time. With an infant, you must express love in all five languages; that's how he will develop emotionally. And yet, even then you may begin to see clues of your child's preferred language—if you are liberally using all of them. For instance, one child may show little response to his mother's voice while another child may find her voice incredibly soothing. One baby may be calmed by the nearness of another person, while another will seem not to notice very much.

As your child grows, you will begin to see that one of the love languages speaks far more deeply of your love than the others; also, when that one is used negatively, your child feels very hurt. Remember those two truths about the five love languages and you will become more effective in expressing your love and less destructive when you feel angry or frustrated with your child.

Discovering your child's love language is a process; it takes time, especially when your child is young. Young children are just beginning to learn how to receive and express love in the various languages. This means that they will experiment with actions and responses that are satisfying to them. That they engage in a particular response for a period of time does not mean that this is their primary love language. In a few months, they may specialize in another one.

Stages in Loving: Cami's Story

In the Campbell family, we were intrigued by watching our granddaughter, Cami, interact with the elderly persons at the nearby nursing home where her great-grandmother lived. Even when she was two and three years old, Cami loved to draw pictures for the residents and give each of them one. She also would make sure that her great-grandmother received enough cards and presents for her birthday and Christmas, even though her great-grandmother had Alzheimer's and did not really know Cami. It would have been easy for us to assume that Cami's primary love language was acts of service. However, that would have been a mistake, since she was too young for anyone to have an accurate reading on this. Also, we observed her need for attention from her parents, especially physical touch, eye contact, words of affection, and quality time.

As Cami grew, we enjoyed watching her ways of showing and receiving love, all the while remembering that children go through periods where their primary love language can temporarily change, especially during adolescence. We mention this because we want you to remember that a love language is not set in stone. While you need to look for your child's primary language, you also need to keep in mind that children go through stages in loving, as they do in everything else. They experiment in reaching out, just as they do in their hobbies and academic interests. They may seem to prefer one language for receiving love and another for giving it. You want to make sure you do not "peg" a child when he or she may be changing.

> We want you to remember that a love language is not set in stone.

As we emphasize your child's primary love language in this chapter, please remember that, as we have said, you cannot ignore the other four. Your child needs to learn to give and to receive love in all the languages. This is crucial because as he matures, he will encounter people whose primary love language is different from his own. The more effectively he can speak love in all the languages, the more effective he will be as a communicator of love and appreciation to his future spouse and children, work associates, and friends.

The supreme value of discovering your child's primary love language is that it gives you the most effective means of communicating emotional love. When you perceive that your child is discouraged and feeling distant, and you want to express emotional warmth to her, you will know how to focus your love.

Don't Be Fooled!

As you begin to look for a child's primary love language, it is better not to discuss your search with your children, and especially with teenagers. By nature children are self-centered. If they see that the concept of love languages is important to you, they may well use it to manipulate you to satisfy their momentary desires. The desires they express may have little to do with their deep emotional needs.

For example, if a child has been begging you for an iPhone, he may see the love language idea as a way to manipulate you to buy the device. All he has to do is to tell you that his primary language is gifts and that if you really love him, you will buy the iPhone. As a conscientious parent wanting to find his primary language, you are likely to buy the phone before you realize that you have been hoodwinked. Remember, positive parenting does not mean giving your children everything they want.

You can employ the following methods as you seek to discover your child's primary love language.

1. Observe How Your Child Expresses Love to You.

Watch your child; he may well be speaking his own love language. This is particularly true of a young child, who is very likely to express love to you in the language he desires most to receive. If your five- to eight-year-old frequently gives you words of appreciation such as, "Mommy, you're pretty," or "Daddy, thanks for helping me with my homework," or "I love you, Mommy," or "Have a good day, Dad," you can rightly suspect that his primary love language is words of affirmation.

This method is not as effective with fifteen-year-olds, particularly those who are accomplished in manipulation. They may have learned by trial and error that if they say positive words, you are more likely to give in to one of their desires, even if you are not completely convinced that you should. For this reason, this first method is best used for children who are between five and ten years of age.

2. Observe How Your Child Expresses Love to Others.

If your first-grader always wants to take a present to his teacher, this may indicate that his primary love language is receiving gifts. However, be careful that you are not suggesting presents for the teacher. If you are, your child is merely following your lead and the gift is not an expression of love, nor is it a clue to his primary love language.

A child whose language is gifts receives tremendous pleasure from getting presents and wants others to enjoy this same pleasure. He assumes that they will feel what he does when they receive a gift.

3. Listen to What Your Child Requests Most Often.

If your child often asks you to "look what I'm doing," play outside together, or sit and read a story to her, she is requesting quality time. If her requests seem to fit this pattern, she is asking for what she needs most emotionally, namely, your undivided attention. Of course, all children need attention, but for one who receives love most deeply this way, the requests for time together will greatly outnumber all the others.

If your child constantly solicits comments on his work, then his love language may be words of affirmation. Questions such as, "Mom, what do you think of the paper I wrote?" or "Does this outfit look okay?" or "Dad, how did I do in the game?" are all requests for words of affirmation. Again, all children need and want such words and will occasionally ask for them. But if your child's requests tend to focus in this area, this is a strong indication that his love language is words of affirmation.

4. Notice What Your Child Most Frequently Complains About.

This approach is related to the third, but, instead of directly asking for something, this time your child is complaining that he is not receiving something from you. If he complains, "You're always busy" or "You always have to take care of the baby," or "We never go to the store together," he is probably revealing more than a simple frustration at the coming of a new baby. He is expressing that since the baby arrived, he is feeling less love from you. In his complaints, he is clearly requesting quality time.

An occasional complaint about the lack of quality time does not indicate the child's primary love language. For example, "Daddy, you work too much" may repeat what a child has heard the mother say. Or, "I wish our family took vacations like Ben's family" may express a desire to be like Ben.

Every child complains now and then. Many of these complaints are related to immediate desires and are not necessarily an indication of a love language. But if the complaints fall into a pattern so that more than half the complaints focus on one love language, then they are highly indicative. Their frequency is the key.

5. Give Your Child a Choice Between Two Options.

Lead your child to make choices between two love languages. For example, a father might say to a ten-year-old, "Eric, I'm going to get off early Thursday afternoon. We could go to the gym together or I could help you pick out some new basketball shoes. Which would you prefer?" The child has a choice between quality time and a gift. A mother might say to her daughter, "I have some free time this evening. We could take Daisy to the dog park or I could help you study for the test. Which would you prefer?" This obvious choice is between quality time and an act of service.

As you give options for several weeks, keep a record of your child's choices. If most of them tend to cluster around one of the five love languages, you have likely discovered which one makes your child feel most loved. At times, your child will not want either option and will suggest something else. You should keep a record of those requests also, since they may give you clues.

If your child wonders what you are up to, giving such choices so frequently, and asks what is going on, you might say, "I've been thinking about how I invest my time with the family. When we have time together, I thought it would be good if I knew your thoughts and feelings about what we do with that time. It has been helpful for me. What do you think?" You can be as philosophical or as simple as you wish. However, what you are saying is true. As you seek to discover your child's love language, you are also giving him an exercise in choice.

Using Choices to Discover the Love Language
Choices at 6

The choices you offer your child depend on age and interest. The following are merely examples to stimulate your creativity. To a first-grader you might say:

"Would you like for me to make you some cupcakes *(acts of service)* or for us to have lemonade on the deck *(quality time)*?"

"Would you rather wrestle *(physical touch)* or read a story together *(quality time)*?"

"While I am out of town for two days, would you rather I bring you a present *(gift)* or send you a special email *(words of affirmation)*?"

"Would you like to play our game, 'I like you because . . .' *(words of affirmation)* or would you like me to put up new shelves in your room *(acts of service)?*"

The game, "I like you because . . ." is one in which parent and child take turns completing the sentence, "I like you because . . ." For example, the parent says, "I like you because you have a beautiful smile." Then the child may say, "I like you because you read stories to me." The parent says, "I like you because you are kind to your sister." This is an enjoyable way of giving affirming words to the child and teaching him to affirm the parent. The game may also incorporate the ABCs so that the first "I like you . . ." must start with an A, as in, "Because you are active." The second begins with a B, as in, "Because you are beautiful."

Choices at 10

If your child is closer to ten years old, you might ask questions such as:

"For your birthday, would you rather have a new bicycle *(gift)* or a trip with me to Washington, D.C. *(quality time)?*"

"Would you rather I fix your computer this evening *(acts of service)* or that we play basketball together *(quality time* and *physical touch)?*"

"When we see Grandma this weekend, would you prefer that I tell her what a great job you did in school this quarter *(words of affirmation)* or that I buy you a surprise when we are there for doing so well *(gift)?*" You may choose to do both.

"Would you prefer I watch you practice your gymnastics *(quality time)* or that we buy you a new pair of jeans *(gift)?*"

Choices at 15

For a fifteen-year-old, the following choices might be appropriate: You and your child have bought an old car that you are trying to get in good condition by the time he is sixteen. The option is, "This Saturday, would you like us to work on the car together *(quality time)* or would you rather that I work on it while you spend time with your friends *(acts of service)*?"

"Would you prefer we buy you a jacket Saturday afternoon *(gift)* or that the two of us spend time at the cabin while Dad is away *(quality time)*?"

"Since you and I are the only ones at home tonight, would you rather that we eat out *(quality time)* or that I fix your favorite pizza *(acts of service)*?"

"If you were feeling discouraged and I wanted to build you up, which would be more helpful to you—if I sat down and told you how much I love and appreciate you, and then mentioned some of your positive traits *(words of affirmation)* or if I simply gave you a bear hug and said, 'I'm with you, man' *(physical touch)*?"

Giving choices will be helpful only if you do it often enough to see a pattern showing a clear preference in love languages. You will probably need to offer twenty to thirty choices before you can see a clear pattern emerging. Isolated answers may just indicate the preference of the moment.

If you decide to be very creative about this, you could draw up thirty of the either/or choices, being sure that you include an equal number of options for each love language. Then present it to your child as a sort of research project on choices. Most teens will cooperate in such an effort, and the results may give you a clear reading on your child's love language.

A Fifteen-Week Experiment

If none of the above suggestions give you much clue as to your child's primary love language, this one may work for you. But if you begin it, be prepared to continue for the full term, fifteen weeks.

First, choose one of the five love languages to focus on for two weeks, as you express love to your child. For example, if you begin with quality time, each day you will seek to communicate your love by giving your child at least thirty minutes of your undivided attention. One day take her to breakfast. Another day, play a computer word game or read a book together. As you give this amount of undivided attention, observe how your child responds. If, by the end of the two weeks, your child is begging for freedom, you know you have to look elsewhere. If, however, you see a new twinkle in her eye and you are getting positive comments on how much she enjoys your time together, you may have found what you were looking for.

After the two weeks, take a week off, not totally withdrawing but giving about one-third the time you did before. This allows the relationship to move closer to what it was before. Then select another love language and focus on it for the next two weeks. For example, if you choose physical touch, you will touch your child in some meaningful way at least four times every day. So, before he leaves for school, you give him a hug and kiss. When he comes home, you greet him with another quick hug. When he sits down to dinner, rub his back for a minute. Later, when he is doing homework, pat him on the shoulder. Repeat this process every day, varying your expressions of physical touch, but always giving meaningful touches at least four times a day.

Then observe his response. If by the end of the two weeks he is pulling back and saying, "Stop touching me," you know this is not his primary love language. But if he is going with the flow, letting you know that it feels good, you may be on the right track.

The following week, draw back somewhat and notice your child's response. Then choose another love language and follow the same scenario. Keep observing your child's behavior as you move through the next weeks. He may begin requesting one language you spoke previously. If so, he is giving you a clue. Or he might complain that

If your child wonders what you are up to, you can respond, "I want to love you in every way I can, so that you will know how much I care about you."

you stopped doing what you did two weeks ago; that's a clue too.

If your child wonders what you are up to, you can respond, "I want to love you in every way I can, so that you will know how much I care about you." Don't mention the concept of primary love languages. And, as you are pursuing this experiment, keep in mind that your child still needs love shown through all the love languages— soothing words, focused attention, acts of love, appropriate gifts, and physical touch along with loving eye contact.

If You Have Teenagers . . .

If you are rearing teenagers, you know that this job is like none other in the world. Because of the changes they are experiencing, your teens' giving and receiving of love may also change with their moods. Most teens go through periods that can best be described as "grunt stages," because all you can get out of them is a couple of muffled words that sound like grunts.

Mom: "Hi, honey, how are you doing?"

Tim: "Okay." *(Barely audible)*

Mom: "What have you been up to this morning?"

Tim: "Nuthin'." *(Barely audible)*

A teenager in this difficult stage may not be able to receive any love language except physical touch, and only then if you are quick about it. Of course, these teens do come up for air now and then, and during their more coherent times you will want to show them all the love you can, particularly in their own primary language.

Teenagers at times make it difficult for you to fill their emotional love tank. They are testing you, to see if you really love them. They may do this by acting sullen for no obvious reason, making something more difficult for you than it should be, or simply by being passive-aggressive in their behavior. Such behavior may be their subconscious way of asking, "Do you really love me?"

These behaviors are always a test for parents. If you can remain calm, cool, and kind (firm but kind), you pass the test and your teens will eventually mature beyond that difficult stage.

When Dan was thirteen, he began testing his parents. His father, Jim, felt some initial frustration but then realized that he had let Dan's love tank go dry. Knowing that Dan's primary love language was quality time, he decided to spend a whole weekend with his son, filling that tank up—quite a challenge since teenagers have a large love tank. After their weekend together, Jim felt that he had done what he set out to do, and resolved that he would never again let Dan's love tank run dry.

The evening they came back, Jim had an important meeting, one that Dan knew about. Just as Jim was leaving, Dan called, "Dad, got a minute?" Here was the test. Dan was really asking, "Dad, do you really love me?" So many parents are trapped by this test and blow their cool.

Fortunately, Jim realized what was happening and set a time to talk with Dan. He said, "I have to get to my meeting right now; let's get together as soon as I come home, about 9:30."

If Jim had lost his patience with Dan and said, "I just spent the whole weekend with you! What else do you need?" he could have punctured a hole in the love tank he had just spent forty-eight hours filling.

Becoming Multilingual

Whatever your child's love language may be, remember that it's important to speak all five languages. It is easy to make the mistake of using one love language to the exclusion of the others. This is especially true of gifts, because they seem to take less of our time and energy. But if we fall into the trap of giving our children too many gifts, we deprive them of healthy and full love tanks, and we can also cause them to see the world through materialistic eyes.

In addition, learning to speak all five love languages will help us to nurture people throughout our lives, not only our children but spouses and friends and relatives. Right now, our emphasis is on nurturing our children, but we know that in a few years they will be reaching out to all sorts of people, most of them quite different from themselves.

As parents, we need to remember that learning the love languages is a maturational process, and that becoming mature is a slow, painful, and often difficult journey. As we become multilingual, we also will be helping our children to learn how to give and receive in all the love languages. As we are faithful in loving and providing examples, we can then envision our children moving into their adult lives able to share love with others in so many ways. When this happens, they will be outstanding adults!

THE 5 LOVE LANGUAGES OF CHILDREN

physical touch
words of affirmation
quality time
gifts
acts of service

discipline and the love languages

Which of the following words is negative: *love, warmth, laughter, discipline?*

The answer is—none. Contrary to what many people think, *discipline* is not a negative word. *Discipline* comes from a Greek word that means "to train." Discipline involves the long and vigilant task of guiding a child from infancy to adulthood. The goal is that the child would reach a level of maturity that will allow him one day to function as a responsible adult in society. Now that's a positive goal!

To train your child in mind and character to become a self-controlled and constructive member of home and community requires that you use every type of communication with the child. You will employ guidance by example, modeling, verbal instruction, written request, teaching and preaching right behavior, correcting wrong behavior, providing learning experiences, and much more. Punishment is also one of these means and does have its place, but in many homes punishment is greatly overused. In fact, many parents assume that discipline and punishment are synonymous. Punishment is a type of discipline, though the most negative (see page 138).

Some parents, particularly those who did not receive much love in their own childhood, tend to skip the importance of nurturing a child. They regard the main task of parenting as punishment, instead of using other, more positive forms of discipline. To be effective in discipline, parents must keep the child's emotional love tank filled with love. In fact, disciplining without love is like trying to run a machine without oil. It may appear to be working for a while, but will end in disaster.

Because of the confusion about discipline, we are focusing in this chapter on the common, corrective meaning of the word, and in the next chapter on the teaching/learning aspects of discipline. In both instances, we will explore how your child's love language can help you to develop discipline in your child.

Keeping Johnny Out of the Street

The common, popular definition of discipline is the establishing of parental authority, the developing of guidelines for behavior, and then helping children live by these guidelines. Every culture historically has held expectations for mature behavior and has devised means through which this would be achieved.

Historically, all kinds of societies have regarded human beings as moral creatures. Within the larger community, some things are considered right and others wrong; some are acceptable while others are unacceptable. While standards differ from place to place, no society is amoral. Each has its codes, rules, laws, and ethical understandings. When individuals choose to live immoral lives, they do so to their own detriment and to the harm of their society.

Parents play the most important role in the discipline of their children because it is they who interpret to their offspring their culture's generally accepted standards. Babies are not capable of deciding how to live, and without parental rules, a child will not survive to adulthood. During infancy, parents must totally enforce the rules and control the behavior of the child. This means that they will not allow Johnny to crawl into a fire, no matter how attracted he may be to the rising flames. Later, as a toddler, Johnny must be kept out of the street lest he be hit by a passing car. His parents must put medicines and toxic substances out of reach.

From this infantile stage requiring total control, parents move toward devoting more than a decade to rearing their child to an acceptable level of self-discipline. This road to maturity is one that every child must walk and for which every parent needs to accept responsibility. It is an awesome task, requiring wisdom, imagination, patience, and great amounts of love.

Many parents are confused about the "best" way to raise children. They don't trust themselves and are ready to listen to the latest expert. Yet even the experts offer clashing theories and often contradictory advice. This has yielded much disagreement as to the standards for discipline in American families. Thus the patterns of discipline vary greatly in America. It is beyond the scope of this book to deal with the full arena of discipline. If you want to read more about this, you will find suggested books in the appendix.

Before You Discipline

Love looks out for the interests of another; so does discipline. So discipline is certainly an act of love. And the more a child feels loved, the easier it is to discipline that child. The reason is that a child must identify with her parents in order to accept their guidance without resentment, hostility, and obstructive, passive-aggressive behavior. This means that we must keep the child's love tank full before we administer discipline.

We must **keep the child's love tank full** before we **administer discipline.**

If the child does not identify with his parents, he will view each parental request or command as an imposition and will learn to resent it. In extreme cases, the child comes to consider a parental request with such resentment that his total orientation to parental authority—and eventually all authority—becomes one of doing the opposite of what is expected.

Michael is ten years old. His father, Paul, is a lawyer who works long hours. On the weekends, he mows the lawn and does other household jobs. Occasionally he attends a football game on Saturday and often spends time working in his home office. Michael doesn't see much of his father. Since Michael's primary love language is quality time, he doesn't feel much love coming from his dad. By the time the weekend rolls around, his father is physically and emotionally tired—not in a mood to put up with childish pranks. His discipline is typically accompanied with harsh words said in an angry voice. Paul thinks that his discipline is what his son needs to become a responsible young man. However, the reality is that Michael greatly resents the discipline and is afraid of his father. He has little desire to obey his wishes and spends most of the weekend avoiding his dad.

Even a casual observer can see the connection between Paul's seeming lack of love and Michael's lack of respect. The father's harsh words and angry tones might be tolerated by a child who felt secure in his father's love, but when the love tank is empty, as in Michael's case, such discipline creates anger and bitterness rather than responsibility.

If Michael felt secure in his father's love, he would know that the discipline he received was, at least in Paul's mind, for his well-being. But since he does not feel loved, he views his dad's discipline as an act of selfishness. More and more, Michael is seeing himself as little more than a bother to his dad, and this is seriously affecting his self-esteem.

Clearly it is crucial that you love your child unconditionally. You can do this much more effectively if you know and speak all the love languages. Every child needs this unconditional love to keep his or her emotional love tank full. Then you will be able to discipline with the best possible results. First things first, fellow parents. Practice unconditional love; then discipline.

How a Child Loves

Before we are able to effectively discipline a child in love, we need to ask two questions:

1. *How does a child love?*
2. *What does my child need when he misbehaves?*

Well, how does a child love? In an immature fashion. In contrast, adults seek to love in an unconditional manner. Often we fail and settle for what is called a reciprocating love. For instance, David has a deep affection for Danielle, whom he wants to fall in love with him. Wanting to put his best foot forward, he tries to be pleasant, calm, helpful, kind, respectful, and considerate to her. Because he is not sure of Danielle's love, he does not resort to immature behavior but seeks to earn her love. This rational approach to obtaining love is called reciprocating love because John is doing his best to secure Danielle's's love in return.

But a child loves with neither reciprocating nor unconditional love. Being immature, a child loves in a self-oriented fashion. She is instinctively aware of her own need to feel loved—to have a full emotional love tank. She is not aware that her parents also have love tanks that need to be filled. Her only real concern is the status of her own love tank. When it is on low or empty, she is compelled to frantically ask, "Do you love me?" How her parents answer that question determines a great deal about the child's behavior, since the main cause of misbehavior is an empty emotional tank.

Some parents think a child should try to earn their love and affection with good behavior, but this just isn't possible. A child by nature continually tests our love by his or her behavior. He is asking, "Do you love me?" If we respond, "Yes, I love you," and fill his love tank, we take the pressure off and make it unnecessary for him to continue testing our love. We also make it much easier to control his behavior. However, if we fall into the trap of thinking our child should "earn" our love by good behavior, we will be continually frustrated. We will also see our child as bad, as disrespectful and unloving, when actually he needs to be reassured of our love.

When a Child Misbehaves

When a child asks through his behavior, "Do you love me?" we may not like the behavior. If the child feels desperate enough, his behavior will turn inappropriate. Nothing makes a child more desperate than a lack of love. However, it does not make sense to demand good behavior from a child without first making sure he feels loved.

> It does not make sense to demand good behavior from a child without first making sure he feels loved.

The second question we must ask in order to discipline with love is, "What does my child need when she misbehaves?" Instead, when a child misbehaves, many parents ask, "What can I do to correct her behavior?" If they ask that question, the logical answer is, "Punishment." This is one reason that punishment is so overused, rather than parents' selecting more appropriate ways of training a child. When we resort to punishment first, later we cannot easily consider the real needs of the child. A child will not feel loved if we handle misbehavior this way.

However, when we ask, "What does this child need?" we can proceed rationally and decide on a proper course. A child who misbehaves has a need. To overlook the need behind the misbehavior can prevent us from doing the right thing. Asking ourselves, "What can I do to correct my child's behavior?" often leads to thoughtless punishment. Asking, "What does my child need?" lets us proceed with confidence that we will handle the situation well.

Why a Child Misbehaves: An Empty Love Tank

When your child misbehaves and you have asked yourself, "What does my child need?" the next question should be, "Does this child need her love tank filled?" It is so much easier to discipline a child if she feels genuinely loved, particularly if the cause of the misbehavior is an empty love tank. At such a time, you need to keep the love languages in mind, especially physical touch and quality time, and the use of eye contact.

When a child obviously misbehaves, what he has done should not be condoned. However, if we deal with it wrongly—either too harshly or too permissively—we will have further problems with that child, and those problems will worsen as he grows older. Yes, we need to discipline (train) a child toward good behavior, but the first step in that process is not punishment.

Young children are not subtle about asking for our love. They are noisy and often do things that seem inappropriate to an adult way of thinking. When we realize that they are really pleading for us to spend time with them, to hold them, to give ourselves to them in a personal manner, we will remember that they are children and that we have the precious responsibility to fill their love tanks first, and then train them to move on in their journey.

Why a Child Misbehaves: Physical Problems

But what do we do when misbehavior is not caused by an empty love tank?

After you have asked yourself, "What does this child need?" and you have determined that the child's love tank is not depleted, ask yourself, "Is this a physical problem?" The second most common cause of misbehavior is a physical problem, and the younger the child, the more behavior is affected by physical needs. "Is my child in pain? Hungry or thirsty? Fatigued? Ill?" Misbehavior cannot be condoned, even if it is caused by a physical problem, but the problem behavior can usually be quickly relieved if its source is physical.

A Child's Remorse, a Parent's Forgiveness

Let's assume that you determine that your child's misbehavior is not caused by physical reasons. What's the next question? "Does my child feel sorry for what he has done?" When a child feels genuinely sorry for what he has done, there is no need to proceed further. He has learned and repented; punishment now could be destructive. If your child is truly sorry and shows genuine remorse, you should rejoice. This means his conscience is alive and well.

What controls a child's (or adult's) behavior when he doesn't have to behave appropriately? Right, a healthy conscience. And what is the raw material from which a normal conscience is formed? Guilt. A certain amount of guilt is necessary for the development of a healthy conscience. And what will wipe away guilt, as clean as a new slate? You guessed it—punishment, especially corporal punishment. However, punish the child when he already feels genuinely guilty for his behavior, and you hinder his ability to develop a good conscience. In such a situation, punishment usually produces only anger and resentment.

When your child is truly sorry for her misbehavior, instead of punishing her, forgive her. In your example of forgiving her, you are teaching beautiful lessons about forgiveness she can take into her adult years. By experiencing forgiveness from her parents, she is learning to forgive herself and later to forgive someone else. What a beautiful gift this is. Have you seen a child who was truly remorseful about a wrong she did and then experienced a parent's forgiveness? This is a rare and unforgettable experience. The love that flows from the child's heart is overwhelming.

The only other way you can teach your child how to forgive is to ask forgiveness when you have wronged her. While you should do this occasionally, it should not be necessary often. If it is, you are unduly offending your child and not learning from your own mistakes.

Five Ideas on Controlling Your Child's Behavior

As parents we are responsible for so much that happens with our children, often more than we want to admit. We can learn ways to help our children avoid bad behavior and subsequent punishment. Here are five methods you can use to effectively control your child's behavior. Two of these are positive, two are negative, and one is neutral. As you read this section, you will want to think about the methods of control that you have employed with your children; you may want to change or add to your approach.

1. Making Requests

Making requests is a very important, positive means of controlling behavior. It greatly benefits both parent and child. Requests are pleasant to the child and help to ease the anger that may be stirred by a parent's commands. And it is so much easier for parents to be pleasant when using requests, thereby remaining "kind but firm."

When you make requests, you are sending three nonverbal messages to your child. The first is that you respect his feelings. You are saying, "I respect the fact that you have feelings, and your feelings about this matter in particular." The second nonverbal message is the fact that you realize your child has a brain and is able to form opinions. "I respect that you have an opinion about this."

The third message is the best of all. Requests tell your child that you expect her to take responsibility for her own behavior. This kind of responsibility is so lacking today. Your child can learn to be a responsible person when you give her the opportunity to do so. By the use of requests, you are guiding and encouraging her to take responsibility.

> By the use of requests, you are guiding and encouraging her to take responsibility.

A child who is raised in this way comes to feel that he is in partnership with his parents in the molding of his character. This kind of child rearing is not permissiveness. The parent is not giving up authority or respect. In fact, the child will have much greater respect for his parents because he will feel that they are not simply telling him what to do, but are interested primarily in what is best for him.

Also, requests are the best way of giving instructions. Since requests are more pleasant, thoughtful, and considerate than commands, you can use them to instruct your child almost endlessly. No other method of control allows this.

2. Issuing Commands

Issuing commands is necessary and appropriate at times. Requests are vastly superior when you have a choice, but commands are necessary when requests fail. Then you must be more forceful. Commands are a negative means of control because they require harsher tones than requests, with a downward voice inflection at the end of the statement. This combination almost always elicits irritation, anger, and resentment in the child, especially if used frequently. Also, the nonverbal messages that accompany commands are generally negative. Because you are telling a child what to do, with no choices or opportunity for feedback or discussion, you are conveying that the child's feelings and opinions are not important to you. Most of all, you are taking all the responsibility on yourself and essentially saying, "It doesn't matter what your feelings or opinions are about this. I don't expect you to take responsibility for your own behavior. I simply expect you to do what I am telling you."

The more you use authoritarian techniques such as commands, scolding, nagging, or screaming, the less effective you become. But if you normally use pleasant requests, then the occasional use of commands will generally be effective.

As parents, you have only so much authority. If you waste it being negative, you will not have enough left for the difficult, critical times. *Being kind but firm* not only conserves your authority, but it *enhances your authority, because you are gaining your children's respect and love as well as their gratitude.*

Children are great observers. They see and hear how other parents resort to unpleasant, authoritarian, and angry discipline with their children. When you are kind but firm with them, you can't imagine how much they appreciate you and how thankful they are to have you as their parents!

3. Gentle Physical Manipulation

Gentle physical manipulation can move a child in the appropriate direction. It's especially effective with young children who often do things that are not necessarily wrong—but are not to your preference. For instance, the negativism of two-year-olds can be easily confused with defiance. "No," Henry says, but then he will do what you request of him. Sometimes there is a delay after Henry says it, and then he responds to your request. It may seem to you that he is

Please **be careful not** to **confuse negativism** with **defiance.**

being defiant, but this is not so. Negativism in two-year-olds is a normal step of development, one way the child begins to separate psychologically from his mother or father.

This simple ability to say no is important. If you punish a small child for this, you are not only hurting him but directly interfering with his normal development. Please be careful not to confuse negativism with defiance. They are completely separate.

Let's say that you want your three-year-old daughter to come to you. You begin with a request, "Come to me, will you, Honey?" Your child answers, "No." You move to a command, "Come to me now!" Again she answers, "No." At this point it is a real temptation to punish her, but you should resist. Instead of taking a great risk and hurting your child, why not gently guide her to where you want her to be? If she resists, then you know it may be defiance and you can take an appropriate course. But, the vast majority of the time, you will discover that the child was not being defiant but was just saying no. And you haven't hurt a thing.

Negativism usually starts when children are two, but you can see examples of it in virtually every age. When you are not sure how to handle a situation, you can try gentle physical manipulation. It is particularly helpful when a small child acts up in a public place. Instead of giving in to frustration, her parents can simply move her on.

4. Punishment

Punishment is the most negative and also the most difficult method of control. First, the punishment must fit the crime because children are so aware of fairness. They know when a punishment is too lenient or severe. They can also detect inconsistency in their parents' attitudes toward the children in the family.

Second, the punishment may not be appropriate for the particular child. Sending a child to his room, for example, may feel very painful to one sibling and seem like a playtime to another. Third, punishment brings with it variation, since parents often rely on their feelings when they are dishing out a punishment. When everything is going their way and they are feeling good, they tend to be more lenient. On bad days, when a parent isn't feeling very good, the punishment meted out is harsher.

As difficult as it may be for you to decide when and how punishment should be used, you still must be prepared to use it and to use it appropriately. This can be facilitated by planning ahead so that you can avoid the "punishment trap." This means sitting down with a spouse or good friend to decide appropriate punishments for various offenses. Such planning will keep your anger in check when your child does something that upsets you.

When your child misbehaves and you quickly ask yourself the questions we suggested earlier, and come up with negatives on all of them (including a two-year-old's constant "No"), you should ask one more question, "Is this child being defiant?" Defiance is openly resisting and challenging parental authority.

Of course, defiance cannot be permitted and the behavior must be corrected. But a child's defiance does not automatically mean that punishment is indicated. You want to avoid the punishment trap. If a request will break the defiance, and it often does, great. If gentle physical manipulation or a command is appropriate, good. If punishment is indicated, do it with care. For more on this, we recommend *Kids in Danger* by Ross Campbell.

Finally, do not use punishment as your primary way of disciplining your young child or teenager. You will provoke great amounts of needless anger. You will also force your child to "stuff" his anger; he may develop passive-aggressive attitudes and behaviors, trying to get back at you indirectly. (We will discuss passive-aggressive behavior in chapter 10.)

5. Behavior Modification

Behavior modification can also control a child's behavior. It utilizes positive reinforcement (placing a positive element into a child's environment), negative reinforcement (withdrawing a positive element from the child's environment), and punishment (placing a negative element into the child's environment). An example of positive reinforcement is to reward a child for an appropriate behavior by giving her a piece of candy or fruit. One negative reinforcement could be withdrawing television privileges from a child for inappropriate behavior. An example of punishment (sometimes called aversive technique) would be sending a child to his room.

Behavior modification can be helpful at times, particularly for specific, recurring behavioral problems for which a child shows no remorse. But we believe it should be used sparingly. If parents overuse behavior modification, their child will not feel loved. The first reason for this is that the very foundation of behavior modification is conditional—the child receives a reward only if he behaves a certain way. Second, behavior modification does not deal with a child's feelings or emotional needs and cannot convey unconditional love. If parents control their child's behavior primarily by trying to modify it, the child will develop a warped value system in which he does things primarily for reward. A "what's in it for me?" orientation will follow.

> Behavior modification cannot convey unconditional love.

Behavior modification can also teach children to use the same method on their parents. They will do what the parents wish in order to get what they want. This leads to manipulation.

Because of all the cautions about this method, you may be surprised that we suggest using it at all. Again, it can help with specific, recurring behavioral problems for a defiant child. However, working with a system of rewards takes time, consistency, effort, and persistence. An excellent book on this topic is *Don't Be Afraid to Discipline*, by Ruth Allen Peters.

Love: Before and After Punishment

Because discipline is most effective when it happens in the context of love, it is wise to give a child a conscious expression of love both before and after administering punishment. We have noted that the most effective way to communicate love is by using the child's primary love language, so speak it even when you must correct or punish the child.

Larry is an electrical engineer and by nature his personality is quite rigid. In his early years of parenting, he tended to be stern and matter-of-fact in disciplining his children. After learning about the five love languages, he determined that his son's primary love language was physical touch. He tells how he applied this in disciplining his son. "Kevin had broken the neighbor's window while playing baseball in the backyard. He knew it was against the rules to play baseball there—the park was just a block away and the place to play ball. On several occasions, we had talked about the dangers of playing ball in the backyard. When our neighbor saw Kevin hit the ball that broke the window, he called my wife to inform us.

"After I got home, I calmly went into Kevin's room where he was working on his computer. I walked over and started rubbing his shoulders. In a minute or so, he turned from the computer and gave me his attention. 'Stand up,' I said. 'I want to hug you.' I wrapped my arms around him as I said, 'I've got to do something really tough, and I want you to know that I love you more than anything.'

"I kept hugging him for a long minute—it felt good to be close.

Then I released him and said, 'Mom called today to tell me what happened to Mr. Scott's window. I know it was an accident, but you are well aware of the rule about not playing baseball in the yard. Therefore, I have to discipline you for breaking that rule. It hurts me to do this, but it is for your good. No baseball for the next two weeks. And you must use your money to pay for repairing the Scotts' window. We'll call the window company to find out how much it will cost.'

"Then I hugged him again. I know he felt my tears running down his neck. I said, 'I love you, Buddy.' And he said, 'I love you too, Dad.' I left the room knowing I had done the right thing; somehow it felt so much better when I assured him of my love before and after the discipline. Knowing that physical touch was his primary love language, I felt the discipline was received in a positive manner. I remember well previous times when I have disciplined him out of my anger and said harsh and bitter words and sometimes spanked him in a heat of rage. I thank God that I now know a better way."

If Kevin's love language had been words of affirmation, Larry's encounter with him might have gone something like this: "Kevin, I need to talk with you for a few minutes. I want you to know how much I love you and appreciate the hard work you do at school. I know when you come home you want to relax, and that you enjoy playing baseball. You usually follow our house rules and I really appreciate that. It is rare that I have to discipline you. What I am trying to say is that what we need to talk about is an isolated incident and not typical of your behavior, and I'm grateful for that.

"You probably know that Mr. Scott called your mother this afternoon and told her that he saw you hit the baseball that broke his window. While it was an accident, you do know the rule about playing baseball in the backyard. It is hard for me to do this, but because you disobeyed, I have to discipline you. No baseball for two weeks. And, you will have to use your own money to pay for having the

Scotts' window repaired. I'll call the window company to find out what it will cost.

"Do you understand that I am not angry with you? I know that you didn't mean to break the window, and also that you probably weren't thinking when you started playing ball in the yard. I love you very much and I'm proud of you. I know you will learn a good lesson from this experience." Their conversation may end with a hug, but the primary expression of love is in the words of affirmation both before and after the discipline.

Using your child's primary love language doesn't mean that you may not also use some of the other love languages; it does mean that you are giving your child the most effective expression of love you possibly can, both before and after the discipline. Because you know that you will be showing love to your child, you will probably be more careful about the type of discipline you choose to administer, and the way in which you do it.

Respecting Your Child's Love Language

Understanding your child's primary love language will help you choose the best method of discipline. In most cases, do not use a form of discipline that is directly related to your child's primary love language. Respect the child's love language by not selecting it as a method of discipline. Such discipline will not have the desired effect and may actually cause extreme emotional pain. The message your child will receive is not one of loving correction but one of painful rejection.

For example, if your child's love language is words of affirmation and you use condemning words as a form of discipline, your words will communicate not only that you are displeased with a certain behavior, but also that you do not love your child. Critical words can be painful to any child, but to this child, they will be emotionally devastating. Thus Ben, age sixteen, told us his father didn't love him, citing his dad's discipline, which included a raised voice and cutting words: "If I happen to do something he thinks is wrong, his screaming can go on for hours. I remember the day he told me he wasn't sure I was his son because he couldn't believe his son would do anything that terrible. I don't really know if I am his son, but I know that he doesn't love me."

As he talked further, it became obvious that Ben's primary love language was words of affirmation. When his father used words to communicate his displeasure with Ben's behavior, he destroyed the boy's sense of being loved.

Be careful. If your daughter's primary love language is quality time, you don't want to discipline her with isolation, such as sending her to her room each time she misbehaves. If it's physical touch, don't discipline by withholding your hugs. We remember Carlos, a ten-year-old whose primary love language is physical touch. He often walks up behind his mother and puts his arms around her or rubs her shoulders. His mother is also physically demonstrative and often communicates love to Carlos by physical touch. But Carlos's father Joe was raised in a home where spanking was the normal method of discipline; consequently, that is his primary method of discipline when Carlos disobeys.

These spankings are not abusive, in that they do not break the skin or leave Carlos with welts. However, when Carlos receives one of Joe's spankings, he may cry for three hours. What his father does not understand is that he is taking his son's primary love language, physical touch, and using it in a negative way. Consequently, Carlos feels not only punished but also unloved. His dad never hugs him after a spanking, for this would seem incongruous in his philosophy of discipline.

Joe is sincere in his efforts to discipline his son, but he doesn't recognize how much emotional distance he is putting between himself and Carlos. As parents, we must constantly be reminded that the purpose of discipline is to correct the wrong behavior and to help a child develop self-discipline. If we do not apply the love language concept, we may well destroy a child's sense of being loved, in our efforts to correct bad behavior. Understanding the primary love language of your child can make your discipline far more effective.

THE 5 LOVE LANGUAGES OF CHILDREN

physical touch

words of affirmation

quality time

gifts

acts of service

9

learning and the
love languages

Parents are a child's first and most important teachers. Researchers now agree that the optimum time for the stimulation of basic learning abilities in a child is before the age of six. Dr. Burton White, a famed pioneer in early learning research and the founder of the Harvard Preschool Project, says, "It appears that a first-rate educational experience during the first three years of life is required if a person is to develop to his/her full potential."[1] And sociologists and educators, convinced such stimulation of the very young can spur learning abilities, have created programs such as Head Start designed to help disadvantaged children during their preschool years.

Yes, we parents are the primary teachers. And one of our primary teaching aids is proper discipline, administered with love.

In chapter 8, we considered discipline as guiding to maturity. Now let's consider the other half of the classical idea of discipline: teaching our children. True discipline can help to develop a child's intellect and social skills that will serve him for a lifetime.

The increased awareness in recent years of the importance of early childhood learning underscores our crucial role as parents in our child's developing intelligence. This does not mean you must conduct formal lessons with your young child. But you should try to understand your child's innate drive to learn, to explore, and then to satisfy his developing brain's urgent need for sensory stimuli and enjoyable learning experiences.

Many parents watch their child's primary occupation of play and think learning can be left for first grade. But small children love to learn. They are born with an innate hunger for learning that remains strong—unless adults bore, spank, train, or discourage it out of them. A careful observation of infants and toddlers reveals that most of their activity is not merely child's play. Rather, our little ones are working at learning a new skill, whether it is to flip from the stomach to the back; to crawl; to pull up and later walk; or to touch, feel, and taste the world around them.

> A careful observation of **infants** and **toddlers** reveals that most of their **activity is not merely child's play.**

Once they learn to talk, their minds are filled with questions, and three- and four-year-olds can ask dozens of questions every day. When they reach the imitative stage and pretend to be adults, they seldom copy grown-ups at play. Rather, they imitate adults at work: teaching, driving a truck, being a doctor or nurse, caring for babies, working as a "businessman," and more. If you observe your child's activities for just one day and ask, "What seems to make her happiest? What holds her attention the longest?" you will likely find that it is an activity in which she is learning.

The Key to Your Child's Learning: You

Children discover life through the five senses. A home environment that is rich in stimulation of vision, hearing, touch, taste, and smell will feed their natural desire to discover and learn. Language development depends to a great extent on the verbal stimulation children receive from adults in these early years. Thus, talking to them and encouraging them to say words cooperates with their natural desire to learn. Cheering their efforts to say words and giving corrective feedback are part of the process. In this kind of rich verbal environment, their vocabulary grows and their ability to use sentences develops. They later learn to employ this skill to express emotions, thoughts, and desires.

What is true of verbal development is true in all areas of intellectual growth. If the home does not provide this kind of basic intellectual stimulation, a child is likely to be handicapped in his later learning, and the prognosis for his educational development is poor. School programs offer only a small compensation for an unstimulating home environment.

A supportive environment and attitude will help our children learn at home. Children are more emotional than cognitive—that is, they remember feelings more readily than they do facts. This means that your children remember how they felt in a particular situation much more easily than they recall the details of the event. For instance, a child listening to a story will remember exactly how she felt long after she forgets the lesson.

Your daughter may forget the details but remember the teacher. In your teaching, this means treating her with respect, kindness, and concern. It means making her feel good about herself, and ensuring that you never criticize or humiliate her. When a teaching situation is boring or degrading, a child is likely to reject even the best teaching, especially if morality or ethics are involved. When you respect your child, she will respect you and your viewpoint.

The key to your child's learning is you, from infancy on through all the years of formal training. Learning is a complex feat that is influenced by many factors. One of the strongest of these is your total involvement.

How the Love Languages Aid Learning

The most important fact to know about a child's learning ability is this: For a child to be able to learn well at any age, he must be at the emotional maturational level of that particular age. As the child grows, his ability to learn increases because of several factors, the most important of which is his emotional maturity. And parents have the greatest effect on the child's emotional growth.

We can prime our child's learning pump by continually filling his emotional tank.

This is not to say that all learning problems are the fault of parents, since many factors can affect a child's learning ability. However, emotional development can make a tremendous difference in the child's learning readiness and process, and this is where parents can help the most. We can prime our child's learning pump by continually filling his emotional tank.

As you consistently speak the five languages of love—physical touch, words of affirmation, quality time, receiving gifts, and acts of service—you are giving your child much intellectual stimulation. In the early years, when you probably don't know your child's primary love language, you regularly give all five. In so doing, you are not only meeting your child's emotional need for love but are also providing him with the physical and intellectual stimuli needed to develop his emerging interests. Although your emphasis is on love, you are also teaching and training your child.

Parents who do not take time to speak the five love languages, but simply seek to meet a child's physical needs, are neglecting her intellectual and social development. A child who is starved for love and acceptance from his parents will have little motivation to accept the challenges of learning in the early years or later in school.

Many parents do not realize that a child can fall behind emotionally. And it is certainly possible for a child to fall behind to such an extent that he can never catch up. What a tragedy! A child's emotional maturation affects everything else—his self-esteem, emotional security, ability to cope with stress and change, ability to socialize, and the ability to learn.

Perhaps nowhere else is the connection between love and learning more clearly demonstrated than when a child's parents separate or divorce. This traumatic break ruptures the child's emotional tank and drains his interest in learning. In place of love, the child often feels confusion and fear, neither of which are good companions for learning. A child whose parents have divorced will usually show lessened academic interest for several months until some measure of security and assurance of love can be restored to his world. Sadly enough, some children never fully recover.

As parents, we have the greatest influence in a child's life. If you are a single parent, by practicing your child's love language you can help to restore your child's sense of security. (A cooperative ex-spouse also will help.) This full love tank will then enable him to reach each succeeding emotional level in time to be ready to take the next step in learning.

"Tiger Mothers" and Others

Studies repeatedly show that parental involvement in education helps children thrive in school. Recently, books like *The Battle Hymn of the Tiger Mother*, by Amy Chua, have shone a spotlight on the extremes some parents go to in order to ensure their children's academic success, and have sparked debate about exactly how involved parents should be. In an era where there is intense attention to American competitiveness in a global marketplace and concern about American student achievement as compared to students in other countries, parents feel unease about their roles and sometimes will go to extraordinary lengths to help their children succeed. At the same time, young people growing up in less-privileged environments fall further and further behind.

Often, the missing piece in these environments is the presence of a father. Research consistently demonstrates that greater attention from fathers results in less delinquent behavior and higher levels of education for the children. And while the children get blamed for delinquent behavior, it is usually the fathers who are the delinquent ones in relation to the children.

But whether you are married, remarried, or a single parent, as a parent concerned with giving your children the love they need, you want to be sure to spend the time necessary to fill their love tanks with all five love languages. You are the key to your children's ability to learn and succeed in every way. And you have a great advantage over people outside your family—you know and understand your own children and have the home environment in which you can meet their needs.

If Your Child Is Anxious

A child who is doing well emotionally will have the concentration, motivation, and energy she needs to use her abilities to the maximum. In contrast, if she is distressed with anxiety or melancholy, or feels unloved, she probably will have problems with concentration and attention span and feel a decrease in energy. It will be more difficult for her to keep her mind on the task at hand. Studying may seem uninteresting. She will tend to be preoccupied with herself and her emotional needs, and her ability to learn will suffer.

If this anxiety continues, it will become more evident when the child enters a new learning experience. Such learning-related anxiety often appears among children who are moving from the third to the fourth grade. This grade step usually involves a change in the content and in the methods of teaching. The primary difference is the move from thinking and learning concretely to the inclusion of thinking and learning abstractly. Concrete learning deals with plain facts: Baltimore is in the state of Maryland. Abstract thinking is symbolic: words and phrases represent ideas and concepts. Moving from concrete to ab-stract thinking is a huge step, and not all children can accomplish it on cue.

> Moving from **concrete** to **abstract** thinking is a huge step, and **not all children** can accomplish it on cue.

When a child fails to make this step with ease, he suffers in many ways. He cannot fully understand the content of the lessons. He senses that he is falling behind, and this damages his self-esteem, as he feels inferior to his peers. Unless this is corrected quickly, the child will develop depression, more anxiety, and will begin to feel like an overall failure. Because the move to fourth grade is one of the most critical periods of academic transition, it is worth special notice by parents.

Your child's level of emotional maturity can make a significant dif-ference in how he or she weathers this transition. By "emotional ma-turity" we mean the ability to control their anxiety, withstand stress, and maintain balance during times of change. The more your chil-dren can do these things, the better they can learn. And the best way to help your children mature emotionally and maintain a good moti-vational level for their age is to keep their emotional love tanks full.

One sign of anxiety in children is an inability to easily make eye contact. An extremely anxious child will have problems approach-ing others, adults as well as peers. The emotionally deprived child will have difficulty in the simplest communication. Routine learn-ing is bound to be affected by this tension and anxiety.

Some of these children have been helped by special attention from their teachers that includes eye contact and physical contact. As their emotional needs are met, their fears and anxieties will lessen and their security and confidence increase. They are then able to learn. Of course, it is far preferable for these needs to be met at home by loving parents.

How Can You Motivate Your Child?

A question parents often ask is, "How can I motivate my child?" We can motivate only after we have filled our children's love tanks and trained them to manage their anger. Failing these two essentials, it is nearly impossible to understand how to motivate children.

The key to motivating a child is to get her to take responsibility for her own behavior. A child who will not or cannot take this responsibility cannot be motivated. A child who is taking responsibility for herself is motivated.

Encourage Your Child's Interests

You can help your child to be responsible (and therefore motivated) in two ways. The first is to patiently observe what your child is drawn to; that is, what your child enjoys, appreciates, or likes to do. Then you can encourage him in that direction. If you see an interest in your child in studying music, you can encourage that. But the key is to let the child take the initiative. When parents take the initiative to convince a child to take music lessons, the results are rarely positive.

Allow Your Child to Take Responsibility

A second way to help your child be motivated is to remember both you and your child cannot take responsibility for the same thing at the same time. If you wait and allow your child to take the initiative, she may then be motivated because you have allowed her to take responsibility. If you take the initiative and try to convince her to do something, *you* are assuming responsibility. A child is seldom motivated when this happens.

Let's apply this to the area of homework and grades. Most children go through periods when doing homework becomes a problem. This is especially true when passive-aggressive behavior enters the picture. And remember, a certain amount of passive-aggressive behavior is normal in thirteen- to fifteen-year-olds.

Passive-aggressive behavior goes for the jugular; that is, it aims at what will most upset the parents. Most parents care about their kids getting good grades. So that the more importance parents place on schoolwork, the more the child will tend to resist it. And remember this: ***The more responsibility the parent takes regarding the homework, the less the child will take.*** And, the less responsibility the child takes in doing his homework, the less motivated he will be.

If you want your child to take responsibility and be highly motivated, you must realize that homework is your child's responsibility, not yours. How do you accomplish this? Let your child know that you will be happy to help with his homework if he asks you. Since you want him to take responsibility for his work, even when he asks for help, you want to avoid taking any of the work on yourself, but want to place it back on your child.

For example, let's say your son has a math problem. You shouldn't solve the problem for him. Instead, you can look in the math book and show him the explanations for doing that type of problem. Then you can hand back the book so that he is able to assume responsibility for doing the problem. Eventually this will teach him to take more responsibility for himself. If you feel that the teacher has not adequately explained the concepts, you might suggest that your child ask for help the next day.

Of course, there will be times when you must clarify points of confusion or give a child additional information. This is fine as long as you are not assuming the responsibility your child should be taking. If you realize that you have been intensely involved in your child's homework, try to gradually shift responsibility to your child. You may see a temporary reduction in grades, but your child's ability to assume the responsibility and become self-sufficient will be well worth it. As you take this approach, your child should need less help as time goes on. And you can spend some of your time together exploring subjects of special interest to you both that are not included in a school curriculum.

Helping a child to be well motivated by permitting her to take both initiative and responsibility for her own behavior seems to be a well-concealed secret today. Most children are placed in a position where a parent or teacher takes the initiative and then assumes responsibility for her learning. Adults do this because they genuinely care for the children and mistakenly believe that the more they take initiative and responsibility, the more they are doing for the children. However, this is a serious mistake.

Using Your Child's Love Language

Your children will reach their highest motivation and success in learning at school when they are secure in your love. If you understand your children's primary love language, you can enhance their daily experiences by speaking their primary language as they leave for school in the morning and as they return in the afternoon. Those are two important times in the lives of school-age children. To be touched emotionally by their parents on leaving and returning home gives them security and courage to face the challenges of the day.

Julia is nine years old. After her mother, Kelly, learned about the five love languages, she made some changes in their daily routine. "I simply can't believe the difference it made in Julia's life," she told us later. "Even after I heard about the love language concept and discovered that Julia's language was acts of service, I never thought that applying this concept would be that helpful at school. But then, a friend mentioned that she was speaking her child's love language before her daughter left for school and when she came home in the afternoon. I decided to try this and the results were almost immediate.

"Mornings at our house were always rather hectic; my husband left home at 7:00, Julia's bus came at 7:30, and I left about 7:50. We all did our own thing and about the only meaningful contact we had with each other was a good-bye as we left the house."

Knowing that Julia valued acts of service, Kelly asked Julia, "If I could do one thing for you in the morning that would help you, what would it be?"

Julia thought a moment. "Um . . . I guess having all my stuff ready to go. Because it seems I'm always looking for things, then I have to run for the bus."

The next morning Kelly made sure Julia's lunch, homework, and anything else she needed were safely stowed in her backpack, which waited by the door. Soon, she said, "I could tell a difference in her morning attitude. She even said thank you most days. And, when she left for school, she seemed to be in a better mood.

"Three days later, I did an act of service in the afternoons when she returned home. The first day I had bought some fruit at the farmers' market. When she came in and dropped her backpack, I said, 'Julia, I got those apples you like. Want to try one?' Then we sat down to talk about her day. The next afternoon, I had found a book of hers she had thought was lost. When she came in, I said, 'Look on the kitchen table.' I had left her book there and she said, 'Oh, thank you! Where did you find it?'"

Kelly began listening to her daughter's requests more attentively, writing them down. And the after-school time became a highlight of their day.

"All of this began four months ago," she said. "The biggest difference I notice is that when we talk about school, her comments are much more positive than they were before. It seems to me that she is having a better time and is more motivated than she was. Also, I feel that our relationship is closer."

If Julia's primary love language had been physical touch, then a warm hug as she left for the bus each morning and open arms as she walked into the house in the afternoon would have served the same emotional purpose. Of course, she would have enjoyed the treats too.

Perhaps you cannot be home when your children return after school. If so, the next best thing is to show a sincere expression of love when you walk in the door. If your last encounter in the morning and your first encounter in the evening is to speak the primary love language of your children, you will be performing one of your most meaningful deeds of the day. And, this just may have a positive impact on their motivation for learning.

THE 5 LOVE LANGUAGES OF CHILDREN

physical touch

words of affirmation

quality time

gifts

acts of service

anger and love

Anger and love. The two are more closely related than most of us want to admit. We get angry at the people we love. You may be surprised to find a chapter on anger in a book about love. But the truth is, often we feel anger and love at the same time.

Anger is the most troublesome emotion in family life. It can lead to marital conflict and to the verbal and physical abuse of children. Mishandled anger is at the root of most of society's problems. Yet we must realize that anger has a positive place in our lives and in rearing our children. Not all anger is evil. You can feel anger because you want justice and care for someone's (including your child's) welfare. The ultimate and righteous purpose of anger is to motivate us to set things right and to correct evil. Thus, angry mothers formed MADD, Mothers Against Drunk Driving, to try to stop this scourge on our highways. Their organization began after one woman channeled her anger over her child's death by an intoxicated driver in a positive manner, lobbying for tougher laws against drunken motorists.

The primary **lifetime threat** to your child is **his or her own anger.**

However, anger more commonly creates problems than solves them. As an emotion, anger is not always expressed for righteous reasons. It often becomes irrational and we do not control it; it controls us. In the heat of anger, people often throw reason to the wind and take a destructive course that actually makes things worse. Also, we don't always judge properly what is the greatest right for ourselves and other people, or we seek to correct wrongs in selfish ways.

Anger is a little-understood emotion—why we feel it, how we express it, and how we can change the way we deal with our frustrations. Unless we as parents know what anger is and how we can handle it in appropriate ways, we will not be able to teach our children what to do when they feel angry. Yes, *when*, because all of us, parents and children, get angry every day.

It may surprise you that the primary lifetime threat to your child is his or her own anger. If your child does not handle his own anger well, it will damage or destroy him. The mishandling of anger is related to every present and future problem your child may have—from poor grades to damaged relationships to possible suicide. It is imperative that you do all you can to safeguard your child now and in the future.

However, the good news is that if your child learns to handle anger well, he will have a great advantage in life. Most of life's problems will be averted and your child will be more able to use anger to his advantage, rather than to have it work against him.

Is This Your Family?

Equally important, we parents must learn to handle our own anger as we respond to our children. Few adults have mastered appropriate ways to handle anger. One reason is that most anger is expressed subconsciously, below the level of our awareness. Another is that few adults have made the transition from immature to mature means of dealing with anger. Typically this affects our dealings with our spouse and children. Consider how the Jacksons deal with their anger.

After a day's work, a tired Jeff Jackson is playing word games on his iPhone in the den. A tired Ellen Jackson is cleaning up after dinner. Neither is very happy with the other. Will comes in and asks Mom for some cookies. She is not in a cookie-giving mood and says, "You didn't finish your supper and so you can't have anything else." Feeling the cause is lost, Will goes to the den where he finds a candy jar. Dad asks, "What are you doing? You heard your mother. No candy!"

Will leaves the room but returns in five minutes, bouncing his basketball. "Can I go to Jack's house?"

"No, you can't. You haven't finished your homework. And stop bouncing that ball!"

Will takes his ball and leaves. In five minutes he is back, this time bouncing his ball in the kitchen. "Mom, I need a book to finish my homework and I didn't bring mine home. Jack has one. Can I go over there and borrow his?" Just then the basketball hits the table, knocking a glass to the floor.

Hearing this, Jeff is out of his chair and into the kitchen. "I told you to stop bouncing that ball!" He grabs Will by the hand and pulls him into the den where he starts flailing him on the bottom, yelling, "How many times do I have to tell you? You're going to learn to listen to me!"

Ellen is in the kitchen crying. She calls, "Stop it. Stop it. You're gonna kill him!" When Jeff stops, Will runs to his room, also crying. Dad plops onto the couch and stares at the TV. Mom goes to the bedroom, still crying. The family anger has not served a constructive purpose.

Many emotions were swirling in this household and everyone was angry. Ellen was angry at Jeff for not helping her clean up. Jeff was angry with Will for disobeying their house rule about the basketball. And Will was the angriest of all because his dad's discipline was far out of line with his crime. Ellen was also angry at her husband's actions toward their son.

Nothing is resolved. Everything is worse. What Will does with his anger remains to be seen. Even if he shows compliance on the surface and acts as if everything is all right, you can be sure that his anger will show up later in his behavior.

Now let's imagine this scene with a different response to anger.

Early in the evening, Ellen leaves the kitchen and joins Jeff in the den, speaking his primary love language for a moment, and then saying to him, "I have a problem. I'm feeling quite angry right now, but don't worry, I'm not going to attack you. I just need your help in solving my problem. Is this a good time to talk?" Then she may return to the kitchen or go to another room and read for a while.

When they do talk, Ellen calmly shares her sense of unfairness that he is not helping her clean up, especially since she worked all day too and then prepared supper. She tells him that she expects more of him and asks that he make a practice of helping her in the future.

> Parents who have **not** learned to control their own anger are not likely to **train their children** how to do it.

If Ellen and Jeff had had this talk, Will's request for a cookie might have received a different response. When he bounced the ball for the second time in the kitchen, Dad could have come in and taken the ball in his hand, spoken Will's primary love language for a moment, explained to him his disobedience and let him know that his ball would be locked in the trunk of Dad's car for the next two days. Then he could have spoken his son's primary love language again for a moment. What a different situation there would have been in this home.

Parents who have not learned to control their own anger are not likely to train their children how to do it. And yet, this kind of training is essential for the well-being of children and of society. If you have never learned how to manage your own anger, we strongly urge you to get some help in this area, so that you will be able to teach your children by example and by word how to best handle their anger.

The Right Kind of Anger

How your child learns to handle anger will largely influence the development of his personal integrity, one of the most important aspects of character. Train your child to manage anger appropriately and he will then be able to develop good character and strong integrity. However, if the child is not taught to handle anger in a mature way, he will always have pockets of immaturity in his character—that is, in his personal value systems, ethics, and morals. Such immaturity will manifest itself in a lack of integrity.

This lack will critically affect the child's spiritual development; the less able a child is to deal with anger well, the more antagonistic will be his attitude toward authority, including the authority of God. A child's immature handling of anger is a primary reason the child will reject the parent's spiritual values.

However, the good news is that when we parents do our job of training our children to manage their anger, we will see them thrive in life. Realize that anger itself is a normal human reaction; it is neither good nor bad. The problem is not the anger but the way it is managed. It can have beneficial results, if it energizes and motivates us to take action when we would otherwise remain silent.

We remember Jill, a shy fourteen-year-old who dreaded confrontations and conflict. She is truly a people-pleaser, and was struggling in her history class, where the teacher made a habit of putting down all religious faiths, especially Christianity. He frequently ridiculed well-known Christians whom Jill admired. As a Christian, Jill at first felt confused by her teacher's antagonism and later even began to question her own faith.

Then, about midyear, the teacher made a caustic remark about "preachers' kids." One of Jill's friends was the daughter of a pastor and this made Jill angry. In fact, she was furious! That evening she called some other Christian kids in the class and laid out a plan in which they agreed to participate. The next time the teacher began his belittling remarks, these students spoke up, though in a respectful way. They let the teacher know his comments were offensive. His first response was to try to ridicule the young people, but he soon realized how foolish he sounded and changed the subject. For the rest of the year, he made no more derogatory comments about religious faiths. Jill had used her anger constructively, to educate her teacher and to protect her personal freedom.

The Passive-Aggressive Child

Unfortunately, most people do not manage their anger as well as Jill did. A more common and destructive way to handle anger is called passive-aggressive behavior. Passive-aggressive behavior is an expression of anger that gets back at a person or group indirectly, or "passively." It is a subconscious determination to do exactly opposite of what an authority figure wants. An authority figure is a parent, teacher, minister, boss, policeman, laws, societal norms—any person or value system that represents authority. Of course, for a child or teenager, the primary authority figures are parents.

Ben, fifteen, is bright, has no learning problems, and is capable of making good grades. He brings home his books most nights and does his homework. But he is angry at his parents, and he is bringing home grades well below his ability. His parents are frustrated. His behavior is a classic passive-aggressive response.

Why Ben Didn't Do His Homework

There are several ways for parents to decide if they are dealing with passive-aggressive behavior, and a correct identification is important, since there are many other reasons for behavioral problems. First, passive-aggressive behavior does not make sense. This was certainly true in Ben's case—with his ability and hard work, his poor grades were very difficult to understand.

Second, you can suspect passive-aggressive behavior when nothing you do to correct the behavior works. Because the purpose of passive-aggressive behavior is to upset the authority figure, no matter what action that authority figure takes, it will make no difference. Nothing that Ben's parents or teachers did improved his grades. They helped him with his homework, they promised to reward him for good grades, and they even tried punishment. Each new method seemed to improve the situation briefly, but in the long run, nothing worked. This is the reason passive-aggressive behavior is so difficult to deal with. Subconsciously, Ben was making sure that nothing would work, since the underlying purpose was to upset the authority figures.

Third, although the purpose of this behavior is to frustrate authority figures, the person acting in this way is the one who will ultimately be defeated and whose future and relationships will be seriously affected.

Passive-Aggressive Behavior during the Early Teen Years

There is only one period of life when passive-aggressive behavior is normal: early adolescence, when a child is thirteen to fifteen years old. And it can be considered normal only if it does not cause harm to anyone. It is essential that the child learns how to handle anger in a mature fashion and grows out of the passive-aggressive stage. If he does not, this behavior will become a permanent part of his character and personality for life, used against employers, spouse, children, and friends.

Teens of bygone eras may have acted out this behavior in ways like putting Farmer Brown's cow on top of the barn or overturning his outhouse. In the city, boys sometimes formed teams to take a Volkswagen bug apart and then reassemble it in the owner's bedroom. Today teenagers have many more options for passive-aggressive behavior, and some of these are dangerous: drugs, violence, alcohol, crime, sexual activity resulting in venereal disease or pregnancy, school failure, and even suicide. Often, when the teens move out of this stage, serious life damage has been done.

As parents, you need to distinguish between harmless passive-aggressive behavior and that which is abnormal and harmful. For example, toilet-papering trees is a normal outlet during a teen's passive-aggressive stage. A messy room may be aggravating, but it is harmless. Also, strenuous physical activities can help teenagers to satisfy their desire for excitement and danger. Teens may be helped through this stage by involvement in mountain climbing, rope courses, long-distance biking, and team or individual sports.

> Many parents have made the tragic mistake of thinking that all anger is wrong and should be disciplined out of children.

As you seek to help your young teenagers through this stage, remember that your objective is to train them to manage their anger by the time they are seventeen years old. They can't leave the passive-aggressive stage unless they learn other, more mature and acceptable ways to replace the behavior. Unfortunately, many people never grow out of this stage—passive-aggressive behavior among adults is all too common.

The truth is that most people do not understand anger or the ways in which it can be managed. Many parents have made the tragic mistake of thinking that all anger is wrong and should be disciplined out of children. This approach does not work and it does children no favors. It does not train children to handle their anger in constructive ways; consequently, they continue to mishandle it into adulthood, just as their parents did before them. Passive-aggressive behavior is a primary cause of failure in college, problems at work, and conflict in marriage.

Because passive-aggressive behavior is the hidden source of most of life's worst difficulties, we as parents must train our children and teens to manage anger appropriately. We can't discipline it out of them.

Begin Early

Obviously, you can't wait until the teenage years to teach your children about anger management. You have to begin when they are very young, although you can't expect them to be able to handle anger with any level of maturity until the age of six or seven.

Anger management is the most difficult part of parenting because children are limited in the ways they can express anger. They have only two options, verbal or behavioral expression, and both are difficult for parents to handle. Parents find it hard to understand that the anger must come out some way—that it cannot be totally bottled up. As a result, many parents respond to children's expressions of anger in wrong and destructive ways.

As you consider the two options, recognize that it is better for your child to express anger verbally rather than behaviorally. When your child vents anger in words, you are able to train her in the direction of mature anger management. You want to avoid passive-aggressive behavior at all costs.

Until the age of six or seven, you are working primarily to keep passive-aggressive behavior from taking root in your child. The first and most important way you do this is to keep his emotional love tank full of unconditional love. The prime cause of anger and of misbehavior is an empty love tank. Speak your child's love language clearly and regularly and you will fill that tank and prevent passive-aggressive behavior from taking root. When that love tank is full, the child is under no pressure to display his unhappiness by asking, through his behavior, "Do you love me?" The child whose love tank is empty is compelled to ask, through misbehavior, "Do you love me?"

Next, realize that your children have no defense against parental anger. When you dump your anger on your child, it goes right down inside the child. If you do this often enough, this bottled anger will probably come out as passive-aggressive behavior. Listen to her calmly; let her express her anger verbally. It may not be pleasant to hear her anger, but it's preferable to her acting it out.

Unfortunately, when children let their anger out verbally, too many parents lash out and say something like, "How dare you talk to me like that? I never want to hear you speak to me that way again. Do you understand?" The children then have only two choices. They can obey and not express anger verbally, or they can disobey. What a corner to be in!

Helping Children Climb the Anger Ladder

Thousands of parents have been helped in their understanding of a child's anger by visualizing an Anger Ladder (see illustration on page 171). As you work with your children in the coming years, you will always be seeking to help them climb from one rung of the Anger Ladder to the next, away from the most negative expressions of anger to the more positive. The goal is to move the child from passive-aggressive behavior and verbal abuse to a calm, even pleasant response that seeks resolution. This is a long process that involves training, example, and patience.

You will notice that passive-aggressive behavior is at the bottom of the ladder. It represents totally unmanaged anger. Because this

THE ANGER LADDER

1. PLEASANT • SEEKING RESOLUTION • FOCUSING ANGER ON SOURCE
   • HOLDING TO PRIMARY COMPLAINT • THINKING LOGICALLY

2. PLEASANT • FOCUSING ANGER ON SOURCE
   • HOLDING TO PRIMARY COMPLAINT • THINKING LOGICALLY

POSITIVE AND NEGATIVE

3. FOCUSING ANGER ON SOURCE • HOLDING TO PRIMARY COMPLAINT
   • THINKING LOGICALLY • Unpleasant, loud

4. HOLDING TO PRIMARY COMPLAINT • THINKING LOGICALLY
   • Unpleasant, loud • Displacing anger to other sources

5. FOCUSING ANGER ON SOURCE • HOLDING TO PRIMARY COMPLAINT
   • THINKING LOGICALLY • Unpleasant, loud • Verbal abuse

6. THINKING LOGICALLY • Unpleasant, loud
   • Displacing anger to other sources • Expressing unrelated complaints

PRIMARILY NEGATIVE

7. Unpleasant, loud • Displacing anger to other sources
   • Expressing unrelated complaints • Emotionally destructive behavior

8. Unpleasant, loud • Displacing anger to other sources
   • Expressing unrelated complaints • Verbal abuse
   • Emotionally destructive behavior

9. Unpleasant, loud • Cursing • Displacing anger to other sources
   • Expressing unrelated complaints • Verbal abuse
   • Emotionally destructive behavior

10. FOCUSING ANGER ON SOURCE • Unpleasant, loud • Cursing
    • Displacing anger to other sources • Throwing objects
    • Emotionally destructive behavior

11. Unpleasant, loud • Cursing • Displacing anger to other sources
    • Throwing objects • Emotionally destructive behavior

NEGATIVE

12. FOCUSING ANGER ON SOURCE • Unpleasant, loud • Cursing
    • Destroying property • Verbal abuse
    • Emotionally destructive behavior

13. Unpleasant, loud • Cursing • Displacing anger to other sources
    • Destroying property • Verbal abuse
    • Emotionally destructive behavior

14. Unpleasant, loud • Cursing • Displacing anger to other sources
    • Destroying property • Verbal abuse • Physical abuse
    • Emotionally destructive behavior

15. Passive-aggressive behavior

Note: Phrases in capital letters indicate positive ways to express anger feelings.
Source: Ross Campbell, How to Really Love Your Angry Child *(Colorado Springs: Cook, 2003).*

behavior is common during the teenage years, you will have to deal with that level at some point, but you should not let your teenage child stay there. If you do, you could be heading for serious problems.

You need to remind yourself that your child can climb only one rung at a time. If you want the process and training to be finished soon, this will be frustrating. You may wait some time before your child is ready to take the next step. This calls for patience and wisdom, but the results are well worth the wait. As you watch your child express anger, you need to identify where she is on the Anger Ladder, so that you will know the next step.

In the Campbell household, I remember one particularly unpleasant experience when my son, David, was thirteen. He verbalized his anger only when a particular event upset him. Sometimes he was verbalizing his anger at me in ways that I didn't want to hear. I had to do some self-talk. I knew letting him express that anger would help to determine where he was on the Anger Ladder. Inside myself I would say to him, *Attaboy, David, attaboy. Let that anger out, because when it is all out, I've got you.* Of course, I didn't say this to David.

Another reason I wanted the anger to come out was that as long as it was inside of David, it controlled the house. But once it was outside, he felt silly and I could regain control. He had gotten all the anger out verbally and was asking himself, "Now what do I do?" It was then that I was in a great position to train him.

Letting David roll those words out of his mouth helped in another way. The more anger he expressed verbally, the less there would be to come out in destructive attitudes and behaviors.

That will be true for your child too. Let him or her verbalize the anger and you'll see where the child stands on the Anger Ladder, and you can limit potential passive-aggressive behavior.

Let Your Child Show Her Anger

Fellow parents, this way of dealing with children is not always easy to accept. Allowing a child to express anger verbally may seem permissive. It really is not. Remember that children of any age will naturally express anger in immature ways. You can't train them to express their anger in mature ways simply by getting upset at them and forcing them to stop venting their anger. If you do, their anger will be over-suppressed and passive-aggressive behavior will be the result.

> Allowing a child to **express anger verbally** may seem **permissive.** It really **is not.**

If you want to train your children to manage anger in a mature fashion, you must *allow them to express it verbally, as unpleasant as that may be.* Remember, all anger must come out either verbally or behaviorally. If you don't allow it to come out verbally, passive-aggressive behavior will follow.

When your child speaks in anger, it does not necessarily mean that he is being disrespectful. To determine whether he is respectful, ask yourself, "What is the child's attitude toward my authority most of the time?" Most children are respectful over 90 percent of the time. If this is true of your child, and now he is bringing verbal anger to you about a particular situation, this is exactly what you want to happen. For once your child has gotten the angry feelings out, you are then in an excellent position to train him.

Isn't it unfair, you may wonder, *to expect me to feel thankful that my daughter is expressing the anger verbally and then to control myself?* We acknowledge this is not easy. But as you behave this way, you are forcing yourself to mature. And you are saving yourself and your family from some of life's worst problems later on.

You may be wondering about children who verbalize anger most of the time, upset or not. It's true: some children express anger to manipulate their parents and get their own way, and that is unacceptable. Angry verbal expressions motivated by a desire to upset and hurt others are inappropriate and must be corrected. Handle those words like any misbehavior. But in the correction, practice the basic parental parameters: be kind but firm.

This may seem confusing, but letting your child bring his anger to you verbally when he is upset about a particular problem will provide you an opportunity to train him, as we will discuss below. Be sure to control yourself as your child expresses his anger verbally. And always remain kind but firm.

Seize the Moment

After an angry outburst, seize the moment to help your child learn to handle her anger. As soon as things are stable between you, sit down together and do three things. Each will help your child deal with her anger in a positive way.

1. Let her know that you are not going to condemn her. Especially if a child is very responsive to authority, she may feel guilty about what she has done and never express her feelings again. Part of training is to let her know that you accept her as a person and always want to know how she is feeling, whether happy or sad or angry.

2. Commend your child for the things she did right. You may say, "You did let me know that you were angry, and that is good. You didn't let your anger out on your little brother or the dog. You didn't throw anything or hit the wall. You simply told me that you were angry." Mention whatever she did that was right. Anytime a child brings verbal anger to you, she has done some right things and avoided some wrong ones.

3. Help your child take a step up the Anger Ladder. The goal is to move your son or daughter toward a more positive anger response. So you want to give your child a request rather than a pro-

hibition. Instead of saying, "Don't ever call me that name again!" you say, "From now on, Son, please don't call me that name. All right?" Of course, this doesn't guarantee that he will never again say what you have asked him not to. But it does ensure that when he is sufficiently mature, he will take that step. That may be the next day or several weeks or months down the road.

This kind of training is a long and difficult process, but, after you have done it enough times, your child will begin to do right without your reminder. The combination of your training, plus your good example of handling anger in a mature fashion, will help your child do her own self-training after a while.

For more information on helping children to handle anger, we recommend two books by Ross: *How to Really Love Your Child* and *How to Really Love Your Teenager.*

Love and Anger

Again, the most crucial element in training your children to manage their anger is your unconditional love for them. When they know that they are loved in this way, when they truly feel loved all the time, they will be far more responsive to your training. Also, you will be much more likely to achieve your goal of bringing them to emotional maturity by age seventeen.

We define love as looking out for another person's interests and seeking to meet her needs. With this definition, all wrongful words and deeds are actually a lack of love. We cannot be loving a child and at the same time be treating her poorly. To insist that we are still loving her when we are behaving badly toward her is to make the word *love* meaningless. A child treated this way does not feel loved. Rather, she feels angry, because she thinks that she is unloved.

We all know adults who are angry because they felt unloved by their parents. They may give very valid reasons for their anger, but at the root of those specifics is a lack of love. Their conclusion is, "If they loved me, they would not have treated me the way they did."

We are not suggesting that children who receive unconditional love, spoken in the primary and other love languages, will never get angry. They will, simply because we live in an imperfect world. Nor are we saying that in order to resolve your children's anger you must agree with their viewpoint. However, you must hear their viewpoint and come to understand their concern. Then you can judge whether they were wronged or misunderstood. At times you may need to apologize to your children. At other times, you may need to explain your reasoning for a decision you have made about their best interests. Even if they do not like your decision, they will respect it if you have taken time to fully hear and understand their complaints.

Processing anger and then training your children to deal with it in a mature way is one of the hardest parts of parenting. But the rewards are great. Speak your child's love language, keep his love tank filled, and watch him develop into a loving and responsible adult who knows how to process anger and helps other people do the same.

THE 5 LOVE LANGUAGES OF CHILDREN

physical touch
words of affirmation
quality time
gifts
acts of service

11

speaking the love languages in *single-parent* families

Filling a child's love tank can seem difficult at times: you are tired, your child is demanding, and you may feel that you need love yourself. At least you have your spouse to help you. Or do you?

In millions of single-parent homes, the answer is no. Instead of two parents filling a child's emotional tank on a regular basis, one does it alone. Instead of two parents giving love that flows through their marriage relationship, the love now is coming from a single mother or father who is wounded and lonely and pressured and without sufficient adult nurture.

Yet you can still speak your child's love language, filling his love tank. Everything we have said about loving your children is true, whether they reside with one parent or two. Single-parent families face many added issues, yet the power of the five love languages is no less. We emphasize this, realizing that single-parent households comprise 29.5 percent of all households with children, according to

2009 U.S. Census statistics.[1] Because so many children are living in single-parent homes, we feel compelled to address some of the special needs of these families, including how to practice the love languages with your children.

We realize one-parent homes are not all equal. Some were created by divorce and others by the death of a spouse. Some parents have never married—in 2008 40.6 percent of all children were born to unmarried parents.[2] In those one-parent homes that resulted from divorce, some of the children have an ongoing positive contact with the noncustodial parent, while others suffer from a negative contact or total lack of relationship. Some single-parent families live near relatives and enjoy the benefit of closeness to grandparents, aunts and uncles, and cousins. Many others live far away from relatives and have to pretty much fend for themselves.

No matter what your situation, if you are a parent raising your children alone, we know you can effectively show love to your family, particularly by speaking your children's primary love language.

When It's All Up to You

The single mother or father trying to meet the needs of children while at the same time maintaining a career and some semblance of a personal life knows the tensions on the home front. If this is your situation, you know all too well the time pressures, the economic demands, and the social and personal changes you and your children have experienced. You know the doubts about whether you can do an adequate job of parenting. You have heard all the judgments from supposed experts about the pitfalls awaiting your children. At times, you feel the loneliness and exhaustion of having to do everything yourself.

Most single-parent homes today are the result of divorce, and research continues to show that divorce can be traumatic for children, especially when the divorce is not handled well by the two parents.

When a parent dies, the child knows that there was no choice. Usually the death was preceded by an illness, and this helped the child to understand death. Divorce is a choice on the part of one or both parents, even when that "choice" does seem to be a necessity. A parent who has been widowed will have to deal with a child's memories, but not with the quality of an ongoing helpful or hurtful connection with the one who is gone. A parent who has been divorced faces years of decisions in relationship to the noncustodial parent.

It would be hard to name another change that has more deeply affected the nature of our society today than divorce. Yet the increasing number of single-parent families created through divorce is a many-layered social problem beyond the scope of this book. Our focus is on what to do now: How can we help the children who find themselves in circumstances they never chose and cannot change? Our concern is also for the millions of single parents who are valiantly working to keep their families intact and to raise happy and responsible children.

> How can we help the children who find themselves in circumstances they never chose and cannot change?

Healing the Wounded

The needs of children in such homes are the same as of children from intact families. It is the *way* that these needs are met that changes; one parent is the primary caregiver instead of two. And the caregiver, whether single through divorce, death, or never being married, is usually wounded. Wounded parents are trying to minister to their wounded children and at the same time hoping to convince them that life can be fairly normal. Instead of the children having to cope with just the ordinary challenges of growing up, they now take on another whole set of concerns that ideally should not be part of their world.

Judith Wallerstein, founder of The Center for the Family in Transition, has done the most extensive research about the effects of divorce upon children. In her book *Second Chances: Men, Women, and Children a Decade After Divorce*[3] she indicates that she entered her research with the notion commonly held among many adults: Divorce brings short-term pain, but eventually it provides greater happiness and fulfillment for everyone involved.

Wallerstein's years of research have found that this assumption is not true. In many ways, children never get over the pain of divorce.

Most of the children whom Wallerstein, Sandra Blakeslee, and their associates interviewed saw themselves as being in a special category, "Children of Divorce." They felt a bond with others who had gone through the same experiences. The most common emotions of these children were fear, anger, and anxiety. As long as ten years after the parents divorced, these feelings still frequently surfaced.

Helping Your Child through the Grief

Such feelings can readily drain love from a child's emotional tank. As you speak your child's primary love language in order to refill her tank, be aware much love is needed. Denial, anger, then bargaining, and more anger—these are common responses to grief, which is felt by both children of divorce and those who have experienced the death of a parent. Eventually children find some level of acceptance to the loss of one parent. Some children can move through these stages of grieving more quickly if significant adults in their lives seek to openly communicate with them about their loss. They need someone to talk with and cry with. If family members cannot be involved in a helpful way, then a sympathetic pastor, friend, or counselor may fill this role.

Let's consider each of the responses and how parents and other adult friends can help the child move toward acceptance. Significantly, speaking the child's primary love language along the way will help the child in processing his grief.

Denial

Typically, the first response is *denial*. No child wants to believe that his parents are splitting up, or that one parent has died. He will talk as if his parents are simply separated for a season, or that the deceased parent is on a journey and will soon return. In this stage, the child is very frightened and feels a profound sense of sadness and loss. He may cry often from his intense longing that his parents be reunited. In the case of divorce, he may also sense that he is rejected.

Anger

The denial stage is accompanied and followed by intense *anger.* The child is angry at the parents for violating the unwritten rules of parenthood: Parents are supposed to care for their children, not abandon them. This anger may be expressed openly in words or may be held inside, for fear of upsetting the parents or fear of being punished for angry words and behavior. A child who is openly angry may have temper tantrums, verbal explosions, and may even be physically destructive. The child feels powerless— she has no say in what is happening to her. She also has a sense of profound loneliness and feels unable to talk with anyone.

The child's anger may be directed at the parent who left or at the custodial parent or both. In the case of death, the anger may be directed toward God. The child intensely needs to feel loved, to know that someone really cares. He is not likely to receive this from the parent who left. The child may or may not receive meaningful love from the custodial parent. And if a child believes that the parent who

> The child intensely needs to feel loved, to know that someone really cares.

is present bears responsibility for the divorce, he may not be open to loving expressions from either parent. For that reason, grandparents and other family members, teachers, and religious leaders need to be sensitive to their opportunity to significantly meet the child's need for love. If they are aware of the child's primary love language, their efforts at meeting his emotional needs will be more effective.

Robbie's love language was physical touch. His father left when he was nine years old. Looking back, Robbie says, "If it had not been for my granddaddy, I'm not sure I would have made it. The first time I saw him after my father left, he took me in his arms and held me for a long time. He didn't say anything, but I knew he loved me and would always be there for me. Every time he came to see me, he hugged me and when he left, he did the same thing. I don't know if he knew how much the hugs meant to me, but they were like rain in the desert for me.

"My mom helped a lot by letting me talk and by asking me questions and encouraging me to share my pain. I knew she loved me, but in the early stages, I wasn't willing to receive her love," Robbie admitted. "She would try to hug me and I'd push her away. I think I blamed her for my father leaving. It wasn't until I found out that he left for another woman that I realized how I had misjudged her. Then I started receiving her hugs and we became close again."

Bargaining

Denial and anger are followed by *bargaining*. When parents separate, the child will make every effort to bring them back together. This may involve talking with the parents separately and together, pleading for them to work out their differences and reestablish the family unit. If verbal bargaining doesn't work, the child may subconsciously try manipulation by misbehaving in radical ways to get her parents' attention. She may also be testing the parents to see if they really care about her well-being. Her response could be drug use, petty theft, vandalism, sexual activity, or even suicide.

More Anger

Following bargaining will be *more anger.* In the hearts of children whose parents divorce, anger runs deep and lingers long. For at least a year after the divorce, they will probably struggle with emotions of guilt, anger, fear, and insecurity. Channeling so much energy into these feelings may result in lower grades at school, more aggressive negative social behavior, lessened respect for all adults, and intense loneliness. It is within such a painful setting that single parents seek to meet their children's need for love and at the same time establish some semblance of normalcy to the home. Theirs is not an easy task.

Wallerstein recently wrote: "After divorce you walk alone. All you've got is you. And it's scary." At the same time, "Little children need you more often . . . They are jittery and moody, and more clinging . . . Raising children always requires more time than you expected. They have more crises than you ever dreamed of. They demand sacrifice of time, money, hours spent at adult work and play."[4]

Learning to fill your child's love tank while your own is running low may seem difficult. But, like Robbie's mother, the wise parent will come to understand what her child uniquely needs—and seek to meet that need.

How Stories Help

Children who are overwhelmed with negative feelings have a hard time thinking clearly. If you are the single parent of such children, reading together can help your children begin to think clearly about their pain and loss. You will want to have a storybook they can understand. Select stories, songs, and poems appropriate to the ages of your children, through the early teen years. This can be a warm, bonding time. Many enjoyable stories have strong ethical and moral lessons, such as "Pinocchio" and stories by Beatrix Potter. There are several guides to help you choose good literature. We recommend *Honey for a Child's Heart,* by Gladys Hunt; *Books That Build Character,* by William Kilpatrick; and *The Book of Virtues,* by William Bennett.

Be alert to your child's reactions as you read to her. Ask what she is thinking, to open opportunities for discussion at her level. If you are reading about a child or animal that is lost and your child expresses concern, you have a great opportunity to praise her for her caring heart. You can also talk about what it feels like to be lost, or to lose someone dear to you.

Children also need help in playing the blame game. Anger can confuse their thinking. It is not uncommon for them to believe that blaming other people is justified, simply because they feel angry. When they are calm, you can explain different sides of a situation, not only about other children but also about what has happened in your family. Especially when children feel terribly wronged by a parent they think has abandoned them, they need to know that their sense of loss is natural and nothing to feel guilty about.

And, as you read together, you can talk about what is happening in your children's daily lives. You can also make up stories together. This will help you to understand what is going on inside your children, at levels they may be unable to articulate in discussion.

Ask for Help!

No parent can single-handedly meet a child's need for love. As we said before, some children may choose not to accept love from either parent; their hurt and anger are so great that they will not allow the possibility of love. This is where grandparents and other extended family members, as well as church and community resources, come into play.

If you are a single parent, don't wait until people ask if they can help. Some may be holding back, not wanting to interfere in your family. Others may not be aware of your situation. If you or your children need help, you may want to investigate the resources available in your community. Someone at your children's school or your church can guide you in your search.

Extended family members are always important, but they become even more crucial when children suffer losses. For instance, nearby grandparents can help the grandchildren in several ways during the school week, and their presence can cheer their own single-parent son or daughter. They may be able to come over and help the children get ready for school in the morning or help chauffeur in the afternoon. They also take some of the emotional burden off the single parent.

There are many people who would be glad to help single-parent families if they know that their help is needed. They want to feel useful, and you need some help. The only problem is getting these two together. A local church is a good place to make this happen, and some churches are networking in just such a way. If you find it difficult to make your needs known, just remember that you are doing this not primarily for yourself but for the well-being of your children.

> There are **many people** who would be glad to **help single-parent families** if they know that their help is **needed.**

Love Languages in the Single-Parent Household

A child's need for emotional love is just as important after the divorce as it was before. The difference is that the child's love tank has been ruptured by the severe trauma of divorce. The love tank will have to be repaired by hours of sympathetic listening and processing of the emotions we have talked about. Someone must nurture the child through the grief process if that child is ever again to believe that he or she is truly loved. The process of repairing the love tank is itself an expression of love. Listening much, talking less, helping your child face reality, acknowledging hurt, empathizing with pain is all part of it.

Of course, the primary way to refill the love tank is to speak your child's love language. Keep in mind that the child's primary love language does not change simply because the parents have separated due to divorce or death. Learn your child's love language and then tell the significant adults in your child's life what the child's primary love language is.

In the early weeks following a divorce, when a child may be unable to receive love from either parent, other significant adults may be the only ones able to express love to the child. If your child receives love primarily through affirming words, he may well receive them from grandparents or other adults yet temporarily reject them from you. A child whose primary love language is gifts may actually throw a gift back in the face of a parent recently divorced. Do not be angered by this but realize the behavior is part of your child's grieving process. Once the child has reached the acceptance stage and understands that he cannot put his parents' marriage back together, and that he is going to be living in a single-parent home, he may perhaps receive love on an emotional level from both parents.

If children receive the right kinds of love at times when they especially need it, they can come through the pains of family separation intact and go on to satisfying adult lives. One example of this is Bob Kobielush, president of the Christian Camping Foundation. Bob's father was a successful businessman and his mother was a homemaker. When Bob was young, his father gave up his business to join a cult, moving the family of five boys several times. When his father

> In the early weeks following a divorce, other significant adults may be the only ones able to express love to the child.

became ill with polio and was completely disabled, the family returned to their home state of Wisconsin to be near extended family. When Bob was nine, his parents divorced.

About this time, Bob and his brothers came under Christian influence and they all received Christ as their Savior. With no means of support, their mother was forced to go on welfare until she was able to get enough odd jobs. She later finished her academic preparation and became a teacher.

Today Bob and his brothers are all happily married, well educated, and productive. Bob says, "Mom always majored on the majors in positive ways. She didn't talk about the negative things. It seemed as if we were a normal family. I didn't know we weren't. I don't know how we would have turned out without a godly mother and extended family to model the practical Christian life. I thank God for my background and for my single mom."

Archibald Hart, dean emeritus of the School of Psychology at Fuller Seminary in California, credits the power of family and God for his growing strong in a single-parent home. Originally from South Africa, the Hart family broke up after years of conflict. Archibald's mother seemed happier after the divorce, but economic worries compelled her to send Archibald and his brother to live with their grandparents. They were a strong Christian influence, motivating the boys by saying, "There is nothing you can't do."

> Your children can become more resilient, productive, and creative if the circumstances are right.

Hart gives this advice to single parents: "Nothing is unchangeable. If you have no support network now, build it, and you will be amazed at how many will respond. Your children can become more resilient, productive, and creative if the circumstances are right. A life that is too easy is not good for the soul."[5]

Keep up your hope and hold on to your dreams for your children.

While things may seem rough now, there is another day, another year. If you and the children are making steady progress away from the sense of loss, if you are all growing in the many areas of life, you can feel assured that the growth will continue. It has become a pattern, a habit that will not easily be forgotten.

Meeting Your Own Need for Love

While we have talked primarily about the child whose parents have divorced, we are keenly aware that the single parent seeking to meet the child's needs is also a creature of need. While the child is working through the emotions of guilt, fear, anger, and insecurity, one or both parents are also working through similar emotions. The mother who has been abandoned by a husband may have found a new male interest; the mother who forced a physically abusive spouse to leave now struggles with her own feelings of rejection and loneliness. A single parent's emotional need for love is just as real as anyone else's need. Because that need cannot be met by the former spouse or by the child, the single parent often reaches out to friends. This is an effective way to begin to have your love tank filled.

A word of caution as you make new friends. The single parent at this point is extremely vulnerable to members of the opposite sex who may take advantage in a time of weakness. Because the single parent so desperately needs love, there is grave danger of accepting that love from someone who will take advantage sexually, financially, or emotionally. It is extremely important that the newly single parent be very selective in making new friends. The safest source for love is from long-term friends who know members of the extended family. A single parent who tries to satisfy the need for love in an irresponsible manner can end up with tragedy upon tragedy.

With your children, you have a tremendous resource of love. For deep down they do love you. And they need your love. As psychologists Sherill and Prudence Tippins say, "The best gift you can give your child is your own emotional, physical, spiritual, and intellectual health."[6] As painful as it may seem, the truth is that you may be a single parent for many years. During this time, long or short, you will want to give your children the example of integrity and responsibility that can be a model for them in their journey to responsible adulthood.

THE 5 LOVE LANGUAGES OF CHILDREN

physical touch

words of affirmation

quality time

gifts

acts of service

12

speaking the love languages in *marriage*

Someone has said, "The best way to love your children is to love their mother [father]." That's true. The quality of your marriage greatly affects the way you relate to your children—and the way they receive love. If your marriage is healthy—both partners treating each other with kindness, respect, and integrity—you and your spouse will feel and act as partners in parenting. But if you are critical, harsh, and unloving toward each other, you are not likely to be in accord as you raise your children. And the children, always sensitive to feelings, will sense it.

It's probably obvious now: The most essential emotional element in a happy and healthy marriage is love. Just as your child has an emotional love tank, you do too. And so does your spouse. We want to feel deeply loved by our mates, for then the world looks bright. But when the love tank is empty, we have the gnawing feeling, "My spouse doesn't really love me," and our whole world begins to look dark. Much of the straying and misbehavior in marriages grows out of these empty love tanks.

To feel loved and to strengthen your child's sense of being loved, you need to speak your spouse's primary love language as well. We conclude *The 5 Love Languages of Children* by talking about the love languages of adults. As a husband or wife, you will find that one of the five love languages speaks more deeply to you emotionally than the others. When your spouse expresses love to you in this primary language, you really feel loved. You like all five languages, but this one is special.

As children differ, so do adults. Seldom do a husband and wife have the same primary love language. Don't assume your spouse speaks your language or a language you learned from your parents. Those are two common mistakes. Maybe your father said, "Son, always give a woman flowers. Nothing is more important than flowers." And so you give your wife flowers and it seems to be no big deal to her. The problem is not in your sincerity but that you are not speaking her primary language. She appreciates the flowers, but one of the other languages would speak more deeply to her.

If spouses do not speak each other's primary language, their love tanks will not be filled; when they come down off the "in love" emotional high, their differences will seem bigger and their frustration with each other will mount. They may think about the warm emotions they used to experience and seek to recapture that "in love" feeling so they will be happy again. And yet, they don't know how to do it with their spouse, since life at home has become dull and predictable and far less than satisfying.

"In Love" or Loving?

Too many people enter marriage through a "falling in love" experience, during which they see the object of their love as perfect. While they are blind to any imperfections, they are also sure that their experience of love is unique and that they are the first to love anyone so deeply. Of course, in time their eyes are opened and they come down to earth where they can see the other person as he or she really is, warts and all. The vast majority of "in love" experiences end up "out of love."

Most people have fallen in love, maybe several times, and they look back on those experiences with thanksgiving that they didn't do anything foolish while the sensation was at its peak. But too many people today are acting on the obsession and causing great harm to their families. That's how marital affairs begin, seeking after an elusive feeling they may have had during their dating years or early months of marriage. But lesser feelings do not mean dwindling love.

There is a difference between love and being "in love." The "in love" feeling is temporary, a primitive emotional reaction that often has little logical basis. Genuine love is quite different, in that it places the needs of the other person first and desires for the partner to grow and flourish. Genuine love allows the mate to choose to return the love. In marriage, we all need a partner who will choose to love us. When that happens, we can happily receive love from the other one and feel thrilled that our mate benefits from our efforts to love and make him or her happy.

This kind of love takes sacrifice and hard work. Most couples reach a point where they lose those exhilarating "in love" feelings and wonder if they still love the one they married. It is then that they need to decide whether they are going to make their marriage work, to care for their mates regardless of everything else, or if they are just going to let the relationship go.

You may find yourself thinking, "But this sounds so sterile. Love as an 'attitude' with appropriate behavior?" As I mentioned in the book *The 5 Love Languages,* some spouses really like and desire the fireworks.

Where are the shooting stars, the balloons, the deep emotions? What about the spirit of anticipation, the twinkle in the eye, the electricity in a kiss, the excitement of sex? What about the emotional security of knowing that I am number one in my partner's thoughts?[1]

That's not wrong, of course. Such feelings at times reward our commitment to relationship. But we shouldn't expect them. Yet we do need our mate to fill our love tank. He will do it if he speaks the love language we understand.

That's what Carla was missing in her marriage. "I just don't feel that Rick loves me anymore," she told her sister one day. "Our relationship is empty and I feel so alone. I used to be number one in Rick's life, but now I rank about twenty—after his job, golf, football, Scouts, his family, the car, and just about everything else. I think he is glad that I'm here, doing my part, but he takes me for granted. Oh, he gets me nice gifts on Mother's Day, my birthday, and our anniversary, and he sends me flowers on all the right days, but the gifts seem empty.

"Rick never has any time for me. We don't go anywhere together, never do anything as a couple, and hardly talk anymore. I get angry just thinking about it. I used to beg him to spend time with me, and he said I was criticizing him. He told me to get off his back and leave him alone. He said I should be thankful that he has a good job, isn't on drugs, and doesn't run around on me. Well, excuse me, but that's not enough. I want a husband who loves me and acts as if I am important enough to spend time with."

Do you spot the love language Carla understands best, that Rick does not speak? Rick is speaking the language of gifts; Carla is crying for quality time. In the early years, she received his gifts as expressions of love; but because he ignored her primary love language, her love tank is now empty and his gifts no longer count for much.

If Carla and Rick can discover each other's primary love language and learn to speak it, the emotional warmth of love can return to their marriage. No, not the obsessive, irrational euphoria of the "in love" experience, but something far more important—a deep inner feeling of being loved by their spouse. They will know that they are number one to the other; that they respect, admire, and appreciate each other as persons, and want to be together, living in an intimate partnership.

This is the kind of marriage people dream of, and it can be a reality when couples learn to speak each other's primary love language on a regular basis. And it will make them stronger parents, working more as a team while giving the children security and a greater sense of love. Let's look at how this can play out with each of the love languages.

Words of Affirmation

"I work hard," Mark said, "and I've been fairly successful in my business. I'm a good father and, in my opinion, a good husband. All I ever expect from my wife is a little appreciation, but instead, what I get is criticism. It doesn't matter how hard I work or what I do, it is never enough. Jane is always after me about something. I just don't understand it. Most women would be glad to have a husband like me. Why is she so critical?"

As frantically as he can, Mark is waving a banner that reads, "My love language is words of affirmation. Will somebody please love me?"

But Jane doesn't know about the five love languages any more than Mark does.[2] She can't see his banner and hasn't the foggiest idea why he feels unloved. She reasons, "I'm a good homemaker. I take care of the kids, work full-time, and keep myself looking attractive. What more could he want? Most men would be happy to come home to a good meal and a clean house."

Jane probably doesn't even know that Mark feels unloved. She simply knows that periodically he explodes and tells her to stop being critical of him. If he were asked, Mark would probably admit that he enjoys the good meals and appreciates a clean house, but these do not meet his emotional need for love. His primary language is words of affirmation, and without such words, his love tank will never be full.

To the spouse whose primary love language is words of affirmation, spoken or written expressions of appreciation are like rain falling on a spring garden.

"I'm so proud of you and the way you handled the situation with Robert."

"This is a great meal. You deserve a place in the chef's hall of fame."

"The lawn really looks nice. Thanks for all your hard work."

"Ohhh, don't you look amazing tonight!"

"I haven't told you this in a long time, but I really appreciate that you work regularly and help pay the bills. I know it is hard on you sometimes, and I do thank you for your great contribution."

"I love you so much. You are the most wonderful husband/wife in the world!"

Affirming words may be written as well as spoken. Before we were married, many of us wrote love letters and poems. Why not continue or revive this expression of love after marriage? If you find writing difficult, buy a card and underline the words that express your feelings and perhaps add a brief note at the bottom of the card.

Speak words of affirmation in the presence of other family members or friends and you gain an extra benefit. Not only does your spouse feel loved, but you have given others an example of how to speak affirming words. Let her mother hear you brag about your wife, and you may have a fan for life!

If such words are sincerely spoken or written, they speak volumes to a person whose primary love language is words of affirmation.

Quality Time

John wrote me after reading the book *The 5 Love Languages*. "For the first time I realized why Beth had complained so much about our not spending time together—her primary love language was quality time.

"Before, I had always accused her of being negative, of not appreciating all that I did for her," John wrote. "I'm a person of action—I like to clean up messes and get things organized. From the early days of our marriage, I have always been good at fixing things around the house, keeping the yard looking good. I never understood why Beth didn't seem to value all this but always complained that we didn't spend time together.

"When the lights came on in my mind, I realized that she really did appreciate those things, but that they didn't make her feel loved because service was not her love language. And so, the first thing I did was to plan a weekend away, just the two of us. We hadn't done that in several years. When she knew I was making the arrangements, she was like a kid going on a vacation."

After that special weekend, John looked at their finances and decided to have weekend getaways every couple of months. The weekend treks took them to different parts of their state. His letter continued:

"I also told her that I wanted us to spend fifteen minutes every night sharing with each other about the day. She thought this was great but could hardly believe I would initiate it.

"Since our first weekend away, Beth's attitude has been totally different. She expresses appreciation for all the things I do around the house. Also, she is no longer critical—yes, my primary love language is words of affirmation. We haven't felt this good in years. Our only regret is that we didn't discover the five love languages earlier in our marriage."

Beth and John's experience is similar to that of thousands of other couples when they discover each other's primary love language. Like John, we must both learn our spouse's primary love language and learn to speak that love language regularly. As you do so, the other four languages will have enhanced meaning, because your spouse's love tank will be kept full.

Gifts

All human cultures incorporate gift-giving as an expression of love between husband and wife. This usually begins before marriage, whether during the dating phase as in Western cultures or during the period before a prearranged marriage. In the West, gift-giving has been emphasized more for the male than for the female, but the receiving of gifts may also be a primary love language of men. Many husbands have admitted that when their wives come home and show them the clothes they have bought for themselves, their silent thought is, "I wonder if she will ever think about getting me a shirt, tie, or pair of socks? Does she ever think of me when she is shopping?"

For spouses whose primary love language is receiving gifts, a present says, "He was thinking about me." Or, "Look what she bought for me." Most gifts require a good deal of thought, and it is this thoughtfulness that communicates the love. We even say, "It is the thought that counts." However, it is not the thought left in your head that counts—the gifts actually should be presented.

> Many husbands wonder, "Does she ever think of me when she's shopping?"

You may be unsure what to give. If so, get help. When Rob discovered that his wife's primary love language was gifts, he was at a loss as to what to do because he didn't know how to buy gifts. And so he recruited his sister to go shopping with him once a week to buy his wife a gift. After three months of this, he was able to select his own presents.

Cindy's husband, Bill, enjoyed golf, and Cindy knew he would like something related to his hobby. But what? She had never learned much about the game. So twice a year she asked one of his golfing buddies to secure a golf-related gift which she in turn gave to Bill. He was always elated at how in tune she was with his desires.

Bart was a suit-and-tie man five days a week. Once a month his wife, Annie, visited the store where Bart bought his suits and asked the salesman to pick out a tie for him. The salesman kept a list of the suits, so that the ties always matched. Bart told everyone what a thoughtful wife Annie was.

Of course, buying a husband gifts assumes that the wife has available cash. If she does not work outside the home, this may mean that in a budget discussion with her husband, they should agree on a monthly amount from which she can buy gifts. If his primary love language is gifts, her husband will be happy to make that budget adjustment.

There is always a way to learn to speak your spouse's primary language. It may take some creativity, but there is no law that says you have to do things just like other people do. Make the gifts you select tie in with your spouse's hobby or some interest he or she is just beginning to explore. Or shop for a gift when you are away together for a day or more. You might buy a gift card for a restaurant you both like, or tickets to a play or concert. Or even a handmade certificate good for a certain amount of work to be done in the house or yard by you or by a professional. Or a couple of quiet days at a retreat center for a mother of young children. Your gift to your spouse could be a new sound system or work to be done on an older piano that he or she values.

Acts of Service

Andy was livid as he talked with a counselor. "I don't understand it. Sarah said she wanted to be a full-time mom and that's fine with me, since I make enough money to support us. But if she is going to stay at home, I don't understand why she can't keep the house in decent order. When I come home in the evening, it's like walking into a disaster area. The bed is unmade. Her nightgown is still lying on the chair. Clean clothes are piled on top of the dryer, and the baby's toys are scattered all over. If she went shopping, the groceries are still in the bags. And she's watching TV, giving no thought to what we are going to have for supper.

"I'm sick of living in a pigpen. All I'm asking is that she keep the house in a halfway decent condition. She doesn't have to cook every night—we can go out a couple of times a week."

Andy's primary love language was acts of service and the gauge on his love tank was reading empty. He didn't care if Sarah stayed home or worked outside the home, but he wanted to live in a greater degree of order than they did. He felt that if she cared about him she would show it by having the house in better order and preparing meals several times a week.

By nature, Sarah was not an organized person. She was creative and enjoyed doing exciting things with the children. She placed the relationship with the children on a higher level of priority than keeping the house clean. Speaking Andy's primary love language, acts of service, seemed almost impossible to her.

Their story may help you understand why we use the metaphor of language. If you grew up speaking English, then learning German or Japanese could seem very difficult. In a similar way, learning to speak the language of acts of service can be difficult. But when you come to understand that service is your spouse's primary language, you can decide to find a way to speak it eloquently.

For Sarah, the answer was to work out an arrangement with a teenager next door to come over late in the afternoon to play with the children, so that Sarah could give the house a "Let's love Andy" treatment. In exchange for the child care, she tutored the teenager in algebra several times a week. Also, Sarah began to consciously plan three dinner meals each week, preparing them in the morning and leaving only the finishing touches for evening.

Another wife in a similar situation decided, along with a friend, to take a course in basic meal preparation at a local technical institute. They cared for each other's children while they were in class and also enjoyed the stimulation of meeting new people in the class.

Doing something that you know your spouse would like is one of love's fundamental languages. Such acts as emptying the dishwasher, running to the drugstore to pick up a prescription, rearranging furniture, trimming shrubs, and cleaning the bathrooms are all ways of serving. It can be little things like straightening up papers in the home office or changing the baby's diaper. It is not difficult to find out what your spouse would most desire. Just think of what they have most complained about in the past. If you can do these acts of service as expressions of love, they will seem far more noble than if you think of them as humdrum tasks that have no special meaning.

> Doing something that you know your spouse would like is one of love's fundamental languages.

Physical Touch

We must not equate physical touch simply with the sexual part of marriage. To be sure, lovemaking involves touch, but physical touch as an expression of love should not be limited to sexual intercourse. Putting your hand on your spouse's shoulder, running your hand through her hair, massaging his neck or back, touching her arm as you give her a cup of coffee—these are all expressions of love. Of course, love is also expressed by holding hands, kissing, embracing, sexual foreplay, and intercourse. For the spouse whose primary love language is physical touch, these are love's loudest voices.

"When my husband takes time to massage my back, I know he loves me. He is focusing on me. Every movement of his hands says, 'I love you.' I feel closest to him when he is touching me." Jill is clearly revealing her primary love language, physical touch. She may appreciate gifts, words of affirmation, quality time, and acts of service, but what most deeply communicates on an emotional level is her husband's physical touch. Without that, the words may seem empty, the gifts and time meaningless, and the acts of service as so much duty. But if she is receiving physical touch, her love tank will be full and the love expressed in other languages will cause it to overflow.

Because a man's sexual drive is physically based, whereas a woman's sexual desire is emotionally based, husbands often assume that their own primary love language is physical touch. This is particularly true for those whose sexual needs are not met regularly. As their desire for sexual release overpowers their need for emotional love, they think this is their deepest need. If, however, their sexual needs are met, they may well discern that physical touch is not their primary love language. One way to tell is how much they enjoy physical touch that is not associated with sexual intercourse. If this is not high on their list, physical touch is probably not their primary language.

Discover and Speak Your Spouse's Love Language

You may be asking, "Does this really work? Will it make a difference in our marriage?" The best way to find out is to try. If you don't know your spouse's primary love language, you could ask him or her to read this chapter and then you can talk about it. If your mate is not willing to read or to talk about it, you may have to guess. Think about his complaints, his requests, and his behavior. Also, the love language he speaks to you and others may give you a clue.

With that educated guess in mind, focus on the likely primary language and see what happens over the next few weeks. If you have judged correctly, you will probably see a change in the attitude and spirit of your spouse. If he asks why you are acting strangely, you can just say that you read something on love languages and are trying to be a better lover. The chances are good that your spouse will want to know more, and you may want to read *The 5 Love Languages* together, as well as this book.

Speak each other's primary love language regularly and you will see a profound difference in the emotional climate between the two of you. With full love tanks you are better able to fill your children's love tanks. We believe you will find your marriage and family life much more enjoyable.

Speak your spouse's primary love language; speak your children's love language. And as you find it making a difference, share the message of this book with your extended family and friends. Family by family, we can create a more loving society. What you do in loving your family will make a difference in our nation.

THE 5 LOVE LANGUAGES OF CHILDREN

physical touch

words of affirmation

quality time

gifts

acts of service

what might be is still *ahead*

As you recognize and begin to speak the primary love
language of your child, we know the outcome will be
a more solid family relationship and benefits for you and your children. As we said in chapter 1, speaking your child's love language
won't end all problems, but it can bring stability to your home and
hope to your child. It's a wonderful opportunity.

But you may have doubts and other concerns as you begin to
speak a new love language, concerns about your past or your abilities in the present. Such concerns also represent opportunities. We
now look at those special opportunities you have, no matter your
past or present situation.

It would seem that the ideal reader for this book is a couple just
starting a family or who have very young children. We know, however, that some of our readers have older children in the home or
even adult children. You may be thinking, *If only I had read this
book earlier . . . but it's sort of late now.* Many parents look back

at the way they raised their family and realize that they didn't do a very good job of meeting their children's emotional needs. And now, those children may be grown and have families of their own.

If you are among those parents with regrets, you probably look back and ask why things went wrong. Maybe your work took you away from home too much in those critical child-rearing years. Or perhaps it was your own turbulent childhood that left you so unequipped to be a parent. You may have lived all your life with an empty love tank so that you never learned how to speak love to your children.

> The wonderful thing about human relationships is that they are not static.

Even though you have learned a lot since those years, you may have concluded, "What happened, happened, and there's not much we can do about it now." We would like to suggest another possibility, "What might be is still ahead." The opportunities are still there. The wonderful thing about human relationships is that they are not static. The potential for making them better is always present.

Developing a closer relationship with your teenage or adult children may require tearing down walls and building bridges—some very hard but rewarding work. Maybe it is time to admit to your children what you have already admitted to yourself—that you did not do a very good job of communicating love on an emotional level. If they are still in your home or live nearby, you can do this face-to-face, looking into their eyes and asking their forgiveness. Or you may need to write this in a letter, making a sincere apology and expressing a hope for a more positive relationship in the future. You can't undo the past, but you can forge a different kind of future.

Perhaps you were not only poor communicators, but you actually abused your children, emotionally, physically, or sexually. Perhaps alcohol or other drugs were your cohorts in crime, or maybe your own pain and immaturity rendered you victims to your anger. Whatever your failure, it is never too late to tear down the walls. You can never build bridges until you get rid of the walls. (If you are still abusing your children, you likely will need a trained counselor to help you break this destructive pattern.)

The most positive thing to do with a past failure is to confess it and ask forgiveness. You cannot erase the deeds any more than you can erase all their results. But you can experience emotional and spiritual cleansing through confession and the possibility of forgiveness. Whether or not your children verbally express forgiveness, the fact that you have been mature enough to admit your failures gives them a bit more respect for you. In time, they may be open to your efforts to build bridges. And who knows, the day may come when they allow you the privilege of a closer relationship with them—and their children.

You can **never build bridges** until you get **rid of the walls**.

Even if you were not the parent you wish you had been, you can begin now to love your children in ways that will make them feel truly valued. And as they have children, you will know that you are influencing another generation of your family, those little ones who now will have a better chance at receiving unconditional love all their days.

With full love tanks, your grandchildren will be more receptive and active intellectually, socially, spiritually, and relationally than they would be without this. When children feel genuinely loved, their whole world looks brighter. Their inner spirit is more secure and they are far more likely to reach their potential for good in the world.

I (Gary) dream of a day when all children can grow up in homes filled with love and security, where their developing energies can be channeled to learning and serving rather than craving and searching for the love they did not receive at home. It is my desire that this book will help this dream to become a reality for many children.

Gary has mentioned the opportunity of emotional and spiritual cleansing through forgiveness. I (Ross) encourage you to remember the spiritual dimension of parenting. The greatest source of encouragement I have found in my own parenting is the promises of God. My wife, Pat, and I have had many difficult bridges to cross, including the birth of a profoundly retarded daughter, and we can assure you that God is always near, ready to help and honor each of His wonderful promises. My favorite promises for parents are in Psalm 37:25–26.

I was young and now I am old,
yet I have never seen the righteous forsaken
or their children begging bread.
They are always generous and lend freely;
their children will be blessed. (New International Version)

The Revised Standard Version of the Bible renders the final line, "and his children become a blessing." I have stood on those two Scripture verses for many years and have tested those promises countless times. I have never seen the righteous forsaken. And I have seen the children of the righteous blessed and becoming a blessing.

As I have seen my children grow and mature in every way, I have been heartened not only that God is keeping His promises and blessing my children, but that I am truly His child also. Pat and I have gone through many trials in which we had real difficulty seeing our way, but God always came through and brought us out of them.

I want to encourage you in your parenting. No matter what your situation is now or will be in the future, God will never forsake you. He will always be there for you and see you through to the end. As you raise your children, there are opportunities to develop the spiritual aspects of their lives—and your own.

The Old Testament prophet Isaiah, declaring God's words, wrote:
Fear not, for I am with you;
Be not dismayed, for I am your God.
I will strengthen you,
Yes, I will help you,
I will uphold you with my righteous right hand.[1]

Such a verse can carry you through some rough periods in life and in parenting; that verse certainly has sustained Pat and me. Without God's assurances and promises, I know our story would be quite different than it has been.

The psalmist calls children "a gift of the Lord," a "reward," a "heritage."[2] Children are the most wonderful gift we can have. If they mean so much to God, they should mean everything to us, their parents. I would like to suggest that you make a list of "requirements" for being a good parent. Don't let the word *requirement* put pressure or guilt on you as a caring parent. These "requirements" should help you feel good about your authority and role as a parent. Relax and really enjoy your children.

When I was a fledgling dad, I found myself worrying; I was insecure in my parenting. But then I discovered that once a parent understands what a child needs, it is not that difficult to meet those "requirements." The best news is that almost any caring parent is able to do this.

I urge you to make up your own requirement list. Start with a few items and then add to the list as you want to. When you see that you are meeting those requirements, you can be assured that your child is receiving good parenting, and you can relax and enjoy your child. It would be hard to describe to you how much this assurance has helped me. In fact, I soon found that I was a better parent than I ever thought I could be.

Most of the "requirements" for good parenting are in this book.

If you want to make a list, I can give you a start. But the list won't be complete or be yours until you frame it in your own thoughts and words. Here is my personal list, my own "Requirements to be a Good Parent":

1 Keep my child's emotional love tank full—speak the five love languages.

2 Use the most positive ways I can to control my child's behavior: requests, gentle physical manipulation, commands, punishment, and behavior modification.

3 Lovingly discipline my child. Ask, "What does this child need?" and then go about it logically.

4 Do my best to handle my own anger appropriately and not dump it on my child. Be kind but firm.

5 Do my best to train my child to handle anger maturely—the goal is sixteen and one-half years.

I hope you will make your own requirement list soon. As you realize that you are able to do what you have written on your list, you will be able to relax and enjoy your children. And they will become increasingly secure in every way.

A study guide, with questions and exercises for parents and groups, is available online at www.5lovelanguages.com

notes

CHAPTER 1
1. Lori Gottlieb, "How to Land Your Kid in Therapy," *Atlantic* (July/August 2011), 64–78.
2. First John 3:18.

CHAPTER 2
1. Mark 10:13–16.

CHAPTER 3
1. Proverbs 18:21.
2. Proverbs 15:1.
3. Helen P. Mrosla, "All the Good Things," *Reader's Digest*, October 1991, 49–52.

CHAPTER 4
1. Sandy Dengler, *Susanna Wesley* (Chicago: Moody, 1987), 171.

CHAPTER 6
1. Luke 14:12–14.

CHAPTER 9
1. Burton L. White, *The Origins of Human Competence* (Lexington, Mass.: D.C. Heath and Company, 1979), 31.

CHAPTER 11
1. Research from *census.gov*.
2. Ibid.
3. Judith Wallerstein and Sandra Blakeslee, *Second Chances: Men, Women, and Children a Decade After Divorce* (New York: Ticknor & Fields, 1990).
4. Judith Wallerstein, "Parenting After Divorce: What Really Happens and Why," *huffingtonpost.com*, November 29, 2010.
5. Lynda Hunter, "Wings to Soar," *Single Parent Family*, May 1996, 7.
6. Sherill and Prudence Tippins, *Two of Us Make a World* (New York: Henry Holt, 1995), 56.

CHAPTER 12
1. Gary Chapman, *The 5 Love Languages* (Chicago: Northfield, 2010), 37.
2. If after reading this chapter you feel you need to learn more about spotting your spouse's primary love language and practicing that language, read *The 5 Love Languages*. It's written specifically for married and engaged couples.

EPILOGUE
1. Isaiah 41:10.
2. Psalm 127:3; see New King James and New International Versions.

more helps for **parents**

Ross Campbell, *How to Really Love Your Child*. Colorado Springs: Cook, 2004.

Ross Campbell, *How to Really Love Your Angry Child*. Colorado Springs: Cook, 2003.

Les Carter and Frank Minirth, *The Anger Workbook*. New York: Wiley & Sons, 2004.

Gary Chapman, *The 5 Love Languages*. Chicago: Northfield, 2010.

Gary Chapman, *The Family You've Always Wanted*. Chicago: Northfield, 2008.

Foster W. Cline and Jim Fay, *Parenting with Love and Logic*. Colorado Springs: NavPress, 2006.

Mary DeMuth, *You Can Raise Courageous and Confident Kids*. Eugene, Oreg.: Harvest House, 2011.

focusonthefamily.com: This website is packed with helpful resources on a wide variety of family-oriented topics.

John Fuller, *First-Time Dad*. Chicago: Moody, 2011.

Willard F. Harley, *Mom's Needs, Dad's Needs: Keeping Romance Alive Even After the Kids Arrive*. Grand Rapids: Revell, 2003.

Tim Kimmel, *Grace-Based Parenting*. Nashville: Nelson, 2005.

Kevin Leman, *Have a New Kid by Friday*. Grand Rapids: Revell, 2008.

Kevin Leman, *Single Parenting That Works*. Grand Rapids: Revell, 2006.

James R. Lucas, *1001 Ways to Connect with Your Kids*. Wheaton, Ill.: Tyndale, 2000.

John Rosemond, *Parenting by the Book*. New York: Howard, 2007.

Tedd Tripp, *Shepherding a Child's Heart*. Wapwallopen, Pa.: Shepherd Press, 1995.

H. Norman Wright, *Helping Your Kids Deal with Anger, Fear, and Sadness*. Eugene, Oreg.: Harvest, 2005.

for **parents** and **kids:** the love languages mystery game

For parents of children 5 to 8 years old:

So many parents wonder about their child's love language, and admittedly, determining the love language of a young child requires some educated guesswork. Why? Because young children can't yet verbalize their love language. However, for children ages 5 to 8 years old, you might try the following exercise. Ask him or her to draw or call out some ways parents love their children. You should try not to guide their drawings or answers, limit their responses, or require more responses than what he or she is prepared to give at the time you ask. Depending on the child's attention span and the time of day, you may get many answers, or you may get very few. If it seems like slow going, then you may want to secretly explore the subject of love with your child for a week or so until you can deduce what he or she perceives as love.

You may find yourself reading books or watching programs with your child and asking the question, "How do you know that mommy or daddy loves that little boy or little girl?" Or you may intentionally experiment by expressing love in each of the five ways over a week's period of time. This will be a subjective measure, but the combination of all these suggestions—studying your child's answers or drawings, listening to his or her answers about other parents and children, and "measuring" his or her response to your expression of each of the five love languages—should be enough to help you accurately assess your child's primary love language. If you are lucky enough to catch your child in a talkative or expressive mood, you may be able to get him or her to identify several ways parents show love. You'll be looking for a theme or a repetition in their answers, and from this, you can accurately determine your child's love language.

For parents of children 9 to 12:

By the time a child is 9 years old, he or she is better able to identify and express his or her feelings about love than when he or she was younger. Parents still have to keep in mind that children this age have a limited attention for and limited interest in such things as helping you determine their love language. The following "game" should help you in your research.

Tell your child you would like help solving "The Love Language Mystery Game." Explain that you need him or her to look at a list of "clues" and that these clues are comments that parents sometimes make to their children. Your child will see a set of 20 clue boxes, each with two comments. He or she must pick one of the two comments in each clue box based on which comment they like better. Explain that at the end of all the clues, you and your child can count the clues he or she circled and solve the mystery. If your child asks what the "mystery" is or what it is about, you can simply explain that it's a game in which parents are trying to learn what makes kids happy or what they like to hear their parents say.

To give this a game-like effect, you should secretly write on a piece of paper what you think your child's love language is (words, touch, time, service, gifts). That is, which letter will he or she most often circle? Do not let your child see your guess but tell him or her that you have written down your guess and will find out at the end of the game if you guessed right. After your child has gone through the set of clues, help him or her count and transfer the answers to the appropriate blanks. Reveal your guess and tell your child if you guessed correctly. For your knowledge, **A** = Physical Touch, **B** = Words of Affirmation, **C** = Gifts, **D** = Acts of Service, and **E** = Quality Time.

This activity will have been little more than a game to your child to see if he or she got the same answer to the "mystery" that you got. He or she will have little clue that you're using this information to further confirm or clarify your guess about his or her love language. Because children expect games to end in a "reward," tell your child at the end of the "mystery solving" that, whether or not you guys ended up with the same answer, you'll celebrate by doing something fun together (i.e., eating a favorite snack, watching a movie, playing a game of your child's choosing, etc.).

Some children will help "solve the mystery" and be satisfied not asking any questions. If your child happens to inquire about this so-called mystery you wanted help with, give a brief explanation of the love languages and tell your child that you just want to make sure he or she recognizes and receives your love. Depending on your child's maturity level, he or she may be able to share his or her thoughts on the matter and further clarify his or her love language.

You are now ready to introduce your child to "The Love Language Mystery Game." At the top of the "game" or profile, you'll see a brief set of instructions that explain to your child how to take and score the profile. Because of your child's age and potential questions he or she may have, be prepared to read the instructions to him or her and answer any questions he or she may have. Also be prepared to help your child score the profile by helping him or her count the number of times he or she circled each letter (A, B, C, D, E). Finally, if your child needs help transferring his or her scores to the appropriate blanks at the end of the profile, then offer to assist with that as well. Have fun, and enjoy unlocking the mystery of your child's love language!

The Love Language Mystery Game

Each clue box has two comments that parents sometimes make to their children. Read each clue box and, of the two comments, pick the one you like better and wish your mom or dad would say to you. Then circle the letter that goes with that comment. Be careful and only circle one letter in each clue box! After you've gone through all 20 clue boxes, go back and count how many A's, B's, C's, D's, and E's that you circled. Then write your scores in the blanks at the end of the game. Ask your mom or dad for help if you have any questions. And have fun unlocking the love language mystery!

1
Give me a hug! — A
You are terrific! — B

2
I've got a special birthday present for you! — C
I'll help you with your project. — D

3
Let's go to a movie. — E
Give me a high five! — A

4
You are so smart! — B
Have you made your Christmas list? — C

5
Would you help me cook dinner? — D
I like going to fun places with you! — E

6
Give me a kiss! — A
You are #1! — B

7
I've got a surprise for you. — C
We can make something really cool. — D

8
Let's watch TV together! — E
Tag, you're it! — A

| 9 | You did a great job! | B |
| | You've earned a special surprise! | C |

| 10 | You can invite your friends. | D |
| | Let's go to your favorite restaurant. | E |

| 11 | I'm going to give you a big hug! | A |
| | You are an awesome kid! | B |

| 12 | I made your favorite food. | C |
| | I checked your homework, and it looks great! | D |

| 13 | You are fun to hang out with! | E |
| | I'll race you! | A |

| 14 | Wow! You did it! | B |
| | Check under your bed for a special present! | C |

| 15 | I cleaned up your room for you. | D |
| | Let's play a game together. | E |

| 16 | Would you like for me to scratch your back? | A |
| | You can do it! Don't give up! | B |

| 17 | What would you like for your birthday? | C |
| | We can pick up your friend on the way to the movie. | D |

| 18 | I always like doing stuff with you. | E |
| | You are so huggable! | A |

| 19 | How did you know how to do that? You are brilliant! | B |
| | I can't wait to give you your present! | C |

| 20 | Don't worry! I'll pick you up on time! | D |
| | Let's spend the day doing whatever you want to do! | E |

How many A's did you circle? _____

A's stand for physical touch. People whose love language is physical touch like to receive hugs, kisses, and high fives.

How many B's did you circle? _____

B's stand for words of affirmation. People whose love language is words of affirmation like for others to use words to tell them that they are special and that they do a good job.

How many C's did you circle? _____

C's stand for gifts. People with the love language of gifts feel good when someone gives them a special present or surprise.

How many D's did you circle? _____

D's stand for acts of service. A person whose love language is acts of service likes it when others do nice things for them such as helping with chores, helping with school projects, or driving them places.

How many E's did you circle? _____

E's stand for quality time. People with the love language of quality time like it when others do things with them like watch a movie, go out to eat, or play a game.

Now ask your mom or dad what letter he or she guessed you would circle the most? Write the letter he or she guessed in this blank. _____

Did your mom or dad guess the same letter that you chose most often when playing the love language mystery game? Circle: Yes or No

CONGRATULATIONS! You've solved the love language mystery and figured out what your love language is! Good job!

The Love Language Mystery Game

Each clue box has two comments that parents sometimes make to their children. Read each clue box and, of the two comments, pick the one you like better and wish your mom or dad would say to you. Then circle the letter that goes with that comment. Be careful and only circle one letter in each clue box! After you've gone through all 20 clue boxes, go back and count how many A's, B's, C's, D's, and E's that you circled. Then write your scores in the blanks at the end of the game. Ask your mom or dad for help if you have any questions. And have fun unlocking the love language mystery!

1	Give me a hug!	A
	You are terrific!	B
2	I've got a special birthday present for you!	C
	I'll help you with your project.	D
3	Let's go to a movie.	E
	Give me a high five!	A
4	You are so smart!	B
	Have you made your Christmas list?	C
5	Would you help me cook dinner?	D
	I like going to fun places with you!	E
6	Give me a kiss!	A
	You are #1!	B
7	I've got a surprise for you.	C
	We can make something really cool.	D
8	Let's watch TV together!	E
	Tag, you're it!	A

9 You did a great job!   B
    You've earned a special surprise!   C

10 You can invite your friends.   D
    Let's go to your favorite restaurant.   E

11 I'm going to give you a big hug!   A
    You are an awesome kid!   B

12 I made your favorite food.   C
    I checked your homework, and it looks great!   D

13 You are fun to hang out with!   E
    I'll race you!   A

14 Wow! You did it!   B
    Check under your bed for a special present!   C

15 I cleaned up your room for you.   D
    Let's play a game together.   E

16 Would you like for me to scratch your back?   A
    You can do it! Don't give up!   B

17 What would you like for your birthday?   C
    We can pick up your friend on the way to the movie.   D

18 I always like doing stuff with you.   E
    You are so huggable!   A

19 How did you know how to do that? You are brilliant!   B
    I can't wait to give you your present!   C

20 Don't worry! I'll pick you up on time!   D
    Let's spend the day doing whatever you want to do!   E

How many A's did you circle? _____

A's stand for physical touch. People whose love language is physical touch like to receive hugs, kisses, and high fives.

How many B's did you circle? _____

B's stand for words of affirmation. People whose love language is words of affirmation like for others to use words to tell them that they are special and that they do a good job.

How many C's did you circle? _____

C's stand for gifts. People with the love language of gifts feel good when someone gives them a special present or surprise.

How many D's did you circle? _____

D's stand for acts of service. A person whose love language is acts of service likes it when others do nice things for them such as helping with chores, helping with school projects, or driving them places.

How many E's did you circle? _____

E's stand for quality time. People with the love language of quality time like it when others do things with them like watch a movie, go out to eat, or play a game.

Now ask your mom or dad what letter he or she guessed you would circle the most? Write the letter he or she guessed in this blank. _____

Did your mom or dad guess the same letter that you chose most often when playing the love language mystery game? Circle: Yes or No

CONGRATULATIONS! You've solved the love language mystery and figured out what your love language is! Good job!

The 5 Love Languages of Teenagers

The 5 Love Languages
of Teenagers

GARY CHAPMAN

NORTHFIELD PUBLISHING
CHICAGO

Editor of 2010 edition: Randall J. Payleitner
Cover and interior design: Smartt Guys design
Cover photo: Aldo Murillo/iStockphoto
Author photo: Boyce Shore & Associates

ISBN: 978-0-8024-7313-4

We hope you enjoy this book from Northfield Publishing. Our goal is to provide high-quality, thought-provoking books and products that connect truth to your real needs and challenges. For more information on other books and products written and produced from a biblical perspective, go to www.moodypublishers.com or write to:

Northfield Publishing
820 N. LaSalle Boulevard
Chicago, IL 60610

Printed in the United States of America

to
Shelley and Derek,
without whom I never would have written this book

Contents

Acknowledgments

Through the years, people have asked, "When are you going to write a book on parenting teenagers?" My stock answer has been, "When I finish with my own." Now that our children are grown and married, I think I am far enough removed from the process that I can write objectively, both from my successes and my failures. Karolyn and I were not perfect parents. Our years with teenagers were not without trauma, but through it all we sought to love, and love has made all the difference. Today we enjoy relating to our former teens as mature, caring young adults. They bring us much joy and encouragement. I write this volume with confidence that if parents are successful in loving teenagers, they will be successful parents.

Much of what you will read in this book I learned from Shelley and Derek. Without my experience of walking with them through the teen years, I would not have been able to empathize with other parents or write with passion. Thus, I have dedicated this book to them. I take this occasion to publicly acknowledge my indebtedness to each of them for letting me "practice" on them. Because of what they taught me, I hope to do even better with my grandchildren.

I am also deeply grateful to Dr. Davis McGuirt, who rendered invaluable help as my research assistant on this project. His expertise in exploring both current and historical studies on parenting teens, and his exceptional organizational skills in digesting this material made my task much easier. "Thanks, Davis. I hope that all your research will help you and Mary

Kay as you raise your own teenagers."

As always, I am deeply appreciative of those parents who have shared with me their successes and struggles in raising teens. Both in the counseling office and "on the road," hundreds of parents have been my teachers. Your pain has made me more sensitive. Your success has given me encouragement.

A special tribute is due Tricia Kube, my administrative assistant for the past twenty-six years, who computerized this material and gave technical advice. She and her husband, R. A., have raised their own teenager, Joe, who is now a successful young adult, and who with his wife, Angela, have made Tricia and R. A. grandparents. "I can see it now, Tricia. In a few more years, you will be reading this manuscript again, as your granddaughter becomes a teenager."

A final word of appreciation to Randall Payleitner, whose editorial skills made a good book better. His updating of statistics and tweaking of content has helped make this latest edition relevant to contemporary parents of teenagers.

Introduction

I think it is safe to say that the task of parenting teenagers today is more perplexing than it has been in any previous generation. Teenage violence is no longer limited to the fictional world of the movies, but it is now a regular part of our daily news intake. Reports of teens killing teens, parents, and sometimes themselves have become commonplace. Such behavior is no longer limited to the impoverished areas of our major cities, it has now come to permeate middle-class suburbia, and deep concern has been raised in the hearts of parents of all social classes.

As I lead nationwide marriage seminars, many of the parents I meet are in a panic mode. This is especially true of parents who have discovered that their own teenager has a sexually transmitted disease, is pregnant, or has had an abortion. Some parents have discovered that their teenager is not only using drugs but is a known drug pusher in their high school. Others are distraught when they get a call from the local police department saying that their teenager has been arrested and charged with possession of a firearm. The question these parents are asking does not come from a philosophical, detached, or intellectual interest in today's social problems, but rather it flows from deep pools of personal pain: *"What did we do wrong?"*

"We tried to be good parents; we've given them everything they wanted. How could they do this to themselves and to us? We just don't understand," they say. Having been a marriage and family counselor for the past forty years, I am deeply sympathetic with these parents. I also feel great empathy for the thousands of parents whose teenagers are not specifically involved in the destructive behavior noted above, but who live with the reality that if it happened to those teenagers, it could also happen to their teenagers.

There is no simple answer to the unrest in the soul of the contemporary teenager. The reality is that today's teenager lives in a world unknown to his predecessors (that's you, parents). It's a global world with mobile Internet, satellite television, and much more. Modern technology is exposing our teens to the best and worst of all human cultures. No longer does the homogeneous environment of the Deep South or the expansive Northwest exist. The ethnic boundaries of the Midwestern teenager are nearly irrelevant. Pluralism—the acceptance of many ideas and philosophies as all being on equal footing, with none being superior to the others—has replaced common beliefs and patterns as the wave of the future. This pluralism of beliefs, morals, and lifestyles will remain, and its waters are much more difficult to navigate than the commonality it is replacing. No wonder many teenagers have lost their way.

It is my observation that never before have parents of teenagers felt so helpless, but it is also my opinion that never before have the parents of teenagers been so important. Teenagers need their parents now more than ever. All research indicates that the most significant influence on the life of a teenager comes from his or her parents. It is only when parents become uninvolved that their main role of guidance is replaced by someone or something else (the gang, the peer group, or the friend at school). I am deeply committed to the premise that the teenager's best interest is served when parents assume their role as loving leaders in the home.

This book focuses on what I believe to be the most foundational building-block of parent-teen relationships—love. I believe that love is concurrently the most important word in the English language and the most misunderstood word. It is my hope that this book will remove some of the confusion and help parents focus effectively on how to meet their teenager's emotional need for love. I believe that if this need is met, it will profoundly affect the behavior of the teenager. At the root of much teenage misbehavior is a teen's empty love tank. I am not suggesting that parents do not love their teenagers; I am suggesting that thousands of teenagers do not feel that love. For most parents, it is not a matter of sincerity but rather lack of information on how to communicate love effectively on an emotional level.

A part of the problem is often that many parents do not feel loved themselves. Their marriage relationship has been sabotaged, and emotional love does not flow freely between Mom and Dad. It was this need to effectively communicate emotional love in a marriage that motivated me to write my original book, *The Five Love Languages: The Secret to Love that Lasts*. This book, which has now sold more than six million copies, has changed the emotional climate for millions of marriages. These couples have learned how to speak each other's "primary love language" and have found that in so doing they have become effective communicators of emotional love. As an author, this has been extremely gratifying for me, especially in hearing the stories of couples that were estranged from each other but have found renewed emotional love as they have read and applied the principles from *The Five Love Languages*.

I've also been greatly pleased by the response to my later book, *The Five Love Languages of Children*, which I coauthored with Ross Campbell, a psychiatrist with thirty years' experience with children and their parents. Both Dr. Campbell and I have been encouraged, not only by the number of parents who have used this book to discover the primary love language of their children, but also the number of educators who have used this book as a basis for teachers' workshops as they learn to effectively encourage and get through to their students by using the love languages concept. It is many of these parents and teachers who have encouraged me to write this present volume on the five love languages of teenagers. As one mother said, "Dr. Chapman, your book on the five love languages of children really helped us when our children were younger. But now, we have two teenagers and it's just not the same. We've tried to do what we've always done, but teenagers are different. Please write a book to help us learn to love our teenagers more effectively."

This mom was absolutely right. Teenagers are different, and loving teens effectively takes some new insights. Teens are going through a tremendous transition, and parents who will be effective in loving them must also make transitions in the manner in which they express their love. It is my hope that this book will do for the parents of teenagers what the first book did for millions of marriages and the second book did for parents of children. If this happens, I will be fully repaid for the energy I have invested in this volume.

I have written primarily to parents, but I believe grandparents and teachers—indeed all adults who care about teenagers—will become more effective in their relationships by reading and practicing the principles found in this book. Teenagers need to not only feel the love of their parents but also the love of other significant adults in their lives. If you're a grandparent, remember that teenagers desperately need the wisdom of older, more mature adults. Show them love, and they will listen to your words of wisdom.

In this book you will enter the closed doors of my counseling office and meet scores of parents and teens who have allowed me to share their journey toward understanding and love. Of course, all names have been changed to protect the privacy of these individuals. As you read the candid dialogue of these parents and teens, I believe you will discover how the principles of the five love languages can really work in the lives of your teens and family.

And Now a Preview of Where We're Going . . .

In chapter 1, parents will explore the world in which their teenager lives. We will look not only at the developmental changes that take place as your child becomes an adolescent, but also at the contemporary world in which the teenager must experience these developmental changes.

In chapter 2, we will learn the importance of parental love in the emotional, intellectual, social, and spiritual development of the teenager.

In chapters 3 through 7, we will look at the five languages that communicate love and appropriate ways to speak these love languages to teenagers.

Chapter 8 will offer suggestions on how to discover your teen's primary love language—the most effective way to fill their emotional love tank.

Chapters 9 through 12 will explore key issues in your teenager's life—including the desire for independence and the need for responsibility. We will also consider how love interfaces with the teenager's understanding and processing of anger; how love fosters independence; the relationship between freedom and responsibility; and how love sets boundaries—boundaries that are enforced with discipline and consequences.

In chapter 13, we will explore what is often love's most difficult task: loving in the midst of failure.

And the final two chapters will deal with the unique application of these love languages for single parents and parents with a blended family.

I believe that if the teenager's emotional need for love is met through the years of adolescence, he or she will navigate the waters of change and come out on the other side of the rapids as a healthy young adult. That's the shared vision of most parents. I believe this is your vision. Now let's plunge into the waters, entering the teenager's world and learning the challenge and opportunities to communicate love to our teens.

CHAPTER 1

Understanding Today's Teenagers

Teenagers didn't even exist seventy years ago . . . well, sort of. At least they weren't given their own separate generational distinction until the very recent past. The word *teenager* first came into popular use around the time of the Second World War. (See *Appendix 1* for a fascinating history of the term and a description of the first teenagers.) Though many changes have taken place since the first teenagers arrived formally on the social scene, there are plenty of similarities between the teens of the 1940s and those of the twenty-first century.

From the early days of emerging teenage culture to its contemporary counterpart, the underlying themes have been the same: *independence* and *self-identity*. Throughout the years, teenagers in our American society have been active in searching for their identity while trying to establish independence from their parents. Neither of these themes played too loudly in the "pre-teenager" era.

Before the industrial age, teens worked on their parents' farms until they were married and were given or inherited their own acreage. Identity was not something the teen sought; he was a farmer from the time he was old enough to work in the fields. The adolescent boy or girl was a child until he or she married—then the child became an adult.

The Search for Independence and Identity

Until the early 1940s, independence was unthinkable until the adolescent was married, and at that juncture real independence was only possible if the parents were benevolent enough to help out financially.

However, a lot of that changed with the coming of industrialization—one's identity became more a matter of choice. You could learn a trade and work in the factory, thus becoming a machinist, a weaver, a cobbler, etc. Independence was also more of a reality because securing a job could mean moving to a neighboring village where, with monies earned, one could establish a separate residence from parents. Thus, the larger cultural changes became the backdrop for an emerging teenage culture.

Since the 1940s, teenagers have followed this paradigm of developing independence and identity, but they have done so in a rapidly changing world. One by one electricity, telephones, automobiles, radios, airplanes, televisions, computers, and the Internet have expanded the possibilities of developing new styles for seeking independence and identity. The contemporary teenager lives in a truly global society. Interestingly, however, his focus continues to be upon himself—his identity and his independence. There will be much more about this later.

The places where the teenager expresses independence and identity have changed through the years, but the means continue to be basically the same: music, dance, fashion, fads, language, and relationships. For example, the musical genre has expanded through the years from big bands to rhythm and blues, rock and roll, folk, country, heavy metal, rap, and so forth. The teen continues to have much more variety from which to choose. But you can be certain that, no matter what, the teen's musical taste will be different from that of his parents: it's a matter of independence and identity. The same principle is true in all other areas of teenage culture.

So what characterizes the contemporary teen culture? How is your teenager similar to and different from teenagers of other generations?

Then and Now: Five Similarities

1. *Facing Physical and Mental Changes*

The basic challenges facing today's teenager are very similar to the challenges you faced when you were a teenager. First, there is the challenge of accepting and adapting to the changes that take place in the teen's body. Arms and legs, hands and feet are all growing, sometimes at a disproportionate rate, producing the reality of "teenage clumsiness" (which can be a source of extreme embarrassment for the teenager). Sexual characteristics are also developing, which may be both exciting and anxiety-producing. And what parent has not felt the pain as they watched their teenager struggle with that most devastating of enemies—acne?

These physiological changes produce numerous questions in the mind of the teenager. "I'm becoming an adult, but what will I look like? Will I be too tall or too short? Will my ears protrude too far? Will my breasts be too small? What about my nose? Are my feet too big? Am I too fat or too skinny?" The parade of questions marches on and on through the mind of the developing teenager. The manner in which a teenager answers these questions will either have a positive or negative effect upon his/her self-identity.

With this physical growth, there is also an accompanying "intellectual growth spurt." The teenager is developing a new way of thinking. As a child, she thought in terms of concrete actions and events. As a teenager, she begins to think in terms of abstract concepts like honesty, loyalty, and justice. With abstract thinking comes the expanded world of unlimited possibilities. The teen now has the ability to think about how things could be different, what a world without war would look like, or how understanding parents would treat their children. The world of expanded possibilities opens all kinds of doors for self-identity. The teenager realizes, "I could be a brain surgeon or a pilot or a garbage collector." The possibilities are unlimited and the teen may envision himself in numerous vocational settings.

2. Entering the Age of Reason

Adolescence is also the age of reason. The teenager is able to think logically and to see the logical consequences of different positions. This logic is applied not only to his own reasoning but also to the reasoning of his parents. Do you see why a teenager might often be perceived as "argumentative"? In reality, he is developing his mental skills. If the parents understand this, they can then have meaningful and interesting conversations with their teenagers. If they don't understand this, they can develop an adversarial relationship, and the teenager must go elsewhere to flex his newfound intellectual muscles. With this rapid growth in intellectual development and the gleaning of new information, the teenager often believes himself to be smarter than his parents and in some areas, he may be right.

This advanced level of thinking leads the teenager into a whole new arena of challenges in the field of social relationships. The discussion of "ideas" with his peers and listening to their point of view gives rise to new levels of intimacy on the one hand and opens the possibility of an adversarial relationship on the other. Thus, development of cliques (small, close social groups) among teens has far more to do with agreement over intellectual ideas than it does with things like dress and hair color. Teens, like adults, tend to feel more comfortable with those who agree with them.

3. Confronting Personal Morality and Values

The intellectual ability to analyze ideas and actions in a logical manner and to project outcomes of certain beliefs gives rise to another common teenage challenge: examining the belief systems with which one was raised, and determining if those beliefs are worthy of one's commitment. "Were my parents right in their views of God, morality, and values?" These are heavy issues with which every teenager must wrestle. If parents do not understand this struggle they will often become a negative influence and actually push the teenager away.

When the teenager questions the parents about basic beliefs, wise parents welcome the questions, seek to give honest answers in a nonauthoritarian manner, and encourage the teenager to continue to explore these ideas. In other words, they welcome the opportunity to dialogue with the teenager about the beliefs that they have espoused through the years. If, on the other hand, the parents reject the teenager's questions, perhaps heaping guilt upon him for even thinking that the parents' beliefs may be incorrect, the teenager is forced to go elsewhere to share his questions.

4. Thinking About Sexuality and Marriage

Another important challenge for the teenager is beginning to understand his own sexuality while learning masculine or feminine social roles. What is appropriate and not appropriate in relating to members of the opposite sex? What is appropriate and inappropriate in dealing with their own sexual thoughts and feelings? These questions, often ignored by parents, cannot be ignored by the teenager.

The teen's emerging sexuality is a part of who he is, and relating to members of the opposite sex is an ever-present reality. Most teens dream of someday being married and having a family. A few years back, when a survey asked teens to rank a number of the important issues in their future, "eighty-six percent said that having a stable family will be the most important item on the blueprint of their future lives."[1] Making the journey from early adolescence to that stable marriage and family that the teen desires occupies many hours of teenage thought.

Parents who want to help will use the normal flow of family conversation to address issues related to sexuality, dating, and marriage. They will also guide their teenager to the right printed materials and websites that speak on the teenage level while providing practical and sound information. For those teenagers who are involved in church or youth group, caring adults and youth ministers often provide sessions relating to sex, dating, and marriage. These classes provide a social context in which teens can learn and discuss this important aspect of teen development in an open and caring way.

5. Questioning the Future

There is one other common challenge faced by teenagers of the past and present. It is grappling with the question: "What will I do with my life?" This question does involve choosing a vocation, but it is far deeper than that. It is ultimately a spiritual question: "What is worth the investment of my life? Where will I find the greatest happiness? And where can I make the greatest contribution?" As philosophical as these questions may appear, they are very real to our teenagers. More immediately, teenagers must answer the questions: "Will I go to college, and if so, where? Should I join the military, and if so, which branch? Or should I get a job, and if so, which job?" Of course, teenagers understand that these choices all lead somewhere. There is something beyond the next step and somehow, the next step will influence where teenagers end up. It is an awesome challenge for these young minds.

Parents who wish to be helpful will share something of their own struggle, their own joys, and their own disappointments. As a parent, you cannot and should not offer easy answers, but you can encourage the teenager's search and perhaps introduce your son or daughter to people of various vocations who can share their journey. You can encourage your adolescent to take advantage of vocational counselors both at high school and later at the university. But ultimately, you should encourage your teenager to follow the example of Samuel. The ancient Hebrew prophet heard God's call as a teenager, and said, "Speak, for your servant is listening."[2] The men and women who have made the greatest impact upon human history have been men and women who had a sense of divine call and who lived out that call in their vocation.

Five Fundamental Differences

With all these similarities, let's not forget that a mighty gulf exists between the contemporary teenager and teenagers of the past (even the recent past); that gulf is the modern cultural setting in which teens face the challenges noted above. What are some of these cultural differences?

1. Technology
One of the most observable differences is that contemporary teenagers have grown up in a world of highly advanced technology. Their parents grew up with the telephone, radio, and network television, but for the contemporary teenager, cable, satellite television, and the Internet have cre-

ated a much more globalized world. A plethora of radio stations and TV channels provide access to every conceivable type of entertainment within our own culture. But the teenager is not limited to these programmed outlets. Every movie ever produced is available on the web or at the local video store, and every song ever sung can be purchased, downloaded, and heard on the teenager's ever-present iPod or smartphone.

The contemporary teen has also grown up with no "pre-Internet" memories; the teenager and the Internet have both come of age together. What we used to call the "information superhighway" has grown into a vast mobile web with both positive and negative influences upon the contemporary teenager. Besides giving our teens immediate access to the latest in movies, fashion, music, and sports, it allows them to have up-to-the-second updates on where their friends are, and who has broken up with whom. In fact, with the proliferation of social networking and mobile updates, the Internet has not only outpaced the traditional telephone as the teen's method of communicating with friends and discussing ideas, but it has literally taken it over. You are much more likely to see your teenager texting, browsing, and/or playing a video game (often at the same time) on their telephone, than you are to see them talking on it. These technological realities put your teenager in touch with the world and the world in touch with your teenager. The contemporary teenager is exposed to far more cultural stimuli than his parents ever could have dreamed at his age.

2. Knowledge of and Exposure to Violence

A second cultural difference is that your teenager is growing up with far more knowledge of violent human behavior. Part of this is because of the technological advances, that is, more violence is reported through the media, but a part of it simply reflects our culture's thirst—almost obsession—for violence. Our movies, songs, and novels often rush toward violent scenes. One youth survey found that 36 percent of teenagers had seen a movie or television show containing a lot of violence in the past month.

Interestingly, the survey said that eight in ten teens, 78 percent, told the Gallup organization that they "do not have a problem watching violent movies or television programs." However, 53 percent of the same teenagers agreed "violence on television and in movies sends the wrong messages to young people." The same survey indicated that 65 percent of the teens surveyed believe that "movies and television have a great deal of influence on the outlook of young people today."[3]

Exposure to violence is not limited to the media and movies. Many contemporary teenagers have experienced violence on the personal level. They have watched their fathers physically abuse their mothers or they themselves have suffered physical abuse from fathers, stepfathers, or other adults. Most teenagers acknowledge that the public school is often the scene of violent behavior.

Some teens are even perpetrators of violence—including homicide. While the overall homicide rate in the United States has remained somewhat steady for the past thirty years, the youth homicide rate has continued to increase. The period of greatest growth was from the mid-1980s to the mid-1990s, when youth homicide increased 168 percent. The FBI reported that there are about 23,000 homicides each year in the United States, and in 25 percent of these killings, the perpetrator is 21 years of age or younger.[4] Thankfully, in more recent years, statistics show a decline in youth violence—but in many communities, youth violence remains the most serious challenge.

3. The Fragmented Family

A third cultural factor that influences the contemporary teenager is the fragmented nature of the modern American family. According to a Gallup youth survey from a few years ago, four of every ten American teens (39 percent) are living with only one of their parents. In eight out of ten cases, the absent parent is the father. The same survey indicated that 20 percent of American teenagers live with a stepfather or some other adult male who lives with their mother.[5]

Sociologists have observed "in unprecedented numbers, our families are unalike: we have fathers working while mothers keep house; fathers and mothers both working away from home; single parents; second marriages bringing children together from unrelated backgrounds; childless couples; unmarried couples with and without children; and gay and lesbian parents. We are living through a period of historic change in American family life."[6] Another researcher noted, "The data is not yet in on the residual of this fragmentation, but a sociological view suggests a direct link with many of the social strains we see every day. Some of the attitudes, stress, alienation . . . and shortened attention spans are directly related to strains of adjusting to new kinds of families."[7]

In addition to the fragmentation of the nuclear family, today's teen is growing up largely without an extended family: grandparents, aunts, uncles, and other relatives. With advanced mobility, more and more nuclear families are living at greater distances from the extended family compared with earlier generations. Also, whereas neighbors once served as surrogate parents, watching out for each other's children, busy neighbors can rarely do that now. At one time the local school was more homogeneous and the community offered a safe environment for young people to relate to others. That's far less the case now. All these positive influences beyond the home are fast disappearing.

James Comer, director of the Yale Child Study Center, sees this breakdown as a factor nearly as critical as the breakdown of the nuclear family. Speaking of his own childhood, Comer said, "Between home and school, at least five close friends of my parents reported everything I did that was unacceptable. They are not there anymore for today's kids."[8] In the past, teenagers could depend upon extended families, healthy neighborhoods, churches, and community groups. The contemporary teen most often does not have these nets of support.

4. Knowledge of and Exposure to Sexuality

Today's overtly sexual atmosphere, the one in which our teens are growing up, is a vastly different situation. The baby boomers of the 1960s rebelled against the traditional sexual mores of their parents, but they remembered what the sexual rules were and sometimes even experienced guilt in breaking them. But the contemporary teenager has grown up in a world without sexual rules. Movies, media, and music all equate sex with love and depict sex as an expected part of a meaningful dating relationship. Thus, vast numbers of teenagers are sexually active.

Teenagers who are not sexually active struggle with thoughts such as *Am I missing out on something important? Is there something wrong with me?* Meanwhile, those teens who are sexually active have other negative feelings: They often feel used, abused, and empty.

The contemporary teen lives in a world where sex is not only an expected part of the dating relationship but living together before marriage is more and more common, and homosexual relationships are being promoted as alternative lifestyles. Indeed, the words bisexual and transgender are common vocabulary for the modern teen. In a very real sense, sex has become the American goddess, and the shrines and venues for worship are as varied as the mind can imagine. This is the world in which the contemporary teenager must navigate the already scary waters of his/her own emerging sexuality.

5. Neutral Moral and Religious Values

Finally, the contemporary teen is growing up in a world that is truly post-Christian. In the area of religion and morals, there is no sure word. In past generations, most Americans could have defined moral and immoral behavior. These moral judgments were primarily based on the Judeo-Christian Scriptures. This is not true for the contemporary teenager. For the first time in American history, an entire generation is growing up without certain moral values. Values are often neutral; the teen is told that what feels good—is good. Right and wrong are relative.

The teenage years have always been the time to explore religious beliefs. Teens are asking questions about the religious beliefs—or disbeliefs—of their parents. As in other areas of life, they are seeking to clarify their own identity. The difference in the contemporary world is that because of the global nature of today's world, our teens are exposed to numerous religious beliefs—both by means of modern technology and through friends who are involved in other religious groups.

Religion is important to the contemporary teen. A recent survey indicated that about half of teenagers (51 percent) see religious faith as important in shaping their daily lives.[9] More than three quarters of teenagers (82 percent) identify themselves with an organized religious group. A third of the teenagers (36 percent) say that they feel "very" or "extremely" close to God and more than half have made a personal commitment to live their life for God (55 percent).[10] Four in ten teenagers (40 percent) reported that they attend services for religious worship at least once per week.[11] Today's teenagers are more interested in the experiential, relational nature of religious groups than abstract religious belief. If the group is accepting, caring, and supportive, they are drawn to the spiritual group even though they may disagree with many of the group's religious beliefs.

Parents *Can* Guide

This is the world into which your teenager has come of age. The good news is that contemporary teenagers are looking to parents for guidance. In a recent survey, teens reported that parents have more influence than peers do in the following areas: whether to attend college, whether to attend religious services, whether to do homework, and whether to drink. Parents also had an impact on the teens' job or career plans. Friends had more influence on their decisions in terms of immediate issues such as whether or not to cut classes, who to date, hairstyles, and what kind of clothes they wore.[12]

The survey found that when teenagers were asked to report "Who has the greatest influence on your decisions? Parents or friends?" the decisions most heavily weighted toward parental influence were those that appear to have a major effect on what kind of person the teen will be. Yes, your teenager will be influenced by friends on some issues, but parents are still the major influence on their teenager's thoughts and behavior. The remaining chapters of this book are designed to help you learn to effectively meet your teenager's need for love and thus lay the foundation for influencing your teen more effectively in all other areas of life.

CHAPTER 2

The Key: Love from
Parents

Becky, a mother of two, had all the symptoms of parental trauma. "Dr. Chapman, I'm frightened to death," she said. "My son is twelve; my daughter is eleven. I've been reading books about teenagers and I'm scared. It seems like all teenagers are having sex, using drugs, and carrying guns to school. Is it really that bad?" Becky asked the question during a marriage seminar in Moline, Illinois. Then she added, "I've been thinking that maybe I should homeschool my children through high school but that also scares me. I don't know if I am ready for my children to become teenagers."

Over the past five years, I have met a lot of parents like Becky. Many parents are reading more books about parenting teenagers. They are hearing more about teenage violence on television. They are reading their local newspaper, and frankly, they are terrified. If you happen to be one of these scared parents, or if you are asking yourself, "Should I be scared?" I hope this chapter will allay some of your fears. Anxiety is not a good mental attitude with which to parent teenagers. I hope that this chapter will relieve some of your anxiety and give you more confidence in the positive role you can play in the life of your teenager.

The Good News about Families and Schools

Let me begin by reporting that not all of the facts are negative. While it is true that a recent Gallup Youth Survey found that only 57 percent of American teenagers live with both of their parents, it is also true that 87 percent of teens have contact with their fathers even when they are not living together all the time.[1] A solid majority of teens (70 percent) say that they feel "extremely" or "very" close to their fathers.[2] Another recent survey indicated that the majority of teens ages thirteen to seventeen say that they usually have good feelings in school. A sizeable majority of teenagers report that they feel happy (85 percent) and supported at school (82 percent). Nearly as many say that they feel appreciated (78 percent), interested (77 percent), encouraged (76 percent), and challenged (72 percent).[3] Two statistics that should warm the hearts of all education-minded parents are that 97 percent of teenagers will graduate from high school, and 83 percent of them consider a college education to be "very important" today.[4]

After reviewing these findings, George Gallup Jr. characterized contemporary youth as being motivated by idealism, optimism, spontaneity, and exuberance. "Young people tell us that they are enthusiastic about helping others, willing to work for world peace and a healthy world, and they feel positive about their schools and even more positive about their teachers." Concerning teens' attitudes toward their future, Gallup concluded: "A large majority of American youth report that they are happy and excited about the future, feel very close to their families, are likely to marry, want to have children, are satisfied with their personal lives, and desire to reach the top of their chosen careers."[5]

Lawrence Steinberg, a senior research associate at the Center for Research in Human Development and Education, is a nationally recognized expert on adolescence. He has noted, "Adolescence is not an inherently difficult period. Psychological problems, problem behavior, and family conflict are no more common in adolescence than at any other stage of the life cycle. To be sure, some adolescents are troubled and some get into trouble. But the great majority (almost 9 out of 10) do not." Steinberg, who is also professor of psychology at Temple University, added: "The problems we have come to see as a 'normal' part of adolescent development—drugs, delinquency, irresponsible sex, opposition to any and all authority—are not normal at all. They are both preventable and treatable. The bottom line is that good kids don't suddenly go bad in adolescence."[6]

The reality is that most of what we read in the newspaper and hear via the media deals with the 10 percent of troubled teenagers—most of whom were also troubled children. You and your teenager *can* have a positive relationship. That's what your teenager wants, and I assume that is what you want. In this chapter, we're going to look at what I believe to be the most important aspect of that relationship, namely, meeting your teen's need for emotional love. If this need is met, then the teenager will effectively navigate the cultural waters that we talked about in chapter 1.

When teens know their parents love them, they will have confidence to face the negative influences in our culture that would keep them from becoming mature, productive adults. Without the love of parents, the teenager is far more likely to succumb to the evil influences of drugs, perverted sex, and violence. In my opinion, nothing is more important than the parent learning how to effectively meet the teen's emotional need for love.

What do I mean by "emotional love"? Deep within the soul of the teenager is the desire to feel connected, accepted, and nurtured by parents. When this happens, the teenager feels loved. When the teen does not feel connected, accepted, and nurtured, his inner emotional tank is empty—and that emptiness will greatly affect the behavior of the teen. Let me describe each of these in more depth.

The Teen's Desire for Connection

The Presence of Parents

Much has been written about the importance of the young child "bonding" to the parents. Most child psychologists agree that if this emotional bonding does not take place, the child's emotional development will be plagued with feelings of insecurity. The opposite of connection is abandonment. If the young child's parents are not available because of death, divorce, or desertion—obviously emotional bonding cannot take place.

The prerequisite for bonding is the presence of the parents. In short: *Bonding requires time together.*

In the teenage years, the same principles are true. Parents who are around little because of divorce, work schedules, etc., jeopardize the teenager's sense of feeling connected to parents. It is a simple reality that for a teen to feel connected, and thus loved by the parents, they must spend time together. The teen who feels abandoned will wrestle with the question, "What's wrong with me that my parents don't care about me?" If parents want their teenager to feel loved they must make time to be with them.

The Connecting Power of Communication

Obviously, physical proximity between parents and teens does not *necessarily* result in connection. Emotional connectedness requires communication. You may be a stay-at-home mother, or a father at home on a two-week vacation, and still be disconnected if there is little communication.

I was encouraged a few years back, while examining a research project, to find that 71 percent of teens surveyed indicated they eat at least one meal a day with family. But my encouragement was short-lived when I discovered that fully half of all teens surveyed watched television the last time they had dinner with their parents. In addition, one in four said they listened to the radio while 15 percent read a book, magazine, or newspaper while dining.[7] It appears that most parents are not using mealtimes as a means for building connection with teenagers.

In my opinion, the meal table is one of the best places to build emotional connectedness with teenagers. What teenager doesn't love to eat? A little talking with parents is a small price to pay for a good meal. If your family does not fall into the 71 percent who has at least one meal together every day, let me encourage you to work toward this ideal. And for those who are eating, but not talking, let me suggest a new guideline for family mealtimes. Announce to the teenagers and younger children that you are starting a new tradition at mealtimes: "First, we talk to God (yes, teach your children to be grateful for their food), then we talk to each other; after that, if we wish, we can revert to TV, newspapers, and radio."

Begin by having someone volunteer to thank God for the food and the person or persons who prepared it. Then each family member shares with the others three things that happened in their life that day and how they feel about them. *Rule #1:* When one family member is talking, the others are listening sympathetically. *Rule #2:* The others may ask questions to clarify what they are hearing, but they don't give advice unless the person who is sharing solicits it.

This one new tradition may be enough to help you establish and maintain a sense of connectedness with your teenager.

The Teen's Desire for Acceptance

The Power of Acceptance...and Rejection

A second element of emotional love is feeling accepted by parents. One fourteen-year-old boy said, "The main thing I like about my parents is that they accept me for who I am. They don't try to make me like my older sister." This teenager feels loved, and this love comes from being accepted by his parents.

"My parents like me. I'm OK." These are the messages played in the mind of the teenager who feels accepted. The opposite of acceptance is rejection. Its messages are "They don't like me. I'm not good enough for them. They wish I were different." The child who feels rejected obviously does not feel loved.

Anthropologist Ronald Rohner has studied rejection in more than a hundred cultures around the world. His findings are clear that although cultures differ in how they express rejection, rejected children everywhere are at heightened risk for numerous psychological problems. These problems range from low self-esteem to deficient moral development, and from difficulty in handling aggression to confused sexual identity. Rohner believes that the effects of rejection are so strong that he calls rejection a "psychological malignancy that spreads throughout a child's emotional system, wreaking havoc."[8]

James Garbarino, professor of human development at Cornell University, has spent many years studying the inner life of violent teenagers. He concluded that the feeling of rejection is a major element in the psychological makeup of the violent teenager. Often this rejection grows out of being compared with another sibling.[9]

Accepting the Teen ... Correcting the Behavior

Many parents think showing total acceptance is wrong. Bob, a concerned parent of two teenagers, spoke with great candor when he said to me, "Dr. Chapman, I don't understand how you can accept a teenager when his behavior is despicable. I don't want my teens to feel rejected, but frankly I don't like their behavior and I don't like them when they engage in that behavior. Maybe I am rejecting them, but in my heart that is not what I feel. I feel love and concern. I don't want them to destroy their lives."

Bob was speaking for thousands of parents who have not yet learned how to communicate acceptance while at the same time correcting the misbehavior of their teen. We will explore this further as we get into the five love languages of teenagers, and also in chapter 12 where we deal with discipline.

For the moment, let me seek to clarify our goal by using a theological illustration. Paul, a first-century apostle of the Christian faith, said of God, "He made us accepted in the Beloved."[10] He was alluding to the central Christian doctrine that the God who is holy has accepted us who are unholy because He sees us as being a part of Himself because we have accepted His Son—the Beloved. Since we have accepted His Son—God has accepted us. Paul's idea is that though God is not always pleased with our behavior, God is always pleased with us because we are His children. As parents, this is what we are trying to do. We want to communicate with our children that we are happy to be their parents, no matter what, without respect to their behavior patterns. This is what we typically refer to as *unconditional love*.

The idea of unconditional love is "I love you, I care about you. I am committed to you because you are my child. I don't always like what you do, but I always love you and care about your well-being. You are my son or daughter and I will never reject you. I will always be here doing what I believe is best for you. I will love you no matter what."

Ken Canfield, president of the National Center for Fathering, said, "Never forget the great question of adolescence: 'Who am I?' Your teenager will have to answer that question for himself. What he wants to hear from you is 'Whoever you end up being, I still love you.'" Then Canfield noted a great fear every teen has: "Never forget the great fear of adolescence—'Am I normal?' The likely answer to that question is 'Yes.' But what the teenager wants to hear from his dad is 'Even if you were abnormal, I'd still love you.'"[11]

Canfield was talking about unconditional acceptance and unconditional love. I will give other suggestions later, but let me share a simple approach that may greatly affect the way your teenager hears your verbal messages of guidance or correction. Before you give your profound statement of what you wish your teenager would do, always preface it with these words (or some other words like these that are better suited to your personality), "I love you very much. I will love you even if you don't follow my advice. But, because I love you, I must give you my advice." Then share your words of wisdom. Your teenager needs to hear that you accept him even when you don't approve of his behavior.

The Teen's Desire to Be Nurtured

The third aspect of loving your teenager is nurturing him or her. Nurture has to do with feeding the inner spirit of your teen. We nurture plants by enhancing the soil in which they are planted. We nurture teenagers by enhancing the climate in which they grow. Teenagers who grow up in a warm, caring, encouraging, and positive emotional climate are more likely to produce beautiful flowers and luscious fruit as they reach maturity.

Never Abuse

The opposite of nurture is abuse. An abusive atmosphere is like spraying poison on the soul of a teenager. Teenagers who receive hostile, cutting, harsh, or demeaning words from their parents will eventually make it to adulthood, but the scars of verbal abuse will follow them for a lifetime. Parents who indulge in physical abuse by slapping, shoving, pushing, beating, or shaking their teenager may well harm the young person's physical development, and they will at least harm the teen's emotional development, which will make their lives as adults far more difficult.

Few things are more detrimental to the teenager's developing psyche than abuse. Teenagers draw conclusions based on what they observe and what they experience at the hands of their parents. Research indicates that most teenagers who turn violent have themselves been traumatized by abuse and are starved for love. James Garbarino describes violent boys in this manner: "They take drugs. They engage in violence. They steal. They gorge themselves on sex. They join gangs and cults and when no one is watching or listening to them, they suck their thumbs and cry themselves to sleep."[12] Behind many violent teenagers is an abusive parent. *Love does not abuse; love nurtures.*

Be a Nurturing Parent

To nurture your teenager first requires that you nurture yourself. If you are going to create a supportive and positive climate in which your teenager can accomplish the developmental tasks of adolescence, you will first have to grow in the areas of your own emotional weaknesses. The fact is that many parents of teenagers did not grow up in nurturing families; consequently, they have developed negative patterns of responding to teenagers, which come across as abusive. If you see this in yourself, the first step is to deal with your own pain and learn to process your own anger.

This may involve reading books on resolving anger,[13] joining support groups through your local church or community center, or going for personal counseling. It is never too late to deal with the dark side of your own history. Your teenagers deserve your best, and your best is not possible until you have dealt with your past.

Nurturing parents have a positive attitude. I do not mean that they deny the realities of life, but they choose to see the hand of God behind the scenes of human events. They look for the sun behind the clouds and they communicate this spirit to their teenagers. Nurturing parents are encouraging, looking for the positive things their teenagers do and say, and commending them.

Nurturing parents are caring parents—constantly looking for ways to enhance the lives of their teenagers. In the chapters that follow, we will look at the five love languages and help you to discover the primary love language of your teenager. Speaking this language is the most powerful way to nurture your child's inner spirit and to enhance his life.

Understand the Impact of an Empty Tank

One of the reasons emotional love is so important for your teenager is because it affects every other aspect of his life. When the teenager's love tank is empty he thinks "no one really cares about me." Motivation for learning is dissipated. "Why should I study at school? No one cares what happens to me anyway." High school guidance counselors hear statements like these every day.

An empty love tank also affects the teen's ability to empathize with others. When the teen does not feel loved, he will have greater difficulty appreciating how his negative actions might affect someone else's feelings. Research indicates that most violent juvenile delinquents display very little empathy.[14] Empathy is one of the foundations for what Daniel Goleman calls "emotional intelligence." He defines emotional intelligence as the ability to read emotions in others, to communicate effectively in the nonverbal realm, to handle the ups and downs of daily life, and to have appropriate expectations for relationships.[15] Thus, lack of emotional intelligence affects the teen's ability to relate positively to others.

Lack of empathy, in turn, affects the teenager's development of the conscience and moral judgments. It is during the teenage years that the standard for one's conscience is being internalized. In the childhood years, standards are given by parents. Now the teen is wrestling with her own concept of what is moral and immoral. If, because of a lack of emotional love, she is not able to empathize with others, there will be little sense that it is wrong to hurt others. In the realm of spirituality, if the child's emotional need for love has not been met, then the theological idea of a loving God will have little meaning to the teenager. This is one reason why teenagers who are starved for emotional love will often turn away from the parent's religious beliefs and practices.

In summary, the teenager's intellectual, emotional, social, moral, and spiritual developments are greatly enhanced if the teenager has significant amounts of emotional love. Conversely, the teen is greatly impaired in all of these areas if the emotional need for love is not met.

Your Nearest Neighbor

Sociologists, psychologists, and religious leaders all agree that the most fundamental need of the teenager is to feel emotional love from the significant adults in his life. David Popenoe, professor of sociology at Rutgers University and cochair of the Council on Families in America, wrote, "Children develop best when they are provided the opportunity to have warm, intimate, continuous, and enduring relationships with both their fathers and their mothers." Psychologists Henry Cloud and John Townsend add, "There is no greater ingredient of growth for your youngster than love." And in *Lost Boys*, James Garbarino asked: "What tools does a boy have to make sense of his life if he has no sense of being loved and appreciated?"[16]

When the religious leaders of that day asked Jesus of Nazareth, "Which is the greatest commandment in the law?" the founder of the Christian faith replied, "'Love the Lord your God with all your heart and with all your soul and with all your mind.' This is the first and greatest commandment. And the second is like it: 'Love your neighbor as yourself.' All the Law and the Prophets hang on these two commandments."[17] Thus, Jesus summarized all the teachings of the Old Testament books of law and the words of the Jewish prophets in these two commandments. I would like to suggest that the teenager living in your house is your nearest neighbor.

"My Whole Life I Felt Alone"

If parents and other significant adults do not meet a teen's need for love, he or she will go looking for love in all the wrong places. After sixteen-year-old Luke Woodham killed his mother and then opened fire at his high school in Pearl, Mississippi, killing three and wounding seven a little more than a decade ago, he later told an ABC News correspondent that he felt so isolated and rejected in his community that he was easily drawn into a group of boys who were self-proclaimed Satanists. He said, "My whole life I felt outcasted, alone. Finally, I found some people who wanted to be my friends."

Garbarino adds, "Emotionally needy boys who are rejected by teachers and parents are prime targets for anti-social older youth and adults. These negative role models recruit vulnerable boys, and they exchange self-affirmation for loyalty to the anti-social cause. Many violent and troubled boys have stories of how they were befriended by older boys who accepted them in return for their involvement in criminal enterprises."[18]

After years of trying to understand violent and delinquent teenagers, Garbarino concluded, "Nothing seems to threaten the human spirit more than rejection, brutalization, and lack of love."[19]

Nothing is more important in parenting teenagers than learning how to effectively meet the teen's need for emotional love. What you are about to read in the next five chapters will introduce you to the five basic love languages—the five most effective ways to fill up the emotional love tank of your teenager. Then I will address the matter of discovering your teen's primary love language—the one language that is most effective in meeting his/her emotional need for love. As I have shared this material in parenting lectures across the country, many parents have found that the application of these truths has radically changed the behavior of their teens and has given the parents feelings of deep satisfaction that whatever else they are doing as parents, they are being effective in meeting their teens' most important emotional need. That's my desire for you as well.

CHAPTER 3

LOVE LANGUAGE #1:

Words of
Affirmation

Fifteen-year-old Brad was in my office at his parents' request. His feet fit loosely into his dark-colored sandals. His multipocketed pants hung precariously on his thin frame. His T-shirt read: "Freedom is having all the jelly beans you want." I was not at all sure that he wanted to be in my office, but I was pleasantly surprised that Brad listened carefully to my inquiries and freely shared his thoughts and feelings. (I've had other teenagers in my office whose answer to every question was: "It's okay.")

Brad's parents had complained that he had become extremely rebellious toward them, he had lashed out in anger several times, and had even threatened to leave home. It was this threat that motivated them to insist that he talk with me. The thought of Brad leaving home had traumatized them, and to use his father's words, "He's the kind of kid who would do it. He's never met a stranger. He would find someone to take him in. But the thought terrifies us."

"We've tried to talk to Brad," his mother continued, "but it seems we always get into an argument and one of us ends up losing control and saying things we don't mean. We later apologize and try to go on, but Brad seems so unreasonable every time we don't agree with him."

After a brief introduction, I assured Brad that my role was not to tell him what to do but that I did hope I might help him understand his parents a little better and perhaps help them understand him as well. I indicated that his parents "seemed concerned"—which is why they had asked the two of us to get together. He nodded in an affirming manner. Wanting to connect with Brad, I decided to begin with the present rather than probing the past. So I said, "Your parents tell me that you are thinking of leaving home. I was wondering if you could tell me a little bit about that."

"I'm not going to leave home," Brad said, shaking his head from left to right. "I said that one night when I was really mad and they weren't listening to me. Sometimes I do think about leaving home, but I don't think I'd ever do it."

"What do you think about when you think about leaving home?" I inquired. "What do you envision your life would be like if you weren't living with your parents?"

"I'd be free to do what I want to do," Brad said. "I wouldn't have to argue with them about every little thing. That's what I don't like about living at home, all the arguments."

I was beginning to sense that negative words were very painful to Brad, which led me to guess that his primary love language was *words of affirmation*. Typically when teenagers are deeply hurt by negative words, it is an indication that affirming words speak most deeply to the teen's emotional need for love.

"Do you feel that your parents love you?" I asked. Brad paused a moment and then said, "I know they love me but sometimes I don't feel loved, especially in the last few years."

"When you were little, how did your parents show their love to you?" I asked.

"They told me how great I was," he said with a chuckle. "Now I think they have changed their minds."

"Do you remember some of the positive things they told you?"

"I remember one time when I was playing youth football, my dad told me that I was the best player he had ever seen. He said that I could play pro football someday if I wanted to."

"Do you play football in high school?" I asked. Nodding his head, Brad then admitted he was playing but dismissed his chances to go further in the sport. "I'm OK but I'm not that good." When I asked him to recall positive things his mother said to him as a child, Brad replied, "Mom always said, 'I love you, I love you, I love you.' She always said it three times really fast. Sometimes I thought she wasn't sincere but mostly I knew she was."

"Does she still say those words to you?" I asked.

"Not lately," he said. "All she does now is criticize me."

"What does she say when she criticizes you?" I asked.

"Well, last night she told me that I was irresponsible and that if I didn't change, I would never make it in college. She tells me I'm sloppy and disrespectful."

"Are you?" I inquired.

"I guess I'm sloppy," he said slowly, "but I wouldn't be disrespectful if they weren't on my back all the time."

"What else do your parents criticize you about?" I asked.

"Everything. They say I spend too much time texting, too much time on the computer, and too much time with my friends. I don't come home when they think I should. I don't call them when I'm late. I don't spend enough time on homework. They say I don't take school seriously. Like I said, everything."

"So with all of these criticisms, how do you feel toward your parents?"

"Some days I'd just like to get away from them," Brad said. "I just get tired of the constant hassle. Why can't they let me be who I am? I don't think I'm all that bad. I wish they would just back off."

"What would you do if they backed off?" I inquired.

"I don't know," Brad said. "Just be a normal teenager, I guess. I'm not going to do something stupid like drugs or get some girl pregnant or blow some kids away with a shotgun. I think my parents watch too much violence on television. They watch the crazies and think all teenagers are like that. I'm not crazy. Why can't they trust me?"

Running on Empty

After three more sessions with Brad, I concluded that he was a pretty normal teenager. He was just living with an empty love tank, not because his parents did not love him, but because his parents had stopped speaking his primary love language—*words of affirmation*. In his childhood, they had often affirmed him verbally. Their words of affirmation were vivid memories, but now, in his mind, all of that had changed. What he heard were negative words and what he felt was rejection. His love tank had been full as a child but as a teenager, he was running on empty.

After thoroughly hearing Brad's story, I shared my assessment with him. I explained to him that all of us have an emotional love tank and when that love tank is full—when we really feel loved by the important people in our lives—the world looks bright and we can discuss our differences in a positive way. But when the love tank is empty and we feel rejected rather than loved, it becomes extremely difficult to discuss differences without stooping to argument and slander. I also told Brad that his parents had their own emotional love tank and that my guess was that they were also running on empty. In the early years, he had probably spoken their love languages and they felt his love, but now their emotional tanks were empty too.

"When parents have empty love tanks," I said, "they often exhibit unhealthy behavioral patterns toward their teenagers." I assured Brad that I believed all of this could be changed and that his relationship with his parents could return to being positive and supportive. I suggested that the next three years of his life could be the best three years yet, and that when he was ready to leave for college he might even "miss" his parents. Brad laughed and said, "I'd like that!"

I told Brad that I would seek to help his parents understand my assessment of the situation, and I challenged him to express his love for his parents in spite of negative feelings he had toward them at the moment. I explained that his growing independence from his parents was best fostered in a climate of love rather than hostility. "Love is a choice," I said, "and I think that if you will choose to love your parents and express it in their primary love languages, you can be a part of the solution. Remember love, not hate, equals peace."

Brad nodded, smiled, and said, "Yeah, man! That makes sense." (It was one of those affirming moments when I realized that I was still able to communicate with a teenager.)

"In about six weeks, after I've spent some time with your parents, I want us to get together again and see how things are going," I said to Brad.

"OK," he replied, as he opened the door and left my office with his pant legs dragging on the floor.

What I sought to communicate to Brad's parents in the three sessions we had together is what I'd like to communicate to you in the remainder of this chapter. I was deeply sympathetic with Brad's parents—as I am with thousands of parents of teenagers who face similar struggles. Brad's parents, like most of you who are reading this book, were conscientious parents. They had read books on parenting, attended parenting seminars, and shared their parenting experiences with their peers. In fact, they had been excellent parents the first twelve years of Brad's life. But they were caught off guard when the teenage years rolled around. When childhood flowed into the white waters of adolescence, their parenting canoe was dashed against the rocks and they found themselves struggling for survival.

They Aren't Kids Anymore . . .

Many parents believe that when their children become teenagers, they can continue to parent in the same manner that has served them well in the child's preschool and elementary school years. But this is a serious mistake because the teenager is not a child. He/she is in transition toward adulthood. The melody playing in the mind of a teenager is independence and self-identity. This melody must be harmonized with all the physiological, emotional, intellectual, spiritual, and social changes that are taking place inside the teenager (which we discussed in chapter 1). When parents do not account for this new song that is being played in the teenager's mind, they set the stage for some major parent/teenager conflict.

Parents who treat the teenager in the same manner in which they treated the child will not experience the same results they received earlier. When the teenager does not respond as the child responded, the parents are now pushed to try something different. Without proper training, parents almost always revert to efforts at coercion, which often lead to arguments, loss of temper, and perhaps, verbal abuse. Such behavior is emotionally devastating to the teenager whose primary love language is words of affirmation. The parents' efforts to verbally argue the teenager into submission are in reality pushing the teenager toward rebellion.

Without realizing it, the parents are removing the teenager's emotional support system and replacing it with verbal warfare. Consider the change as your teen sees it: As a child, he felt the warm loving security of his parents but as a teenager, verbal grenades explode in his soul and his love tank is ruptured. As parents, our intentions may still be good, but the results are definitely bad. Unless we parents change course, we will most certainly end up with a rebellious teenager and often an estranged young adult.

But this need not happen. Thousands of parents have done what Brad's parents did—realized they needed a midcourse correction and took action. The first step for Brad's parents was to recognize what had happened. I explained to them that, in my opinion, Brad's primary love language was words of affirmation. In his childhood years Brad's love tank had been filled by their many affirming words. However, in the turbulence of the teenage years, they had replaced affirming words with condemning words, accepting words with words of rejection, and in so doing they had not only emptied Brad's love tank, they instead filled it with resentment.

The lights came on, and Brad's father said, "Now I understand what has happened. It seems so clear. But how do we turn it around?" I was glad he asked, because the parent who wants to learn, can!

What Brad's Parents Did

I suggested that the first step was a cease-fire: stop the condemning, negative bombshells. Second, they should call for a family conference and openly share with Brad their deep regret that even though they were sincere parents and had nothing but his best interests in mind, they realized they had gone about parenting him in the wrong way. They could further say that they had a lot to learn about parenting during the teenage years, that they sincerely wanted to learn and, more than anything, they wanted him to know that they loved him no matter what he did, and that they would always love him.

"I encourage you to tell Brad that you care first and foremost about his well-being and that you intend to eliminate critical, condemning, demeaning, and harsh words from your vocabulary.

"Be honest with Brad. Tell him that you won't be perfect in doing this over the next few months, but when you fail, you will sincerely apologize because that is not your intention. You may want to say to him, 'We still recognize that we're your parents and we want to help you through these teenage years to mature adulthood. We plan to be there for you when you need advice, and we intend to continue to set guidelines that we believe are for your benefit.'"

Then I told Brad's parents to be careful not to argue about these guidelines. "Let him know you want to learn to work with him in open communication and negotiation. Tell him, 'Brad, we want to treat you as the emerging young man you are; your ideas and feelings are important. We know this will take time and all of us will stumble occasionally in the process, but we're committed to being the parents you deserve.'"

His parents did just that. Later they told me that this family conference was the turning point in their relationship with Brad. They felt that Brad genuinely forgave them for their failures—although he was not overly optimistic about their abilities to change. They understood this and acknowledged that it would be difficult, but they were committed to growth in their parenting abilities.

I know that some of you are thinking, "But if we are not going to verbally condemn our teenager's wrong behavior, then how are we going to discipline them?" As one mother said to me, "Dr. Chapman, surely you are not suggesting that we simply let teenagers do whatever they want to do?" I responded with a resounding: "Certainly not."

Teenagers need boundaries. Parents who love them will see that they live within the boundaries. But there is a better way to motivate teenagers to do so than by yelling cruel, bitter, condemning words when they misbehave. We will discuss this more thoroughly in chapter 12 when we discuss the relationship between love and responsibility. What we are talking about in this chapter is how to keep the love tank of the teenager full.

Harsh, argumentative words are obviously not the way to do it. Negative, condemning words are harmful to any teenager, but they are devastating to the teenager whose primary love language is words of affirmation.

Most teenagers are struggling with self-identity. They are comparing themselves with their peers physically, intellectually, and socially. Many are concluding that they simply do not "measure up." Many feel insecure, have little self-esteem, and blame themselves. If there is a stage of life where humans need more affirming words, it would certainly be during the teenage years. Yet this is the very stage at which parents often turn to negative words in their efforts to get the teenager to do what parents believe is best. I cannot overemphasize the need for parents to give teenagers affirming words. Even if your teen's primary love language is not words of affirmation, she will appreciate your affirming statements. The ancient Hebrew proverb was right. "Death and life are in the power of the tongue."[1]

How to Affirm Your Teenager

How then do we speak words of life to our teenagers? Let me suggest some ways to water the soul of your teenager with words that affirm.

Words of Praise

First, there are words of praise. Praise has to do with recognizing your teenager's accomplishments and commending her. All teenagers do some things right. Look for these noble actions and reward them with verbal praise. Two factors are important in giving words of praise to teenagers. *First and foremost is sincerity*. Teenagers are looking for adults with integrity and authenticity. You may have gotten away with flattery when she was three, but it will not work when she is thirteen. To tell a teenager, "You did a good job cleaning your room," when in fact she did not, is a slap in the face to your daughter's intelligence. She is smarter than that. Don't play those games.

This brings me to the second important factor in praising teenagers: Praise specifics. Sweeping general statements of praise such as "You did a good job cleaning your room" are seldom ever true. The truth is far more often found in the specifics. "You did a good job of getting the coffee stain out of the carpet." "Thanks for putting the dirty clothes in the hamper; it was a real help when I did the laundry this morning." "Thanks for raking the leaves out of the side yard Saturday. It really looks nice." These are the kinds of specific praises that ring true with the teenager. Train yourself to look for specifics.

Bob's son Barry plays on the high school baseball team. Recently he had a particularly bad day. In batting and in fielding, it seemed like everything went wrong. But there was one play where Barry was perfect. He was at his third base position with a runner on first and one out. When the batter sent a sizzling ground ball to third base, Barry scooped it up, made a perfect throw to the second baseman, who in turn made a perfect throw to first base, and the inning was over. It was the only play in the whole game where Barry performed well, and his team lost the game.

Barry rode home on the bus with the team. His dad and younger brother drove home in the car, but when Barry walked in the house several hours later, his younger brother met him at the door and said, "Dad said, 'It's the greatest play I've ever seen.'"

"What are you talking about?" Barry asked.

"Your double play," his younger brother replied.

Barry's dad heard the conversation, turned the TV off, and walked into the room. "That's right," he said. "I'll remember that play the rest of my life. I know you guys lost. I know you had a rough evening, but I'm telling you— that was the most spectacular play I've ever seen! That ball was hot, but you played it like a pro. It was exciting. I'll never forget it."

Barry walked into the kitchen for a drink of water. His dad walked back to the family room, but in the kitchen Barry was drinking more than water. His love tank was filling up as he thought about the words of his father. Barry's father had mastered the art of looking for specifics and praising teenagers. Think of how different that encounter would have been had Barry's father done the easier task of criticizing Barry's abilities.

It takes effort, especially for parents who tend to be negative themselves, but any parent can learn to locate specific actions worthy of praise and use them as occasions for words of affirmation.

However, there is a third aspect of giving praise: When you can't praise results, praise efforts. For instance, your thirteen-year-old has mowed the grass. It's not as perfect as if you had mowed it, and in fact it's quite atrocious. You have a little more experience than he. But most of the grass is cut, and your teenager invested two hours of life laying the grass low. Get hold of yourself—don't point out the grass that was missed. You can do that next week before he starts mowing again. Now is the time to say, "Nathan, you're really coming along in your grass-mowing skills. I really appreciate your hard effort. I want you to know it is a real help to me and I appreciate it." Nathan walks away and somehow mowing the grass seems worthwhile. His love tank is filling up as he senses he is important to his father and his work was noticed.

Someone asks, "But won't he always be a mediocre grass mower if I don't point out the grass he missed?" My response is, "It is a matter of timing." After two hours of lawn mowing, no one is encouraged to hear that his job was not done perfectly. To do so is almost surely to make the teenager hate mowing grass. When his efforts are rewarded with praise, he feels appreciated and motivated to mow the grass again. He is even open to instruction as he begins next week on how he can do an even better job.

(Side note to the parents who are reading this: I would like to suggest that the same principle is true in your marriage relationship. Reward each other for effort rendered rather than pointing out the imperfections of the completed task. Try it. It works. I promise. For example, the husband spends three hours washing the car. His wife comes outside, points out a spot he missed. Prediction: that's the cleanest car she'll see for awhile. Or the wife fixes a meal for her husband. He sits down at the table and says, "Did you forget the slaw?" Prediction: I hope he likes fast-food restaurants. He's going to spend a lot of time there the next three months. Case closed. Reward for effort, not perfection.)

Teenagers need to hear words of praise from parents. There are always teenage actions worthy of praise. Some parents are so focused on the teenager's failure to reach their expectations that they cannot see the teenager's positive actions. That's narrow tunnel vision. Focusing on the negative has been the downfall of many parents and has resulted in an empty love tank for many teenagers. No matter what is going on in the life of your teenager that brings you pain, disappointment, or anger, continue to look for those actions worthy of praise, and give your teenager affirming words.

Words of Affection

Whereas praise focuses on the positive behavior of a teenager, affection focuses on the teenager themselves. It is verbally expressing positive regard for the teenager as a person.

The most common statement of verbal affection is the simple "I love you." These three words are always appropriate, though there may be a brief stage in which the teenager does not wish to hear you say these words in the presence of his peers. If your teenager makes this request, by all means honor it. When spoken in private, however, these three words are always appropriate at every stage of teenage development.

In fact, teenagers who do not hear the words "I love you" from parents will often experience deep emotional pain in adulthood. During the past few years I've been privileged to speak at a number of marriage enrichment conferences for professional athletes. One of my saddest experiences has been to look into the eyes of a pro athlete—I'm talking about a really serious, tough athlete—and to see the tears form in his eyes as he said to me, "Dr. Chapman, I've never heard my father say the words 'I love you.'" I wanted to take him in my arms and say, "Here, let me be your father. I love you." I can say the words and I can hug him (though with the football players, I cannot get my arms around them), but my hug and my verbal affirmation can never take the place of the words of a father. There is a void in the soul of the man or woman who has never heard the words "I love you" from a father and mother.

Usually mothers speak these words freely to their teenage sons and daughters. Fathers are often reluctant to do so. Sometimes fathers have never heard the words themselves and thus they have difficulty speaking what they have never heard. It doesn't come naturally for them. If you happen to be one of these fathers, I want to encourage you to break the chains of tradition, look your teenage son or daughter in the eye, place your hands on their shoulders and say, "What I am about to say to you is extremely important to me. I want you to hear me carefully." Then with your eyes looking into their eyes say the words, "I love you very much" and then embrace them. Whatever the experience means to you, I can assure you that your words will ring in the heart of your teenager forever. Now that the dam is broken, the waters of love are flowing. Say the words again and again and again. Your teenager will never tire of hearing them and your own love tank will be replenished when you hear your teenager say the same words to you.

Of course, there are other ways to verbally express affection. Vicki Lansky, author of 101 *Ways to Tell Your Child I Love You*, told about the time her thirteen-year-old daughter Dana was feeling blue and she wanted to cheer her up. She said to Dana, "I really enjoyed you today." Why did she say "enjoy" rather than "love"? Lansky explained, "Using the word enjoy rather than the word love really made the difference." Several times after that her daughter would ask, "Did you enjoy me today, too, Mommy?"[2] Make up your own synonym and try it on your teenager. Here are some examples to get you started:

"I adore you."

"I feel proud when I think about you."

"You are my sunshine."

"If I could choose any teenager in the world, I would choose you."

"You are so wonderful."

"I wake every morning and think 'What a privilege to be your father/ mother.'"

"Yesterday I was sitting at my desk thinking, 'I really miss my daughter.'"

"I love it when you are around."

Now think up a few of your own and write them in a notebook and periodically sprinkle them in along with your "I love you's." If your teenager is accustomed to hearing "I love you," then one of these optional statements of affection may fill your teenager's love tank more effectively.

Verbal affection can also focus on various attributes of the teen's body or personality. "Your hair looks like sunshine today" may be especially affirming to a sixteen-year-old who is wondering if she "looks OK." "Your eyes are beautiful" may be the words that return to the heart of the seventeen-year-old who has just been dumped by her boyfriend. "You are so strong" may be the words that change the mood of a fifteen-year-old son who is overly concerned about facial blemishes. Look for physical characteristics of your teenager that you can verbally affirm. It is an effective way of expressing verbal affection.

These words of affection may also focus on the teenager's personality. "I am so happy that you have such an outgoing personality. I know that you think of yourself as being shy, but I've observed that once you start talking to someone, you open up. It's just like the floodgates open and you start talking freely."

Here are other expressions that show love for who your teenager is:

"You are so steady. I like the way you think before you speak."

"Your bubbly personality makes so many people happy."

"You may be quiet, but when you speak, you say something."

"One of the things I really admire about you is that you are dependable. When you give your word, I can count on it."

"I am so happy that I can trust you. Other mothers tell me that they cannot trust their daughters, but I trust you explicitly."

"I love the way you encourage people. I observed you last night talking with Tim after the game was over. You have a real gift of encouragement."

Such statements of affection speak deeply to the inner spirit of teenagers. They give your son and daughter a sense of being valued, admired, and loved.

For some parents, such verbal expressions of affection will not come easily. I challenge you to keep a notebook. Write down the examples I have given above, read them aloud several times in private. Make up your own statements of affection and periodically share one with your teenager.

Words in the Presence of Others

Try affirming your teenager in the presence of the entire family. Give words of praise and appreciation in the presence of younger or older siblings. (I don't suggest you do it in the presence of the teen's peers.) Words of affirmation often speak louder when given in the presence of others. For example, the family is having dinner when Jeremy's father says, "I said this to Jeremy earlier in private but I want to say it in front of the whole family. I was proud of him last night. He had reason to be angry with the official's call but he showed tremendous sportsmanship in the way he responded and I'm proud of him." Jeremy has now been emotionally affirmed and the rest of the family has been reminded of the importance of character.

Or Dad says about his daughter, "Did everyone see my Meredith to-night? She stepped up to the foul line, made both shots and won the game. Yeah!!" Meredith not only had the satisfaction at the game; she relives the satisfaction and feels emotionally affirmed by the family. This may speak even more deeply to Meredith's emotional need for love than if her father had limited his comments to a private encounter between the two of them.

Words of affirmation is one of the five primary love languages. All teenagers need words of affirmation. In the midst of the insecurity of the teenage transition, affirming words are often like rain on the desert soul of a teenager. For those teenagers for whom words of affirmation is their primary love language, nothing is more important emotionally than the affirming words heard from parents.

What They Say

Listen to the following statements by teens who feel loved when they hear their parents speaking words of affirmation.

Matt, a seventeen-year-old senior and member of the wrestling team: "When I win, nothing is more important than hearing my father say, 'Great job, Son.' And when I lose, nothing is more helpful than hearing him say, 'You gave him the best match he's had in a long time.'"

Bethany, age thirteen: "I know my mother loves me. She tells me all the time. I think my dad does, too, but he doesn't say it."

Ryan, age fifteen, lives in Chicago's inner city: "I don't have a dad except these guys at the center. But I know my mom loves me. She tells me how proud she is of me and encourages me to make something of myself."

Yolanda, age eighteen: "I'm going off to college in a few months. I think I am the luckiest girl alive. My parents both love me. Even through the difficult teenage years, they have always encouraged me. My dad says, 'You're the greatest,' and my mom says, 'You can be whatever you want to be.' I just hope I can help some other people the way they have helped me."

Emma, age fourteen and an eighth grader: "My mom left when I was four years old, so I don't remember her, but later my dad married my stepmother. I consider her my mother. Sometimes when I get down on myself she tells me how much she loves me and she tells me good things about myself that I sometimes forget. I couldn't make it without her."

For these and thousands of other teenagers, the love language of words of affirmation speaks deeply. When parents speak such words regularly, the teen's emotional tank will remain full.

If your teenager's love language is
WORDS OF AFFIRMATION

Here are a few more ideas especially for parents of teenagers. Pick and choose among them to try something new you think your teenager will appreciate.

- *Talk about a goal your teenager would like to reach and verbally encourage them to explore it.*

- *Put a Post-it note with some encouraging words on the cereal box they will see in the morning.*

- *Make a habit of mentioning something specific you've observed that highlights your teenager's accomplishments. Examples include, "I really enjoyed the way you picked up your clothes without my asking you," or "I appreciate that you worked so hard to finish your paper for school on time."*

- *Ask what your teenager wants to do after high school. If your daughter says, "I want to work as a physical therapist, helping people recover from difficult injuries," verbally encourage her to find what would be involved in reaching this goal.*

- *Copy or cut out inspirational quotes as you find them in publications and simply attach a note that says, "This really reminded me of you."*

- *If you are artistic, create a painting or drawing that shows how much you love your teenager.*

- *Take a favorite piece of artwork or special note from your teenager to be professionally framed. Then hang it in your home or office.*

- *When you have to be out of town for work or other reasons, leave a series of short notes for your teenager, one for each day you are apart.*

▶ *Call your teenager at home or on their cell phone whenever you think of them just to say, "I love you." (This can also be done with e-mail or a text message.)*

▶ *Place their trophies, best school papers, and other standout works in areas they recognize as important to you such as the refrigerator, the office, or a special scrapbook.*

▶ *When your teenager is feeling down, share five reasons why you are proud of them.*

▶ *Keep a picture keychain (or pictures in your wallet) with current pictures of your teenager that you talk about with your friends—especially when your teenager is around.*

▶ *Create an encouragement jar that you and your teenager can use to drop in notes of praise and read together on a regular basis.*

▶ *When a teenager makes a mistake trying to do something helpful, first use words to recognize that you knew of their good intentions.*

CHAPTER 4

LOVE LANGUAGE #2:
Physical Touch

There's undeniable emotional power in touching those we love. That's why parents are encouraged to hold and cuddle infants—kissing them on the face and stroking their skin. Hugging three-year-olds or letting them sit on your lap while you read a story is a powerful way to fill a child's love tank. On the other end of life, touch is also an emotional communicator. Who has not walked the hallways of "homes for the elderly" and seen senior adults sitting in wheelchairs, extending a hand desiring to be touched? And, of course, in marriage lovers embrace and kiss.

But what about teenagers? Are they different? Does *physical touch* communicate emotionally to the teenager? The answer is yes and no. It all depends on when, where, and how.

For instance, a hug in the presence of the teenager's peers may be embarrassing and motivate the teenager to push the parent away or mumble, "Stop it." However, massaging the teenager's shoulder muscles after he comes home from a game may deeply communicate emotional love.

Trying to touch a teenager when the teen is in an "antisocial mood" will almost always annoy the teenager. But a loving touch after a disappointing day at school will be welcomed as true parental love.

Teenagers are different from children. You cannot continue to give the same kind of touches in the same environments and in the same manner that you gave when they were younger. Again, parents must remember the teenager's themes of independence and self-identity. Thus, parents must ask, "Does my proposed touch threaten my teen's sense of independence? Does it enhance positive self-identity?"

Remember, the teen desperately needs to feel your love. Physical touch is one of the five basic languages of love, but you must speak the language of physical touch at the appropriate time, in the appropriate place, and in an appropriate manner. If your teenager's primary love language in childhood was physical touch, their love language will not change during the adolescent years. However, the dialect in which you speak that language must change if you want the teenager to feel loved. Let's examine each of these.

The Time for Touching

The ancient Hebrew book of wisdom says, "There is a time for everything ... a time to embrace and a time to refrain [from embracing]."[1] Coaches often remind their athletes, "Timing is everything." Similarly, parents of teenagers must learn the art of appropriate timing. Good actions taken at the wrong time often backfire. This is a difficult task for two reasons. First, timing is largely determined by the teenager's mood. And second, the teen's mood is not always easy to figure out. Sometimes it is after parents "make their move" and lovingly touch a teenager that they discover the teenager is in an "anti-touch mood." But "difficult" does not mean impossible.

Wise parents will study their teenager. They will learn to pick up on the teenager's mood by his behavior. One mother said, "I can tell whether my son wants to be touched by the way he closes the door when he enters the house. If he slams the door, it's a 'Don't touch me' mood. If he takes time to quietly close the door, he is saying 'I'm open to a touch, Mom.'" Another mother said, "I can tell when my daughter doesn't want to be touched by the distance she stands from me when she talks. If she stands on the other side of the room while talking, I know she doesn't want to be touched. But if she comes up and stands close to me, I know she's open to a loving touch."

Teenagers communicate mood by their body language—how close they are to you, or whether their arms are folded, for example. The astute parent will observe this body language and learn the appropriate times for touching a teenager. It is not necessary to understand why the teenager is in the "Don't touch me now" mood. What is important is to recognize it and respect it.

It is almost always inappropriate to seek to touch a teenager when he or she is angry. When your teen daughter, for instance, is angry with you or someone else, she won't want to be touched. She is angry because in her mind someone "did me wrong." Anger is the emotion that pushes people away from each other. If you attempt to touch a teenager when she is angry, you will almost always be rebuffed. To an angry teenager, physical touch comes across as an effort to control. It strikes at the teenager's need for independence. Thus, the teenager pulls away from your touch. We will discuss how to process teen anger in a later chapter. What we are saying here, simply, is that it is usually inappropriate to use the love language of physical touch when a teenager is angry.

On the other hand, there are many appropriate times for touching teenagers. One such occasion is when your teenager has succeeded in a major accomplishment. It may be any number of occasions: a victory on the athletic field, a successful piano recital, an exceptionally well-executed dance performance, the completion of a major paper for school, the passing of an algebra exam, the securing of a driver's license. These are the times when teenagers are usually open to loving physical touch from parents. The thrill of accomplishment has thrust them down the road of independence and self-identity. Your celebration of their successes by verbal affirmation and physical touch will be received as further evidence of your recognition of their emerging maturity.

Conversely, times of failure in the teenager's life are also times for expressing the love language of physical touch. The teenager is down on himself because he flunked the calculus exam, his girlfriend just dumped him, or he just had a fender bender. Your teenage daughter is feeling in the pits because her best friend has a date for Friday night and she does not, or, worse yet, her boyfriend has just broken up with her and started dating her best friend. These are occasions when teenagers are open to the love language of physical touch.

In the normal flow of daily life, if the teenager is in a good mood, she is typically open to some form of physical touch as an expression of love. If the teen is in a bad mood, he will be annoyed by physical touch. Thoughtful parents will respect the mood of their teenager and will seek to give physical touch only at appropriate times—learning by trial and error is often the only way.

Here is the experience of one mother: "When Julie turned thirteen, I thought she was on drugs. Her behavior changed radically. In all of her childhood years, she was a 'touchy-feely child.' I hugged and kissed her all the time and often gave her back rubs. But when she turned thirteen, I found her pulling away from me, not wanting me to touch her. I thought something terrible had happened to our relationship. I later realized that she was a normal teenager. I have now learned when Julie is in the mood for touching and when she is not.

"Once in a while, I misread her and she jerks back from my hugs. But most of the time, I connect because I've chosen the right time. Julie is fifteen and a half now, and I feel good about our relationship. I think her primary love language is physical touch. I know she needs it. I just want to continue to be sensitive to do it at the right time."

The Place for Touching

As there is a time to touch and a time not to touch, there is also a place to touch and a place not to touch. I'm talking here about geography—not sexuality. We will deal with that later. The ten-year-old welcomed his mother's embrace after the football game was over. He rushed to wherever his mother was standing and waited for her positive words and affirming touch. But at sixteen when the varsity game is over, he will not be looking for Mom and he hopes that she will not be looking for him. He will be celebrating his independence and self-identity with his teammates and friends. They can slap him on the back, beat him on the head, give him "high fives," but when his mother approaches, his thought is: *Please, Mom, don't even think about it.* In most public settings, teenagers do not want to be hugged or touched affectionately by their parents.

This is especially true in the presence of their peers. The teen's self-identity is tied up with that of his friends. When Mom or Dad enters that world and expresses physical affection, it threatens the teenager's self-identity and strikes at his desire for independence. As one teenager said, "It makes me feel like they think I'm still a kid." A good rule of thumb is to never touch a teenager in the presence of his/her friends unless the teenager initiates it.

Sometimes teenagers are open to physical touch in the presence of extended family members such as grandparents. If you are bragging to the grandparents about the teenager's accomplishments, then the teenager may accept a pat on the back at the end of your speech. Don't assume this to be true, however. Watch your teenager's response and don't pursue touching if they give you the cue to "back off."

Then where is the appropriate place to speak the love language of physical touch to your teenager? Typically in the privacy of your own home or when you are alone with the teenager. Physical touch can be an effective communicator of emotional love when given in private or in the presence of immediate family members. Remember, for some teenagers, physical touch is their primary love language. For these teens it's extremely important that parents learn the appropriate time and place to express love.

Fourteen-year-old Jacob said, "I love going on camping trips with my dad. That's when I feel closest to him." When I asked, "What do you like most about camping with your dad?" Jacob replied, "When we arm wrestle at night by the fire. I especially like it when I beat him." Emotional love is coming through to Jacob by the language of physical touch. Independence and self-identity are being encouraged—especially when he wins.

Fifteen-year-old Jessica said, "Mom and I are really close. I don't think I'd make it without her hugs. School has been hard this year but I always know that when I get home, I'll get a hug from Mom." Jessica's mom has discovered her primary love language and is speaking it in the privacy of their home. Remember, though, when speaking this love language, always do so at the appropriate time and in the appropriate place. Otherwise, it will not be interpreted as love.

The Manner for Touching

Be Flexible

Here we are talking about not only the kinds of touches we give but the manner in which we give them. There are numerous ways by which to express affection through physical touch. Hugs, kisses, back rubs, pats, tender touches, massages, and arm wrestling are all appropriate ways to speak the language of physical touch to a teenager. However, the process is not as simple as it sounds. Teenagers are individuals. They don't all like the same kinds of touches. Some teens like back rubs and others don't. Some like for you to play with their hair and others don't. Your teen is unique, and you will have to learn not only the love language itself, but also the dialects in which he or she best receives love.

We must remember not to force our own love language on the teenager; rather, we must learn the teen's language. What makes it even more complicated is that the kinds of touch you gave when your teenager was a child might not be the kinds of touch your teenager appreciates as a teen. Parents are often frustrated by this. They think they have discovered the child's primary love language, and they have learned how to speak it. Now the teenager is drawing back from the same kinds of touch that earlier she enjoyed. A major reason is the teen's quest for independence and self-identity. When you touch your teenager in the same manner that you touched him when he was a child, these touches may stimulate feelings of dependence and insecurity—the exact opposite of what the teenager wants to feel. Thus, the teenager draws back from these "childish" expressions of love.

Sometime ago I shared this insight at a parenting workshop. I could see the lights come on in Rod's mind. At the break time he came up to me and said, "Now I understand it. My son Matt is now fifteen. When he was young, I used to give him back rubs all the time. He loved it. For the past two or three years, he has not let me give him a back rub. I've felt like he was pulling away from me. I couldn't understand why he had changed so much. Now I see that the back rubs remind him of childhood. He is on a course toward independence and doesn't wish to return to childhood. It all makes sense now."

I suggested to Rod that he find new ways of expressing the love language of physical touch to his son. "Slap him on the back, tap him on the shoulder, trip him when he walks by your chair. If he falls, wrestle him on the floor. You will see his love tank start filling up because you are treating him like the emerging man he is—rather than like the child he used to be. You are fostering his sense of independence rather than sabotaging it." Rod has learned an important lesson about loving teenagers.

If your teenager says, "I don't like that" in response to your efforts to physically touch her, then back off and find another method of physical touch. Don't force a particular kind of physical touch upon your teenager because you think she should like it. The whole concept of the five love languages is learning to speak the other person's language, not your own. The key question is: What makes your teen feel loved? If physical touch is her primary love language, then you must find the particular kinds of touch that communicate love to her. The process of loving a teenager is complicated by the parents' own preferences. Some parents have never "tripped" their teenager and cannot imagine doing so as an expression of love. Others have never "elbowed" their teen. I'm not suggesting that all teenagers like these dialects of physical touch. What I am suggesting is that you discover the kinds of physical touch that your teenager appreciates and speak that dialect regularly.

Obviously, the emotional climate in which you give physical touch is extremely important. If you trip your teen when you are angry, it is not an expression of love. If you slap him on the shoulder because you are frustrated with his behavior, he will not feel loved. The mother who withholds hugs from her daughter because she doesn't like her choice of friends runs the risk of losing her daughter. As parents we are responsible for our own attitudes. If we express love to our teenagers only when they are doing things that please us, we have left the high road of unconditional love and have entered the treacherous world of manipulation.

Use Physical Touch Gently to Correct

The good news about the love language of physical touch is that it can be easily spoken even when your teen's behavior is not pleasing. You can even express your displeasure with the teen's behavior at the same time you are expressing love by physical touch. Marcia is touching her teenage daughter's arm and saying, "I am very upset with the fact that you came home an hour late last night. I understand that you were having a good time with your friends and didn't notice what time it was. But do you understand how troublesome that is to me? We've always agreed that if you are going to be late, you will call me so I won't be worried about you."

Now she turns and faces her daughter. Placing both hands on her daughter's shoulders she says, "Darling, I love you so much. I don't want to make your life miserable. I just want to know that you are all right." Marcia loves her daughter in an extremely effective manner while at the same time addressing her concerns.

The language of physical touch spoken at the right time in the right place and in the right manner speaks deeply to the teenage soul. Physical touch says, "I recognize you as a person of importance. I'm with you. I care about you. I love you." Every teenager needs to hear the language of physical touch. If they don't hear it from parents, they will seek it elsewhere.

A Critical Word to Fathers

There is a tendency on the part of the fathers of this generation to withdraw physical touch from their emerging teenage daughters, particularly when the daughter approaches puberty. Some don't know how to respond to their daughters' ongoing physical change; others think their daughters don't want touch since they are no longer girls. Still other fathers fear someone may accuse them of sexual touches or even abuse. Whatever the reason, withholding physical touch is a serious mistake. The teenage daughter needs to feel good about herself as a female. She needs to sense that she is attractive to the male gender. The father's role is to give her this sense of well-being about herself. Appropriate physical touch is a vehicle for doing this. If the father withdraws physical affection from the daughter—she is far more likely to become sexually active at a younger age.

Fathers, I strongly encourage you to continue to speak the love language of physical touch as your daughter enters her teenage years. She needs those appropriate touches as she develops her independence and self-identity as a woman.

Inappropriate Physical Touch

I wish I did not have to write the next few paragraphs. I wish that the terms physical abuse and sexual abuse were not so commonplace in our society. The reality is that a significant minority of teenagers do experience abuse from their parents. The more dramatic cases, we see on the evening news. But most teenagers suffer silently and sometimes those closest to them are not aware of the abuse.

Physical Abuse and Anger

Physical abuse is causing physical harm by beating, hitting, kicking, etc., out of anger rather than play. The key word is *anger*. Some parents of teens have never learned to handle anger in a constructive manner. When they are angered by the teen's behavior, the flow of vicious words is followed by physical violence. Slaps, pushes, shoves, choking, holding, shaking, and hitting are all abusive behaviors to teenagers. Where this occurs, we can be certain that the teenager's love tank is not only empty, it is riddled with holes. Positive words and expressions of physical affection that follow such angry outbursts will always appear hollow to the teenager. The teenage heart does not easily recover from such physical abuse.

The parent who wishes his teenager to feel loved after such angry episodes must not only render a sincere and honest apology to the teenager, but he must seek help in breaking these destructive patterns and learning positive anger management skills. This is best done through reading books,[2] attending support groups, and/or professional counseling.

Explosive anger will not simply go away with the passing of time. The parent must take initiative to change these destructive outbursts. Nor will the teen's emotional pain subside merely with the passing of time. If the parent does not render a genuine apology and actively change these patterns, the teen will most assuredly continue to feel unloved by the parent who abuses her. Ironically, the teenager often feels unloved by the other parent as well. The teen reasons, "If they loved me, they would not allow this abusive behavior to continue. They would protect me." If you are married to a consistently abusive spouse, I would encourage you to go for personal counseling and gain the emotional strength and knowledge as to how you can take constructive steps to protect yourself and your teenager. You are not serving the cause of love when you continue to allow such abusive behavior to continue. You need the help of a trained counselor or pastor to help you become a positive change agent in your family.

Sexual Abuse

Sexual abuse is taking advantage of your parental role to obtain sexual favors from your teenager in order to satisfy your own sexual desires. Sexual abuse is most often perpetrated by fathers, stepfathers, or a mother's boyfriend. Such abuse is normally focused on teenage girls. Although homosexual abuse does sometimes occur in the nuclear family, it is not nearly as common as heterosexual abuse. Often the parental sexual abuser will seek to convince the teenager that his sexual overtures are expressions of love for the teenager. This message will not "ring true" with the teenager. Something deep within the teenager says, "This is not right."

However, the teenager is often reluctant to discuss the sexual experience with the other parent or another adult. Sometimes teenagers are kept silent by shame, but the most common constraint is the emotion of fear. Often the parental abuser has threatened them. One fifteen-year-old daughter said, "My father told me that if I told my mother or anyone else about what was going on between us, he would deny it and my mother would believe him and not me. He would see to it that I was punished for lying." A seventeen-year-old girl when asked why she did not tell her mother that her stepfather had been sexually abusing her since she was thirteen responded, "If I told my mother, I knew my stepdad would kill me. He told me often it would be easy to get rid of me. I knew he was serious and I didn't want to die." It was not until her stepfather was in prison for another criminal offense that she finally shared with a counselor what had been going on between her and her stepfather.

It should be obvious to all that sexual intimacy with a teenager on the part of a parent figure is not an expression of love to a teenager. It is in fact self-gratification—the opposite of love. The teenager will feel used and abused. Such abuse over a period of time breeds bitterness, hatred, anger, and often depression in the teenager. It also has a drastically negative effect on the teenager's emotional, social, and sexual development.

Dealing with Sexual Abuse

If you are involved in gaining sexual gratification from a teenager who lives in your house, the first step is to acknowledge the wrongness of such behavior. The second step is to make an appointment with a professional counselor, share the problem, and begin the process of trying to heal the relationship with your teenager. Yes, such a bold step will be costly, may bring embarrassment, may disrupt your marital relationship, may create emotional stress for you, and may end up with legal consequences. But failure to do so will be more costly in the long run.

I'm fully aware that most sexual abusers will not take the advice I have just given. Therefore, the other parent must press the issue. Of course, often the other parent is not aware of what is going on. Sometimes they have closed their eyes to revealing clues and have plugged their ears to the teenager's efforts to tell them. Such insensitivity for whatever reason is treason to your teenager. I urge you to listen and probe any statement from your teenager that even faintly resembles a plea for help. And I urge you to keep your eyes open to any evidence that inappropriate behavior is taking place between your spouse and your teenager.

Please be aware that sometimes your teenager will deny it when you ask a straightforward question. Again, that denial is often based on shame and fear. Don't take your teen's immediate response as the final word on the situation. If you have reason to believe that there is inappropriate sexual behavior between your spouse and your teenager, I urge you to contact a professional counselor, share the evidence you have, and let the counselor help you take appropriate steps. Sexual abuse is devastating to your teenager's well-being. If you know of such abuse and do not deal with it, your teenager will not only feel abused by the perpetrator but abandoned by you. Yes, dealing with the abuse will be costly, perhaps embarrassing, and may even destroy your marriage or relationship with the abuser, but it is the only alternative if you love your teenager.

With proper counseling and spiritual help, there can be healing even after such devastating abuse. But without such emotional and spiritual guidance, your teenager may never experience a healthy adulthood. Many of the troubled young adults in our society can trace the roots of their trouble to sexual abuse they suffered when they were teenagers. Often, parents or parental figures did not perpetrate this abuse; it might have been perpetrated by extended family members: aunts, uncles, cousins, or adults the teenager met at school, church, or in other community settings. Most homosexual abuse of teenagers takes place outside the nuclear family. If parents become aware of such abuse, it should immediately be reported to the local mental health/social work authorities. Teenagers should not be left to fend for themselves in the shark-infested waters of the twenty-first century's sexual confusion. Parental love impels us to do all that we can to help our teens develop a positive sexual identity and to keep them shielded from adults who would seek to abuse them for their own personal sexual gratification.

The encouraging news is that most parents are not physically or sexually abusing their teenagers. Most parents love their teenagers by appropriately speaking the love language of physical touch. A survey of American teenagers ages thirteen through seventeen found that 75 percent believed that fathers should hug their teenagers at least once a week. And 55 percent of the same teens said that their own fathers did so.[3]

What They Say

Teenagers need to be touched by parents if they are to feel loved. For some teenagers, physical touch is their primary love language. It speaks more deeply and quickly than the other four.

Listen to the following teenagers for whom physical touch is their primary love language.

Victoria, sixteen, who lives with her single-parent mother: "I love it when Mom gives me back rubs. All my problems seem to go away when Mom rubs my back."

Joel, age seventeen: "I know my dad loves me. He is always picking on me. He elbows me when we are watching a game together. He hits me on the shoulder and trips me when I walk by. Sometimes I'm not in the mood to be touched and Dad respects that. But the next day he bumps me when I walk by. I love it!"

Meredith, who's fifteen: "My dad doesn't hug me as much as he used to. I don't know if he thinks that I'm an adult now and don't need it. But I miss his hugs. They always make me feel special."

Barrett, who has had a rough year with algebra: "The best part of homework is when Mom comes by and rubs my shoulders. I forget all about algebra. It relaxes me. When she walks away, I feel better."

Jessica, age seventeen: "I know that sometimes I'm hard to live with. My parents have put up with a lot of my moods. I guess it's just being a teenager, but when they hug me or even touch my arm, I feel like everything is going to be OK. It's like a calming thing. I know that they really love me."

If your teenager's love language is
PHYSICAL TOUCH
· ·

Need more ideas? Try one or more of these with your teenager this week.

▸ *Hold hands during family prayers.*

▸ *Develop a unique handshake or greeting that is only used between you and your teenager. Use it regularly when you say good-bye or meet after being apart.*

▸ *If your teenager is under stress, gently stroke their head to relax them as your son or daughter tells you about their situation.*

▸ *Hug and kiss your teenager every day when they leave for school for as long as they will let you, but be sensitive to their resistance, especially when in public.*

▸ *Shortly after disciplining your teenager, take a moment to give them a hug to show them the discipline was a consequence of their wrong choice and not against them as a person.*

▸ *Give each other a high five or similar congratulations whenever you catch your teenager doing something positive.*

▸ *Purchase a gift for your teenager that is touch-oriented, such as a soft pillow, blanket, or sweater.*

▸ *Play games or sports together that require physical touch. This will allow both shared time together as well as touch that is meaningful without appearing forced.*

▸ *Offer to give your teenager a shoulder massage when they experience an especially difficult day.*

▸ *For father and son, playful wrestling can often express love, but only if this is an activity enjoyed by the teenager.*

▸ *Provide a positive "pat on the back" as a way of communicating love when your teenager accomplishes something significant. (This can also often be helpful when your teenager has not accomplished a goal. Strive to be unconditional in offering love.)*

▸ *If you see your teenager already in bed, walk in and pull their blankets up around them.*

CHAPTER 5

LOVE LANGUAGE #3:
Quality Time

At 11:45 p.m. I stepped into my teenage son's room. I had spent the day counseling and felt both physically and emotionally drained. I was anticipating a brief "goodnight, I love you" experience. Instead, my son said, "Dad, I don't understand girls." I sat on the floor, leaned against the side of his bed and asked, "What brings you to that conclusion?"

That was the beginning of a two-hour conversation. Derek was seventeen years old at the time. He is now over forty. He still doesn't understand girls. Neither do I. But we've always been close enough to talk, and that is what's important.

To give your teenager *quality time* is to give your teenager a portion of your life. Real, quality time means giving the teenager your undivided attention. Nothing else matters in those moments. Quality time is a powerful communicator of emotional love.

Unfortunately the love language of quality time is much more difficult to speak than either words of affirmation or physical touch for one simple reason: It takes more time. A meaningful touch can be given in a second; words of affirmation can be spoken in less than a minute. But quality time may require hours. In today's hurried world, many parents of teenagers find it difficult to speak the language of quality time. Consequently, many teenagers live in houses filled with the latest technology but have empty love tanks. They often feel like they too are simply a part of their parents' collection of things.

Busy parents who want their teenagers to feel loved must make time to give their teenagers focused attention. Psychiatrist Ross Campbell wrote, "Without focused attention, a teenager experiences increased anxiety, because he feels everything else is more important than he is. He is consequently less secure and becomes impaired in his emotional and psychological growth."[1]

Be There, Really There

The central aspect of quality time is togetherness. I do not mean mere proximity. Being in the same house with your teenager is not quality time. When you are in the same room with your teenager, you are in close proximity, but you are not necessarily together. Togetherness has to do with being in touch with each other. Father and son watching a baseball game on television or even in the bleachers may or may not experience togetherness. If the teen walks away from the experience feeling lonely, thinking *sports are more important to my father than I am,* then togetherness did not occur. But if the teen gets this message, "The most important thing about this game is being with you. I love it when we do things together," the father and the son have connected. And the son will walk away feeling loved. The focus of this chapter is to help you experience *togetherness* when the two of you are together.

What does it mean to be "in touch" with your teenager? Essentially it means that the teenager is feeling that he is the focus of your attention. This does not mean that every time you are together you must have long in-depth conversations. However, it does mean that you, the parent, must intentionally seek to communicate by eye contact, words, touch, and body language that the teen is more important than the event.

Fifteen-year-old Clint illustrated this when he said, "My father thinks he is doing me a favor when he takes me fishing. He calls it 'our buddy time' but we don't ever talk about us. Our conversations are about fishing and nature, but I don't care about fishing or nature. I wish I could talk to my father about my problems, but he doesn't seem interested in me." I knew Clint's father, and I can tell you assuredly that he thought he was doing a wonderful thing by taking Clint fishing. He had no idea they were not "in touch."

The problem was his focus on the activity rather than his son. He was shocked to learn later in our counseling session that his son actually walked away from the fishing experience feeling empty and rejected. Clint's father had a lot to learn about speaking the love language of quality time.

Quality Conversation

Like words of affirmation and physical touch, the love language of quality time also has many dialects. One of the most common dialects is that of quality conversation. By quality conversation, I mean dialogue between parent and teen where each is free to share their experiences, thoughts, feelings, and desires in a friendly, accepting atmosphere. It requires that parents learn to speak "with" their teens rather than "at" them.

Asking and Listening

Quality conversation is quite different from the first love language. Words of affirmation focus on what we are saying, whereas quality conversation focuses on what we are hearing. If the parent is going to express love by means of quality time and is going to spend that time in conversation, it means the parent will focus on drawing out and listening sympathetically to what the teenager says. The parent will ask questions—not in a badgering manner but with a genuine desire to understand the teen's thoughts, feelings, and desires. Most parents will have to work at this because it is a change in communication style.

When our children were little, we issued instructions and commands, but if we continue this pattern of communication during the teenage years, the teenager will say something like, "You are treating me like a child." And he will be right. We must now learn to treat our child as a teenager, remembering his emerging independence and encouraging his developing self-identity.

This means that we must allow our teenager to think her own thoughts, experience her own emotions, have her own dreams, and be able to share these with us without receiving our unsolicited assessment. We must learn to help her evaluate her ideas, understand her emotions, and take realistic steps toward accomplishing her dreams. And we must learn to do this in a friendly, encouraging atmosphere of dialogue rather than the dogmatic statements of monologue. *For most parents, this is one of the greatest challenges of parenting teenagers.* Many parents have become exasperated in the process of learning.

"I don't know how to parent a teenager," Marlene told me. "I thought I was doing fairly well until Katie turned sixteen. Now I wake up to discover that I am 'stupid, not in touch with the real world,' and trying to control her life. I feel totally frustrated and unappreciated by my daughter. Everything I say is wrong. I don't even know how to talk to her anymore."

I had known Marlene for a number of years and knew that her communication style was what I called "the babbling brook" (whatever comes in the eye gate and the ear gate goes out the mouth gate, and normally there are not sixty seconds between the two). Whatever Marlene saw, heard, or felt she expressed freely and without reflection as to whether others were interested in hearing her thoughts, feelings, and impressions. Katie, who had accepted this as normal in her childhood years, was now trying to discover her own identity and establish a measure of independence from her mother. She no longer accepted her mother's word as "the gospel." She now had a few thoughts of her own, and she expressed them as freely as her mother.

I knew that for Marlene, the learning curve was going to be steep. But I also knew that if she didn't learn a new pattern of communicating with Katie, she was going to lose the warm relationship she had in earlier years. Marlene had to learn to minimize the flow of her own words, and she had to learn the new art of active listening and sympathetic dialogue.

How to Have a Quality Conversation

Here are eight guidelines for better listening and true dialogue. The first five have to do with learning to actively listen to your teenager. Good listening must precede steps 6 through 8. These guidelines helped Marlene learn about quality conversation. Practice them and your conversations with your teen will improve.

1. *Maintain eye contact when your teenager is talking.* This keeps your mind from wandering and communicates that the teen has your full attention. Refrain from rolling your eyes in disgust, closing your eyes when they give you a low blow, looking over their head, or staring at your shoes while they are talking.

2. *Don't multitask while listening to your teenager.* Remember quality time is giving someone your undivided attention. If you are watching, reading, or doing something else in which you are keenly interested and cannot turn from immediately, tell your teenager the truth. A positive approach might be "I know you are trying to talk to me and I'm interested. But I want to give you my full attention. I can't do that right now but if you will give me ten minutes to finish this, I'll sit down and listen to you." Most teenagers will respect such a request.

3. *Listen for feelings.* Ask yourself, "What emotions are my teenager experiencing?" When you think you have the answer, confirm it. For example, "It sounds like you are feeling disappointed because I forgot..." That gives the teen a chance to clarify his feelings. It also communicates that you are listening intently to what he is saying.

4. *Observe body language.* Clenched fists, trembling hands, tears, furrowed brows, and eye movement may give you clues as to what the teen is feeling. Sometimes body language speaks one message while words speak another. Ask for clarification to make sure you know what she is really thinking and feeling.

5. *Refuse to interrupt.* Research has indicated that the average individual listens for only seventeen seconds before interrupting and interjecting his own ideas—parents of teenagers might even be quicker than that! Such interruptions often stop the conversation before it gets started. At this early point in the conversation, your objective is not to defend yourself or to set

the teen straight; it is to understand the teenager's thoughts, feelings, and desires.

6. *Ask reflective questions.* When you think you understand what your teenager is saying, check it out by reflecting back what he has said (as you understand it) in a question: "What I hear you saying is.... Is that correct?" Or "Are you saying ... ?" Reflective listening clears up misunderstandings and your perception of what the teen is saying. Remember, you are trying to answer the questions: "What is my teen thinking? What is my teen feeling? What does my teen desire of me?" Don't share your own ideas until you have clearly answered those questions.

7. *Express understanding.* The teen needs to know that she has been heard and understood. Suppose as a parent you ask the reflective question: "What I hear you saying is that you want to go to the beach with three of your friends, that you want to drive your car because they do not have driver's licenses, and that you would like for me to pay for gas and lodging because none of you have enough money. Is that what you are asking?" If the teenager responds, "Yes," then you can express understanding of their request: "I can see how you would find that very desirable. I'm sure you would have a good time at the beach." In expressing understanding, you are affirming the teen's sense of worth, and you are treating the teen as a person who has desires. Now you are ready for step eight.

8. *Ask permission to share your perspective.* "Would you like to hear my perspective on the idea?" If the teen says, "Yes," you proceed to share your thoughts, ideas, and feelings. If the teen says, "Not really," then the conversation is over and the trip to the beach goes unfunded. If you have expressed understanding of the teen's thoughts, feelings, and desires, it is very likely that the teenager will be open to hearing your perspective. Even though she may not agree with you—she will listen.

Toward a Better Relationship

Some parents find the idea of asking permission to share their perspective ridiculous, or even offensive. "Why should I have to ask my teen permission to speak?" one father asked. The question is not whether the parents have the right to speak to the teenager, they do. The question is: "Do you want your teenager to listen to what you are saying?" Asking permission recognizes that she is an individual, and she has the choice of hearing what is in your heart and mind—or not hearing it. You are recognizing your teen as an individual. You are creating the climate for sympathetic dialogue. Parents certainly have the freedom to preach their sermon without asking permission, but teenagers also have the freedom "to tune parents out" if they choose. Many will do so because they feel they are being treated as a child. When you ask permission to share your perspective, the teen feels that she is being treated as a maturing young person.

Parents still have the final word on things like paying for a beach trip, or for that matter in allowing the teen to go to the beach at all. It is not a matter of parental authority; it is a matter of parent-teen relationships, or how you will express your authority. You can always lord it over your teenager as a tyrant. This will almost certainly result in your teenager feeling rejected and unloved. On the other hand, you can relate to your teen as a loving parent who seeks to foster his healthy, loving transition into adulthood.

Such quality conversations will obviously take time. Twice as much time will be spent in listening to the teenager as in talking to them. The dividends, however, are enormous. The teen feels respected, understood, and loved—the dream of every parent. Such dreams do not come true by simply doing what you've always done. They come by learning new patterns of communication that are more appropriate during the years of teenage development.

Learning to Talk

Talking is an important part of meaningful dialogue with your teenager. However, the manner in which you talk is extremely important. Effective talking focuses on sharing your own thoughts, feelings, and desires, not on attacking those of the teenager. Parents create an adversarial relationship when they begin their talking by condemning the teenager's perspective on the subject. It is far better to take the positive approach of sharing your perspective, thoughts, feelings, and desires.

Speaking "I" Statements

The simplest way to learn this approach to talking is to begin your sentences with *I* rather than *you*: "*I* think . . . , *I* feel . . . , *I* want . . ." These are statements of self-revelation; they are informing the teenager of what is going on inside your head. Conversely, "*You* are wrong, *you* don't understand, *you* are misreading the situation, *you* are being unreasonable, *you* are making my life difficult" are statements of blame and accusation. They almost always lead to one of two responses: explosive argumentation or withdrawal and depression—depending upon the teenager's basic personality.

You statements stop the flow of dialogue; *I* statements open the road to further discussion. It may take some time for you to learn this new way of talking. If you find yourself beginning your sentences with *you*, stop. Tell your teenager that you are trying to learn a new way to talk and that you'd like to try that sentence again. Rephrase the sentence, starting with *I*.

For example, if you hear yourself saying, "*You* make me angry when . . ." you should stop and say, "Let me try that again. *I* feel angry when . . ." Then you say to your teenager, "Do you understand why I'm trying to learn a new way to talk? I don't want to condemn you; I want to understand you. At the same time, I want you to understand my feelings and thoughts." Most teenagers will appreciate parents' efforts to learn new patterns of communication.

Teaching Instead of Preaching

Another important principle in talking with teenagers is to teach rather than preach. I grew up in the rural South where teachers and preachers were highly respected. The difference between the two was not in content, for the secular and sacred were intricately woven together, even at school. Nor was the difference in geography. It is true that the preacher preached at church and the teacher taught at school, but it is also true that the teacher often taught at church and the preacher sometimes preached at school. The difference was in the manner of delivery. The preacher was forceful in delivery—speaking loudly at times and softly at others, sometimes crying, sometimes laughing, but always passionate and dogmatic. The teacher, on the other hand, used a conversational tone, taught the content more "matter-of-factly"—passionate, I'm sure, but never overtly so. Parents of teenagers who wish to be effective communicators must emulate the teacher rather than the preacher.

A parent's raised voice and/or theatrics will typically cause teenagers to turn elsewhere for advice. On the other hand, parents who learn to share ideas in a reasoned and calm manner will often find teenagers asking for their advice. I do not mean that parents cannot be dogmatic about deeply held beliefs. I mean, rather, that their dogmatism must be tempered by openness to others' opinions—especially those of their teenager. "Let me tell you what I've always believed about that and tell you why I believe it to be best and then give me your feedback. I'd be interested in your observations." Such an approach allows the parent to express strong beliefs but also makes it easy for the teenager to share his thoughts, even if they are divergent from those of the parent. The parent must seek to create this kind of climate.

Remember, teenagers are beginning to think abstractly and in logical sequence. They are examining the beliefs with which they grew up and are deciding their own value systems. Parents who wish to influence this process must learn to be teachers rather than preachers. Learn the art of asking questions. Parents who learn how to ask questions will keep their teenagers talking. I don't mean badgering questions, such as, "Where did you go, how long did you stay, who were with you?" I mean questions that solicit the teenager's thoughts, such as, "How do you think most teenagers reacted to the antiwar protest last week by the students at the university?" Listen attentively and you will hear not only your teenager's observation about his peers, but you will also discover his/her thoughts on the subject. Keen interest in the teenager's opinions solicited by thoughtful questions may also lead the teenager to ask for your opinions. Questions beget not only answers, but also other questions.

Offering Reasons

Here's one other idea about talking to teenagers: Replace "Because I said so" with "Let me tell you why." Teenagers are interested in reasons. They are developing their own ability to reason, and they respond to the person who has logical reasons for his beliefs or opinions. The parent who reverts to pure authority without expressed reasons stops the flow of sympathetic dialogue with their teenager, the teenager will then feel rejected by the parent, and the love tank will remain empty.

The parent who learns the art of effectively listening and talking to teenagers is the parent who will most effectively communicate love on an emotional level. Quality conversation is one of the most powerful ways to communicate such love.

Quality Activities

Teenagers are creatures of action. Many parents' most quality conversations will take place in association with some activity. Some of these activities are a part of the normal flow of life—school, athletics, music, dance, drama, community, and church. Teenagers can be active in all these arenas. Parents who wish to spend quality time with teenagers will find these venues offer many opportunities. In the younger teenage years, there are all the hours spent en route to and from such activities. These times in the car need not be riddled with arguments if parents follow the eight guidelines listed above for talking and listening. Often the events themselves offer opportunities for experiencing quality time with your teen. When your teenager understands that you are at the event because you want to see him perform, that you are interested in his pursuits, that nothing is more important to you this afternoon than attending his event, it speaks volumes to him.

One fourteen-year-old said, "My dad always attends my concerts. He is not a musician, but he encourages me. I feel so fortunate." Another teenage daughter in the same orchestra said, "I know my dad loves me, but he never leaves work to attend my concerts. He makes time to play golf with his buddies, but he never makes time for me." The second teenager believes intellectually that her father loves her, but she is living with an empty emotional love tank.

Teenagers know that giving your time to attend one of their activities is giving them a part of your life, and it communicates deeply your love for them. Conversely when parents do not make time to attend the events in which their teenagers are involved, the message is "You are not as important as other things."

Teenagers do better in the normal challenges of development if their parents are involved with them in the normal flow of life. It is interesting that when five thousand adults were asked, "What did you least appreciate from your parents as a teenager?" the number one response was, "They were not involved in my life."[2] The fact is teenagers want their parents to be involved in their lives. Such involvement not only creates memories for the future but deep bonds of love in the present. Helping with homework, attending activities, driving your teens to the mall, and shopping with them, all create opportunities for quality time with teens. Parental involvement says, "Your interests are important to me."

The Right Environment

Parents may also learn to create environments for quality time with teenagers by planning and executing events outside the normal weekly routines. This requires time, effort, and sometimes money, but the dividends are enormous. Camping or hiking trips, rafting, fishing, attending sports, musical or theatrical events in a distant city, or visiting places of historical interest are but a few ways to create environments for spending quality time with your teenager.

Choose Events Your Teen Likes

The key to creating successful environments is to begin with the interests of your teenager. Planning a trip based on your own interests rather than the teenager's interests is planning for a bad experience. Discover your teenager's interests and be creative in planning environments that will motivate your teenager to spend quality time with you.

I remember when our seventeen-year-old son Derek got involved in learning about Buddy Holly—the 1950s singer-musician who died young in a plane crash. I made a trip to the library and read everything I could find about Buddy Holly. I read the lyrics to his songs. Later I engaged Derek in conversation about Buddy's lyrics. He was surprised that I even knew the lyrics. Some time later, I scheduled a marriage seminar in Fort Worth, Texas, and asked Derek if he would like to go with me. "After the seminar,"

I said, "we'll drive out to Lubbock and explore Buddy Holly's roots." I'll never forget the look in his eyes when he said, "Dad, I'd love to do that." (I had no idea how far it was from Fort Worth to Lubbock—talk about quality time, we had plenty of it.)

All across west Texas, we talked about what we expected to find in Lubbock. We talked about Derek's own history and the possibilities of his future. We saw the oil wells, barbed wire fences, railroad tracks, and tumbleweed. But mainly, we talked.

When we arrived at Lubbock, we went to the chamber of commerce and received four pages of information on Buddy Holly. We went to the house where Buddy Holly was born. (The house was actually gone, but we took a picture of the lot where Buddy Holly's house used to stand.) We drove to the radio station where Buddy Holly played his first record. They actually invited us inside and showed us the turntable on which his first record was played. We went to the house where Buddy Holly lived when he cut his first record. I took a picture of Derek in the front yard. The home owner came outside to greet us. We told her what we were doing and she said, "It's all right. They do it all the time." We went to the club where Buddy Holly played his first gig. (It is now a used car lot, but the rusty sign still hangs outside—"Cotton Club.") We went to the high school that Buddy Holly attended, and I took a picture of Derek leaning against the cream-colored brick building. We went to the little Baptist church where Buddy Holly was married and where his funeral was conducted. The youth director's father had been the youth director when Buddy Holly was living. Now the younger youth director told us all about the wedding, all about the funeral.

Then we drove to Buddy Holly's grave at the edge of town. We saw the marble stone and the bronze guitar. I walked away to give Derek some private time—then we slowly walked to the car and drove away. With Lubbock in our rearview mirror, we discussed Buddy Holly: What would have happened if Buddy had not been killed in the plane crash at such an early age? What were Buddy's religious beliefs? Since some people die young, what are the important things about life? We talked and talked and talked, all the way back to Fort Worth. That was a quality-time experience that neither of us has ever forgotten.

Imagine our surprise some years later when we were on another quality-time experience in London to discover the musical "Buddy." All the actors were British, speaking with Texas accents. It was fabulous! Then I remember a little later when Derek got into Bruce Springsteen. I won't bore you with the details, but we went to Freehold, New Jersey, and explored Springsteen's roots.

Create an Environment for Quality Time

Seeking to tap into Derek's interests, I planned a trip for us every year during his teenage years. I highly recommend it as a means for creating an environment for quality time. Even now Derek often looks back and reminisces about our quality-time trips together. We are forever bonded by those memory-building quality-time experiences.

I would encourage you to think of creating a quality-time experience with your teenager. It need not be as expensive or extensive as London, Lubbock, or Freehold. It can be as brief and inexpensive as traveling to a town thirty miles away to experience something your teenager is interested in together. Planned activities provide an opportunity to speak the love language of quality time. Even if your teen's primary love language is not quality time, such activities will let you know your teen better, create meaningful and lasting memories, and let your teen know you love him.

"My teenager won't talk"

One common complaint among parents is that when their child becomes a teenager, they stop talking. "My teenager won't talk. So why even try to have a quality conversation?" It is true that adolescents have a greater need for privacy than younger children. Having thoughts and feelings of their own that differ from those of parents is a part of becoming independent. There are times when teenagers don't want to talk about it because they want to work it out for themselves. On those occasions, parents are unwise to pressure the teen to talk. What we do need to do is to let the teen know that we are available if they want to talk.

Sometimes, though, teenagers do not want to talk with parents because when they have tried to talk, it ended in the teenager feeling put down or rejected. As parents, we must listen to what we say and how we say it. If your teenager comes home discouraged from a failure at school, begins to share about it with you, and you say, "What did you do wrong this time?" the conversation is over, and the teenager walks away feeling misunderstood.

Sometimes parents offer empty reassurances. "By this time next week, you won't even remember what happened today." At other times we are often too quick to give advice. "Moping around won't help. Why don't you go jogging or something?"

These are the kinds of responses that close the flow of communication. Such statements communicate a "know-it-all" attitude. They express no empathy for what the teenager is feeling at the moment. Some teenagers don't talk because they have learned over time that these are the kinds of responses they will receive. So why bother?

As parents, we can help open the door of communication if we are sensitive to the teenager's moods. "Looks like you had a hard day today. Want to talk about it?" is an invitation that many teens will accept. "You look excited tonight. Did something good happen today?" makes it easy for the teenage daughter to talk. Sympathetic listening (which we discussed above) and nonthreatening questions will create a climate that makes it easier for your teenager to talk. Remember, your teenager has the right to keep her thoughts and feelings to herself. Sometimes that will be her choice. Attempting to make her talk on these occasions is denying her individuality and independence from you. Let her know that you are available to talk if she wants to.

Sometimes teenagers are willing to talk but not at the times the parents prefer. Sometimes teenagers want to talk at their own convenience. This is often late at night and in the privacy of his or her room, or in the kitchen after everyone else has gone to bed. Thoughtful parents will take advantage of these opportunities when they arise. Two extra hours of sleep will make little difference in the parent's overall well-being, but two hours of quality time with the teenager may make the difference between the teenager going to bed with a sense of love rather than loneliness and rejection.

"My teenager doesn't want to spend time with me"

Recognize His Need for Friends

Another complaint parents voice when trying to maintain quality time is, "My teenager doesn't want to spend time with me." Of course, during the teenage years your son or daughter will develop deep friendships with those outside the family. Sociologists refer to this as the teenager's peer group. Dr. Eastwood Atwater defines the peer group as "people who regard one another as equals because of their age, grade, or particular status."[3] Dr. Atwater also indicates that peer groups play four primary roles in the teenager's life. These are:

1. The group helps the teen transition to adulthood by providing a social-emotional support group.

2. The peer group provides standards that the teenager can use to judge their own behavior and experiences.

3. It provides opportunities for developing interpersonal relationships and developing social skills.

4. It provides a context in which the teenager can develop his/her sense of self-identity.[4]

Hanging out with friends after church, school, or other activities, going to movies or the mall, spending the night at each other's houses, and talking on the telephone or texting are all activities that automatically increase when a child becomes a teenager. "Adolescents' newfound peer groups help to satisfy their need for companionship and fun, along with emotional support, understanding, and intimacy," notes counselor Gary Smalley. "They still need these things from their families and other adults as well, but it's vital in their development to receive these things from friends."[5]

Parents often misinterpret the adolescent's heightened interest in friends as disinterest in family. They assume that a fifteen-year-old would not be interested in going hunting with Dad or shopping with Mom or on a family picnic. However, research shows that most teenagers would like to spend more, not less, time with their parents than they currently spend.[6]

Consult Your Teen When Planning

A part of the problem is that parents sometimes plan activities without bringing the teenager in on the planning. Consequently, the teen has something exciting planned with their peer group and does not want to go with the parents. The parents interpret this as rejection or lack of desire to be with the family. However, if the parents would have recognized the teenager as a person (someone with independence and self-identity) and consulted with the teenager at the planning stage, the teenager may have been very interested in accompanying the family. It is when we treat our teenagers as children and make plans *for* them rather than treating them as emerging independent persons that we get the impression that they don't wish to be with the family.

Seventeen-year-old Brandon said, "My parents tell me that they are hurt because I don't want to go with them when they plan trips for us. The problem is they don't ever consult my schedule. They make plans and announce them to me on the day before we are supposed to leave. I have things already planned with my friends, and my parents get upset because I don't want to break those plans and go with them."

Consider Your Teenager's Interests

Another reason teenagers are sometimes reluctant to respond to parents' planned activities is that parents fail to take into account the teenager's interests. What parent has not been through the following routine?

Mom says: "We're going down to see Uncle Bob and Aunt Clara on Saturday, and we would like for you to go with us."

The teen replies: "I don't want to go."

Mom: "Why?"

Teen: "It's boring down there. There's nothing to do."

Mom: "You could spend time with your cousin. You enjoy being with each other."

Teen: "Mom, he's a kid. I'm a teenager now. It's not the same."

If parents are in touch with the teenager's interests, with a little thought they can plan into such a trip some activity that would be of interest to the teenager and make the trip more appealing. I'm not saying that teenagers should never be forced to accompany the family on a visit to relatives. I am suggesting that if such a trip is forced upon the teenager, you cannot expect it to be a quality-time experience for the two of you. It is far better to work with the teenager's interests and schedule, planning activities together that will be meaningful for both of you.

What They Say

Let me repeat what I said at the beginning of this chapter: This love language, quality time, is much more difficult to speak than words of affirmation or physical touch. But quality time is one of the five love languages. For some teenagers, it is their primary love language. Without quality time with their parents, these teenagers will not feel loved even though the parents may be speaking other love languages. It is essential for these teenagers that parents make time to give the teenager focused attention. Listen to the following teens for whom quality time is their primary love language.

Marissa, age fourteen, and a would-be fisherman: "I love it when my dad takes me with when he goes fishing. To be honest with you, I really don't like those smelly things. But I like being with Dad. We talk about all kinds of things, and I really love getting up early. It's the best time I have with him."

Kyle, age sixteen, and the proud owner of his first driver's license: "Now that I can drive, I like going places without my parents. But I also like doing things with them. I really like it when Dad and I can do things together. Some of my friends don't have fathers. I think I'm really fortunate."

Monica, age fourteen, lives with her mother and has little contact with her father: "What I like about Mom is that we can talk about everything. We don't keep secrets. I feel really close to Mom. She has helped me with a lot of problems. I know I can always tell her what's bothering me and she will help."

Jennifer, age eighteen, is getting ready to go to college in the fall: "I think the thing I'm going to miss most when I go to school is my talks with Mom and Dad. Sometimes they are late at night and long, but I know they are always there for me. I won't have that at college. I know we can talk on the phone, but it won't be quite the same."

If your teenager's love language is

QUALITY TIME

The biggest commitment in showing love to a teenager desiring quality time is a commitment to change your personal schedule. Sometimes talking together in the car after school or practice to discuss the day is all that is needed, but here are several more creative ideas for your times together.

▸ *Ask very specific questions about your teenager's day that require more than a "yes" or "no" answer.*

▸ *Stop what you are doing to make eye contact with your teenager as they tell you something important.*

▸ *Give your teenager the family video camera and have them record special events. Then watch the video together to see what memories they captured.*

▸ *Have your teenager tell you of places they would like to go and why. Then surprise them occasionally by letting them choose one or arranging it for them ahead of time.*

▸ *Turn off your television show to watch your teenager's favorite show with them.*

▸ *If your teenager is driving, take a road trip together to a location of their choosing.*

▸ *Cook something together for a snack—such as cookies or brownies.*

▸ *Find silly things to laugh about and laugh about them a lot.*

▸ *Make a snack for yourself when you make one for your teenager. Then talk about their day together as you eat.*

▸ If you have more than one child, arrange for care of the others and take your teenager out for a quick breakfast before school or for a shake after school.

▸ Go a few minutes early to pick up your teenager from hockey practice or Student Council. Stay late talking together about his involvement and get to know others involved in the group or on the team, such as teammates, coaches, or teachers. Tell the coach or teacher you appreciate his hard work.

▸ If your family is musically talented, sing or play instruments together at home instead of watching television. Even better, choose a specific time each week and make it a tradition.

▸ Keep your scheduled times with your teenager on your Blackberry and make those dates high priority.

▸ Surprise your teenager with tickets or a trip to a special place. A camping trip, basketball game, or trip to the mall can build lifelong memories. Add pictures of the event to further strengthen this surprise.

▸ If possible, take your teenager to your workplace one day. Introduce your teenager to your coworkers, include them in your meetings, and talk about what it's like to serve in your particular company.

▸ Create "traditions" with your teenager, such as eating ice cream at the same store each time or walking together at a particular park.

▸ Choose one or two board games or card games that you regularly play together.

▸ Focus family vacations to include significant time being together versus a trip focused on divided parent and teenager activities.

▸ Occasionally take family walks or bike rides together. Seek opportunities to spend time together that also include exercise.

▸ *Share more meals together as a family at the table. Make dinnertime a special occasion with lots of pleasant talk about the day. Family prayer can also strengthen this practice.*

▸ *Don't give up "tucking in" your teenager at night. You may no longer read bedtime stories, but you can still talk about the day or pray together.*

▸ *Spend time doing homework together. This both improves their grades and creates additional quality time (you might also learn something new).*

▸ *Plant something together. For those with outdoor oriented teenagers, time together in a flower garden, planting summer vegetables, or landscaping the yard can create lifelong positive memories.*

▸ *Make photo albums or a scrapbook together—either in a book or on your computer. Talk together about the memories you shared in the process.*

CHAPTER 6

LOVE LANGUAGE #4:

Acts of
Service

"I think the thing that made me feel most loved was the way my parents worked so hard to help me with everything." Mark had just started his first full-time job and was contemplating getting married soon. As he talked about his teenage years, he began recalling specifics. "I remember all the meals Mom made even though she worked outside the home, and the time Dad helped me with the old clunker we bought together when I was sixteen. The little things, the big things—they did so much to help me."

Now twenty-four, Mark continued to reminisce. "I realize it now more than I did then. But even at the time, I knew that they were working hard to help me and I always appreciated it. I hope I can do the same for my children someday."

Mark was describing his parents who adeptly spoke the love language *acts of service*.

Parenting is a service-oriented vocation. The day you decided to have a child, you enrolled for long-term service. By the time your child becomes a teenager, you have been speaking this language for thirteen years. If you want to feel really good about yourself, take a few minutes and calculate the number of diapers you changed, meals you prepared, clothes you washed, folded and/or ironed, Band-Aids you applied, toys you repaired, sheets you tucked, hair you washed and combed, etc. Please don't show this list to your teenager. But in the privacy of your bedroom read it aloud, especially on the days when you are feeling like a parental failure. There is the solid, irrefutable evidence that you have loved this child.

However, your child has now become a teenager, and you must learn some new dialects if you are to effectively speak the love language known as acts of service. There are no more diapers but there are plenty of buttons to replace, dresses to mend, meals to prepare, bicycle tires to replace, cars to tinker with, shirts to wash and iron, uniforms to bleach, personal taxis to drive (at least until they are sixteen in most states), etc.

The Powerful Language of Service

All of this hard work takes on a dimension of nobility when you understand that such acts of service are powerful expressions of emotional love to your teenager. Some parents have slipped into performing these routine acts of service out of a sense of parental duty. They are blinded by the trees and cannot see the forest. My hope for these parents is that the following pages will blow away the clouds of the mundane and allow the sunshine of genuine love to create a brighter vision for parenting teens.

History is replete with examples of men and women who learned how to speak the love language known as acts of service. Who does not know of Mother Teresa? Her name is synonymous with acts of service. In Africa, there was Albert Schweitzer, and in India, Mohandas Gandhi. Most people who have studied the life of Jesus of Nazareth, the first-century founder of the Christian faith, agree that His life can be summarized by His simple act of washing the feet of His disciples. He Himself said, I "did not come to be served, but to serve, and to give [my] life as a ransom for many."[1] He instructed His followers, "Whoever wants to become great among you must be your servant."[2]

True greatness is expressed in serving. Acts of service freely given from parents to teenagers are true expressions of emotional love.

Service Freely Given

Because service to a child is constant for so many years and takes place in and around so many other obligations, parents can forget that the daily and mundane acts they perform are expressions of love with long-term effects.

Loving service is not slavery. Slavery is imposed from the outside and is done with reluctance. Loving service is an internally motivated desire to give one's energy to others. Loving service is a gift, not a necessity, and is done freely, not under coercion. When parents serve their teenagers with a spirit of resentment and bitterness, the teens' physical needs may be met but their emotional development will be greatly hampered.

Because service is a daily occurrence, even the best parents need to stop for an attitude-check now and then to be sure that their acts of service are communicating love. I remember Cameron telling me, "My dad will help with my homework if I insist. But he makes me feel guilty and undeserving. I usually don't ask for his help." Those acts of service by Dad don't communicate love. Mothers can also communicate little love in their service. "I wish Mom would help me on my school projects but I feel like she is too busy," said Julia, now in her first year of high school. "When I do ask her, I feel like she is only doing it to get me off her back." If parental acts of service are to be heard as love in the soul of the teenager, they must be freely given.

Manipulation Is Not Love

It is possible to use acts of service as a means of manipulating your teenager. "I will drive you to the mall to meet your friends if you will clean up your room." This is an effort to strike a deal with the teenager, to make a contract: "I will…if you will…." I'm not suggesting that we should never seek to make contracts with our teens, but we must never view this as an expression of emotional love. Your driving the teen to the mall is payment for the services rendered; namely, cleaning the room. It is a bartering system to get the teenager to do something you find desirable—it's not an expression of love.

You are practicing manipulation if your acts of service are always tied to the teen's doing something you desire. Manipulation is never an expression of love. Love cannot be earned. It is a gift freely expressed. We are to love our teenagers unconditionally. Perhaps they are not pleasing us in all their behavior. We can still speak the love language acts of service. In fact, the teenager will feel more deeply loved when she knows that your love is unconditional.

That system of "trying to change your teen's behavior by promising to do something you know she wants you to do" is called *behavior modification*. It has to do with rewarding the teen for what the parent considers good behavior by doing something the teen desires or withholding something when the teen fails to comply with the parent's wishes. This method of parenting was popular during the 1970s but, in my opinion, is not the healthiest way to parent children and is certainly not the best way to relate to teenagers.

I'm not saying that behavior modification should never be used as a parenting style. It may be helpful particularly in breaking ingrained patterns that the parent considers to be irresponsible behavior. Sometimes the reward offered would be enough to motivate a teenager to change behavior that she would not normally be motivated to change. Unfortunately, this behavior change is not always permanent unless you continue to give rewards. (More about this in chapter 12 when we talk about love and responsibility.)

On the other hand, parents must also be warned that teenagers will sometimes try to manipulate you through your acts of service. If there is something they want you to do for them, they may offer to do something that they know you have requested in the past. Sixteen-year-old Bradley said, "If I want Mom to do something for me, all I have to do is offer to clean my room. She'll do anything I want." Bradley has learned to manipulate his mother. If the mother feels that what Bradley is asking is for his good, she may agree to his contract. But parents should never agree to do something that they believe is unwise simply because the teen is agreeing to do something they desire.

Some teenagers are master manipulators. "If you love me, you ..." is the ultimate statement of manipulation for the teenager. The teen is using the parent's desire to be a good parent as a tool to get parental approval of his desires. The best parental response is "I love you too much to do something I believe is detrimental to you no matter how much you want it." Manipulation has nothing to do with love and everything to do with control. It is not a good approach for parent-teen relationships.

Reciprocal Love

Modeling and Guiding

Conscientious parents of teenagers have two main desires: to love and to be loved. We want our teens to feel our love in order to keep their love tanks full, but we also want them to learn how to love others. Parents sometimes ask, "If I continue with acts of service to my teenager, how will he learn to do things for himself and how will he learn to serve others?" The answer to that question is found in *modeling* and *guiding*. We model unconditional love when we do things for the teenager that we know they would like for us to do so long as we believe these actions are good for the teenager. However, we must choose these acts of service wisely. Otherwise, we create a dependent teenager who takes but never learns to give. For example, cooking a meal is an act of service, but teaching a teenager how to cook a meal is an even greater act of service. It is certainly easier to prepare the meal yourself than it is to teach a teenager to prepare the meal. But which is the greater act of love?

A rule of thumb is that you do acts of service for your teenagers that they cannot do for themselves. When they are young, you wash the clothes for them; when they are teenagers, you teach them how to wash the clothes. Parents who don't learn this distinction may actually cripple the teens' maturity in the name of love. This does not mean that you would never do the laundry for them. It does mean that you will not always do the laundry. Instead, you will go beyond modeling to guiding your teen toward independent actions and maturity.

Guiding the Right Way

I think it is helpful for parents to verbally explain to teenagers what they are doing. Mom says to Patrick, age thirteen, "Now that you are a teenager, I want to share some personal thoughts with you. When you were little, I did lots of things for you because I loved you very much. I fixed all of your meals, I did your laundry, I cleaned up your room, etc. I could go on doing all of these things for you until you graduated from high school, but that would not be the loving thing to do. Because I still love you very much, I am going to teach you to do these things for yourself. I don't want you to finish high school and leave home and not have the skills to make it on your own.

"I've made a list of the things I want to teach you, Patrick. I want to show it to you and give you the opportunity to add to the list the things you would like to learn. I also want you to choose the order in which you would like to learn them. I will not push you beyond your limits but as you are ready, I want to teach you these skills."

Patrick's mother has explained her plan for loving him by acts of service. And Patrick probably will respond positively to the plan because Mom has let him be a part of choosing the things he would like to learn and the order in which he would like to learn them. Patrick and his father could also make a similar list of things his father would like to teach him and things he would like to learn from his father.

The teenager who has parents who will take this approach is more fortunate than he probably knows. He will not only feel loved by the parents, but will grow up to be a responsible adult who knows not only how to take care of himself, but also how to love others by acts of service.

In this approach, parents are not only speaking the love language acts of service, they are also guiding the teenager in learning the necessary skills to serve others effectively. This guidance will require both teaching (instruction through words) and training (learning by doing). Parents who follow this approach will give verbal instructions regarding a particular skill. They will demonstrate how it is done, and then they will give the teenager hands-on experience in doing it himself.

For example, the father who wants to teach his son to wash the family car and later perhaps his own car begins with some verbal instructions. "One of the things you will want to always remember is to hose the car first in order to remove sand particles so that the car is not scratched as you soap it. Once you've done this, you will want to begin with the top of the car and work your way to the hood, trunk, and sides of the car, washing only one portion at a time and rinsing it quickly so that the soap does not dry and streak the car." Then the father demonstrates what he has just said, allowing the teenager to help with the process. Perhaps they will wash the car together for a couple of weekends. Then the father allows the son to wash the car by himself. After that, they may wash the car together, the father may wash it alone, or the son may wash it alone, depending on their desires. When the son washes the car alone, the father expresses praise and appreciation. The teenager has learned not only how to wash the car but how to love the father.

Helping Your Teen's Sense of Identity and Independence

In today's hurried society, some parents have failed to teach their teenagers the fundamental skills of life. Consequently, many of these teenagers later find themselves married only to discover that neither they nor their spouse know how to scrub a bathtub, vacuum floors, cook meals, or do laundry. They are totally inept in the basic skills of serving each other. Their parents failed to teach them how to speak the love language of acts of service.

It will be obvious that making the shift from doing things for the child to teaching the teenager how to do things for himself will require much time and energy on the part of the parent. However, few things are more important to the teen's emotional and social well-being. If the teen learns to do acts of service, he will feel good about himself; thus, his self-identity will be enhanced. As the teen serves people outside the family, he will receive positive feedback. Everyone likes the person who serves others. Thus, the teen's self-identity will be further enhanced.

Furthermore, in learning such skills, the teen is able to maintain life on his own and he will then have a greater sense of independence. Parents are making a powerful contribution to the teen's developmental maturity. Parents who fail to do this will have teenagers who become bored with life, have little sense of accomplishment, have low self-esteem, and will struggle in social relationships. I cannot overemphasize how important it is for parents of teenagers to love their teenager enough to teach them the skills of serving others. When parents fail to do this, teenagers will inevitably feel cheated by their parents. Love feeds children when they are little but teaches them to feed themselves when they are teenagers.

Focusing on Acts of Service

For some teenagers, *acts of service* is their primary love language. When parents express love by acts of service, the teenager's love tank is filled quickly. Scott was one such teenager. Upon his sixteenth birthday, his parents had bought him a car, which in their words "was the worst thing we could have done." Six months later, he was in my office because his parents threatened to take away his car if he didn't come (a perfect example of manipulation, but probably the only way Scott would have come to see me). Scott's parents had seen me the week before and shared their concerns. Since getting the car, Scott had been totally irresponsible. He had already received two traffic tickets for speeding and had been cited in one "fender bender" accident.

His parents indicated that Scott's attitude was "very belligerent" toward them. "Now that he has a car, he doesn't want to spend any time at home," his father said. "He works at a fast-food restaurant two hours each afternoon in order to pay for his gas. Then he wants to spend the rest of the afternoon and evening with his friends. He eats at the restaurant so he doesn't feel the need to come home for dinner. We have threatened to take the car away, but we don't know if that is what we should do.

"Actually, we don't know what to do. That's why we came to see you." Both of Scott's parents were highly motivated individuals. They both had good careers, and Scott was their only child.

In my conversations with Scott over the next few weeks, I discovered that he had little respect for his parents. "They are both into their careers," he said. "They don't really care about me." I discovered that his parents typically did not arrive home from work until 6 or 6:30 p.m. Before Scott had his car and part-time job, he would normally arrive home from school about 3:30, do his homework, talk on the phone with his friends, and use the computer. When his parents arrived, they had dinner together. "Most of the time, they picked up food on the way home. Mom doesn't like to cook, and Dad doesn't know how. After dinner, they checked to make sure I had finished my homework. Then Dad worked on his business stuff and watched television. Mom did some reading and made some phone calls.

"I usually went to my room and talked with my friends on the phone," Scott continued. "It was boring. There was nothing for me to do."

In further conversations with Scott, I learned that on numerous occasions, he would ask his parents to help him with various projects, but in his opinion "they never had time." "When I was thirteen," he said, "I asked my dad to teach me how to water-ski, but he told me it was too dangerous and I was too young. When I wanted to learn to play the guitar, he said I didn't have any musical ability and it would be a waste of money. I even asked Mom to teach me how to cook. She said she would but she never did."

It was obvious to me that Scott felt cheated by his parents. They had fed him, housed him, and clothed him, but they had not spoken to his inner need for emotional love. It appeared to me that acts of service was his primary love language, but that his parents had never learned how to speak his dialect. They had served him by providing basic physical needs, but they had not been sensitive to his interests and thus had made little effort to foster the required skills in developing these interests. Consequently, Scott felt rejected and unloved. His behavior was simply a reflection of these emotions.

I wish I could say that things turned around quickly for Scott and his parents. But in reality, things got worse before they got better. I shared my observations with Scott's parents, and I think they understood and made some sincere efforts to try to connect with Scott. But he was not very responsive. Most of their efforts were rebuffed. His attitude seemed to be that what they were doing was too late and too little.

An entire year passed before significant change took place. I visited Scott in the hospital after an automobile accident in which he suffered a broken hip, a broken leg, and a crushed ankle. He had just begun his senior year of high school; now, during his time of recuperation, Scott finally reconnected emotionally with his parents. They apologized for having failed to meet his needs in the earlier years, and Scott admitted that he had shut them out of his life because he felt so rejected by them.

With this emotional reconnection, things improved significantly over the next year. While Scott was in a cast, his parents had ample opportunities to express love by acts of service but more importantly, they discovered Scott's present interests and took steps to help him develop these interests. Scott's senior year in high school was, as he put it, "the worst and best year of my life." Scott experienced great physical pain, but he also rediscovered genuine emotional closeness with his parents. He lived at home the next two years and attended a local college, which also provided numerous opportunities for his parents to express acts of service.

Both of his parents became very involved in helping him with school projects. He and his father spent many weekends on the lake. Scott was no longer interested in water-skiing, but he did learn to drive his father's boat and he became proficient on a Jet Ski. With college, Scott's interests expanded, and his parents stayed in touch with those interests and took every opportunity to serve him by helping him explore his interests. Scott is now in his thirties, married, and is speaking acts of service to his own son.

Scott's parents were very sincere—as are most parents. They loved their son incredibly, but they had failed to discover and speak his primary love language. When they finally discovered it and tried to speak it, Scott did not respond immediately. This is typical when a teenager has felt alone and rejected for a period of time. However, parents must not give up. If they are consistent in making attempts to speak the teenager's primary love language, that love will eventually pierce the emotional pain of a teenager and they can reconnect emotionally.

What They Say

This reconnection will be the turning point in the parent/teenager relationship if it is followed by consistent efforts to speak the teen's primary love language. Listen to the following teenagers whose primary love language is acts of service.

Gray, age thirteen, lives with his mother and younger sister. His father left when Gray was seven. "I know my mom loves me because she washes my messy clothes, fixes supper every night, and helps me with my homework even when I don't ask her. She works hard as a nurse, so we can have food and clothes. I think my dad loves me but he doesn't do much to help."

Krystal, age fourteen, is the oldest of four children. "I know my folks love me because they do so many things for me. Mom takes me to cheerleader practice and to all the games. Daddy helps me with my homework, especially my math, which I hate."

Todd, age seventeen, has his own lawn service in the summer and has bought his first car. "I've got the greatest dad in the world," he said. "He taught me how to mow grass, start a business, and make money so I could buy a car. Last week, he showed me how to change the spark plugs."

Kristin is thirteen. "I know my mom loves me because she takes time to teach me everything. Last week, she got me started on knitting. I'm going to make my own Christmas presents this year."

If your teenager's love language is

ACTS OF SERVICE

While this chapter discusses the need to train your teenager to grow and to serve others, there are many times when a simple act of service to your teenager provides significant impact. Here are several that express love without ignoring your teenager's need for responsibility.

▸ *Acknowledge your teenager's uniqueness by shopping together for new paint colors for their room and helping them paint it.*

▸ *Help your teenager practice for their sports team, such as pitch and catch for baseball, or help rebounding free throws for teenagers participating in basketball.*

▸ *Assist your teenager on a tough homework assignment.*

▸ *Make a favorite snack when your teenager is having a difficult day.*

▸ *Help your teenager choose an outfit for school or a special occasion (especially for mothers and teenage daughters).*

▸ *Occasionally wake up a half hour earlier to make a special surprise breakfast for your teenager.*

▸ *Begin teaching your teenager the importance of serving others through regular involvement in a local community group or church ministry. For the independent teenager, allow them to research different opportunities and select the place of service.*

▸ *When running late for school or other meeting, help your teenager quickly finish what needs to be done so they can arrive on time.*

▸ *During a time when your teenager is sick, go the extra step by setting up their favorite movie or making their favorite soup.*

▸ Connect your teenager with one of your friends or family members who can help them in an area of interest such as dance lessons, soccer, or piano playing.

▸ Choose one special area in which you determine to always serve your teenager above and beyond normal expectations. Examples could include making sure school lunch is always made or making a favorite dessert on a regular basis.

▸ Start a "birthday dinner" tradition where you make your teenager any meal they want on their birthday.

▸ Help your teenager create flash cards for their upcoming test or quiz. Work together with your teenager until they feel confident with the material.

▸ If your teenager calls you at work and is in a crisis, sacrifice more time than usual to listen to their situation.

CHAPTER 7

LOVE LANGUAGE #5:
Gifts

I had an afternoon break during one marriage seminar held in a memorable setting—the NATO Air Base in Geilenkirchen, Germany. It was a minimum two-year assignment for most of the troops, so spouses and families lived on the base. During this afternoon, I spotted thirteen-year-old Alex sitting at a picnic table doing his homework. He looked like a typical American teenager: crew cut, blue jeans, and a well-worn, faded green sweatshirt. I had the feeling he wouldn't mind being disturbed, so I introduced myself and engaged him in conversation.

After some small talk, I commented on the St. Christopher medallion that was hanging on the chain around Alex's neck. "My dad gave that to me for my thirteenth birthday in March," he said. "Dad said that when he had to be away on duty, he wanted it to remind me of him. I wear it all the time."

"Who was St. Christopher?" I inquired.

"I'm not sure," he said. "Some saint in the church who did a lot of good."

I could tell that for Alex, the medallion had little religious significance.

But on the emotional level, its worth was priceless. It was a constant reminder of his father's love. I had the sense that if thirty years from now I happen to encounter Alex again, he will still be wearing that same St. Christopher medal around his neck.

What Makes a Gift a Gift?

Gifts are visible and tangible evidence of emotional love. It is important to understand the essential nature of a gift. The Greek word from which we get our English word "gift" is *charis*, which means grace or an undeserved gift. By its very nature, a gift is not something that the teenager deserves; it is given because the parent desires to share unconditional love with the teen. Some parents fail to realize this; they think they are giving gifts to their teenagers when in reality they are simply paying them for a service rendered. When that happens, they are not really speaking the love language called *gifts*.

For instance, Beverly told her fifteen-year-old daughter, Amanda, "If you go clean your room, as soon as dinner is over, we will go to the mall and I will buy you that dress you want." In reality, she was either trying to manipulate Amanda to do what she wanted, or she was bartering a deal with her: "If you will . . . then I will give you a dress." Or perhaps she was sick and tired of Amanda's harassment about the dress, and this was her way of caving in to the harassment while trying to get a little work out of Amanda in the process. At any rate, the dress will *not* be a gift. It will be payment for a clean bedroom. Beverly set it up that way. She may think she is expressing love to Amanda by giving her a dress, but Amanda will accept the dress as something she deserves—not as a gift.

For some parents, almost all of what they call "gifts" are in fact efforts at manipulating their teenager, bartering for something they desire, or payment for the teenager's work. The only time some teenagers receive true gifts is at Christmas and on birthdays. Other than that, the parents' gifts are not gifts at all. Please don't misunderstand me: I'm *not* suggesting that parents should never repay teenagers for services rendered. I am simply saying that these payments are not to be considered gifts. The teenager could probably work out a similar deal with some adult down the street. Even if the parent gives them a better deal than they could get down the street, it is still a deal and not a gift.

It might help you to ask, "What is the last genuine gift I gave to my teenager?" Once you have the gift in mind, ask yourself, "Did I require anything of my teenager before I gave her the gift?" If so, then mark it off, because it was not a genuine gift. Start over and try to find the last real gift you gave your teenager. Some parents will find it was last Christmas or the last birthday.

Teenagers are not opposed to this deal-making with their parents. In fact, many of them are happy to make deals. It has become their accustomed way of getting what they want. If they can't get it by verbally harassing the parent, then they will get it by "cutting a deal." This is the standard practice in many homes, but it has nothing to do with gift giving or speaking your teenager's primary love language.

The Gift and the Ceremony

Gift giving should be done with some measure of ceremony. Think back on a significant gift you have received in the past. What was the gift? Who gave it to you? How was it wrapped? How was it presented to you? Was the presentation of the gift accompanied by words, touches, or other expressions of love? Chances are the more effort the giver put into packaging and presentation, the more love you felt. The purpose of gift giving is not simply to get an object from one person's possession to another. The purpose is to express emotional love. We want the person to sense deeply, "I care about you, I think you are important, I love you." These emotional messages are enhanced when attention is given to the ceremony accompanying the passing of the gift.

Parents of teenagers will do well to remember this. When we diminish the ceremony, we diminish the emotional power of the gift. Johnny requests a pair of basketball shoes. Mom or Dad drives Johnny to the mall and buys the shoes. Johnny wears them as he leaves the store, and that's that. No ceremony at all. Many teenagers have become accustomed to this procedure. Such gifts communicate little emotional love. If all gifts are given in this manner, it creates an entitlement mentality in the teenager's mind: *I'm a teenager. My parents owe it to me to get me whatever I want.* There is little appreciation on the part of the teenager and the gift has little emotional meaning.

However, if the shoes are taken home, wrapped creatively, presented in the presence of other family members as an expression of love, and accompanied by words of affirmation and physical touch, then the gift suddenly becomes a strong vehicle of emotional love. If you have been a no-ceremony gift giver, let me suggest that you announce to your teenager that you have chosen to bring more celebration into the life of your family and that there will be a new way of giving gifts in the future. Your teenager may laugh or even be annoyed by your early efforts to change the pattern, but I can tell you he will soon come to view your gifts in a different light. And he will learn how to speak the love language of giving gifts, which will serve him well in adulthood.

Gifts and Materialism

Sincere parents often ask, "If I give too many gifts to my teenagers, won't I foster the spirit of materialism that is so prevalent in our culture?" Ours is a largely materialistic society—it doesn't take too much looking around to confirm this fact.

Adults and teenagers alike are busy collecting toys. If we have the latest, the best, and the most technologically advanced, then we are successful. While adults are collecting bigger and multiple houses, more expensive cars, more sophisticated appliances, and the latest notebook computers, teens are collecting faster cars, more powerful audio systems, designer clothes, more capable smartphones, and buying into the latest fad to prove that they are not like their parents. We are all marching to the beat of the same drummer. We are simply collecting different toys.

As parents, we are wise to ask, "Is this what I want to teach my teenager?" We must also ask, "Is this what I want to do with my own life? Is there something more to life than acquiring and playing with my toys?" Most adults believe there is something more, but many are not able to define for themselves or others what it is.

I believe the answer lies in two arenas. First, learning to enjoy the ordinary, and second, learning to share it with others. For thousands of years men and women lived without the "toys" made possible by the industrial and technological revolutions of the nineteenth and twentieth centuries. Without these toys, people enjoyed the ordinary things of life—eating, sleeping, working, music, art, and interacting with nature. Second, they shared this ordinary life with others. Not only was there a sense of connectedness within the extended family, but there was also a sense of community with neighbors. For many, this sense of connectedness also extended to God. God was seen as the Creator and Sustainer of all that existed and the source of moral law that regulated man's relationship with man.

Materialism in the Western world began when humans came to believe that by their own efforts they could accomplish utopia. Industrial and technological advances convinced humans that they no longer needed law and that moral laws were not divine but could be manipulated. Human reason replaced God, and the products of man's hand became his idols. Materialism, then, is the worship of these idols. The fundamental weakness of worshiping idols is that when you most need them, they are not there. When human relationships are fractured by man's inhumanity to man, when drugs and sexually transmitted diseases destroy our teenagers, when divorce destroys our marriages, and disease destroys our bodies—then the toys we have gathered around us speak no word of comfort or meaning. Our idols have deserted us in our time of need.

As our nation grapples with challenging economic times, many adults in our society are concluding that materialism is a poor substitute for the simple fundamentals of enjoying the ordinary aspects of daily life and sharing these joys with others. Many are looking again to the spiritual rather than the material to answer the deep longings of the human heart for ultimate meaning in life. If you agree with these conclusions, then certainly you would be concerned about fostering the spirit of materialism in your teenager by the overuse or misuse of gifts. This does not mean that we can or should "escape" the world of machines and technology. It does mean that the gifts we choose to give, and the manner in which we give these gifts, will be influenced by our commitment to these deeper realities.

Let me suggest two specific areas where I believe parents must take careful consideration in speaking the love language of gifts.

Giving Money

The Value of Cash

In Western society teenagers are major consumers; they are major players in a multibillion-dollar market. Advertisers direct huge chunks of their marketing budgets toward teenagers. Where do teenagers get all this money? By and large, the money comes from their parents. One might think that if giving gifts is one of the primary love languages, and if parents are giving all this money to their teenagers, then the teenager's love tank should be full. Well, probably not.

The problem with this reasoning is twofold. First, most of that money is not given as a gift—it is structured into the family's method of operation and has simply come to be expected by the teenager. Second, because the teenager has not worked to secure the money, the teen places little sense of value on the money. Thus, receiving it from parents does not communicate love at a deep emotional level. So how are parents to address the issue of giving money to their teenagers?

Two Approaches to Giving Money

I believe we approach the problem in two ways. One, we must encourage the teenager to work for money. This is the only way the teen will come to have any sense of the value of money. If the teen works for the $75 she is about to spend on this piece of designer clothing, she has some sense of the effort that goes into earning it. It forces the teen to ask, "Is this object worth the effort?" This is how your teen can then become a discerning consumer. If the teenager must work for money, it also forces him to make choices between material objects. If he cannot have everything, then he must make some discerning judgment about what is most desired. This also, obviously, prepares your teen for the real world of adult living.

If the parent is concerned that after-school work will keep the teenager from enjoying sports, drama, music lessons, dance, gymnastics, or other pursuits, then perhaps the parent can consider paying the teenager for her effort in these venues at the same pay scale of the local fast-food restaurant. All of these pursuits require fully as much diligent effort as the part-time after-school job. Paying a teenager for these efforts has much the same benefits as a part-time job. The point here is that unlimited money ought not be given by the parent, nor expected by the teenager, if we want our teenagers to avoid the dangers of materialism.

The second approach is that when the parent chooses to give money, they give it for specific purposes, such as to pay for a sports camp or church camp, to attend a concert, or to pay for a class in photography, art, and so forth. Then they can present it as a gift, following the guidelines mentioned above; namely, given unconditionally, given with ceremony, accompanied by affirming words, physical touch, and as often as possible, done in the presence of other family members.

Since the teenager has worked, and now knows something about the real value of money, the gift of money can be appreciated on an emotional level. The teenager has some idea of how long it takes to make the money the parent is now giving her as a gift. Thus, there can be genuine appreciation on an emotional level.

When parents freely dish out money—$20 here, $40 there, $100 here—without following these guidelines of effective gift giving, their gifts of money may not be appreciated and they will more than likely fail to meet the teenager's emotional need for love. I am convinced that most parents of teenagers have never learned how to make the gift of money an effective vehicle of emotional love. I believe the suggestions given above will help parents do this far more effectively.

Giving Gifts

Consider Your Teen's Welfare

When it comes to giving gifts other than money, I believe the parent must do so with due consideration. Remember, the purpose of a gift is to emotionally communicate *I love you* to the teenager. Therefore, the parent must ask, "Am I convinced that this gift is for the well-being of my teenager?" If the answer is "no," then the parent cannot conscientiously give that gift to the teenager. Obviously this would rule out giving, say, illegal drugs to our teenagers, but it may also rule out a number of more likely or conventional gifts.

Let's look at a specific and regularly occurring scenario: It has become commonplace in middle-class America for many affluent parents to give a car to their sixteen-year-old. I'm not suggesting that this is always bad for the teenager. What I am suggesting is that parents need to ask the question, "Is the gift of a car good for my teenager?"

There are many factors involved in answering that question. One is the level of maturity and responsibility of the teenager. Some teens are not emotionally ready for a car at age sixteen. Some teens have not demonstrated a sufficient level of responsibility in other areas that warrant the giving of a car.

Assuming the parent concludes that the car itself would be good for the teenager, the parent might then ask, "Is giving the car to my teenager the best way? Would it be better if I required her to work to pay for all or part of the car? Would this help to foster responsible use of the car more than if I simply gave it to her?" These are the kinds of questions that thoughtful parents seek to answer. There is not one pattern that is best for all parents and all teenagers. However, parents who do not give thought to these questions will likely make unwise decisions in whether they should or how they can give a car to their teenagers.

Similar questions arise when we talk about giving our teenager a college education. Is it simply to be expected that, if the parents can afford it, it is their responsibility to pay for the teenager's college education? Again the question needs to be: "What is the best thing for the teenager?" Parents want to do the loving thing—to look out for the interests of the teenager. Is it more loving to let the teenager pay for part of his college experience? If the parents choose to pay for all educational expenses, what can or should be expected of the teenager? Should we be thinking in terms of an unconditional gift or should we be thinking in terms of teaching the teenager responsibility? This may not be the time for an unconditional gift of $40,000 per year for the next four years. This may not be the time for speaking the love language of gifts, but rather a time for the teenager to learn to speak acts of service; or maybe there needs to be a combination of the two love languages. What is important is that we know what we are doing and why we are doing it.

If I choose to give the teenager an unconditional gift—an all expenses paid, first year of college no matter how they respond—then that's my choice. But perhaps I should limit that gift to one year while I observe the teenager's response to the educational process rather than giving her an unconditional gift of four years.

If, as a parent, I understand what I'm doing and why I'm doing it, I am less likely to be disappointed in the long run. If, however, we handle these issues of cars and college without thought, we set ourselves up for disappointment. How many parents have said later, "I gave him four years of college, no strings attached, and he has little appreciation for my gift." Chances are the parents violated the principles of conscientious thought in the giving of such gifts. The teenager sometimes reasons, "I didn't have to go to college. They said they wanted me to go to college. So I found it boring and partied. They are the ones who told me to do it. Why should they be upset?" With little appreciation for the effort parents expended to pay for college expenses, the teenager walks away not only unapprecia-tive, but now feeling rejected by the parents. His love tank is empty, and the parental gift is ineffective.

Consider Their Interests

Another critical factor in gift giving is the teenager herself: What are her interests? Think back to a gift you received from someone in the past, something for which you had little use and no desire. You realize that the giver may have spent considerable monies for the gift. You appreciated their thought, but the gift itself was meaningless. It is possible for us to give similar gifts to our teenagers. If we want our gifts to be emotionally effec-tive in communicating love to our teenagers, then we must consider our teenager's interests. Rather than buying something that strikes your own fancy, why not buy something that speaks right to your teenager?

This can be done in a very overt manner. Simply say to your teenager, "If I should decide to buy you a gift this month, would you make me a list of two or three things you would like to have? Be as specific as possible.

Give me brand names, colors, etc." Most teenagers will be happy to oblige. (Most wives also wish their husbands would ask this question periodically.) If the information your teen gives is ambiguous, there is nothing wrong with asking the teenager to accompany you to the mall and show you precisely what gift he or she would like to have if you should decide to give something. Go back later and purchase the gift and follow the guidelines of packaging and presentation discussed above. Why would you want to buy a CD that your teenager will never play, a shirt he will never wear, or a dress she will find hideous?

Private and Treasured Gifts

Not all gifts should be given in front of the family. The value of some gifts is enhanced by a private presentation. When my daughter Shelley was thirteen, I invited her to take a walk with me in the village of Old Salem (a restored Moravian village in our city). The walk was not unusual for us—we often took walks together through the village. But on this occasion, we sat by the small fishpond, and I presented her with a golden key on a gold chain. I gave her what I thought was a beautiful speech about how much I valued her and how happy I was with her accomplishments in life. I told her that the key was a key to her heart and body and that my desire was that she would keep herself pure and, someday, present the key to her husband.

To say the least, it was a tender moment for both of us. To her own chagrin, a few years later, she lost the golden key, but the memory of my presentation was hers forever. The physical gift was gone, but the symbolism behind the gift was carried in her heart and mind through the years. She now has a daughter of her own, Davy Grace, and I wouldn't be surprised if someday Davy receives a golden key from her father.

Not only are there private gifts, but there are also treasured gifts. Every family has some of these. They are not necessarily gifts of great monetary value, but they are treasures because of what they mean to the family. The treasure may be a ring, necklace, knife, book, pen, Bible, or anything else that has special significance to the parent. These may have been items that have been passed down from former generations, or they may simply be items that are purchased for the explicit purpose of giving them to the teenager. They are the kind of gifts to which we attach emotional value.

Such gifts may be given in private or in the presence of other family members. But they should definitely be given with ceremony, including speeches about the significance and symbolism of the gift. They may also be accompanied by warm verbal and physical expressions of affection for the teenager.

These treasured gifts become symbols of love in the heart of the teenager for years to come. When the teenager is going through periods of emotional upheaval, these gifts sit in their rooms as reminders of the genuine love of parents. Often when the teenager looks at the treasure, the affirming words of parents come back. Every teenager needs a few of these treasured gifts.

Counterfeit Gifts

There is one kind of gift that no teenager needs. They are what I call counterfeit gifts. These are gifts designed to take the place of true love. They are given by busy and sometimes absentee parents—parents who are so caught up in the busyness of life that they have little time for speaking the love language of quality time, acts of service, words of affirmation, or physical touch, so they try to make up for this deficit by giving the teenager gifts—sometimes expensive gifts.

One single mom said, "Every time my sixteen-year-old goes to visit her father, she comes home with a suitcase full of gifts. He is not willing to help me with her medical and dental bills, but he always has money for gifts. He seldom calls her on the phone and only spends two weeks in the summer with her. But somehow the gifts are supposed to make everything right." This kind of gift giving on the part of noncustodial parents has become commonplace. The teenager typically receives the gifts, expresses verbal appreciation, and goes home with an empty love tank. When gifts are given as a substitute for genuine love, the teenager sees them as the shallow counterfeit they are.

This phenomenon happens not only where parents are divorced, but also it often happens when both parents are living in the same house with the teenager. It occurs most often when both parents have demanding vocations. They are awash in money but bereft of time. The teenager fixes his own breakfast, goes off to school, returns, unlocks the door, walks into an empty house, and does what he wishes until his parents return home depleted of energy. The family eats a fast meal together, each goes off to their own computer, and tomorrow the process will be repeated. Counterfeit gifts are regularly given in this type of family situation. The money is laid down freely, gifts are quickly purchased, and the teenager has all that he desires—except the love of his parents. Such counterfeit gifts will never fill the love tank of the lonely teenager, nor will they ultimately remove the guilt of the uninvolved parent.

This is a good time for me to restate what I said at the beginning of our discussion of the five love languages. Teenagers need to receive love from parents in all five of these love languages. To speak only the primary love language of the teenager and ignore the other four is not the message of this book. What I am trying to say is that the primary love language of the teenager will speak more deeply and will more quickly fill the emotional love tank. But the primary language must be complemented by speaking the other four languages as well. Once the teenager is receiving a sufficient amount of love in his/her primary love language, then the other love languages become even more meaningful. On the other hand, if the parent ignores the primary love language of the teenager, the other four are not likely to fill the teenager's love tank.

If the primary love language of your teenager happens to be receiving gifts, then the principles of this chapter will be extremely important for you. In many ways, this is the most difficult of the love languages for parents to speak to their teenagers. Few parents actually speak this language fluently. Many parents bungle in their efforts to communicate love emotionally by giving gifts to their teenagers. If you even suspect that your teenager's primary love language is gifts, I suggest that you not only reread this chapter but that you discuss it thoroughly with your spouse and together you should evaluate your past patterns of gift giving.

What They Say

As you seek to identify weaknesses in your pattern of giving gifts and to implement some of the positive suggestions contained in this chapter, you will learn how to speak the love language of giving gifts effectively. In the next chapter, I will share with you how to discover your teenager's primary love language. But first, listen to these teenagers who indicate that their primary love language is receiving gifts.

Michelle, fifteen, was asked how she knew her parents loved her. Without hesitation, she pointed to her blouse, skirt, and shoes. Then she said, "Everything I have they gave me. In my mind, that's love. They have given me not only the things I need, but far more."

Serena is a senior in high school. In speaking of her parents, she said, "I look around my room and I see constant reminders of my parents' love. My books, computer, furniture, and clothes have all been given to me by my folks over the past few years. I still remember the night they gave me my computer. My father had already connected it and my mom had wrapped it in golden paper. When I cut the ribbon, the computer screen read, 'Happy Birthday, Serena. We love you.'"

Ryan, age fourteen, said, "I guess the reason I know my parents love me is that they give me so much. They often surprise me by giving me things that they know I would like to have. It's not just what they give me, but it's the way they do it. My family makes a big deal out of giving gifts, and it doesn't even have to be my birthday."

Jeff is seventeen and proud of a certain car. As he explained, "This car is a collection of my family. My dad and I bought the car 50–50, but everything else I received as gifts. The mats on the floor were given by my sister to celebrate my buying the car. Mom and Dad gave me the stereo on my seventeenth birthday. The wheel covers, my mom gave me one each week for four weeks, always on a different night of the week so I would be surprised."

Sean is fifteen and in the eighth grade. He has had a lot of physical problems and has missed a lot of school. "I know I have a lot of problems. Most guys my age are playing ball and stuff. In school, I'm a year behind most guys my age. But as I see it, I'm the lucky one. My parents love each other, me, and my sister. They are always surprising me with things. I'm a computer geek but somehow my dad finds out about new applications before I do. When I see a candle burning on the table, I know that after supper, there is going to be a celebration. Usually, Dad has found a new application for me so we have a party and celebrate."

If your teenager's love language is
GIFTS
· ·

When it comes to gift giving, many parents need to be reminded that the gift is as much about the love behind the giving as it is about the gift itself. Creativity is more important than money when it comes to gift giving for your teenager.

▸ *Select presents that fit the interests of your teenager—choosing gifts that are perceived as appropriate by your teenager.*

▸ *When on a shopping trip, give your teenager a set "allowance" that you will pay toward an item they select.*

▸ *Keep a small collection of inexpensive gifts packed away for your teenager. Then give them one at a time as you sense there is a need.*

▸ *Carry candy or gum you can give away as a small gift when away from home.*

▸ *Make a special meal you know your teenager likes, go to a special restaurant, or make their favorite dessert.*

▸ *Start a collection of unique gift boxes and wrapping papers that can be used to package even the most simple of presents.*

▸ *When away from home, mail a small package to your teenager with their name on it in large letters.*

▸ *Keep a "gift bag" of small, inexpensive gifts your teenager can choose from as a reward for doing something positive. These gifts can also include "coupons" for special privileges, like allowing three friends to stay over that weekend or choosing where the family eats the next time you go out.*

▸ *Give your teenager a "song," either one you make up or a special song you select that reminds you of them.*

▸ Create a scavenger hunt for a gift that includes a map and clues along the way to the main surprise.

▸ Hide a small gift in your teenager's coat pocket with an encouraging note attached.

▸ If you are away from your teenager a few days, leave a small package for each day with a special gift and note reminding how much you love them.

▸ Instead of spending money on a larger gift for a birthday, host a large birthday party with their friends encouraging each person to bring a gift or card.

▸ Consider a gift that lasts, such as a tree you can plant together, a board game you can play together in the future, or a picture they can hang in their room.

▸ Buy a ring or necklace for your teenager to wear that is just from you.

▸ For a birthday or Christmas, shop together for a special gift that includes your teenager's opinion in the process. This special gift plus personal involvement in the decision can create a highly meaningful gift.

▸ During the Christmas holiday season, shop together to purchase a gift for someone in need, partnering with Angel Tree, The Salvation Army, or a similar organization.

▸ Give hints leading toward a special upcoming gift. A "countdown" of notes such as, "Only four more days until present day," help create huge anticipation and a tremendous amount of love for those who especially enjoy receiving gifts.

▸ Send flowers or candy to be delivered at school with a note that recognizes an academic or extracurricular achievement.

CHAPTER 8

Discover Your Teenager's Primary Love Language

"I don't know how I can ever determine her primary love language," Kristin said about her fourteen-year-old daughter, Kayla. "It seems like it changes every day. What she seemed to like yesterday she withdraws from today. She seems so moody, I never know what to expect."

Discovering the primary love language of teenagers is not as easy as discovering the primary love language of younger children. Our teens are just like Kayla—in a state of radical transition. When a person is in a state of transition—things in their external world are changing while their inner world of thoughts, feelings, and desires are in a state of disequilibrium—the person responds differently in different situations.

The Challenge

Moody Teens

Most teenagers are in this state of disequilibrium for several years. Sometimes this emotional instability is more intense than at other times—

teenagers are often unpredictable in how they will respond in a given situation. As adults, we assume that if a fellow employee responded positively last month to my pat on the back, he will have a similar response this month. While that is usually true with adults, it is not true with teenagers. The teenager's response is greatly influenced by his moods, and these moods are fluctuating, often several times within a day. The loving expression he accepted after breakfast may be rejected after dinner.

Since the teenager is in transition, attitudes quickly change, often driven by changing emotions. Desires also fluctuate greatly. Yesterday the most important thing in the world was getting a specific brand of basketball shoes. Your teenager was so insistent that you dropped your own plans for the evening and went to the mall. Two days later your teenager is leaving for the basketball court wearing a pair of old well-worn basketball shoes, and you are shaking your head saying to yourself, "I don't understand this kid." Kristin's experience with Kayla reflects the typical frustration of relating to a normal teenager, who may not seem normal at all.

Independent Teens

In addition to the teen's fluctuating moods, desires, and behavior, that developing sense of independence is another reason parents find it difficult to determine the teenager's primary love language. We have alluded to this reality several times in the preceding chapters. The normal process during adolescence is this "breaking away" from parents and establishing a personal identity. Kayla no longer wants to be known merely as Kristin's daughter. She is trying to establish an identity apart from her mother. Gaining independence is a step toward developing this self-identity.

Because self-identity is also in process, Kayla is trying to decide if she wants to be known as, "Kayla the basketball star, Kayla the honor roll student, Kayla the caring friend, Kayla the girl with short blond hair, or Kayla the dancer." Because Kayla has not determined which or how many of these identities she wishes, she often fluctuates between any one of these self-identifying characteristics. When she thinks of herself as Kayla the basketball star, she may not want quality time with her mother. But when she thinks of herself as Kayla the caring friend, she may be very responsive to quality time. Thus, the teenager's emerging independence and developing sense of self-identity often makes the task of determining her primary love language extremely difficult.

Withdrawing or Angry Teens

Sometimes it seems the teenager draws back from all expressions of love. You give him an affirming word and he says, "Don't get mushy" or "You're embarrassing me." You try to hug him and he shoots out his fingers like a prickly cactus. You give him a gift and receive nothing more than a mechanical, "Thank you." You ask if you can take him out to dinner, and he responds, "I'm having dinner with my friends." You ask if you can sew the buttons on his jacket and he responds, "Don't need buttons." You try all of the five love languages and are rebuffed.

Sometimes the teenager draws away from parental love because of unresolved anger between the parent and teenager. (We will discuss this in chapters 9 and 10.) But most often, the teen's rejection of all expressions of parental love can be explained in terms of the teen's fluctuating moods, thoughts and desires, emerging independence, and developing self-identity. In short, the teenager is simply being a teenager.

Fortunately, most teenagers do have moments of sanity when they will respond to parental expressions of love. It is not a lost cause. You *can* determine the primary love language of your teenager.

"Has his primary love language changed?"

I am assuming that a number of parents reading this book might also have read my book, *The Five Love Languages of Children*. Perhaps when your teenager was a child, you determined her primary love language and spoke it fluently for a number of years. Now you're wondering, "Has her love language changed?" The good news is that your child's primary love language did not change when she became a teenager. I know that some of you are saying, "But I'm doing the same thing I did when she was a child, and now she is not responding." I understand and I am going to address that reality in a moment. But first, let me affirm that the primary love language does not change when the child becomes a teenager.

Why Teens Seem to Change Their Primary Love Language

There are several reasons why parents sometimes assume that the primary love language of their teenager has changed. *First, the teenager may be drawing back from the love language that earlier seemed to fill his/her love tank.* This resistance can be explained by the reasons we have just discussed: fluctuating moods, thoughts and desires, emerging independence, and developing self-identity. In fact, the teen may temporarily draw back not only from his primary love language but also from all expressions of love.

There is a second reason the teenager's primary love language may seem to have changed from that of his childhood. *When a person is receiving enough of his primary love language, the secondary love language then becomes more important.* Fifteen-year-old Jared is a "toucher." His parents learned when he was ten that his primary love language was physical touch. Both of his parents found that language easy to speak, so from childhood they have spoken Jared's primary love language. Lately Jared has complained, "You know, I work hard around here but nobody ever appreciates it." Jared is asking for words of affirmation. This is not the first time his parents have heard this complaint. His parents are wondering if Jared's love language has changed. The reality is that for Jared, words of affirmation is a strong secondary love language. If his parents want to effectively meet Jared's need for emotional love, they must give Jared more words of affirmation while they continue to speak his primary love language: physical touch.

The third possibility is that parents originally misread the child's love language. This is not uncommon because parents tend to see their children through their own eyes rather than the child's eyes. It is easy to think that because our language is physical touch, that will be true of our child. We tend to believe what we want to believe rather than what is true from the child's perspective. As long as the parents expressed their love to the child in all five languages, the child may have received enough of his or her primary love language and the love tank may have stayed full. However, in the teenage years, because the parents felt rebuffed, they may have drawn back from speaking one or more of the languages while still focusing on what they believed to be the teenager's primary love language. In this case the teenager's primary love language has not changed. The problem was an incorrect diagnosis.

Time to Learn a New Dialect

Now what about the parent who said, "I'm doing the same thing I did when he was a child but now he is not responding"? This was Patti's experience. "I've known for a long time that Teddy's primary love language is words of affirmation. I've always verbally affirmed him but now that he's fourteen, he is saying to me, 'Mom, don't say that. Mom, stop saying that. Mom, I don't want to hear that.' It's very confusing to me," she said.

"Tell me some of the words of affirmation you give Teddy," I said to Patti.

"I say things like, 'You are the greatest. I'm so proud of you. You are so smart. You are so good-looking.' Things I've always said."

There's the problem: Patti is speaking the same words she has always given her son. Seldom do teenagers want to continue hearing the same dialects as when they were children. Since these were the words they heard as children, they associate these words with childhood. They are trying to be independent and don't want to be treated as children.

Parents who want teenagers to feel loved must learn new dialects. I suggested that Patti eliminate the dialects she had used through the years and come up with new verbal expressions of love, using more adult words, such as, "I admire the strong stand you took for that boy who was being picked on at school . . . I appreciate your hard work on the lawn . . . I trust you because I know you respect the rights of others." These statements express high regard for the teenager but don't have the ring of childishness. I also suggested that she might want to start calling him Ted instead of Teddy. She looked shocked and said, "You know, Teddy has been telling me the same thing. It's hard to call him Ted when I've called him Teddy all his life." I knew that Patti had some hard work ahead of her, but I was also confident that she would make the necessary changes.

Roger also demonstrated the need for learning new dialects when he told me about his son's new responses as a teenager. "For a long time, I've known that Brad's love language is acts of service," Roger said. "When he was younger, he would bring me his toys to fix. I think he believed that I could fix anything. When he walked away with a repaired toy or a homework assignment completed, I could tell he felt loved because of the twinkle in his eye. However, since Brad has become a teenager, I'm noticing that he is not asking for my help very much. The other day he was working on his bicycle. When I offered to help, he said, 'Thanks, Dad, but I can do it.' He seldom ever asks for my help with his homework anymore. I don't feel as close to him and I wonder if he feels close to me."

If Brad's love language is acts of service, he may not be feeling his father's love as much as he did earlier. However, it is obvious he does not want from Roger what he wanted as a child. He has learned to do things for himself, which feeds his emerging independence and maturing self-identity.

Roger must now learn how to speak new dialects of acts of service. I suggested that he look for things that Brad does not yet know how to do and offer to teach him how. Obviously, Brad wants to do things for himself. This enhances his sense of maturity. If Roger offers to teach Brad how to replace spark plugs, how to change oil, how to build a bookcase, or anything else in which Brad expresses interest, he will likely find that Brad is very open to receiving acts of service. His emotional closeness with Brad will be enhanced. And Brad will feel secure in the love of his father.

Learning new dialects may be difficult. All of us are creatures of habit. To continue to express love to our teenagers in the same ways we did when they were children is very natural. It seems comfortable to us. Learning new dialects means effort and time, but if we want our teenagers to feel loved, we must be willing to expend the energy to learn new dialects of their primary love language.

Finding Your Teen's Primary Love Language

If this book is your first exposure to the concept of the love languages—you didn't look for his primary love language when he was a child—and you haven't a clue about how to figure out his primary love language now that he's a teenager, let me suggest three steps. First, you've got to ask questions; then make some observations; and third, experiment.

1. Ask Questions

You have to ask questions if you want to know what is going on inside your teenager's head. "Forget that," one father said. "No matter what question I ask, I get one of three answers: 'I don't know'; 'Okay'; or 'Whatever.' These three answers are used to explain anything, everything, and nothing." I understand the frustration of this father, and it is true that teens sometimes speak with *grunts* instead of words. But the only way to know for certain what a teenager is thinking and feeling is if the teenager chooses to reveal those thoughts and feelings—so don't give up.

Teenagers are more likely to reveal what's up if they are asked questions. Not many teenagers initiate a conversation by saying, "Let me sit down here and tell you my thoughts and feelings." On the other hand, they are very likely to say, "Let me tell you what I want." Teens are much more likely to share their desires than they are to share their thoughts and emotions. Often these are locked inside their mind until the parent asks the right question.

Questions may be your greatest ally in the effort to discover your teenager's primary love language. Andrea said to her fifteen-year-old daughter, Kerstin, "I've been reading some books on parenting. I realize that I'm not a perfect parent. My intentions have been good, but sometimes I have done and said things that have hurt you. On the other hand, I'm not always certain that you feel I'm available to you when you need me. I want to ask you a serious question: *From your perspective, what would make our relationship better?*"

Kerstin's response was one that Andrea will always remember. "Mom, if you really want to know, I'll tell you, but don't get mad at me. When I try to talk with you, I never feel like I have your full attention. You're always knitting, reading a book, working on the bills, watching TV, washing clothes, or doing something else.

"You are always doing something. I feel like I am bothering you when I try to talk. I wish that sometimes you could just sit down and talk with me without doing something else."

Andrea asked for it and Andrea got it. The answer to her question revealed Kerstin's primary love language—she was aching for quality time, her mother's undivided attention.

Andrea's husband Mark asked a different question of their sixteen-year-old son, Will, but he found the same openness exhibited by Kerstin.

One night while driving his son to an athletic event, Mark began, "Lately I have been thinking about some changes I need to make in my life. More specifically, I've been thinking about how I can be a better husband to your mother and a better father to you and Kerstin. I'd like to have your input, so I want to ask you this question: *If you could change anything about me, what would you change?*"

Will thought about it for what seemed like an eternity, but eventually he said, "In a lot of ways you are a good dad. I appreciate your hard work and the things you give me. But sometimes I feel like I don't ever please you. No matter how hard I work, what I get is criticism from you. I know you want me to do my best, but when you constantly criticize me, I feel like giving up."

Fortunately, Mark was sincere in asking his question, and he was in a listening mode. He responded, "What I hear you saying is that I give you too much criticism and often don't express appreciation for the hard work you do" to which Will responded, "Yeah. I don't mean that you shouldn't ever criticize me, Dad, but once in a while it would be nice to know that I did something that pleased you." Inside Mark was reeling from Will's statements, so he said simply, "I appreciate your sharing that. I'm going to give some thought to that and I'm going to work on that." Then he reached over and patted Will on the back as they drove into the parking lot of the stadium.

All that evening, the word *criticism* kept running through Mark's mind. He wasn't aware that he criticized Will that much. In fact, he didn't really see it as criticism. *Yes, I do correct Will,* he told himself. *I pointed out the spots Will missed when he washed the car. And I reminded him that the recycling bin needed to be taken to the street, but criticism?* Mark was carrying on a dialogue in his own mind while he and Will watched the game. *Yes, criticism. That's what Will hears, criticism. That he never pleases me, that what he does is never good enough.* Mark had almost forgotten that he originally asked the question in hopes of discovering some clue to Will's love language.

All of a sudden, it dawned on him that Will had revealed his love language: words of affirmation. He wanted to be appreciated. *What I've done,* Mark told himself, *is to give him negative, critical words rather than positive, affirming words. No wonder I've sopmetimes felt that Will did not want to be with me.* Mark promised himself that he would talk to Andrea and ask her to help him recognize times when he gave Will critical words and to help him learn how to affirm Will verbally. Mark felt a tear forming in his eye. He brushed it away and as the crowd around him roared, he turned to Will and said, "I love you, son. I really enjoy being with you."

Will hit his dad on the shoulder, smiled, and said, "Thanks, Dad."

With one question, Mark had discovered his teenager's primary love language.

There are innumerable other questions parents can ask that may stimulate information from the teenager which will reveal the teen's love language. "Who would you say is your best friend?" When the teen says "Paul," then you ask, "What does Paul do that makes you feel he is your best friend?" Your teen responds, "He listens when I talk and tries to understand." Your teen has just revealed that quality time is his primary love language.

You might ask your daughter, "If you wanted to show your grandmother that you really loved her, how would you do it?" Such questions may reveal the teen's primary love language. They also create an atmosphere for further communication between parent and teen.

I do not suggest that you explain the five love languages to your teenager and ask her, "So what is your primary love language?" First of all, such a question may come across as a game. Remember, the teen is looking for authenticity and sincerity. Second, if the teenager genuinely understands the love language concept, she may choose to use it as a means of manipulating your behavior. What parent has not heard a teenager say, "If you loved me, you would . . ."? On rare occasions, what the teenager is requesting reveals his or her primary love language, but far more likely it is an effort to satisfy a momentary desire. Once granted by the parent, the teenager seldom feels loved. Almost any question is better than the question: "What is your primary love language?"

2. Make Observations

Consciously observe the behavior of your teenager. Look for ways in which he expresses love or appreciation to others. Keep notes on what you observe. If you find that five times in the last month, your teenager has given a gift to someone else, there is a good chance that your teenager's love language is gifts. Most people have a tendency to speak their own love language. They do for others what they wish others would do for them. This is not always true, however. For example, sometimes a teenage son will give gifts as expressions of love because his father emphasized gift giving. He remembers his father's words, "Son, if you want to make a woman happy, give her flowers." So he gives gifts not because that is his own love language but because he has learned to speak that language from his father.

Also, be sure to observe the complaints of your teenager. What a person complains about is a clue to his or her primary love language. This was seen earlier in Will's response to his father when he said, "But sometimes I feel like I don't ever please you. No matter how hard I work, what I get is criticism from you. I know you want me to do my best, but when you constantly criticize me, I feel like giving up." Will's complaints reveal that his love language is words of affirmation. He was complaining not only about his father's criticisms, but also that he seldom gives compliments.

Typically, when teenagers complain, parents get defensive. The teenager says, "You have no right to go in my room and move my things around. Now I can't find anything. You don't respect my personal property. It's not right." Many parents respond, "If you would clean your room, I wouldn't have to go in there. But when you don't clean it, then I'm going to clean it." The conversation now moves to a full-blown argument, or it is dropped and both walk away in silence.

However, if the parent would observe the complaints of the teenager, the parent may find that these complaints fall into a pattern. This is not the first time the teenager has complained about someone "moving my things." It may be that the primary love language of this teenager is gifts. Keep in mind that almost everything in a teenager's room was a gift. For this teenager, there is a special place for each gift, and when someone moves his stuff, it is like moving an expression of love (it might also be perceived as an attack on his budding self-identity or independence).

It's important to look for patterns of complaints. When several of the complaints fall into the same category, they likely reveal the teenager's primary love language. Observe the following complaints. "You don't ever help me with my homework anymore. That's why I make poor grades ... If you would take me to the game, I could be with my friends and wouldn't have to sit around the house all the time ... I couldn't clean behind the desk because you weren't here to help me move it ... If you show me how to fix my bicycle, I could ride to school." This teenager's primary love language is probably acts of service. Each of the complaints is asking the parent to do something for the teenager.

Also be sure to observe the teenager's requests. What a person requests most often indicates her primary love language. Renee is saying to her mother, "Mom, can you and I go to the walking trail this afternoon? I want to show you some flowers I discovered down by the lake." Renee is requesting quality time. If she often requests activities which put her and her mother together alone, her love language is quality time. Similarly, when thirteen-year-old Peter asks, "Dad, when are we going on another camping trip?" or "When can we go fishing again?" or "Can we play catch now?" he is revealing that his primary love language is quality time.

If parents observe how the teen expresses love and appreciation to others, what the teen most often complains about, and what the teen most often requests, chances are the parent can discover the teenager's primary love language.

3. Experiment

A third way to discover a teenager's primary love language is to experiment by focusing on one of the five love languages each week and observing the teenager's response. Spend a week giving the teenager more *physical touches* than normal. Seek to touch them several times a day.

The next week, draw back from touching and give them *words of affirmation*. Spend some time each day coming up with new expressions of affirmation that you will give your teenager each evening.

The following week, seek to do as many *acts of service* as you can for your teenager, especially things you know the teenager would like for you to do. Fix a special meal. Iron that hard-to-iron shirt. Give extra help on algebra. Wash the dog for your teenager (with a positive attitude). Do as many things as you can for your son or daughter.

The next week, make an effort to give the teen *quality time*. Take walks together, play ball with each other. If he requests something that takes time — do it. Do things *together* as often as you can. Have as many in-depth conversations as the teen will allow. Give the teen your focused attention.

Then focus on *gifts* during the last week. From a list you have accumulated, purchase some of the key items your teenager has requested. Wrap them with colorful paper, present them to the teen in front of other family members. Make a big deal of it. Have a party every night.

During the week that you are speaking your teenager's primary love language, you will see a difference in your teen's countenance and attitude toward you. The love tank is being filled, and the teenager is responding far more warmly to you than normal. The teenager is also probably wondering what has happened to you—why you are acting so weird. You don't have to fully explain yourself. Just tell the teen you have been working at being a better parent.

Another experiment is to give the teen choices between two options and keep a record of what they choose. For example, a father says to his thirteen-year-old son, "I have two hours free this afternoon. Would you like to fly your new kite together or go to the store for batteries for your new camera?" The choice is between a gift and quality time. The father does what the son chooses and keeps a record as to whether he chose the gift or quality time. Three or four days later, the father gives the teenager another choice. "Since you and I are the only ones at home tonight, would you rather we eat out (quality time) or that I fix your favorite pizza (acts of service)?" Next week the father says. "If you were feeling discouraged and I wanted to make you feel better, which would you prefer? That I write you a note reminding you of all the positive things you have done or would you rather I give you a big bear hug?" The choice is between words of affirmation and physical touch.

As you keep a record of the teenager's choices, they will likely fall into a pattern which will reveal the teen's primary love language. I know some of these things sound laborious and, more than likely, a little bit out of the normal routine—but it'll be worth it. Adjust your experimentation to your own comfort level and give it a try.

Once you have discovered your teenager's primary love language, you will want to learn as many dialects (different ways of speaking this language) as you can. And you will want to speak this love language regularly, keeping in mind that your teenager may sometimes draw back even from his primary love language. Respect his wishes. Never force expressions of love on an unwilling teenager. For example, if you know your teenager's primary love language is physical touch but when you put your arm on your teenager's back, he jerks away, that is not the time to try to give him a bear hug. That's the time to walk away and respect the fact that for the moment, the teenager does not want to be touched. Try not to take things like this personally.

Try a different tactic the next day. When the teenager is in the mood for physical touch, pour it on. If you speak the teenager's primary love language as often as you are allowed, the teenager's love tank will be full. But if you withdraw from physical touch because you don't like the awkwardness of being rebuffed, in time your teenager's love tank will empty and they will come to resent you. To effectively love a teenager, parents must speak the teen's primary love language regularly and in whatever dialects that communicate love to the teenager.

Speaking All Five Languages

The Benefits to Your Teen

Let me emphasize what I said earlier. I am not suggesting that you *only* speak the one primary love language of your teenager. Teenagers need to receive love in all five love languages, and teens need to learn to speak all five love languages. They learn best by seeing it modeled by their parents. What I am suggesting is strong doses of the teen's primary love language and speaking the other four as often as possible. If the teenager has a clear secondary love language, the parent will also want to give heavy doses of that language. As the parents speak all five love languages to the teenager, the teenager is learning how to speak those languages to others.

This is exceedingly important to the teen's future relationships. In the future, the teen will have neighbors, work associates, friends, dating partners, most likely a spouse, and later children to whom they will need to speak love and appreciation. If teenagers become fluent in speaking all five love languages, their relationships with people will be greatly enhanced. If, on the other hand, they are limited to speaking only one or two of the love languages, their relationship potential will be diminished. There will be certain people with whom they will not connect emotionally. These people may be significant people, even people with whom they would like to have a meaningful and lasting relationship. The teen who learns to speak the love languages fluently will have a decided advantage in all future relationships.

This may prove to be a formidable challenge for the parent who has not learned to speak all five love languages. I suggest you reread the chapters on each of the five languages—especially those that are difficult for you to speak. Note the ideas on how to speak the particular language and practice speaking it not only to your teenager but to other family members as well. Eventually you can learn to speak each of the love languages. Few things are more rewarding than expressing love to others in a language that meets their need for emotional love.

The Benefits to Your Marriage

In their efforts to more effectively love teenagers, some couples have found their own marriage reborn. It is never too late to learn (or relearn) how to speak your spouse's primary love language. Couples who learn to speak each other's primary love language can see the emotional climate of their marriage radically change in a brief period of time.

One husband said, "Dr. Chapman, we have been married for thirty-three years. The last twenty-five years have been utterly miserable. A friend gave me a copy of *The Five Love Languages*. When I read it, the lights came on. I realized that I had not spoken my wife's language and she had not spoken mine for all these years. I shared the book with her, we discussed it, and agreed to begin speaking each other's primary language. If anyone had told me that our marriage could be turned around in two months, I would never have believed it. But within two months, I had warm feelings for her and she had warm feelings for me. Our marriage has been totally changed.

We can't wait to share this with our married children."

Since love is our most basic emotional need, when another person meets that need, we have warm emotional feelings toward that person. The emotional climate of marriage and family life can be greatly enhanced when members of the family learn and speak each other's primary love language.

CHAPTER 9

LOVE AND ANGER—PART ONE:

Breaking Destructive Patterns

Teenagers get angry with parents, and parents get angry with teenagers. I don't think this is a surprise to anyone. Both parents and teens can say and do things to each other that hurt very deeply. Ambrose Bierce once said, "Speak when you are angry and you will make the best speech you will ever regret."

Most parents and teenagers have made a few of the kind of speeches that Bierce described. We wish we could pull the words back. We wish we could undo the painful action. *Mismanaged anger is behind many of the broken relationships between parents and teens.*

How does all of this relate to love? In the minds of most people, love and anger are antonyms—they just don't seem to go together. In reality, they are opposite sides of the same coin. Love seeks the good of the other person in any relationship, and rightly directed anger seeks the good of the other person as well. We experience anger when we encounter what we perceive to be wrong behavior on the part of others. Parents get angry with teenagers when the teen does or says something considered irresponsible. Teenagers get angry with parents when the parents' behavior is considered to be unfair or self-serving.

The purpose of anger is to motivate us to take loving action, that is, to do something to try to turn the teenager or parent in the right direction. Unfortunately, many of us have never learned how to take such loving action, and we end up taking destructive action. Sometimes in our response to anger we end up making the situation even worse. The purpose of this chapter is twofold: to help parents manage their own anger in a loving way and to give parents practical ways of teaching their teenager to handle anger positively.

Me, My Teenager, and Anger

We are not likely to teach our teenagers what we have not learned for ourselves. Many parents can identify with Marvin, an Idaho potato farmer, who once said to me, "I never experienced intense anger until I got married. And I never experienced super-intense anger until I had teenagers." Though we may experience anger in all arenas of life, some of our most intense anger is toward family members, and particularly teenagers.

Why Teens Anger Us

Why do we often experience more anger toward our teenagers than we do toward our younger children? This is primarily because of the changes that are going on inside the teenager—which we have discussed in earlier chapters. The teen's increased intellectual abilities to reason and think critically about issues allow him to question our judgment in a way he did not do as a child. This intellectual growth is accompanied by the push toward independence and self-identity that may lead the teenager not only to question our judgment, but also to choose noncompliance. Not only is he thinking for himself—he is now deciding for himself. This often puts the teenager in conflict with the parent and stimulates anger within the parent that never happened like this when he was a child.

The parent sees the teenager's behavior as defiant, rebellious, or irresponsible. The parent reasons, *This is not good for my son [daughter]. He is going to wreck his own life. This is not a pattern I can allow to continue.* Anger motivates a father or mother to take action. Unfortunately, if the parent does not realize that he or she is now dealing with a teenager rather than a child, the parent's action may in fact make the situation worse.

Why We Must Change First

When the teenager does not readily comply to the parent's requested change in his course of action, the parent often resorts to cold, harsh commands. "You do it or else," the parent loudly proclaims. Not wanting to be a child, the teenager chooses "or else," and the battle between parent and teenager rises to another level. Before the battle is over, parent and teen are hurling harsh critical words at each other like enemy soldiers throwing grenades. Both leave the battlefield wounded, feeling rejected and unloved. The situation has become much worse because of misguided anger. Verbal explosions and/or physical abuse on the part of parents never produce positive results.

In more than thirty years of marriage and family counseling, I have often wept as teenagers have recounted the painful words and destructive behavior of parents whose anger was out of control. What is even more tragic is the many young adults who were abused as teenagers and now find themselves treating their own children in the same manner their parents treated them. I will never forget seventeen-year-old Eric who said, "Dr. Chapman, I used to think that my father loved me but now I know that he doesn't. All he thinks about is himself. If I do everything he wants, the way he wants it done, then he's OK. But how can I ever grow up if I don't have the right to think and make decisions on my own? I sometimes wish he would die or I would die. Either way, the pain would be over."

Patterns of misguided anger are often passed from generation to generation. These patterns must be broken. I cannot tell you how strongly I feel about this issue. As parents, we must come to grips with our own anger and learn how to handle it in a responsible, positive way. If we don't, we *will* jeopardize all our good efforts at parenting. The teenager who is verbally or physically abused by an angry parent will no longer remember the acts of service, words of affirmation, quality time, gifts, and physical touch that were received in childhood. All they will remember are the cutting words of rebuke and condemnation and the screaming voice of their parent. They feel no love—only painful rejection.

If you recognize such misguided anger in your own life, I urge you to read this chapter carefully and take the hard steps required to bring healing in your parent-teen relationship.

Negative patterns from the past can be broken. We need not be slaves forever to misguided anger. If we are willing, we can change destructive patterns into loving actions.

Breaking Our Destructive Patterns

Let me suggest the following steps in breaking destructive patterns and establishing loving patterns of anger management.

1. *Admit the Truth*

First of all, we must admit the truth. We will not change our trajectory until we admit we are going in the wrong direction. Admit it to yourself, admit it to God, and admit it to family members. "I have mismanaged my anger. I have often been out of control. I have said and done things that are wrong. My words were not kind and they were certainly not loving. They were destructive and hurtful. And with the help of God, I want to change." Don't hesitate to bring God into the process. You need all the help you can get.

Write the above words on a sheet of paper. Modify them if you wish to express it in your own words. Then read it out loud to yourself and acknowledge the painful truth . . . "I have mismanaged my anger." Then admit it to God and confess your wrong behavior and ask His forgiveness.

Then one evening when the family is all together, tell them there is something you need to share. Pull out your paper and read it. Tell them that you have admitted this to yourself, you've admitted it to God, and now you are admitting it to them. Tell them that you sincerely want to change. You might wish to say something like the following. "Over the next few weeks, I am going to be working on this. But if I lose my temper with any of you and start to yell and scream, you will help me if you will put your hands over your ears, walk out of the room, and if you like, take a walk around the block. I assure you that by the time you return, I will be in control and I will not resume the harsh words. I will ask you to forgive me, and we'll go on from there. It may take me a little time but with God's help, I'm going to change." Once you make this humbling speech, you are on the road to positive change.

2. Develop a Strategy

Now you are ready for step two: Develop an effective strategy for breaking destructive patterns. You have admitted to yourself that what you have done in the past is not acceptable. So how will you break those negative patterns? You have already initiated one strategy when you asked your spouse or children to walk out of the room if you begin to "lose it." Each time this happens in the future, you are reminded to confess your failure. There is something humiliating about confessing failure. The very act of confessing motivates you to change the behavior in the future.

But what can you do to head off your anger before you explode? Sometimes all that is needed is a "pause in the action." I met a man named Rueul and his wife at a marriage conference in Spokane; he acknowledged that he would often "explode and say hurtful things" to his wife and children. I gave him some practical ideas on how to "stop the flow" of angry words and how he might channel his anger in a more positive manner. Two years later, I saw Rueul at another marriage seminar, this time in Seattle. His "anger update" was very encouraging.

"Well, you know the idea about counting to one hundred before you say anything? I've been doing that," he said. "When I get angry, I start counting and I start walking as you suggested. I've walked in the rain, I've walked in the snow, and I've walked in the sunshine—counting aloud. If people heard me, they would probably think I was insane. But what I was doing before is what was really insane. I was destroying my wife and children. The walking and counting gives me time to cool down and take a more positive approach to my anger."

Rueul had found a strategy for breaking his destructive patterns of verbal abuse. He was substituting a new strategy for his old destructive patterns. There are plenty of other very practical strategies besides counting to one hundred. Jim told me, "When I get angry, I get on my bike and just start riding. I ride until I've cooled down. Sometimes I ride several miles." Amy said, "When I get angry at my husband I simply tell him, 'Excuse me. I've got to go to the park.' I get into the car, drive to the park, take a walk, or sit on the bench until I've had time to cool off. My husband agrees that this is much better than what I used to do."

Brenda told me, "My husband and I have agreed that when we get angry with each other, we will call a 'time out,' and one of us will walk out of the room. We have agreed that within five hours, we will come back and ask for an opportunity to discuss the issue. If we get heated again, we will call time out a second time. We have agreed it is better to call 'time out' than to verbally destroy each other." Meanwhile, when Ashley became angry with a family member, the first thing she did was to go water her flowers. "The first summer I tried this, I almost drowned my petunias, but that's better than drowning my family with angry words."

All of these people have found a strategy for replacing their destructive behavior with an activity that allows them time to cool off.

3. Analyze Your Anger and Look at Your Options

The third step is to analyze your anger and look at your options. You may still feel angry after you have counted to one hundred—or even five hundred—but now you are calm enough to begin to ask questions about your anger.[1] *Why am I angry? What wrong has the other person committed? Am I judging their behavior without having all the facts? Do I really know their motive? Has my teen misbehaved or am I being overly sensitive? Are my expectations too high for the developmental level of my teen?* (Sometimes parents get angry with teens who are simply being teens.)

Take some time to think about the situation—then you can decide what action would be constructive. Among your many options, only two represent positive responses to anger. One is to release the anger ("let it go"), realizing that it is your problem, not their problem. Your problem may be due to a bad attitude, a lot of stress, a lack of sleep, a short fuse, or any number of other reasons.

Whatever the reason, recognize the anger is your problem and release it. You may say aloud or to yourself, "My anger reveals my selfishness. Therefore, I choose to release my anger realizing that it is distorted. The family member has done me no wrong; I have simply been irritated by his (her) behavior." Sometimes it is helpful to state your conclusions to God in the form of a prayer. "Dear God, I realize that my anger is not valid. I have been self-centered and overly demanding of my family. Forgive me for my wrong attitude. I release my anger to You. Help me to be loving toward my family members. Amen." You have made the conscious decision to release your anger, and you have confessed what you believe to be your own failures.

On the other hand, your anger may be valid. The family member may have wronged you. You have the "right" to be angry. You have counted to five hundred, you have taken your walk, you have analyzed your anger, and you know that this is an issue that must be discussed. You cannot simply overlook it. A wrong has been committed; you have been hurt and the issue must be resolved. So the second positive response is to address the issue by talking with the family member. Before you initiate a conversation with your teen, however, it is helpful to think about how you will approach the situation.

Make sure to honestly acknowledge what is happening with your teenager. Explain to him or her that you are angry, assure them that you are not going to explode, and acknowledge the need to process the issue at hand. If it is not a good time to talk, then you set a time to talk.

4. Engage the Family Member in Conversation

Step four is actually engaging the family member in conversation. It is laying the matter before the person so it can be discussed. Try to choose a time when the two of you can be alone, not in the presence of other family members. This may mean waiting a few hours for the appropriate time and place. If you insist, "We are going to talk about this now," you are sabotaging the conversation before you ever start.

Once you find the time and place, let me suggest that you say something like the following. "I want to share my feelings with you because I value our relationship. I know that I may have misunderstood or misinterpreted the situation. But I want to tell you what I saw and how I felt. Then I would like for you to tell me your perspective. Perhaps I've missed something and I need your help in understanding it."

As you present your concerns, be as specific as possible. Talk about what you heard, what you saw, how you interpreted it, what your feelings are, and why you are upset. Limit your presentation to this one event. Don't go back and share similar events from the past. To do so is to overwhelm the other person with a sense of condemnation. They are likely to fight back for self-preservation, and the conversation can become an argument. Most of us can handle one incident, but we are overwhelmed when all of our past failures are paraded before us.

After you have shared your concerns about this particular infraction, then say to the family member, "I think you hear my concerns. Again, I realize that I may be missing something or I may have misinterpreted something. So please tell me your perception of the situation." Such a statement makes it easier for the other person to be open and honest with you. As he shares his perspective, please refrain from "butting in." If he makes one statement and you jump in to say: "That's not right," you are creating a battle rather than working for a peace treaty.

When you call a family member a liar, you stimulate strong negative emotions inside the person. Rather, listen carefully to what he is saying. Use reflective questions that will develop further understanding, such as "Are you saying . . . ?" or "What I hear you saying is . . . " You are trying to get the individual to share further, and you are indicating an effort to understand his thoughts and feelings about the matter.

If indeed you disagree with the other person's perception, then it is fine to say, "It appears that we see this very differently. I guess that's because we are two different people. What can we learn from this that will make things better for the both of us in the future?" Such an approach will likely lead to a positive solution. If, however, you insist that your perception is the right perception and that your family member is wrong, you have won and he has lost, but no solution has been reached. The distance between you is as great as ever.

On the other hand, if you insist on looking for a solution and learning something positive from the experience, you both come away better off than before. Your anger is processed and the results are positive. It is this kind of positive anger management that sets a model for teaching your teenager to handle anger.

Two Key Relationship Skills: Love and Anger

Obviously we cannot wait until we are perfect in our anger management skills before we begin teaching our teenagers—most of us would be waiting a very, very long time. In fact, some parents do not realize that they have a problem with anger until they see their own behavior mirrored in their teenagers. When you see your teens yelling and screaming at you in anger, the logical question is "Where did they learn this?" Chances are they are following the model of one of their parents. It is this frightening thought that "my teenagers might turn out to be like me" that motivates many parents to begin to change their own patterns of anger management. Often we must learn how to handle anger in a constructive way right alongside our teenagers.

Two of the most important relationship skills a teenager can learn are how to express love and how to process anger. The two are not unrelated. If the teenager feels loved, then he has a much better opportunity of learning how to handle anger in a positive way. However, if the teenager's love tank is empty, the teenager will almost certainly handle anger poorly. It is so important for parents to learn the primary love language of their teenager and to speak it regularly.

Unfortunately, a full love tank does not mean the teenager will automatically know how to handle his anger. Positive anger management is a relationship skill that must be learned. Parents who love their teenagers are usually in the best position to teach the teenagers these skills. So, you ask, what must parents know in order to be successful in this arena?

1. Start Where They Are

First and fundamentally, *the parent must start where the teenager is at right now.* By the time a child reaches the teenage years, she has already developed methods of responding to anger. As one mother said to me recently, "Dr.

Chapman, how do you get a teenager to talk about her anger? When my fifteen-year-old daughter gets mad, she clams up. When I ask her 'What's wrong?' she refuses to talk about it. I don't know how I can ever help her if she won't talk about it." Another mother said, "I have the opposite problem. When my teenage daughter gets angry, everyone knows it. She goes ballistic. She screams and yells and sometimes jumps up and down like a two-year-old having a tantrum." These mothers have witnessed the two ends of the continuum. Most teenagers lean toward one of these destructive approaches to anger: implosion or explosion.

I use the word *implosion* for the silent teenager because when anger is held inside, and goes unprocessed, it will eat away at the inner spirit of the teenager. Remember, anger is stimulated when the teenager perceives that the parent or someone else has wronged her. This sense of being wronged, if it is not processed with the parent or the individual who wronged her, often leads to feelings of resentment, loneliness, isolation, and ultimately depression. Implosive anger may also lead to passive-aggressive behavior. The teenager is passive on the outside, refuses to deal with anger, but expresses the growing resentment by becoming involved in behaviors that are sure to hurt the person at whom they are angry: often the parent or themselves. Passive-aggressive behavior may involve such dissimilar things as loss of interest in things that were previously important (maybe schoolwork or sports), drug use, or becoming sexually active, all of which are aggressive expressions of anger toward the parent. Sometimes after months of depression, these teenagers who have held anger inside often erupt with violent behavior.

On the other hand, numerous teenagers have explosive patterns of handling anger. When the parent does or says something that the teen perceives to be wrong, the teen responds with loud, harsh, sometimes cursing words that express their displeasure at what the parent has done or failed to do. Some teens also throw bottles, break writing utensils, drive cars at breakneck speed, "accidentally" drop dishes, run lawnmowers over water hoses, and exhibit their anger in other physically destructive ways. If these destructive patterns are not changed, these are the teenagers who will, in a few short years, verbally and physically abuse their own spouses and children.

Not all teenagers go to the extremes that we have described in the preceding two paragraphs, but virtually all teenagers lean toward one of these two directions: implosion or explosion. Few teenagers have yet learned to manage their anger in a more mature and productive way. For some parents, the task of teaching their teenagers proper anger management is a formidable task. The first step is to recognize the patterns that presently exist in your teenager. You are not likely to lead them to patterns of mature anger management until you first identify where they are. Thus, I suggest to parents that you observe your teenager when he is angry and keep a record of how he processes his anger toward you or toward others. Two months of observation will show you where your teenager is in the development of positive anger management skills.

This is the first step in becoming a positive change agent for the teenager. In the next chapter we will learn three other steps that will help parents help their teens learn to manage their anger well.

CHAPTER 10

LOVE AND ANGER—PART TWO:

Forging Constructive
Paths

Tom approached me after I had given a lecture on anger. I noticed the tears in his eyes as he spoke: "I have failed. I realized tonight for the first time that I have caused my daughter to withdraw in silence. Earlier in her life, when she would get angry with me, I would tell her how stupid she was. I would tell her she needed to grow up, that she shouldn't be so sensitive. I realize now that I pushed her away. For the past six months, she has shared almost nothing with me."

How do we help our teen when she has imploded with her anger, completely withdrawn, and wants no communication with us? Once we recognize how our child handles her anger—whether holding it in (implosion) or spewing it out (explosion)—we can help her. This chapter looks at the ongoing steps in helping your teen develop skills for positive anger management.

2. The Hard Work of Listening

Once you have identified your child's faulty method for dealing with anger (we looked at this in point #1 in the previous chapter), you should take the next step in helping her to learn healthy skills in anger management: *You must now do the hard work of listening to angry teenagers.* I can assure you this will not be easy.

We'll address the issue of the implosive (withdrawn) teenager shortly; in some ways that's the greater challenge. But let's begin with listening to the explosive teenager. This is the one with which I have the most personal parental experience. Our son was an exploder.

Listening to Fierce, Exploding Words

I am a marriage and family counselor. I have been trained to listen, but it was no easy task to listen to the angry expressions coming from the mouth of my teenage son. The "hard work" of listening may make it sound too easy. In reality, listening to my explosive teen was a colossal task. Yet I was convinced that the only way to have a positive influence on an angry teenager was to hear his concerns no matter how harshly they were delivered. The poem found at the end of this chapter, written by our son many years later, assured me that my listening was not in vain.

I still believe we must hear our teenagers' concerns no matter how harsh they sound. Why is listening to the teenager's expressions of anger so important? Because the anger cannot be processed unless the concerns that stimulated the anger are addressed. Parents cannot address these concerns until they have first heard them. Let's begin at the beginning. Why is the teenager angry? Something happened that the teenager perceived to be unfair, stupid, or inhumane. Granted, the teenager's perception may be distorted, but in the teenager's mind, a wrong has been committed. (The teenager gets angry for the same reason the adult gets angry: a perceived wrong.) Thus, when an angry teenager is expressing that anger verbally— even if the teen is yelling—the parents should be thankful. Because if they will listen, there is a good chance they will learn what is going on in the mind and spirit of the teenager. This information is essential if parents are to help the teenager process anger.

The parent must discover why the teenager is angry: What wrong has occurred in the teenager's eyes? What seeming injustice has the parent perpetrated? Indeed, what act of treason has the parent committed? If the parent does not discover this important information and resolve the matter with the teenager, the teenager's anger will be stored inside, and the explosive words will have been spoken in vain. If, on the other hand, the parent hears the teenager's concerns and gets to the root issue, then the parent can have an intelligent response.

Losing Our Cool

The difficulty is that most of us as parents of teenagers respond negatively to our teen's explosive words before we ever hear their concerns. We get angry at the way our teenager is talking to us, and we often "lose our cool" by yelling at them. The parent says, "Shut up and go to your room. You are not going to talk to me like that." In so doing, the parent has stopped the flow of communication and eliminated the possibility of discovering the source of the teenager's anger. The household may get quiet, but anger is brewing inside both parent and teenager—anger that will not go away until it is processed further.

This is like putting a cap on the bottled-up anger inside the teenager. The teenager is now doubly angry. He is angry about his original concern, but he is also angry about the way the parent treated him. The parent has compounded the problem rather than teaching the teenager how to handle anger positively.

The wise parent will focus on what the teen is saying, not the manner in which he is saying it. What is important at the moment is discovering the source of the teenager's anger. The teenager is the only one who can give you this information. If the teen is yelling at you, he is trying to tell you something. The wise parent will shift into the listening mode. I suggest that you reach for paper and pen and begin to record what you hear the teenager saying. This will help you direct your attention to the message being delivered rather than the manner in which it is delivered. Write down what you hear the teenager saying. What is it that the teen believes to be unfair? Don't defend yourself. This is not the time to fight; this is the time to listen. Negotiation or fighting may come later, but now we are gathering the information that will be necessary for us to reach a future peace agreement with our teenagers.

Round Two of Listening

When the teenager finishes the initial explosion of angry words, share with the teen what you think you have heard him say and let him clarify. You might say, "What I think I hear you saying is that you are angry because I . . . Is that what you are saying?" Such a statement indicates to the teenager that you are listening and that you want to hear more. The teenager will inevitably oblige and give you more. It may be with the same intensity or the intensity may be somewhat reduced, but your teen will continue to share with you why he is so upset.

Continue to write down what you are hearing. Refuse the temptation to defend yourself. Remind yourself that you are in round two of listening.

When the teen subsides, again repeat what you think he is saying and give him another opportunity to make sure you are getting the full message. After the third round of listening, the teenager will sense that you have taken him seriously. Your teenager will now be shocked by the fact that you have taken notes and are intently giving him your attention. When the teenager senses that you have genuinely heard his concerns then, and only then, are you ready to move to the third step (which we'll get to after we talk about how to interact with your silent teen). I cannot overemphasize the importance of listening intently to your teenager when he or she is angry.

Dealing With the Silent Teen

What if your teen's anger is implosive rather than explosive? In some ways, the silent teenager is even more difficult to help. His refusal to share the things that concern him, the issues that stimulated his anger, renders the parent powerless. That is, the parent cannot respond to what is going on inside the teenager's mind until he or she has learned the teenager's thoughts and feelings. In some cases, this is precisely why the teenager is using the silent treatment.

Silence and Power

When the parent is extremely controlling of the teenager's life, making all decisions for him, the teenager feels powerless. The teen is unable to develop independence and self-identity, and he believes silence is the only way to gain the upper hand with his parents. With silence, the teenager is in control, at least for the moment. He has something the parent wants and he refuses to give it up. Control.

When the parent panics and woefully moans to the other parent or other concerned adults that the teenager will not talk, or when the parent verbally explodes and says loudly, "I can't help you if you don't tell me what's wrong," the teenager is winning the battle. That is precisely what the teen wants: to be out of your control. He is tired of your parental control; he wants to be independent. At the moment, silence is one way he can establish this independence.

Parents of silent teenagers need to ask the hard questions: Am I being overly controlling of my teen? Am I giving her enough freedom to think and make some decisions for herself? Am I allowing her to be a teenager or am I treating her as a child?

For the overly controlling parent, the best approach is to communicate the following message: "I know that sometimes I get too involved in your life. I know that you are a teenager now and may not want to share all of your thoughts and feelings with me, and that's all right. But when you do want to talk, I want you to know that I am available. I am willing to listen when you want to talk." Then give the teen an expression of love, using the teenager's primary love language. Such a statement, accompanied by an expression of love, creates an atmosphere where the teen feels a sense of recognition. If the parent will maintain this position, I can almost guarantee you the teenager will begin to open up when he or she is angry with the parent.

Another reason why some teens choose silence when they are angry is that they have learned from experience that when they share their anger with the parent, the parent will explode. These teens, tired of past explosions, choose to be silent rather than face the tirade of the parents' condemning words. The teens have felt embarrassed, shamed, and/or condemned by the parents' words. They do not wish to go through that again. The easier approach is to clam up and refuse to share why they are angry.

The parents of such teenagers will never be able to drag the words out of their teens. Their efforts will be considered nagging and will push the teenager further into silence. The parent must confess his own past failures. Tearing down the wall of negative behavior is the first step in creating an atmosphere where the teenager will again share his/her anger.

A Time to Confess

That's what Tom decided to do. He went beyond his tears of regret to take some humbling yet healing action in front of his daughter, Tracy. After admitting to me, "I have failed," he told me his plan. "I'm going to go home tonight and confess my failures to her. Maybe she will give me another chance." He asked me to help him work out a confession statement so that he would not be guided totally by his emotions.

Here is the statement we came up with. Something like this could help any parent who is trying to end the silent treatment and is willing to confess his own responsibility.

"Tracy, have you got a few minutes that I could share something with you that is really important to me? If this is not a convenient time, I'd be willing to wait." Once Tracy gave permission, Tom would proceed. "I went to a meeting the other night where the speaker was discussing anger. And I realized that I have done you a disservice in the past. When you have come to me with your concerns, I have often been very insensitive and have cut you off. I remember specifically the times I told you that you were stupid and needed to grow up and not be so sensitive. I realize now that was very immature on my part. You were the mature one when you shared your concerns with me, and I'm sorry for the way I made you feel.

"I want you to know that when you are angry with me in the future, I want to be a listener. I will try to hear your concerns and respond in a positive way. I know sometimes you have gotten upset with me, and I am certain that will happen in the future. If you'll tell me why you are upset, I will try to listen. I will try to respect your feelings and we can deal with the issue together. OK?"

I told Tom that his daughter might not have any verbal response to his speech. I encouraged him not to pressure her to talk at that moment. But I asked him to give her an expression of love, using her primary love language. The step Tom took that night with his daughter was the first step in restoring the possibility of his daughter sharing her anger with him.

When teenagers realize that it is safe to share anger with their parents, they will do so. But when they feel threatened, intimidated, put down, shamed, or ill-treated, many teens will choose the route of silent withdrawal. The objective of the silent teenager's parent is to create an emotional atmosphere where the teenager feels free to share anger. When the silent teenager begins to talk again, the parent must now do the hard work of listening that we discussed above.

3. Affirm That Their Angry Feelings Are Valid

Step three in teaching your teenagers a positive response to anger—after you've identified your teen's faulty method for dealing with anger and listened intently to the teen's expressions of anger—is to *affirm the validity of their anger*. I can hear some parents thinking, "Wait a minute. Often I don't believe my teen's anger is valid. I think they have misunderstood my actions. Sometimes they don't even have the facts straight. How can I affirm their anger when I don't agree with their perception?"

I'm glad you asked, because this is where many parents make a serious mistake. They confuse facts with feelings. The result is that parents get in arguments with teenagers about the facts, and the feelings get ignored. If the argument gets heated, it stimulates even more feelings that are also ignored.

Ignored feelings do not build positive relationships between parents and teenagers (that is why step three is so important). If you don't understand how to affirm the angry feelings of your teenager, you will never teach your teenager to handle anger positively. Keep reading—this next part is *extremely* important.

When you are angry, it is because you believe a wrong has been committed. Otherwise, you would not be angry. Granted, your perception of the situation may not be correct, but if I don't affirm your right to be angry, then you are not likely to be open to my presentation of the facts as I see them. It is my affirmation of your right to be angry that creates the emotional climate where you can hear my perception.

One of the best ways to be able to genuinely affirm another person's emotions is commonly called *empathy*—putting yourself in the shoes of the other person and trying to see the world through his eyes. For the parent, this means becoming a teenager for a moment, remembering the insecurities, the mood shifts, the desire for independence and self-identity, the importance of being accepted by peers, and the desperate need for love and understanding from parents. The parent who does not seek to have empathy with his teen will have difficulty affirming the teenager's feelings of anger.

Curtis demonstrated the power of empathy when he said to me, "It's amazing what happened when I tried to empathize with my daughter. She was angry with me because I had taken her driving privileges away for a week. She was yelling at me about how unfair it was and how embarrassed she was going to be to tell her friends that she couldn't drive them to school this week because her father had impounded her car. In the past, I would have argued with her and told her that she should be glad that I took it away for only one week. I would have told her that her friends could get another ride and that she deserved to feel embarrassed. This would have created more anger in her. She would have yelled nasty things at me. I would have said a few more words to her, then walked out of the room and left her crying. That's happened more times than I want to admit. But having listened to your lecture on empathy, I put myself in her shoes and remembered how hard it was to lose driving privileges for a week.

"I didn't have a car when I was her age, but I remember the time my father took my driver's license for two weeks and wouldn't let me drive the family car. I remembered how embarrassed I felt. It's amazing when I tried to see the world through her eyes, I could understand her emotions," Curtis continued. "So I said to her, 'Sweetheart, I understand why you are angry with me. And I can understand how it will be embarrassing for you to not be able to drive your friends to school. If I was a teenager, and I was once, I would be angry and embarrassed also. But let me tell you where I am as a parent.

"'We agreed that if you got a speeding ticket, you would lose your driving privileges for a week the first time. And if it happened a second time within a year, you would lose your license for two weeks. You knew the rules; we all agreed on the consequences. I would be a poor parent if I didn't hold you to the consequences, because the reality of life is that when we break the rules we have to suffer the consequences. I love you so much, and that is why I have to enforce the rules even though I am very sympathetic with what you are feeling right now.'

"I gave her a hug and walked out of the room," Curtis said with tears in his eyes. "But for the first time, I felt I had handled my daughter's anger in a positive way."

Such an empathetic statement by a parent does not remove the teenager's feelings of embarrassment, but it does take the edge off of the teenager's anger. When the parent identifies with the teenager's anger and affirms it as being OK rather than arguing with the teenager, the teen's anger subsides because she has been treated with dignity and not ridicule. It will be apparent that step two (listening to the teenager) is a prerequisite to step three (affirming the teenager's anger). Parents cannot honestly empathize with the teen's anger if they have not heard the teen's perception of the situation.

Marie's teenage daughter was angry with her because she would not buy her another outfit that she "needed." It was the third such "needed purchase" her daughter had requested in as many weeks; Mom had already bought the first two. But not this time. The budget simply would not allow it, Marie explained. When her daughter poured forth her angry words, accusing her mother of not loving her, Marie listened (instead of following her normal pattern of retaliation). She took her notepad and wrote down the key concerns her daughter expressed. Then, rather than arguing with these concerns, she said to Nicole, "I think I understand and I can see why you could be so angry with me. If I were in your position, I would probably be angry with my mother also." Such an empathetic statement would not have been possible if Marie had not first listened to Nicole's concerns. Listening creates the possibility of empathy.

4. Explaining Your Perspective and Seeking Resolution

When the teenager has been thoroughly heard and then receives an empathetic statement regarding his anger and other feelings, you can more readily take the final step in processing anger: Explain your perspective and seek resolution.

Now and only now is the parent ready to share his or her perspective with the teenager. If the parent does this before following the first three steps, the results may be an extended argument with the teenager that will typically end with harsh, cutting, and regrettable words. If you have listened carefully, and affirmed the teenager's anger, then the teenager will listen to your perspective. Your teen may not agree with you, but he will hear you and the issue can be resolved.

In Marie's situation, having expressed understanding and affirmation of Nicole's feelings, Marie said, "If I had unlimited resources I would buy you the outfit. But I don't. The fact is that in the last two weeks, I bought you two other outfits you wanted. There are always limits to what we can buy and we have reached our limit." Nicole may not be happy with her decision. She may still choose to be angry, but in her heart, the teenager knows that her mother is right. Because her mother has listened to her carefully and affirmed her feelings, the teenager will not be sitting around with bitterness toward her mother. However, suppose that when Nicole asked for the outfit Marie would have exploded with, "I'm not getting you another outfit. I've bought you two outfits in the last two weeks; that's enough. You think you have to have everything. I can't believe how self-centered you are. Don't you know the rest of the family needs clothes also?" Nicole would have felt rejected by such a response, and almost certainly she would have held bitterness in her heart toward her mother.

Sometimes They're Right...and Sometimes They Aren't

Sometimes when parents have listened to the teenager's concerns, they realize that the teenager is right. Beth said, "I will never forget the day my daughter Christy got angry with me because I went into her room and cleaned up her desk. She told me in no uncertain words that she was angry with me, that I had violated her space, that I had no right to go into her room and mess with the things on her desk, that I had thrown away some things that were very important to her, and that if I ever did that again, she would leave home. That's when I realized how deeply I had hurt her and how strongly she felt about the matter. I could have argued that I had the right to go into her room and do anything that I wanted to do. I could have argued that if she had straightened up her own desk, I wouldn't have to do it for her. But instead I listened to her.

"I think that was the day that I realized for the first time that my seventeen-year-old daughter was becoming a young adult, that I could not treat her as a child any longer. So I said to her, 'I am sorry. I realize now that what I did was wrong. At the time I was just trying to get the desk clean, but I understand what you are saying and I realize that I had no right to throw away some of your things. In fact, I had no right to clean your desk. If you will forgive me, I promise I will not do that again.'"

Because parents are not perfect, we often make mistakes, which in turn stimulate anger in our teenagers. If we honestly listen to the teenager, we will recognize our wrong behavior. Confession and requesting forgiveness always form the most positive approach when we realize we have wronged our teenager. Most teens will forgive if parents make a sincere apology.

On the other hand, the parent will often have a totally different perspective from that of the teenager. This perspective needs to be shared openly and freely in a kind but firm manner.

John listened carefully as his son Jacob poured out his anger toward his father. Jacob was angry that his father would not loan him the money to pay for his car insurance. When Jacob turned sixteen, John had bought him a car with the understanding that Jacob would pay for gas, oil, and insurance. That was eighteen months ago. The insurance payment was due every six months. Jacob made the first two payments without any problem, but now he was short on cash and felt that his father should loan him the money so that he could continue to drive the car. Jacob knew that his father had plenty of money; it would not be a problem for him to make the payment.

John listened to Jacob carefully, making notes as Jacob talked. Then John responded. "So you think that I should make the loan because I have plenty of money and it wouldn't hurt me to do so?"

"That's right," Jacob said. "It's a little thing for you; it's a big thing for me. And if you don't loan me the money, I can't drive the car for at least two weeks."

John listened again as Jacob explained his thoughts. Then John said, "I can understand why you would want me to do this. I know it will be very inconvenient for you not to drive your car for two weeks. But let me tell you where I'm coming from. As a parent, my responsibility is to help you understand how to manage money. We agreed at the very beginning that you would pay the gas, oil, and insurance. You have known for six months that the insurance payment was coming due. Instead of saving the money, you spent it. That was your choice. That's fine. I'm not complaining about how you spent the money. But since you made that choice, you don't have enough money to pay the insurance.

"I think I would be doing you a disservice to bail you out," Jacob's father continued. "I think this is a strong lesson for you on learning to handle money. During the next two weeks, I am willing to loan you my car when I can; I will drive you places when I cannot loan it to you. But I'm not going to loan you the money for your insurance. I think I would be failing you as a parent if I did that. Do you understand what I'm saying?"

Jacob dropped his head and mumbled, "I guess so." Jacob wasn't happy but he understood what his father was saying. He was willing to accept it because his father had listened carefully, affirmed his concerns, and expressed understanding.

Our goal is always to help our teenagers work through their anger to the point of resolution. Unresolved anger in the heart and mind of the teenager is one of the worst things that can happen. Unresolved anger breeds feelings of bitterness and resentment. The teenager feels rejected and unloved. The teen's unresolved anger makes it almost impossible to receive expressions of love from the parent. Many parents are frustrated by the teenager's refusal to accept parental love so they try harder—only to be further rebuffed. If the parent is going to successfully communicate love to the teenager, the parent must seek to deal with the teenager's unresolved anger. If the teenager's anger has been stored over a period of time, the parent will have to create a climate where the teenager is free to share the issues about which he is angry.

Acknowledging past failures may be a part of creating this environment. For instance, you might say, "I realize that in the past, I have not always listened to you when you were angry with me. Sometimes I have said very hurtful and critical things that I deeply regret. I know that I have not been a perfect parent, and I would very much like to deal with my failures. If you would be willing, I would like for us to have a conversation sometime in which you can honestly share with me where I have hurt you. I know that such a conversation may be painful for you and for me, but I want you to know that I am willing to listen."

Statements like these open the door to the possibility of the teenager revealing stored anger and giving the parent a chance to process the issues. If the teenager does not eventually respond to such parental overtures, perhaps professional counseling will be required. If the teenager is not willing to go for counseling, the parents can show their own sincerity by going for counseling themselves. Eventually the teen may be willing to join them in the counseling process.

Teaching your teenager to accept anger and process it in a positive way is one of the greatest contributions you will ever make to the emotional, social, and spiritual life of your teenager. The teen learns to process anger by experience. We start where the teenager is now and help our son or daughter process anger even if it involves listening to the teen's initial screams. Later we can teach better methods of communicating anger. But we must never allow the teen's language to keep us from listening to the teen's message.

The poem on the next page was written to me when my son was in his twenties. It's one reason why I am a believer in the healing power of listening to teenage anger.

Dad

You listened way past dark.
This is what you gave to me.
You had ears to hear
the exploding symphony of my youth—
Knife words, scissor syllables slicing thin air.
The others left.
You stayed
and listened.

When I blew holes in the ceiling—shotgun screams
rapid firing flames
ripping angels' wings open,
you waited,
mended the wings,
and we continued somehow.
To the next day
The next meal
The next bomb.

And when they all ran for cover
For shelter
For protection
you stayed out on the battlefield
exposed to fire from all sides.
You risked your life
When you had me.
You risked your life listening
Way past dark.

— Derek Chapman

CHAPTER 11

Love and the Desire for
Independence

Matt and Lori had requested a consultation with their family physician at which they poured out their concerns about their thirteen-year-old son, Sean. "His personality has changed," began Matt. "He is so unpredictable."

"He has never been rebellious," added Lori, "but now he questions almost everything we say. And his language has changed. Half the time we don't know what he's really saying. A couple of weeks ago, he cursed at me. Sean has never cursed."

"We're afraid that Sean has some neurological problem," Matt said.

"Like maybe a brain tumor," Lori added. "We wondered if you would examine him and let us know what you think."

Their doctor agreed, and two weeks later Sean came in for an examination. After a thorough physical exam, including a CAT scan, the physician informed Matt and Lori that Sean was a perfectly normal teenager. There were no neurological problems. What they were experiencing were actually signs of normal adolescent development. Matt and Lori were both relieved and confused. Relieved that there was no physical problem, but confused as to how they should respond to this frightening stage of Sean's development. They knew they could not just ignore his behavior.

Matt and Lori were experiencing the normal trauma of parents whose children *suddenly* become teenagers. Everything changes so fast—seemingly overnight. What worked before suddenly no longer works, and the child they thought they knew so well has suddenly become a stranger.

We have been talking about the teenager's emerging independence and desire for self-identity. And in this chapter, we want to focus on the changes that typically occur during this period of the teen's development. When parents know the ways that their teen's independence and quest for self-identity manifest themselves, they can then learn better ways to affirm their teens and show love. And, yes, they will be able to more effectively speak their teen's love language.

The Need for Independence . . . and Love

Do you know the two periods in which parents often have heightened conflict with their children? Researchers say the first occurs during what is typically called the "terrible twos," and the second occurs around the time of puberty. These two periods are tied together by one common thread: *independence*. During those terrible twos, the child is struggling to demonstrate physical independence from the parents. Little legs take them places their parents cannot see, and little hands do things that greatly frustrate parents. What parent does not have stories about trees painted on wallpaper with mother's lipstick, powder dumped on the bedroom carpet, drawers opened and ransacked, and so on?

Now jump from that toddler year to the onset of puberty—the second stage of heightened parent-child conflict. These conflicts still revolve around independence. Of course, the teenager is at a greatly advanced stage of life, so the messes he makes, the rules he breaks, and the intensity of the parent-teen conflict are of much greater consequence. According to experts Steinberg and Levine, the good news is "confrontations between parent and child usually peak in the eighth or ninth grade, then decline."[1]

At both of these frustrating stages of the child's development, it is helpful if the parent knows what to expect and has some strategy for responding in a positive manner. Our concern here, of course, is with the second stage, during the early teen years.

First, let's look at some of the common behavioral patterns you can expect. The teenager's need to be independent will be expressed on many fronts. Along with this need for independence, the teenager continues to need parental love. Often, however, the parent interprets the teenager's move toward independence as an indication that he no longer wants parental affection. This is a serious mistake.

Our goal is to encourage the teenager's independence while at the same time meeting the teen's need for love. The behavioral characteristics that accompany the teen's search for independence normally cluster around the following familiar areas.

The Desire for Personal Space

The teenager wants to be a part of the family but at the same time wants to be independent from the family. This often expresses itself in the need for personal physical space. Teenagers may not want to be seen in public with their parents. This is especially true if they think they will run into their friends. The reason is not that they don't want to be with you, but because they want to look older and more independent. It might sound like this: "Drop me off in the parking lot, and I will meet you at the car in two hours."

The mother who thought she was going shopping with her teenager may be greatly upset by the teenager's attitude. But if she understands the teenager's need to be independent, Mom will respect this request and express love to the teenager, using the teen's primary love language as they leave the car. The teen will feel both loved and independent. The parent who expresses hurt or anger at the teenager's request will probably precipitate a verbal battle with the teenager, and the teenager will walk away feeling both controlled and unloved.

Allowing the teen to sit with friends rather than family at the theater or church, if accompanied by an expression of love, is a way of both affirming independence and meeting the teen's need for love. Occasionally allowing the teenager to remain at home or to eat dinner with a friend while the rest of the family goes to a restaurant serves the same purpose.

Their Own Room

Teenagers often request their own room. They may have been content to sleep in a room with a younger sibling for the first twelve years of their lives, but be assured, that if there is any possible way, teenagers will seek their own space. They are willing to move to the attic or the basement; they will even choose the end of a hallway underneath the stairs—anywhere to have their own place. Parents often find these requests frustrating. What the teenager is asking doesn't seem reasonable. Why would they want to sleep in a damp basement when they have a perfectly nice room with a younger sibling? The answer lies in the need to be independent.

I suggest, if at all possible, that parents seek to comply with the teen's request. Once the space is provided, the teen will want to decorate it in keeping with her taste (this is when the parent will be glad that the teenager's space is in the basement)! The teenager is sure to choose colors, forms, and fabrics that you would not have chosen. The reason again is independence.

Providing private space and the freedom to decorate it as the teen desires, if accompanied by meaningful expressions of love by the parent, will foster the teen's independence and keep the teenager's emotional love tank full. However, if the granting of private space and the freedom to decorate it as one chooses comes on the heels of weeks of arguments about the stupidity of doing so, the teenager loses self-esteem, and an emotional wall is erected between the teenager and the parent even when the parent finally acquiesces to the teen's request.

Their Own Car

Teenagers will want their own wheels. In our affluent Western culture, most teenagers will want to have their own car as soon as they are able to obtain a driver's license. Again the push is for independence. "If I have my own car, I can drive myself to school, to swim meets, to church activities, and to the mall. It will save you all kinds of time." (Most parents find this appealing.)

Few things infuse teenagers with a greater sense of independence and power than driving off in their own car. In the next chapter, we will revisit the car issue as it relates to the whole matter of teenage responsibility that goes with freedom. We will discuss the matter of who pays for the car and what are responsible expectations for the teenage driver. At the moment, however, we are talking about fostering the teenager's need to be independent while at the same time communicating love.

Assuming the parent is financially able and the teenager is reasonably responsible, this is an area where the parent can express trust and confidence in the teenager while concurrently fostering independence. Remember, gift giving *is* one of the five love languages. Even if it is not your teenager's primary love language, make much of the gift you are giving when you make it possible for the teenager to have a car. If the teenager can drive away feeling loved, trusted, and independent, the parent has helped him take another step toward adulthood.

The Desire for Emotional Space

Teenagers need emotional space. In the earlier years, your child may have told you everything—what happened at school, the dream they had last night, how difficult her homework is, etc., but in the teenage years, you may feel shut out. When you ask the teen what happened at school, she may respond, "Nothing," or "Same old stuff." When you ask your teenage daughter about one of her friends, she may accuse you of prying. This doesn't necessarily mean that she is covering up misbehavior. One way teenagers establish emotional independence is by keeping their thoughts and feelings to themselves. Parents should respect this desire on the part of teenagers. After all, do you share all of your thoughts and feelings with your teenager? I hope not.

A part of what it means to be an adult is that we choose when and what to share with others. Your teenager is in the process of becoming an adult. A wise parent who has learned the value of giving the teenager emotional space might say something like this: "I know that sometimes you don't want to share your thoughts and feelings with me. I understand and that's fine. But if you do want to talk, I want you to know I'm always available."

Another way in which teenagers express their need for emotional space is to withdraw from expressions of love they formerly received. Don't be surprised when your teenage daughter rejects your efforts to help her do something. For years, your acts of service were taken as an expression of love. Now she wants to do it for herself, and she may choose to do it very differently from the way you have done it. Sometimes it is not because the teenager does not need your help—it is because she does not want to be reminded that she needs your help. She wants to be independent. Rather than pressing the issue, the wise parent will back off and say, "If you need my help, let me know." Such words spoken along with a meaningful expression of love leave the teenage daughter or son feeling independent and loved; they also create an atmosphere where your growing child may indeed request your help.

Your thirteen-year-old daughter may pull herself away from your hugs not because she doesn't want physical touch, but because this is what you did when she was a child. She is now on the way to adulthood and doesn't want to be treated as a child. The wise parent will find new ways of expressing physical touch that the teenager will welcome.

When you give your teen instructions on how to respond to a relative who is to visit tomorrow, be prepared for him to do exactly the opposite of what you have requested. Such requests often seem childish and phony to the teenager. When you give the teenager words of affirmation, make sure your words are sincere. If the teenager senses that you are trying to manipulate his own feelings by giving kind words, he will reject your words as insincere.

Behind all of this is our teenagers' desire for emotional space. They want to be loved, but they don't want to be smothered as if they're children. This is where learning new dialects of the love languages becomes so important in communicating love to your teenager.

The Desire for Social Independence

Choosing Friends over Family

Not only does the teenager want physical and emotional space, the teenager also desires social independence from parents. This desire for social independence is expressed in numerous venues. Teenagers often choose friends over family. The family has always done things as a family. Now the teenager doesn't want to go with the family. You have planned a picnic for Saturday afternoon. On Thursday evening, you tell the children your plans, and the teenager says, "Count me out."

"What do you mean, 'Count you out'?" you reply as a dad. "You are part of the family."

"I know, but I have plans already," the teen responds. "I'm going somewhere with my friends."

"Then tell them there's been a change in plans," Dad says. "This is a family outing, and it is important that you be there."

"But I don't want to be there," the teenager says. This is the first round of what will become a major battle if the parent doesn't quickly realize that he is dealing with a teenager, not a child.

Parents can coerce children into going on family outings. Once the child is there, she will likely have a good time. But if parents try the same tactics with a teenager, they will be picnicking with a reluctant traveler all afternoon and evening. The teenager will not snap back and enjoy the outing. She will exert her independence against your coercion.

In my opinion, it is a far better approach to allow the teenager not to go, especially since you announced it at such a late date. I don't mean that the teenager should never go with the family. On events where you think the teenager's presence is extremely important, then you should expect the teenager to attend. But these occasions should be announced well in advance; this gives your teenager not only chronological time but also emotional time to prepare for the event. Parents should also explain why they feel it is important for the teenager to attend the event. If teenagers feel that their schedule and interest have been considered, they will likely join the family with a positive attitude. On the other hand, teenagers need to do some things apart from the family in order to establish social independence.

The parent who realizes the value of the teen's independence will foster it by agreeing to allow the teenager to do social events apart from the family and will accompany that affirmation with expressions of love rather than argument. The parent who argues with the teenager, and later reluctantly gives in, has neither fostered independence nor expressed love. The teenager's desire to be with friends is not a rejection of parents—it is evidence that his social horizons are widening beyond the family.

Upon reflection, most parents realize this is exactly what they had hoped would happen. What parents would want to keep their teenager socially bound to them forever? Social independence emerges during the teenage years. Wise parents help children build a positive foundation for later social experiences beyond the family.

Playing Their Own Music

Teenagers will choose their own music. Nothing is more central to teenage culture than music. I would not be so foolish as to suggest the type of music to which your teenager will listen. If I told you what is popular today, I can assure you something else will have supplanted it by the time you read this chapter. What I can tell you is that the music your teenager will choose will be different from the music you enjoy. How can I be so certain of this? The answer is found in one word: independence. Your teenager wants to be different from you.

If you have exposed your children to what you consider to be good music throughout their childhood, have no fear. That music will continue to influence your teenager throughout life. Music has a way of touching the heart and soul of man. The influence of good music never fades, but at the moment your child is going through the teenage phase of life. This is a time for establishing independence. Be assured their choice of music will be affected by this emerging independence.

In the preteen and early teen years, parents need to establish clear guidelines as to what is acceptable and not acceptable in musical lyrics. For example, lyrics that depict murder, brutality, and perverted sexual experiences as normal behavior should not be considered appropriate music for teens. The teen needs to know that the purchase of such music will result in parental confiscation and destruction with no financial refunds. With these boundaries in place, I think parents may allow the teen freedom of choice, knowing that the teen will explore various musical styles. Most music downloads and CDs now have ratings that indicate the nature of the content (such as language, sexual, or violent themes). This is a good place to help your teen start his evaluation (and to set reasonable rules).

The parent who criticizes the teen's choice of music will be indirectly criticizing the teen. If such criticism continues, the teenager will feel unloved by the parent. However, if the parent affirms the teen's freedom of choice and continues to express love in the teenager's primary love language, the teenager's sense of independence is fostered and the teenager's need for love is met. I encourage you to read the lyrics of your teenager's music. (I say read because you will probably not be able to understand the words if you listen.) Find out what you can about the musicians who write and sing the music your teenager chooses. Point out things you like about the lyrics, and positive things about those who perform. Listen as your teenager chooses to share his own impressions.

If you will take this positive approach to their music, occasionally you can say, "You know, it troubles me a bit that in this song that is otherwise rather positive, there is this line that seems to be so destructive. What do you think about that?" Since your teenager knows that you have not been critical of their music, in fact you have made many positive comments, he will be inclined to hear your criticism and perhaps even agree with you. Even if he disagrees, you have planted a seed of question in his mind. If one of your teenager's music idols is arrested for drug use, overdoses, or divorces his/her spouse, be sympathetic, not judgmental. Express pain and concern for the person and sadness over the situation. You are empathizing with your teenager's emotions and the teen will feel affirmed. Remember the teenager is already thinking logically; he will draw his own conclusions. You don't need to preach a sermon. If the teenager feels your emotional support then he will feel loved.

Speaking a Different Language and Wearing Different Clothes

Teenagers will speak a different language. When your child becomes a teenager, she will learn a new language. Please don't try to learn it (that would be embarrassing for everyone involved). The whole purpose is to have a language that parents do not understand. Why is this so important?

The answer is social independence. The teen is putting distance between herself and the parent, and language is one means of doing this. If you try to understand the teen's language, you will defeat the whole purpose. Wise parents simply accept the teen's new language as evidence that the teenager is growing up. It is perfectly legitimate for the parent to periodically say, "Would you like to explain that to me in English?" However, if the teen's response is negative, the parent should not press the issue.

Teens understand each other's language, but adults are not supposed to comprehend. The teen is connecting with his peers. He is establishing social relationships outside the family, and this new dialect is a part of these relationships. The wise parent doesn't make fun of this new language, but instead he allows the teen this new expression of social independence and continues to love the teenager.

Teenagers also have a different dress code. I can't tell you what your teenager will be wearing; I can tell you it will be different from what you are wearing. This new wardrobe will be accompanied by hairstyles and colors you have likely never seen before. Their accessories will include colors of nail polish you find outlandish, and their jewelry may be worn in places you have never imagined. If the parent gets "bent out of shape" and accusatory about all of this, the teenager will withdraw. If the parent is highly controlling and demands that the teenager return to "normalcy," the teenager may do so in the presence of the parent (that is, dressing as he did at age eleven), but he will do it with great resentment. And when the parent is not around, the teenager will revert to being a teen.

It is helpful for parents to see the role of dress in the broader social arena. Dress is primarily dictated by culture. If you doubt this, then ask yourself, "Why do I wear the style of clothing I wear?" Chances are it is because people in your social circle wear similar clothing. Look at the people who work with you, live in your community, attend your church, and otherwise interact with you in social settings. Again, chances are you all dress similarly. Teenagers are following the same principle. They are simply identifying with teenager culture.

Parents who create a world war over the teen's clothing are fighting a useless battle that turns a normal developmental phenomenon into a divisive issue between parent and teenager. Such battles do not change our teenagers' ideas, and offer no positive rewards for parents.

Wise parents share their opinions, if they must, but back off and give the teenager freedom to develop social independence. Meanwhile, they continue to fill the teenager's tank by speaking his/her primary love language and sprinkling in the other four languages when possible.

The Desire for Intellectual Independence

Earlier we discussed the teenager's developing intellectual skills. The teen is coming to think more abstractly, logically, and globally. The teen is testing his beliefs. He is looking at things that earlier he accepted without question, and now he is applying the test of reason and logic. This often means that he questions his parents' beliefs as well as those of his teachers and other significant adults in his life. These questions tend to cluster around three significant areas: values, moral beliefs, and religious beliefs.

Values

The teen is sure to question his parents' values. What is important in life? The teen looks at what his parents have said and what his parents have done with their own lives. He often sees discrepancies between the parents' stated values and the parents' demonstrated values. The father who asserts that the most important thing in life is family relationships but who in fact is so absorbed in his vocation that he has little time for family should know that his teen will see this inconsistency. The mother who says that faithfulness in marriage is important but who ends up having an affair with a man at work will most certainly be seen as hypocritical by her teenage daughter. "But you said . . ." is often a part of the teenager's barrage of words at the parent whose actions do not match his or her stated values.

Even if parents are true to their values, the teenager will sooner or later question them. The teen must answer for himself what is important in life. *My parents have said that getting a college degree is the most important thing for my future. But I'm not sure that is correct. Some of the smartest people I know did not go to college and some of the wealthiest people in the world did not attend college. How can I be sure that college is best for me?* Thus reasons the teenager.

Parents who wish to be an influential part of their teenagers' reasoning process must shift from monologue to dialogue, from preaching to conversation, from dogmatism to exploration, from control to influence. Teenagers need and want their parents' input into these important areas of life, but they will not receive it if the parent treats them as a child. In childhood, the parents told the child what was right, and the child was expected to believe it. That is no longer true when the child becomes a teenager. The teenager wants to know why. Where is the evidence?

If parents are willing to enter the world of dialogue, to think critically about their own values, to share reasons and yet be open to the teen's opinions, the teenager will receive the parental input and thus be influenced by the parents' values. However, if the parents maintain the stance "It's true because I say it's true," they will have lost all influence on the teenager's choice of values.

The approach of the parents who want to be a part of influencing their teenager's values might sound like this: "I've always thought this was important and here's the reason why . . . Does that make sense to you? How do you feel about it?" Numerous conversations, each picking up where the last left off, not judgmental or dogmatic, this is the process of parent-teen interaction that allows the teen intellectual independence and at the same time gives the teen the benefit of the parents' thoughts.

When such open dialogue is accompanied by meaningful expressions of love, the parent is both fostering intellectual independence and meeting the teenager's need for emotional love. The parent who says, "I respect your right to choose your own values. You have seen my life. You know my strengths and my weaknesses. I believe that you are highly intelligent and in my heart I know you will make wise decisions," is speaking the love language words of affirmation while encouraging the teenager's intellectual independence.

Morals

While values answer the question "What is important?" morals answer the question "What is right?" Man by nature is a moral creature. Beliefs about what is right and what is wrong permeate all human cultures. I believe that is because man is made in the image of a personal, moral God, so that image is reflected in man. Whatever one's belief about the origin of morals, the cultural reality is that all people hold moral beliefs. Your teenagers will question not only your values, but also your morals. They will examine not only your words, but also your actions.

If you declare it is right to obey civil law, the teenager wants to know why you are breaking the speed limit. If you say it is right to tell the truth, then your teenager asks, "Why did you lie to the person on the other end of the telephone and tell them that Dad was not at home?" If you say it is right to be kind to others, the teenager will ask why you treated the store clerk in an abusive manner. If you say that racism is wrong, then the teenager wants to know why at the shopping mall you walk briskly down the hall and avoid eye contact whenever you see a person of another ethnic group approaching.

All of this can be extremely annoying to parents who have learned to live with their own inconsistencies. Annoying or not, our teenagers will be persistent in pointing out our moral inconsistencies.

Beyond this, our teenagers will question our moral beliefs as well as our practices. They will ask themselves—and us—the hard questions: If murder is wrong, then is abortion murder? If violence that ends in the destruction of human life is wrong, then why are we entertained by Hollywood's versions of violence? If sexual monogamy is the ideal, why have thousands of adults chosen serial sexual partners? Are right and wrong to be determined by the consensus of society? Or is there a natural, moral law that transcends society's opinions? These are the deep issues with which our teens wrestle.

Many parents find it troubling that their teenagers revive these old unsettled moral issues. However, if as parents we refuse to talk about our teens' moral concerns, they are left to the influence of peers and other adults who are willing to discuss these issues. If we are not willing to admit our inconsistencies between belief and practice, our teens will cease to respect our opinions.

We do not have to be morally perfect to influence our teenagers, but we do need to be morally authentic. "I realize that I've not always lived up to my own beliefs in this area, but I still believe that this is right and that what I have done is wrong." Such statements, made by sincere parents, restore the respect of teenagers in the parents' authenticity. Parents who get defensive about their own moral beliefs when teenagers ask probing questions will again drive the teenager elsewhere to seek input on moral issues. Parents who welcome the teenagers' moral questions, who are willing to talk about their own beliefs and practices, who are open to listen to opposing viewpoints, and who give their teenagers reasons for their own moral beliefs—those parents are able to keep the road to dialogue open and thus positively influence their teens' moral decisions.

After such discussions about moral issues, be sure to give affirmations of your emotional love. This will keep your teenagers' love tanks full and create an atmosphere where your teen feels free to come back for additional dialogue.

Religious Beliefs

Whereas values answer the question "What is important?" and morals answer "What is right?" religion seeks to answer the question "What is true?" Humankind is perennially trying to discover the truth about the material and nonmaterial universe. How do we explain our own existence and the existence of the universe? Is there a spiritual reality beyond what I can see and touch? Why has mankind, throughout history, in all cultures had a belief in a spirit world? Is this evidence that such a world exists? And if so, what is the nature of that world? Is there a God? And is the world His creation? If so, is God knowable?

These are the questions teenagers are asking. They are questions that have sometimes lain dormant for years in the hearts and minds of their parents. They are questions that perhaps were never adequately answered by the parents themselves.

Whatever your religious beliefs or disbeliefs, at some point your teenagers will wrestle with these issues. These are the questions humans have always asked, and teenagers are human (I know it's hard to believe sometimes, but they are). Man is incurably religious. The French physicist, Blaise Pascal, once said, "There is a God-shaped vacuum in every heart."[2]

Saint Augustine said, "Thou hast made us for Thyself, and the heart of man is restless until it finds its rest in Thee."[3]

Your teenager is restless. She will question your religious beliefs. She will examine the manner in which you apply your beliefs to your daily life. Again, if she discovers inconsistencies, she may well confront you with these. If you become defensive and refuse to talk about religious issues, then your teenager will turn to peers and other adults. But your teenager will not cease to ask religious questions.

Your teenager may also explore other religious beliefs and may even reject aspects of your own religion. Most parents find this extremely upsetting. In reality, it is a necessary step for your teenager in developing his own religious beliefs. Actually, parents should be more concerned if the teenager simply adopts the parents' religion without serious thought. This might be an indication that religion is simply a cultural façade—serving social purposes rather than addressing the deeper questions of life's meanings.

When the teenager announces that he will no longer go to Mass, the synagogue, Sunday school, or the mosque, he is calling attention to himself as a person independent of his parents. And he is expressing a desire for intellectual independence. It will be comforting for parents to know that research has shown that "while teenage rejections of religion may be dramatic, they are seldom permanent."[4]

It is difficult for most parents to react calmly when their teenager talks about rejecting their religion, but parental overreactions may close the door for dialogue. Remember, the teenager is establishing his independence not only in the other areas that we have discussed, but also in the intellectual area, which includes moral values and religious beliefs. This is simply a part of the teenager's broader process of questioning and exploration. It is more an expression of intellectual independence than it is a rejection of religion. If parents keep this in mind, they are less likely to be overly judgmental of the teenager's religious thoughts at the moment.

A better approach is to listen to the teenager's thoughts. Let them express freely why they find this religious belief to be interesting or satisfying. Share your own thoughts on the subject but in a nonjudgmental manner. Tell your teenager you are glad to see she is thinking about these issues. When you get really bold, ask for her opinions about how well you have lived by your own religious beliefs. You may discover why the teenager is looking in another direction.

This is not a time for dogmatism, although you may hold your religious beliefs very deeply. This is a time for encouraging exploration. If you are deeply convinced of the validity of your own religious beliefs, that indeed what you believe fits closely with what is real about the world, then you should have a measure of confidence that your exploring teenager, if sincere, will eventually end up with beliefs similar to your own. If, on the other hand, your religious beliefs are not held deeply and you are not at all certain about whether they fit with ultimate reality, then perhaps you should be encouraged that your teenager is on such a search. Perhaps he or she will discover what you have not.

The fact is: your teenager is going to explore religious thoughts. The question is: "Do you want to be a part of that exploration and do you want to love your teenager in the process?" If the answer is yes, then you must again shift from monologue to dialogue and create an atmosphere for open, honest discussion about religious issues. You must give your teenager the right to think thoughts differently from your own. You must be willing both to share evidence and listen to opposing evidence. You must acknowledge that your teenager is "in process," and you must allow time for the processing of religious beliefs.

If you do this, all the while filling the teenager's emotional love tank, the teenager will feel loved and will develop intellectual independence. The teenager will develop the religious beliefs by which he will live, and you have been a positive influence during the search.

Our Teens' Need to Decide for Themselves

It will be obvious that in all of these areas—values, morals, and religion—our teenagers will be making decisions. Underlying most of the conflicts between parents and teens is the basic question about the teenagers' right to make independent decisions. If the parent recognizes this right to independent thought and recognizes that the teenager's decisions are "in process" and is willing to invest the time and create the atmosphere for meaningful dialogue in a loving setting, the teenager will continue to be "plugged in" to parental influence.

If, however, parents draw lines in the sand, make dogmatic proclamations about what teenagers are going to believe and do, the parents will create adversarial relationships with their teens. Thousands of parents have walked this road and have experienced estrangement from their teenagers. Teenagers have turned to peer groups (sometimes very destructive peer groups) and other adults (sometimes evil adults who are willing to give the teenager acceptance and a surface love for favors, pleasures, and self-gratification) instead.

Remember, teenagers will exert their independence. It's part of becoming adults. Wise parents recognize this as a developmental stage through which teenagers must pass and seek to cooperate rather than hinder their teenagers' development. Loving the teenager through this volatile process is extremely important. If you can foster your teenager's independence in the ways suggested in this chapter while keeping his love tank full, the teen will grow up to be a responsible adult, finding his place in society, and making his contribution to the world.

Parents who fail at this critical stage may well be estranged from their teenagers for years and see their teenagers struggle with finding their place in the world. Creating an atmosphere where their teenagers can develop social, intellectual, and emotional independence is one of the parents' greatest gifts to teenagers.

At this juncture I know some of you are asking, "But what about boundaries? What about responsibility?" I'm glad you are asking these questions. It reveals that you understand the implications about what I've said in this chapter. And it brings us to the next chapter, where I wish to discuss these very issues. In fact, I request that this chapter and the next one be read and studied at the same time. They go right together: *independence and responsibility*.

CHAPTER 12

Love and the Need for
Responsibility

Michael's father purchased an old clunker for him, and they worked on it together over the course of several weekends. When Michael got his driver's permit, his father taught him some of the finer points of driving. First, they drove during the daylight hours; later Michael got experience driving at night. One weekend he and his father went camping, and Michael drove the whole way to the campsite. It was all going quite well until Michael finally got his driver's license.

Hey, I'm free! Michael told himself. *Dad doesn't have to go along.* He began to dream of driving wherever, whenever, and however he pleased. Michael didn't understand when his father insisted that there would be rules on when, where, and how he would drive the car.

Michael was about to learn that freedom and responsibility are opposite sides of the same coin—one never exists without the other. This is always true in the adult world, and the teenager also must learn this reality. Adults are allowed the freedom of living in a house as long as they take the responsibility of paying the monthly mortgage payments. The electric company allows freedom to have the lights on as long as the customer takes the responsibility of paying the monthly bill. All of life is organized around the principles of freedom and responsibility. The two never stray far from one another. Of course, it is a major part of parenting to help the teenager make this discovery.

As the loving parent encourages teenage independence, so parental love means teaching the teen to be responsible for his own behavior. Independence without responsibility is the road to low self-esteem, meaningless activity, and eventually boredom and depression. We do not gain a sense of self-worth from being independent. Our worth comes from being responsible. Independence and responsibility pave the road to mature adulthood. The teenager who learns to be responsible for his own actions while developing his independence and self-identity will have good self-esteem, accomplish worthwhile objectives, and will make a meaningful contribution to the world around him. Teenagers who do not learn responsibility will be troubled teenagers and eventually troublesome adults.

The Role of Laws (Boundaries)

Responsibility requires boundaries. All human societies have boundaries—typically called laws. Without social boundaries, society would self-destruct. If everyone simply did what was right in his own eyes, the results would be chaotic. When the majority of people abide by the laws, that is, when they are responsible citizens, the society thrives. When a significant number of individuals choose to walk their own way and live irresponsibly, the society suffers the negative consequences. Our own Western society is experiencing the results of irresponsible living on the part of many teenagers and adults. From financial crises to moral failures to violent crimes, and everywhere in between, there are great numbers of people living with little regard for their own actions. Not only does the individual suffer for his/her irresponsible behavior, but the society at large also suffers.

In the family setting, parents are responsible for establishing rules, or boundaries, and seeing that the teenager lives responsibly within these boundaries. The idea that teenagers will rebel if parents establish boundaries is untrue. In fact, research indicates "the majority of adolescents feel that their parents are reasonable and patient with them most of the time. More than half admit 'when my parents are strict, I feel that they are right, even when I get angry.'"[1]

Lawrence Steinberg, professor of psychology at Temple University, observed, "What causes adolescents to rebel is not the assertion of authority but the arbitrary use of power, with little explanation of the rules, and no involvement in decision making."[2] The problem is not parental authority; the problem is parents who express their authority in a dictatorial, unloving manner. When your child was younger, you could make arbitrary rules and your child would seldom question your right to do so, though they may still have disobeyed your rules. However, teenagers will question whether your rules are right. They will question whether your rules were made for the benefit of the teen or simply to satisfy your own whims. "Because I said so" simply doesn't work anymore. If you continue such a dictatorial approach, you can be assured your teenager will rebel.

Forming Rules *with* Your Teen

Because the teenager is developing independence, she needs to be a part of forming rules and setting consequences. Wise parents will bring their teenagers into the circle of decision-making—letting them express their ideas on what constitutes fair and/or worthy rules. Parents should share reasons for their own ideas and demonstrate why they think the rule is good for the teenager. Those who do so will create an atmosphere that fosters the teenager's independence while at the same time teaching the teenager that there is no freedom without responsibility.

In such open "family forums," parents and teens can meet and the parents can still be the authorities. They have the final word, but the parents will be wiser when they know the teenager's thoughts and feelings about the matter. And if the teenager has had a voice in making the rule, he is more likely to believe the rule is fair and less likely to rebel. Studies show "that young people whose parents are willing to engage in discussion with them are more affectionate and respectful, and more likely to say they want to be like their parents, than are young people whose parents insist on always being right."[3]

Parents are not only responsible for establishing the boundaries but also for enforcing the consequences when these rules are violated. Again, if teens have participated in deciding what the consequences will be, they are more likely to believe they are fair and less likely to rebel when the parents enforce the consequences. As parents, we must remember that our goal in raising teenagers is not to win an argument but to teach our teenagers to be responsible while they are becoming independent. The principle is "if you can accept the responsibility, then you can have the freedom. If you cannot accept the responsibility, then you are not ready for the freedom." When our teenagers understand that the two always go together they will have learned a major lesson, which will serve them well throughout the rest of their lives.

The Importance of Love

If this process of teenage independence and responsibility is to move smoothly, parents must help it along with the right language of love. When teenagers feel loved by the parents—when they deeply sense that the parents have their well-being in mind, that rules are made and enforced for the benefit of the teenager alone—then independence and responsibility are more likely to emerge. Keep your teen's love tank full, and his rebellion is likely to be only sporadic and temporary. On the other hand, if your teen does not feel loved—if he views your rules as arbitrary and self-serving, and he senses that you are more concerned about your own reputation and success than his well-being—he will almost certainly rebel against rules and you as the rules enforcer.

Remember, efforts to control teens by coercion will almost certainly fail. Coercion cannot accomplish what love was designed to create, namely feelings of positive regard toward parents. Love is indeed the most powerful weapon for good in the world. Parents who remember this and make conscious efforts to continue to communicate emotional love to the teenager will be taking the first and most important step in teaching them responsibility while fostering independence.

Steinberg, a recognized expert on adolescents, said, "When parents back off, because they think the adolescent doesn't want or need their affection anymore, teenagers feel abandoned. Trite as it may sound, love is the most important thing you can give your adolescent."[4] It is giving the teenager emotional love that creates a climate where we can both cooperate with their emerging independence and concurrently insist on responsible behavior. Having said this, we are now ready to examine the process of establishing and enforcing rules for teenagers.

A Special Family Forum

It should be obvious by now that whatever rules were established when your teenager was a child cannot be arbitrarily carried into the teenage years. The teenager is at a different stage in life; this calls for rethinking and reforming the rules. Parents who simply try to "slide" into the teenager years without reflection, conversation, or attention to family rules will soon see their teenager rebelling. Parents who are proactive will call for a family forum, acknowledging awareness to the teen that he/she is now a teenager and that this calls for rethinking our family rules to allow more freedom and more responsibility.

The parent who acknowledges this reality before it dawns upon the teenager will have the respect and the attention of the teen. Teenagers are interested in more freedom and more responsibility. This is one family forum they will gladly attend.

Some tips on having this family forum and a sample introduction for explaining the purpose to your teen are included in *Appendix 2*. Being proactive by calling such a family forum before the teenager starts to complain about the childish rules he must live by is a strategy of great wisdom. The teenager who is caught off-guard by his parents announcing his emerging independence and responsibility is far more likely to be a friendly participant in such a family forum than the teenager who has insisted for six months that such a forum be called.

However, if your teenager is fifteen and you have never had such a forum, it is never too late to shock him by taking the initiative to reexamine the rules.

Some Rules about the Rules

Let me first suggest three guidelines for making rules that will make the whole process seem both more manageable and purposeful. After this I will lay out three guidelines for setting consequences during such a forum.

1. Rules Should Be as Few as Possible

Sixteen pages of family rules will not only take a long time to write, but they will likely be ignored. This is one area of life where less is better. Too many rules overwhelm the teenager, will not be remembered, will create a nightmare for parents to enforce, and will make life much too rigid. Teenagers need some room for spontaneity and lightheartedness. Too many rules will also make your teenager paranoid and fearful.

What are the really important issues? Typically the answer to this question will cluster around avoiding those things which are physically, emotionally, or socially detrimental to the teenager's well-being and encouraging those things that will foster the teenager's accomplishment of worthy goals. Responsible living is saying "no" to those things that destroy and "yes" to those things that build.

Rules should point the way toward this objective. Later in this chapter, we will look at several areas of teenage responsibility and seek to apply this principle. The objective of rules is not to regulate every moment of the teenager's life; it is to provide important boundaries within which the teenager can make choices. Remember, God only came up with ten rules— they're called the Ten Commandments.[5] And Jesus summarized these in two.[6] Since you are not as wise as God, you will probably have a few more than ten—but try to keep them to a minimum.

2. Rules Should Be as Clear as Possible

Ambiguous rules make for confusion for both the teenager and the parent. "Come home at a reasonable hour" is sure to be interpreted differently by teenager and parent. "Be inside the house at 10:30 p.m." is clear. The teenager may break the rule, but there is no confusion about what the rule means. "Don't ever drive more than three miles per hour above the posted speed limit." Anyone intelligent enough to drive will have no difficulty in understanding this rule (it may be difficult to follow, but it isn't difficult to understand).

When the rule is clear—a teenager is aware when the rule is broken. He may try to cover his mistake. He may even argue that it didn't happen. He may rationalize as to why it happened. But the teenager knows that the rule was broken. However, if the rule is ambiguous, the teenager is certain to argue about the parent's judgment that the rule was broken. Unclear rules set the stage for argument. Teenagers will certainly enter the stage and give a wonderful performance. Clear rules deter such theatrics.

3. Rules Should Be as Fair as Possible

I say "as possible" because none of us is perfect in our understanding of what is fair. You and your teen may well disagree on the fairness of a rule. By means of open dialogue, seeking to understand each other's viewpoint, you and your teenager can arrive at a consensus on what is fair. Don't give in when you are convinced that your rule is in the best interest of the teenager, but be willing to bend up front when you feel that doing so will not be detrimental to the teen's well-being.

Fairness is *very* important to your teenager. As we discussed earlier, the teenager is wrestling with values, morals, logic, and reason. If a teenager's sense of fairness is violated, the teenager will be angry. If the parent cuts off discussion and arbitrarily enforces the rule, and refuses to deal with the teenager's anger, the teenager will feel rejected and will later resent the parent.

Every effort should be made to hear the teenager's concern about fairness in forming rules. If the teenager agrees that the rule is fair, he is not likely to rebel when the parent enforces the rule. Which brings us to the matter of consequences.

Some Rules about the Consequences

Rules without consequences are not only worthless, but they are also confusing. Teenagers will not respect parents who do not seek to lovingly but firmly enforce the rules by letting the teenager suffer the consequences when rules are broken. Suffering consequences is an important reality in adult life. If I do not pay the mortgage payment, next month I will pay additional finance charges. If in three months I haven't made the mortgage payments, I will be evicted. If I break the speed limit and am issued a traffic ticket, I must not only pay the fine but my insurance premiums may also increase. Consequences can be tough, but they foster responsible living. A flashing blue light in the distance causes drivers to take their foot off the accelerator. The fear of paying the consequences is a motivator to follow the rules.

Here are three guidelines for formulating and enforcing consequences:

1. Consequences Should Be Determined Before a Violation

Most social laws incorporate this concept. The amount of additional fees I will pay when I miss the mortgage payment is already determined before I miss the payment. The bank or lending agent does not arbitrarily decide "a late fee" after I have violated my payment contract. In most states and cities, the fine for a traffic violation is determined before the violation occurs. If we are preparing our teenagers to live in the adult world, wouldn't it be logical to apply this principle while they are teenagers?

I am amazed at the number of parents I meet across the country to whom this thought has never occurred. They wait until the teenager violates the rule, then, often in anger, they pronounce the consequences. The nature of the consequence is often determined by the emotional state of the parent at the moment. The chances of the teenager agreeing that the consequences are fair are almost nil. On the other hand, if parents are in a good mood, there may be no consequences at all. The teenager is obviously confused by this arbitrary method of determining consequences.

I suggest that the consequences for violations should be determined at the time the rules are formulated and that the teenager should be a part of the process. If the teenager is going to be a part of formulating the rules, why should she not be a part of determining the consequences? We have already observed that teenagers have a keen concern with fairness. Letting them be a part of setting the consequences is helping them develop their moral judgment. Often teenagers will be harder on themselves than the parent will be. You may think that one week without driving privileges would be a fair consequence for violating a given rule. The teenager may suggest two weeks. The important thing is to agree on a consequence that the teenager believes to be fair.

The value of agreeing upon predetermined consequences is that when the violation occurs, the parent and the teenager already know what is going to happen. The parent is not as likely to overreact in the heat of anger, and the teenager is far more likely to accept the consequence as being fair since he had a part in determining the consequences. If it was determined beforehand that the football is not to be thrown inside the house and that the first violation will result in the football being impounded in the trunk of the car for two days, while the second infraction within the same month impounds the ball for an entire week, then the parent is not as likely to rant and rave about the teenager throwing the football inside the house. She will simply intercept the football and put it in the trunk. The teenager may be momentarily upset, but he will likely acknowledge that the consequences were justified.

Parents save themselves a lot of grief when consequences are determined before a violation occurs. It is a win-win situation. Parents are less frustrated and teenagers have a greater sense that fairness has reigned. Another step has been taken in reaching the goal of teenage responsibility.

2. Consequences Should Be Administered with Love

Parents must not be gleeful in administering consequences. Suffering the consequences of wrongdoing is painful in the adult world and painful in the world of the teenager. What adult would not resent the police officer who laughs as he writes you a ticket for a traffic violation? Teenagers will experience the same resentment when parents seem to take pleasure in administering the consequences of the teenager's wrongdoing. Neither should the parents be harsh and cold in administering consequences. "I told you so. If you had listened to me, you wouldn't be in this mess." Such a statement may alleviate some of the parents' frustration, but it will not have a positive effect upon the teenager.

Our teenagers need to sense that we love them in spite of the fact they have violated the rule. Our teenagers need sympathy and understanding, but they do not need parents to capitulate and alleviate the consequences.

"I know that it will be very difficult for you not to be able to drive the car this week. I wish I didn't have to take your keys. But you know the rule and you know the consequences. Because I love you, I don't have any other option. I must let you experience the pain of having broken the rule." Such understanding and empathy with the teenager helps the teen to accept the consequences as being fair and loving. The teenager, though upset, will not resent the parent who administers the consequences in such a kind, caring manner.

It is also appropriate after such a confrontation to speak the teenager's primary love language as a final gesture of love. For example, if the teen's love language is physical touch, a pat on the back or a hug will speak volumes as you walk away with the keys. If acts of service is the teen's love language, then fixing her favorite dessert will fill up her love tank in spite of the pain she is feeling at having lost the car. If words of affirmation is the teen's love language, then verbally affirming the teenager before and after you administer the consequences will assure her of your love and will make the consequences bearable. This is another occasion when understanding the primary love language of your teenager is exceedingly important. To speak one of the other languages is certainly appropriate but will not be nearly as effective emotionally as speaking the teen's primary love language.

3. Consequences Should Be Administered Consistently

Consequences should not be administered at the whim of the parent. By nature, all of us are influenced by our emotions. If parents are feeling good and are in a positive mood, they are often inclined to simply overlook the teenager's infraction of rules. In contrast, when the parents are in a bad mood or overly stressed and perhaps angry with someone at the office, they often come down hard on the teenager when a family rule is violated. Such inconsistency will create anger, resentment, and confusion in the heart of the teenager. The teenager's sense of fairness is violated. He will feel angry, and an argument and aggressive behavior will probably soon follow.

Parents who determine the consequences before the violation allow the teenager to be a part of determining the consequences, and those who administer the consequences in love are more likely to be consistent. The ideal is to kindly, firmly administer the consequences consistently in love. Parents who do this will be cooperating with the teenager's need to learn responsibility. The teenager, though not always happy, will be a willing participant in the process.

Establishing Areas of Responsibility

Without trying to be comprehensive, let's look at some of the specific areas of family life that will require rules and consequences in order to teach your teenager responsibility and at the same time foster independence. Formulate your rules and consequences in response to these two questions: (1) What are the important issues in helping my teenager develop into a mature adult? (2) What dangers need to be avoided and what responsibilities need to be learned? Yes, some rules will be prohibitions, designed to keep the teenager from words or behavior that will be physically or emotionally destructive to himself or others. But other rules will be designed to help your teenager practice positive behaviors that will enhance his own maturity and enrich the lives of those around him.

Here, then, are some of the more common areas where parents and teenagers will need to formulate rules and consequences.

1. "Around the House" Opportunities

I say opportunities rather than duties because it sounds more positive. In reality, both elements exist. In a healthy family, every member has certain duties that must be performed to keep life flowing in a positive manner. However, such duties also represent opportunities for service. In recent years, our society has lost some of its emphasis on the value of altruistic service. However, it is still true that those who are most honored among us are those who have an attitude of service. In contrast, the self-centered, self-serving person may be financially successful but is seldom held in high esteem.

If teenagers are to learn to serve beyond the family, they must first learn to serve the family. Teenagers need real household responsibilities that enhance the lives of other family members. These will differ in every household but may involve such things as supervising a younger sibling, helping to cook dinner, washing the family car, taking care of the family pet, mowing the grass, trimming shrubs, planting flowers, vacuuming floors, cleaning bathrooms, dusting, and washing clothes. These responsibilities may shift from time to time so that the teenager has an opportunity to learn skills in various areas of household maintenance.

It's important that the teenager sees himself as a part of a family and understands that in a family everyone has responsibility. As a teenager, he is acquiring more and more abilities. This means not only more freedom to do things away from the home but more responsibilities at home. The teenager certainly will have more responsibilities than his eight-year-old sibling. With these responsibilities comes the freedom to stay up later, to spend some time away from the family, etc. In my opinion, such freedoms should always be tied with appropriate responsibilities. If the teenager demonstrates that he is mature enough to take responsibilities seriously, then he is also mature enough to have greater freedoms.

In the family forum where rules are made and consequences determined, this principle should be clearly understood. In this framework, parents are not then inclined to force a teenager to perform household duties. Rather, the teenager has an opportunity to demonstrate maturity by shouldering responsibilities gladly and thus gain more freedom. If the teenager chooses not to perform assigned family responsibilities, then the consequences are determined in terms of loss of freedom. For example, if the driving teenager is assigned the responsibility of washing the family car by noon on Saturday and the predetermined consequence is that failure to do so means that he will lose driving privileges for two days, wise parents will not stay on the teenager's back to wash the car. It's a choice—he chooses to shoulder responsibility and have the accompanying freedom or he chooses to be less mature and lose that freedom. I can assure you that the teenager will seldom wish to lose such freedom, and parents will not waste time and energy fretting over whether the teenager washes the car.

2. *Schoolwork*

What are the important issues regarding the teenager's education? This is the question you and your teenager will answer together. Most parents will feel that graduation from high school is nonnegotiable. In Western culture, the teenager without a high school diploma will be seriously hampered in living a satisfying adult life. If the parent agrees, then this is stated as nonnegotiable. You then ask, "What are the rules that will help the teenager accomplish this objective?" Generally this would involve regular attendance at school and the successful completion of assignments. Typically, both of these are graded on the teenager's report card, which parents receive periodically. Rules could be very simple: attendance at school daily unless sick at home or in the hospital, successful completion of all assignments at school and all homework assignments. If the attendance rule is broken, the consequences might be that for every day missed at school, the teenager will spend Saturday reading a book and making a verbal report to the parent on what was read. They will not be allowed to leave the house for the normal hours they would have been at school. Most teenagers will lose only one Saturday.

Performance of schoolwork is a little more difficult to judge but is normally reflected in grades and/or a visit with the teacher. When the parent discovers that the homework assignments are not being completed and/or the teenager's performance at school is less than satisfactory, the consequence could be that the assignments will be completed on Saturday or Sunday afternoon even though the teacher indicates that they will not improve the grade. The parent will closely supervise the completion of these "not for credit" assignments. Such rules and consequences free the parent from daily harassing the teenager about completing his homework. The teenager chooses to be responsible and have the freedom of Saturday and Sunday afternoon for more pleasurable activities, or the teenager loses that freedom because he was irresponsible.

3. *Use of Automobiles*

The opportunity for a teenager to drive a car is a privilege, not a right. Teenagers are not entitled to have their own car or to drive the family car whenever they wish. Driving is a freedom that is earned by responsible behavior. This reality should be clearly understood by the teenager long before he is old enough to get a driver's license. Again, teenagers need to understand the relationship between freedom and responsibility. Most parents want their teenagers to have the freedom of driving a car, but many parents fail to connect this freedom to drive with responsibility. Consequently, teenagers see driving as an inalienable right.

What are the key issues involved in a teenager's use of the car? The parent and teen probably will agree on some of the following: the teenager's physical safety, the safety of other drivers and passengers, and obedience to all traffic laws. These are fundamental concerns. Other parents and teens may agree on certain rules regarding the teenager helping to finance this privilege by buying gas out of his allowance or earnings. Others will want rules about securing permission from parents on when the car may be driven and when the teenager must return. From these concerns, specific rules will be formed along with appropriate consequences.

The following are suggestive. *Rule:* Obey all traffic laws. *Consequence if violated*: If the teenager receives a ticket for any traffic violation, he will lose driving privileges for one week and will pay for the ticket out of his allowance or earnings. If a second violation occurs within three months, he will lose driving privileges for two weeks and make appropriate payment. *Rule:* Never allow a friend to drive your car. *Consequence if violated:* lose driving privileges for two weeks. Other rules may address such issues as curfews, talking on the phone or sending text messages while driving, payment of car expenses, regular vacuuming of the car, and auto maintenance.

4. Money Management

Money hassles are common between parents and teenagers. Many times this is because parents have not established clear rules and clear consequences. What are the major concerns regarding money and teenagers? The first reality is obvious: money is limited. Few families have unlimited resources, which means the teenager cannot have all that he or she may desire. A second major concern is that the teenager should learn basic principles of money management. One simple fundamental principle is "When money is gone, purchases cease until more money is obtained." The violation of this principle on the part of many adults (in their own lives and in their interactions with their teenagers) has been the source of deep financial problems. That is why, in my opinion, teenagers should never be given a credit card. Credit cards encourage spending beyond one's income, and such spending is an extremely poor practice to teach teenagers.

Fundamentally, a teenager cannot learn to manage money until he has some money to manage. This has led many parents to the decision that the teenager should be given a regular allowance rather than coming to the parent every two days asking for another $20 to buy this or that. The parent who doles out $10 here and $20 there to meet the teen's specific request of the day does not teach the teenager to manage money. A far better approach in my opinion is for parents and teens to agree on a weekly or monthly allowance. With the allowance, there needs to be a clear understanding of what areas of expenditure the teenager is responsible for. This may include clothing, food, music, gas, etc. For example, parents may give the teenager $100 a month (or $25 a week) out of which the teenager will buy all of their meals away from home unless they are accompanied by a family member, all of the gas for their car if they are of driving age, and all of their clothes except what the parents agree to buy. (This should be clearly delineated, such as: "We will buy all of your underclothing, all of your socks, three pairs of shoes per year, and one coat per year. Everything else will be your responsibility." Parents may choose to buy additional clothing items at Christmas or birthdays.) Such an arrangement gives the teenager the ability to learn to manage money.

Parents need to be as realistic as possible in setting the amount they will give the teenager. Once the amount is set, it should not be changed simply because the teenager complains, "It's just not enough." If the teenager wants more than he can purchase with the allowance, then the teenager must secure a means of earning money outside the family. If they are not old enough to work in a fast-food restaurant, they can mow lawns, babysit, deliver papers, or find any number of other jobs available to younger teens. In this arrangement, the teen is not only learning how to manage money, he is learning the value of money by choosing to work to secure additional funds. However, if the parents break down and give the teenager additional funds when the teenager complains, the parent is sabotaging the teen's learning of financial responsibility. In affluent America, thousands of parents have undermined their teenager's fiscal well-being by freely supplying money at the teenager's request.

Be sure you communicate to the teenager that you are giving her an allowance because you love her, and you want her to learn to handle money responsibly. You are not giving it to the teen because of her household duties. That is a totally separate matter of responsibility. I suggest that the teenager not be allowed to earn additional funds from parents. It confuses the issue of normal expected household responsibilities. It is far better to let them earn the money outside the family. I also believe that loaning the teenager money is a mistake. It is teaching the teenager to purchase beyond one's income. This is teaching the teenagers the wrong lesson.

5. Dating

The subject of dating creates trauma in the hearts of many parents. Some parents remember their own dating experience and don't want their teenagers to do what they did. Some parents hear and shudder at statistics like the following compiled by the National Commission on Adolescent Sexual Health a number of years ago: "By the time they are 20 years old, more than 3/4 of adolescents have had sexual intercourse. Every year one million teenage girls become pregnant; more than 1/2 million have a child; and 3 million teenagers acquire a sexually transmitted disease."[7]

Such statistics encourage some parents to vow never to let their teenagers date. "If I can keep them away from the opposite sex until they are twenty, maybe they will be mature enough to handle it," these parents reason. Also, there is much confusion on what constitutes a date. If a date is considered one boy and one girl going out for a hamburger and later spending three hours in the backseat of a car stimulating each other sexually, then one may question whether teenagers should date at all. But if dating is a group of teenagers, male and female, going out for a hamburger and later attending a ballgame or going to a dance, then dating can be a positive experience in building the teenager's self-esteem and developing relationship skills necessary for mature adult romantic relationships.

I won't indicate when your son or daughter should begin dating, though Steinberg warns that girls who begin dating in early adolescence risk being caught up in "a misty, romantic feeling" and will typically date older boys who are "likely to overpower [the teenage girls] psychologically as well as physically."[8] Steinberg also indicates that early dating also affects the girl's relationships with other girls her age. Because she is dating an older boy, she tends to associate with older girls. This may gain her temporary acceptance with the older crowd but will alienate her from girls her own age. As a result, she loses the valuable experience of intimate friendships with girls her age. After thirty years of marriage and family counseling, I am convinced that early adolescence is the time for the teenager to develop same-sex friendships, gradually followed by group activities involving girls and boys, and in later adolescence to one-on-one dating. As teenagers mature, they feel more comfortable with the opposite sex and are more confident about themselves and are better able to handle dates and potential romance. To short-circuit this process of social and emotional development by encouraging one-on-one dating in early adolescence is a serious mistake.

If you happen to concur with my opinion, then the time to paint this picture in the mind of your child is when they are nine, ten, and eleven. Then they enter the teenage years with no pressure for early dating, expecting rather to spend more time away from family and with friends of the same sex under the supervision of the friends' parents or under your own supervision. They will anticipate group activities with members of the opposite sex and feel little pressure to pair off until later adolescence.

Obviously, I am picturing the ideal and this does not account for the teenager's varying personality, insecurities, peer pressures, and other factors which may push the teenager to seek emotional solace in a romantic relationship in the early teenage years. This is another reason why emotional love from parents is so important to the young teenager. This is especially true of the opposite-sex parent. If the teenage girl feels loved by her father, she is less likely to seek emotional love from an older teenager. The teenage boy who feels loved by his mother is less likely to exploit a younger girl for his own emotional or physical pleasure.

So you are having your family conference with your thirteen-year-old teenager, seeking to formulate rules and consequences for his or her dating behavior. What are the central issues? I would suggest that concern for your teenager's physical and emotional health would be at the top of the list. Second, and perhaps equal in importance, is the healthy development of emotional and social maturity that will equip your teenager for a romantic relationship when the time comes.

What rules might foster such healthy social maturation? *Rule:* Same-sex friendships with teenagers of their own age will be encouraged in early adolescence. But for your teenager to spend the night at a friend's house, you must first have met the teenager and talked with their parents. (This safeguards your teenager from getting involved with someone whose values and lifestyle might be detrimental to your teenager.) Any such overnight visit must be done when parents are in the home. *Consequences for violation:* No such overnight visits for three months, and no allowance for one week. *Rule:* The teenager is free to attend group activities involving boys and girls so long as there is adult supervision and the parent approves of the activities. Parents reserve the right to say "no" to any activity they feel would be detrimental to the teenager's well-being. *Consequences for violation:* No such group activities for one month, and no allowance for one week.

As the teenager grows older there will be more and more opportunities, activities, and potential relationships vying for his attention. I think it is important to note here that the "dating scene" that your teenager is confronted with is one that bears only a slight resemblance to the one you faced when you were a teenager.

This is where it becomes so critical that you and your teenager have set up rules and consequences, far in advance, that serve your teenager's best interests. Even though things are so different today than they were a generation ago, teenagers still have the same needs, insecurities, and longings they've always had.

Please understand that these rules and consequences are only suggestive. Each parent and teenager must work out what they believe to be fair and workable. Obviously the earlier these rules and consequences are formed, the more likely the teenager is to see them as fair and for his/her benefit.

6. *Substance Abuse: Alcohol and Drugs*

More and more teenagers are taking more and more drugs at earlier and earlier ages. The results are obvious—more teenaged alcoholics and drug addicts. Nothing destroys independence faster than alcohol and drug addiction. What can a parent do to guarantee that their teenage son or daughter will not get involved with drugs and alcohol? The answer: nothing. Parents cannot follow teenagers twenty-four hours a day and make sure they do not ingest alcohol and drugs. There are, however, things a parent can do to make drug use less likely.

First, and most powerfully, is to model abstinence. Teenagers who watch parents take a drink every night to unwind are far more likely to use and abuse alcohol. Teenagers who watch parents misuse prescription drugs are much more likely to become drug users. I cannot overstate the power of a parental model at this point. Once the model is in place, however, there are other things that parents can do to make their teenagers less likely to be involved in drug use.

Let's come back to our paradigm of rules and consequences. What are the major concerns surrounding alcohol and drug abuse? Usually the key issue is fear of the teenager becoming an alcoholic or a drug addict. This is certainly a legitimate fear. A second concern may be that the teenager will be riding with a drunken driver and be hurt or killed in an automobile accident. A third concern is that the teenager might associate with other teenagers who abuse drugs and alcohol and in that mind-altered state get involved in criminal activities. All of these are very real and legitimate concerns.

What rules might address these concerns? In the family forum, parents should certainly express their desire that the teenager abstain from drug and alcohol use. Parents should explain that this is not because of some ill-founded, illogical, religious, or personal belief but is based on the facts that have been clearly researched. Knowing that the teenager will someday be an adult and can make his own decisions about drug and alcohol use, it is perfectly legitimate for parents to insist that while the teenager is at home, the rule is no alcohol and no drugs.

Consequences for violation should be stringent. It should be pointed out to the teenager that most drugs are illegal and are in violation of state and federal laws. If the teenager is found in possession of illegal drugs, he may suffer not only parental consequences but also judicial consequences. One parent suggested that the first offense would remove driving privileges for one month. The second offense, three months. The third offense, the car that had been purchased by the parent would be sold and never replaced by the parent. If the parents lovingly and firmly administer the first two consequences, chances are the car will never have to be sold. If, however, they let the first two slide, you can be certain that the teenager will proceed further in his substance abuse.

As you explore these and other areas of teaching your teenager responsible behavior, you will want to periodically reevaluate rules and consequences, giving the teenager more freedom and more responsibility as he gets older but never separating the two. All rules and consequences should have the best interest of the teenager in mind and should be formed after much thought with due consideration to the teenager's thoughts and feelings but under the canopy of loving, parental authority. The loving parent cares enough to do the hard work of forming rules and enforcing consequences.

CHAPTER 13

Loving When Your Teen Fails

Daniel was a big man with thick brown hair and a well-trimmed beard. He was a success in business, and he was very highly respected in the community. However, in my office, his tears were now watering the roots of his beard.

"I can't believe it, Dr. Chapman. It all seems like a bad dream. I wish I could wake up, and it would all have been just a nightmare. But I know it is reality. And I don't know what to do. I want to do the right thing, but in my state of mind I don't know if I am capable of doing the right thing. A part of me wants to strangle him and ask, 'How could you do this to us?' Another part of me wants to take him into my arms and hold him forever. My wife is so upset she couldn't even come with me today. He's coming home tomorrow, and we don't know how to respond."

Daniel's tears, anger, frustration, and confusion all focused on his nineteen-year-old son. His son had called home from college the night before and informed Daniel and his wife, Micki, that he had gotten a girl pregnant and that she refused to have an abortion. He told them that he knew this news would hurt them and that he knew what he had done was wrong. But he needed help and he didn't know where else to turn. Daniel and Micki had spent a sleepless night trying to console each other but there was no consolation. Their son had failed and there were no easy answers.

Only those parents who have received similar phone calls can fully empathize with this couple. The pain seems unbearable. Emotions rush through their bodies. Hurt, anger, pity, sorrow, and deep love—the kind of love that brings more hurt, anger, pity, and sorrow—slosh through their minds like socks in a washer. They hope against hope that when the sun rises tomorrow it will all be a colossal hoax, but in their hearts the parents know that they must face the reality of broken dreams.

Teens Will Fail

As I recall Daniel and Micki's pain, I am reminded of what child psychologist John Rosemond said: "Good parenting is doing the *right* thing when a child does the *wrong* thing."[1]

That's what this chapter is about: the right response to our teens' wrong choices. The fact is we cannot keep our children from failing, and we certainly cannot keep our teenagers from failing. Our best efforts at loving and parenting them do not guarantee their success. Teenagers are their own people, and they are free to make choices: good and bad. When teenagers make poor choices, parents suffer. This is the nature of parenting. Because we are related, when the teenager fails, the rest of the family feels the shock waves. No one, however, feels the trauma more deeply than the parents of the teenager.

Not all teenage failures are of the same magnitude. As with physical earthquakes, there are minor tremors and there are 7.5 quakes. Obviously the aftermath of one is not the same as the other. Alex missed three consecutive free throws—any one of which would have sealed victory for his team—as his friends and family watched. Alex failed, but his failure was a small tremor compared to the failure of Daniel and Micki's son. But what if a scout from a major university was in the stands that night? Well, there are different kinds of failures . . .

Kinds of Failures

Failure to Meet Our Expectations

Not only are there different levels of failure, there are also different kinds of failure. Alex's situation illustrates failure to perform up to one's ability or the expectations of parents. These kinds of failures occur all the time in the field of sports, the arts, schoolwork, the debate team, etc. Some of these performance failures occur because parents and/or teenagers have accepted unrealistic expectations. If the goal is unrealistic, then failure is inevitable. Parents should understand from the outset that not every player can win the gold medal. If parents are only satisfied with perfection—they will be dissatisfied with their teenager. Performance goals, if not attainable, will create discouragement.

In competitive events, parents may need to help the teenager reframe the results. Coming in second place in the playoff tournament is not failure. If there are thirty teams in the league, it means your team is better than twenty-eight. Coming in last place in the marathon means that you are a better runner than the one hundred thousand people who didn't enter the race. If your teenage daughter was playing clarinet in the marching band that placed tenth among one hundred high schools in a competition, her band ranked in the ninetieth percentile! That's cause to celebrate, not to bemoan the band's "poor showing."

Of course, everyone would like to win all the time. However, the fact that there can only be one winner does not mean that everyone else is a loser. In our highly competitive "winning is everything" culture, teenagers are often set up to fail by well-meaning adults (usually parents).

Another reason some teenagers experience performance failures is that they have been pushed into areas of performance in which they have little or no interest or aptitude. Because of the parent's interest in athletics, the teenager is pushed into the athletic arena when she really wanted to play in the band. The teenager could have been an excellent trumpet player; instead, she is "sitting on the bench," feeling like a failure in the athletic world. Pushing teenagers into areas where they have no interest is setting them up to fail.

I once knew a father who pushed his son to become a medical doctor.

His son struggled through organic chemistry and physics in college and after two emotional breakdowns finally made it through medical school. On the day of his graduation, he presented his M.D. sheepskin to his father and refused to go for his residency. The last I heard, he was working at McDonald's trying to decide what he wanted to do with his life. Certainly parents may expose the teenager to their own areas of interest—that only makes sense. But they must not seek to manipulate the teenager into following their own desires when they do not coincide with the teenager's interests and abilities. Parents who recognize this tendency in themselves should rent and view the film *Dead Poets Society*. This story of a young high school student who could not please his father will leave you weeping, but wiser.

Moral Failures

A second category of teenage failure is far more devastating to both the teen and the parent. It's what I am calling moral failures. These failures occur when the teenager violates the moral code by which the family has lived through the years. From earliest childhood, parents communicate their moral values to their children. It is the hope of most parents that in the teenage years, though the teens may test these moral values, they will come to adopt them as their own. Obviously, this does not always happen.

Teenagers violate moral codes in two ways. Some make the conscious choice to reject the family's moral values and establish their own. Others, while accepting the family's value system in practice, violate its precepts. Either of these creates pain for the parents and usually for the teenager as well. Parents truly grieve when their son or daughter makes a moral decision that the parents know is wrong. They know that consequences are in store for the teen. And the teen usually senses that the parents feel let down, or at least sense the pain of, or even estrangement from, his parents.

The consequences for moral failures can often be devastating to parents. Most parents have secretly asked themselves the question, "What would I do if my teenage daughter called and said 'I'm pregnant'? Or if my son called and gave me the message his girlfriend is pregnant [the same message that Daniel and Micki received]? What would I do if I learned that my teenager was using or pushing drugs? What would I do if my teenager informed me that he/she had AIDS or some other sexually transmitted disease? What would I do if I received a call from the police department saying that my teen had been arrested for theft or assault?"

In truth, these are questions that thousands of parents will be forced to answer during their child's teenage years.

Bring Redemption to Your Teen's Moral Failures

In the remaining pages of this chapter, I want to suggest some practical ideas that have helped other parents process teenage moral failure in a redemptive manner. We are acting as good parents when we use our teen's failure to show compassion and restoration, "doing the right thing when [our] child does the wrong thing," as Rosemond says.

1. Don't Blame Yourself

Before you help your teenage son or daughter, you must first deal with your own response. The first response many parents have when their teen fails is to ask, "What did we do wrong?" It is a logical question, particularly in a society that has placed so much emphasis on the value of proper parenting. However, many self-help books and parenting seminars have overestimated the power of positive parenting and failed to properly reckon with the teenager's freedom of choice. The fact is that teenagers can and will make choices both in the home and outside the home. These choices always have consequences. Poor choices produce detrimental results, whereas wise choices bring positive fruit.

Parents cannot be in the physical presence of their teenagers twenty-four hours a day and control their behavior. You did this when your daughter was three, but you cannot do it when she is thirteen. As frightening as it may seem, your teen must be given freedom to make decisions.

Choices expand during the teenage years. This is a necessary and usually healthy process, but it does increase the risk of teenage failure. Parents who blame themselves are doing their teenager a disservice. The bottom line is the teenager made a poor decision and is now suffering the results. If the parent takes the blame, the guilt is removed from the teenager. The teenager is more than happy to find someone else who will take the blame for his present woes. When he is able to roll his guilt on your shoulders, the teen is less likely to learn from the failure and more likely to repeat it in the future.

Parents who are most prone to take the blame for their teen's moral failures are parents who realize they did a poor job of parenting in the earlier years. I do not wish to convey the idea that parents do not have a responsibility to be good parents. What I am saying is that you are responsible for your own failure, not the failures of the teenager. If you recognize specific failures in your past parenting patterns, confess these to God and the teenager. Seek forgiveness from both but don't accept responsibility for your teenager's poor choices.

2. Don't "Preach"

Usually the teenager is already feeling guilty. Teens know when their behavior hurts parents. They are aware when they violate the moral codes they have been taught. Preaching is unnecessary. To Daniel, the tearful father we met at the beginning of this chapter, I said, "When your son comes home from college tomorrow, don't let your first words be words of condemnation. Don't say, 'Why did you do this? You know this violates everything we've taught you through the years. How could you do this to us? Don't you know you are tearing our hearts apart? You have ruined everything. I can't believe you could be so stupid.'

"I understand that you may have all of these thoughts and feelings," I continued, "but your son does not need to hear such condemnation. He is already having those thoughts and asking himself those questions. If you make these statements and ask these questions, he may become defensive and stop wrestling with the questions himself."

A teenager who has failed needs to wrestle with his own guilt, but he does not need further condemnation.

3. Don't Try to Fix It

The natural response of many parents is to try to minimize what has happened. Jumping into a "damage control" mode and protecting the teenager is, in my opinion, an extremely unwise move. If you seek to remove the natural consequences of the teen's failure, you are working against your teen's maturity. Teens learn some of life's deepest lessons through experiencing the consequences of failure. When parents remove these consequences the teenager gets another message. The message is one that fosters irresponsibility. "I can do wrong and someone else will take care of the consequences." Such a conclusion makes it difficult for the teenager to learn responsibility.

I know it is difficult to watch our teenagers suffer the consequences of their decisions, but to remove the consequences is to remove one of life's greatest teachers. I remember the parent who said to me, "The most difficult thing I have ever done in my life was to walk out of jail and leave my son behind bars. I knew I could get him out on bail but I knew that if I did, he would be selling drugs again that night. For his own good, I chose to let him suffer the consequences of his own wrongdoing. In retrospect, it was one of the best decisions I ever made on his behalf."

Thus far, we have focused on the negatives: Don't blame yourself; don't preach to the teenager; don't try to fix it. Now let's turn to the positive side.

4. Give Your Teenager Unconditional Love

First, demonstrate unconditional love to your teen. This does not contradict what we have just said. Allowing the teenager to experience the consequences of his own failure is itself an act of love. In so doing, you are looking out for the well-being of the teenager—which is the essence of love. However, what I am focusing on in this section is meeting the teen's emotional need for love. This is where the five love languages are exceedingly important. If you know your teenager's love language, this is the time to speak that primary language loudly, while demonstrating the other four love languages as often as possible.

The teen's moral failure creates feelings of guilt. These emotions push the teenager away from you. As Adam and Eve tried to hide in the garden from the presence of God, so your teenager may try to hide from you. The teen may fear your condemnation. God's response to Adam and Eve is a good model for parents. Indeed, He let them suffer the consequences of their wrongdoing but, at the same time, He gave them a gift. They were trying to hide themselves with fig leaves. He gave them leather coats. The wise parent will give love to the teenager no matter what the failure.

Daniel and Micki told me later that when their son arrived home from college, they met him at the door with outstretched arms. They each gave him a long tearful embrace and said, "We love you." Then they sat down and listened as their son confessed his wrongdoing and asked their forgiveness. Unconditional love creates the climate for open dialogue. The teenager needs to know that no matter what he has done, someone is there who still believes in him, who still believes that he is valuable, and who is willing to forgive. When the teenager senses emotional love from parents, he is more likely to face the failure head-on, accepting the consequences as deserved, and learning something positive from the experience.

5. Listen to the Teenager with Empathy

We said earlier that this is not the time for preaching. It is a time for empathetic listening. Empathy means to enter into the feelings of another. Parents need to put themselves into the shoes of the teenager and try to understand what led to the failure as well as what the teenager is feeling at the moment. If the teenager senses that parents are trying to understand and identify with her feelings, the teenager is encouraged to continue talking. On the other hand, if the teenager senses that parents are listening with a judgmental attitude, ready to condemn her actions, the conversation will be short-lived and the teenager will walk away feeling unloved and rejected.

Empathetic listening is enhanced by asking reflective questions, such as: "Are you saying that this is what you were feeling at the time? Are you saying that you felt we would not understand? Is this what you are saying?" Such reflective questions give the teenager a chance to clarify thoughts and emotions, and they give the parents an opportunity to understand.

Empathetic listening leads to understanding, which creates the platform for being able to truly help the teenager.

6. Give the Teenager Support

Once you have listened and have come to understand the thoughts and feelings of the teenager, you are now in a position to give emotional support. Let the teen know that while you do not agree with what he has done and that you cannot remove all the consequences, you want him to know that you are with him and will stand by his side as he walks through the process of dealing with the consequences of this failure.

After Daniel and Micki had listened to their son's story and had shared their tears of regret, Daniel said to his son, "I want you to know that Mom and I are with you. Obviously we are not happy about what has happened. We don't know all the results that must be faced. But we will walk with you through the process. We hope that you will do the responsible thing by the young lady and the baby, and we will do all we can to support you. This does not mean that we will take care of the financial expenses. That is something we believe to be your responsibility. But we will encourage you, pray for you, and do everything we can to help you become a stronger person on the other side of this."

Those are statements of emotional support. The teenager needs to know that even though he has failed, he is not alone in life. Someone cares enough to join him in his pain and difficulty.

7. Give Guidance to the Teenager

Give your teenager guidance. By guidance, I do not mean manipulation. Parents who tend to have controlling personalities often want to control the teenager's behavior after a moral failure. When the parent decides what ought to be done and tries to convince the teenager to do it, this is manipulation, not guidance. Guidance is helping the teenager think through the situation so as to be able to make wise choices in responding to the consequences of the moral failure.

Parents must take seriously the feelings, thoughts, and desires of the teenager. These must not be swept away as being insignificant. Because the teenager has had a moral failure does not mean that the parents must now make the decisions for the teenager. The teenager cannot become a responsible adult without having freedom to grapple with his situation and make decisions regarding where he goes from here.

One way in which parents may give guidance to a teenager is by helping the teen follow his own thoughts to their logical conclusion. For example, Daniel and Micki's son said, "One of the thoughts I had is simply to leave the state, move to California, and try to start my life over again." Micki was wise not to follow her desire to say, "That is a stupid idea. That won't solve anything." Rather she asked, "If you could find enough money to get to California, what kind of work would you pursue?" After her son shared his ideas on the subject, she said, "Would you see yourself sending money to take care of the child's expenses?" to which her son responded, "Certainly. I'm going to do the responsible thing."

"Perhaps you could research a little online to check out the insurance rates in California," Micki then suggested. "It's probably a good idea to search a little so as to have some idea of what it would cost you to rent an apartment." With these and several other questions, Micki was helping her son think about the implications of his idea of moving to California.

Parents who learn how to give this kind of guidance will continue to influence their teenager's decisions in a positive direction. However, parents who make quick judgments and dogmatic statements about their teenager's ideas will stop the flow of communication and drive the teenager to someone else for guidance. The teen may even make a foolish decision as a purely defensive reaction to the parents' "know it all" attitude.

This kind of guidance is difficult for many parents to give. It is easier to tell our teenagers what we think and to make dogmatic statements about the validity or absurdity of their ideas. This does not help a teenager develop his own decision-making skills. The teenager does not need commands—he needs guidance.

Another way of giving guidance is to share your ideas as possibilities. "One possible approach might be . . . " is far more helpful than "What I think you ought to do is . . . " Remember, in spite of moral failure, the teenager still wants to develop independence and self-identity. Parents must not forget this major motif of the teenage years in trying to help their teenager learn from failure. You may well see possibilities that your teenager does not see. Your teenager could profit from your insights if you share them as possibilities, not as "oughts."

If, after all your dialogue, you see a teenager about to make what you think to be a detrimental decision, one that simply will make the situation worse rather than better, you can continue to give guidance if you share it as advice rather than commands. The issue is to recognize the teenager's autonomy as a person and that ultimately, he will make his own decisions.

In such a situation, a parent might say, "Brad, I certainly want this to be your decision because you are the one who will have to live with the consequences. But I want to share with you my fears if you make that decision." You share your fears and then say, "Those are the things that make me feel it might be better to take another approach." Then you share your own ideas. You have not removed the responsibility of decision making from the shoulders of your teenager nor have you blatantly demanded that your teen do what you want, but you have given the teen the benefit of your thoughts and feelings stated in a way that he is more likely to receive.

If, in the end, the teenager makes the decision that you believe to be unwise then you allow him to suffer the natural outcomes of that decision. If those outcomes turn out to be negative and the teenager fails again, you repeat the process discussed above, remembering that you cannot control the life of your teenager. Being a responsible parent is helping your teenager learn from his own mistakes.

Teenage Failure Through Drugs and Alcohol

Since drug and alcohol abuse is such a major problem in our society, I feel compelled to say a word to parents about helping teenagers who fail in this area. But first a word about prevention. The best thing parents can do is to be proactive in the early teenage years in regards to tobacco, alcohol, and drugs, applying the principles we have discussed about letting the teenager experience the consequences of his choices.

In a family forum, Jack and Sarah explain to their thirteen-year-old that now that he is a teenager, they know he may be pressured by his friends to smoke, to drink, and to use drugs. "Since you are now a teenager, we believe you are old enough to be an informed citizen on these matters. Therefore, one of the things we are going to do as a family is to attend the informational classes at the local hospital on the detrimental effects of smoking cigarettes." Jack added: "Mom and I want you to know the facts before your friends try to pressure you to smoke."

Most teenagers will respond positively to such an opportunity and, having seen pictures of diseased lungs, will choose not to smoke. As a wise parent, you can take a similar approach to both alcohol and drugs, whether it is attending a class that is available in your community, or reading about and discussing the detrimental effects of alcohol and drugs online. Providing your teenager with information about the detrimental effects of alcohol and drugs is information that can lead the teenager to make wise decisions before he is pressured by his peers to drink or use drugs.

After giving your younger teenager such foundational information, you may periodically clip articles from the newspaper about young people who are killed by drunk drivers. You may want to take your teenager for a visit to the local rescue mission and let her sit through a meal and a service with the men or women whose lives have been wrecked by alcohol and drugs. In so doing, you are giving your younger teenager a picture of the other side of drug and alcohol use that she will never see on television or in movies.

You may also talk with your teenager about the way advertisers seek to exploit people by showing her only one side of drinking and drug use. If your teenager can begin to see that advertisers are seeking to exploit her and other young people, she is likely to respond negatively to the lure of TV advertisements and the pressure of peers. This proactive approach is, in my opinion, one of the best things parents can do for younger teenagers.

However, if you did not have such a family forum when your daughter or son was thirteen and you find out that your fifteen-year-old is already smoking cigarettes, you have a choice to make. Rather than ignoring it, hoping it will go away, or searching the teenager's drawers and throwing away the cigarettes hoping they will not return, it is far better to confront the teenager with the knowledge you have received and say to him: "I think you know that it is my sincere desire that you not smoke. My reason is that smoking is so extremely detrimental to your health. However, I know that I cannot make that decision for you. I can keep you from smoking in the house, but I cannot control your behavior when you are away. If you are going to smoke, I want it to be an informed decision. Therefore, I am going to ask you to attend the informational classes held at the local hospital on what happens when people smoke. I know that I cannot make you attend these classes but because I care so much about you, I am going to strongly urge you to attend." If the teenager attends, he can then make an informed decision. Most teenagers will choose not to smoke when they know the facts.

However, if the teenager refuses to attend the classes, the parents can do two things. First, they can make certain the teenager does not smoke in the house—feel free to mention the dangers to other family members of secondhand smoke in the house. Second, until the teenager attends the class, the parent can withhold allowances and privileges as a leverage to encourage the teenager's compliance. Again, you are not making the teenager do anything; you are simply demonstrating that freedom and responsibility always go together. They no longer have the freedom of receiving an allowance until they attend the class.

Perhaps the substance is not tobacco, but alcohol or drugs. Alcohol and drug abuse not only can impair and eventually destroy the life of the user, but either one will harm the lives of all those around the user. If your teenager is an addict, you need professional help. I strongly suggest two steps. One, discover and begin attending a local Al-Anon meeting. Al-Anon is a national group designed to help parents who have teenagers (or other family members) who are hooked on alcohol or drugs.[2] Second, go for personal counseling. Find a counselor who has expertise in helping parents make wise decisions about how to relate to their teenager who is addicted. Parents cannot handle this alone. They need the wisdom of those who are experienced in working with addicted teens. There are programs that can help. These programs are worth exploring, but you need the wisdom of a professional to help you make wise decisions in the process. If the parents of an addict do not get help, they are unlikely to be able to help their teenager.

The Power of Love

Many parents can join Daniel and Micki in saying, "The darkest night of our lives was the beginning of a deeper and more meaningful relationship with our teenager." Love is the key for turning tragedy into triumph. Parents who will love enough not to blame themselves, not to preach, not to try to fix it, who will listen with empathy, give support and guidance—all in the spirit of unconditional love—will likely see their teenager take giant steps toward maturity as they walk through the consequences of teenage failure.

What I have tried to say in this chapter is that the teenager who fails does not need parents who walk behind, kicking him, or condemning her for a personal failure. Nor does the teen need parents who will walk ahead, pulling him, trying to get him to conform to the parents' wishes. What the teenager needs is parents who will walk alongside, speaking the teen's love language with a sincere desire to learn with the teenager how to take responsible steps after failure. Parents who do this will indeed be successful parents.

CHAPTER 14

The Single Parent Family, Teenagers, and the Love Languages

Amanda's world is not easy. It hasn't been easy for a long time. She's a single mom with two teenagers, Marc, age fifteen, and Julie, age thirteen. She has raised them alone since her husband left five years ago.

She felt the trauma of a difficult divorce and worked through her own sense of rejection. Soon, however, she took charge of her life. With the help of her parents, Amanda finished her nurse's training and since then has worked at the local hospital. Without working full-time, she would not have made it because her husband's child support payments were inadequate and often sporadic.

In spite of all that she has accomplished, Amanda lives with an underlying sense of guilt. Because of her job, she was not able to spend as much time with the children as she would have liked. She was not always able to attend their after-school activities. Julie was only eight when her father left, now she's a developing adolescent, and Amanda still can't spend as much time with her and her brother as she would like. She feels that Julie and Marc are growing up, slipping through her fingers, and she wonders if they are ready for what lies ahead. One day she tells herself, *I did the best I could.* The next day she says, *I'm not sure I did enough.* Lately, Marc has been talking back, and he is often critical of his mom. Julie wants to start dating, and Amanda thinks she is too young.

In my office, Amanda said, "I'm not sure I am up to this. I think I've done fairly well up until now, but I don't know if I can endure the teenage years."

I was hearing from Amanda what I have heard from hundreds of single parents through the years. "Will someone please help me? I'm not sure I can do this by myself."

Fortunately, there is help for parents like Amanda. Most communities provide single parent support groups, sponsored by churches and other civic groups. Most libraries have numerous volumes directed to single parents. There are also all kinds of valuable resources available on the Internet. I will not seek to duplicate the information that is available through other resources. The focus of this chapter is to help the single parent effectively meet his or her teenager's emotional need for love.

Common Challenges

Receiving Love from One Parent

Of course, each single parent household is unique. However, there are some common threads running through single adult families that often make this a more difficult task than when both parents are present. Most obvious is the reality that only one parent is the custodial parent. Though joint custody, where the child theoretically spends an equal time with each parent, sometimes works in early childhood, it is seldom workable with teenagers. The most common arrangement is that the mother will be the custodial parent while the father sees the teenager either regularly or sporadically, and in fewer cases, never. Thus in the day-to-day experience of life where the teenager needs to feel loved, there is only one parent available. Ideally, the teenager needs a mother and a father who are expressing love on a daily basis. In a single parent family, this is simply impossible. The noncustodial parent almost never has daily contact with the teenager. The custodial parent must accept this reality. That is one reason why the content of this book is so important for single parents.

If you are the only parent giving love on a daily basis, it is extremely important for you to discover and speak your teen's primary love language. Otherwise, you may love your teenager by acts of service when they are craving words of affirmation. As one single mom said, "I can't believe the difference in my daughter. I attended a workshop where they were discussing the five love languages and how to discover your teenager's primary language. It became obvious to me that my daughter's love language was quality time. I had been giving her words of affirmation and wondering why she was responding so negatively. When I started spending quality time with her, most of which was taking her with me as I ran errands, it is amazing how her attitude changed because I was focusing on her. Within two weeks, she was a different person, and the whole climate in our house greatly improved."

Erupting Emotions

Another common factor in single parent homes is that the feelings buried in childhood often erupt in the teenage years. The emotions of hurt, anger, and rejection, which were seldom expressed in childhood, may give rise to low self-esteem, feelings of inadequacy and depression, or critical words and abusive behavior. These emotions and the resulting behavior are seldom expressed in the presence of the noncustodial parent. This may be because the teenager believes the parent would not understand or perhaps not care, or it may be that the teen does not want to disturb the positive aspects of the relationship with the noncustodial parent. It is the custodial parent who bears the brunt of the teenager's formerly dormant emotions.

This is extremely hard on most custodial parents. Often such parents feel unappreciated and experience anger toward the teenager. The parent who has worked hard to care for the child feels that she is mistreated by the teen.

Please know that you are not alone in having such feelings. Such emotions are common for single parents when their children become teenagers. Remember, your teen's strong emotions are in keeping with his or her developing desire for independence and self-identity. As an emerging adult whose intellectual, spiritual, and moral values are being formed, your teen is forced to grapple with what appear to be the inequities of life. This process can be positive. If the teenager is to enter adulthood with some level of maturity, these hurts from the past must surface and be processed. However, this process may be painful for both teenager and parent.

The Proper Responses

Focus on the Teen's Emotions

The important issue for the custodial parent is to focus on the teenager's emotions—not the teenager's behavior. This is exactly the opposite of what we typically do. Listen to Roberta as she describes her frustration with her fifteen-year-old son, Sam. "He seems so down on himself. No matter how much I praise him—he expresses feelings of inadequacy. He seems depressed much of the time. I try to be happy and upbeat. I try to focus on the positive things about our lives, but he continues to mope around the house. Nothing I do seems to make any difference."

Roberta is trying to change Sam's behavior, but she is ignoring his underlying feelings. Instead, she must realize that behind her teenager's behavior, which is based upon his depression and low self-esteem, are deeper feelings of hurt, anger, and rejection. These are the emotions that need to be discussed. If she continues to focus her attention on trying to talk her son into a more positive self-esteem and more positive actions, by telling him how smart and capable he is, her efforts will produce minimal results. However, if she can create an atmosphere where Sam can talk about his childhood, particularly the emotions centering on the divorce, death, or abandonment of the father, she will begin to see a change in his attitude toward himself.

I'm not suggesting this is an easy process. It is not something that happens in one conversation. The teenager must express these hurtful emotions from the past, and the thoughts and memories surrounding them, again and again while the custodial parent listens sympathetically. The surfacing and sharing of these hurts is necessary if the teenager is to find emotional healing.

Madison complained of a different problem. "My sixteen-year-old has gone ballistic," she said. "The other night, she actually cursed me. I could not believe my ears. Several times she has thrown things, sometimes at me but usually at the wall. This behavior is totally uncharacteristic." As I later talked with Madison's daughter, I discovered that she had recently started dating. The prospects of having a romantic relationship with a male had surfaced all the dormant emotions she had toward her father. Since her father had abandoned her—she feared the abandonment of her boyfriend. The anger she had held under wraps was now erupting. She was angry with her mother, whom she still somewhat blamed for the divorce. She was angry with her father for walking away, and even angrier that he had shown so little interest in her since he left. This angry behavior was actually a positive indicator that she was now beginning to deal with the hurts of the past.

When Madison understood this, she was able to focus on helping her daughter talk about these buried emotions rather than condemning her daughter's negative behavior. The behavior will eventually subside if the inner pain can be processed through talking and sympathetic listening.

Listen and Tell Your Teen the Truth

In processing the teenager's hurts of the heart, the custodial parent must do the hard work of listening, and it is critical that she also tell the truth. When the teen's father left, you gave simple explanations that seemed to satisfy the child at the time. You thought the issues were settled. Now the teenager is bringing all of it to the surface again, only now the teenager will ask much more specific questions. She wants to know what went on before the divorce; she wants to know what the marriage was like in the earlier years. She will ask, "If my father is so bad, then why did you marry him?" If the mother died, the teenager will again ask questions about the nature of the illness or accident. "Tell me again, what was Mom like? What did she say about me?" These are typical questions of the teenager—hard, painful, probing questions, but questions that deserve answers.

Whatever you do, don't make excuses for your own behavior or for the behavior of your ex-spouse. *Tell the truth.* If your teenagers find out later that you lied about the details, and they most likely will, they will lose respect for you. Perhaps you felt that when they were children, they could not handle the truth. But now they are teenagers, and their emotional healing process demands that they know the truth.

Lynn, the mother of a fourteen-year-old, said, "The hardest thing I ever did was to answer my teenage daughter's questions. I know I should have told her earlier, but it never seemed to be the right time. Now she was asking the hard questions, and I had to choose whether I would lie or tell the truth. It was the most painful night of my life when I told her that I was never married to her father, that I met him at a beach party, had sex with him, and never saw him again. Before that, I had always told her that he left when she was young. At first, my daughter was angry. She said I should have told her earlier, but the thing that hurt me most was when she said, 'So you really didn't want me. I was an accident.'

"I listened to her angry words and I told her I understood how she could feel that way, but I hoped my actions since that night had demonstrated to her that I loved her from the very beginning. We had many talks in the weeks following that night. We've cried, laughed, and hugged each other. I've never felt closer to my daughter than now, and I think she loves me in a more mature way than ever before. I always knew the day would come when I would have to tell her the truth. I had hoped I would have the courage. I'm glad I did." The old adage is true: the truth hurts. But the truth also heals.

Knowing and speaking your teenager's primary love language can be an extremely helpful part of this truth-telling experience. A touch, a word of affirmation, a gift, an act of service, or quality time will help create the climate where the painful process of healing the past can take place. Lynn's daughter later said to me, "It was my mom's hugs that brought me through. I have never felt so hurt in my whole life as when she told me the truth. I wanted to run, I wanted to scream, and I wanted to kill myself. But when Mom hugged me, it felt like a blanket of love." Her primary love language was physical touch, and it spoke deeply to her hurting heart. Lynn also spoke the other love languages. She gave her much quality time through these long discussions. She verbally affirmed her love on numerous occasions. There were special gifts and acts of service—all of which played a role in her daughter's healing. But physical touch was the blanket of love.

Respect the Teen's Unrealistic Desires

I'd like to take the time to mention one other challenge for the single parent—along with the parent's proper response. The teenager in a single parent family will experience many unrealistic desires. You may hear your teenage son say, "I wish Dad would come to my games." But you know the reality is his dad lives a thousand miles away, has a new wife, and two children. He is not coming to your son's games. Your sixteen-year-old daughter may say, "Daddy is going to buy me a car," but you know that her father is deeply in debt and could not buy her a car even if he wanted to. These impossible dreams are a part of the teenager's imagination. It is a subconscious attempt to have the kind of family the teenager desires.

The natural response of many custodial parents is to blast these dreams with grenades of reality. In my opinion, this is a serious mistake. It is far better to affirm the teen's desires and let reality dawn a day at a time. "You wish that your father would buy you a new car. That's a good thought. I wish he would too." "You wish that your father could come to your games. I wish he could too. That would really be nice." If you have these kind of positive responses to your teenager's unrealistic desires, you are affirming the teen as a person. If you feel compelled to blast his ideas and say something negative about your ex-spouse, you are encouraging the teenager to keep his desires to himself. In accepting and affirming these desires, you will encourage the flow of communication. Often the teenager already knows that these are impossible dreams, but dreaming is a part of his coping with the less-than-ideal realities.

If you have contact with your former spouse, you can share some of the teenager's desires. This should never be done in a demanding way but simply as a matter of sharing information. "I thought you'd like to know that several times Seth has said, 'I wish Dad could come to my games.' I know that's probably impossible, but if it would ever work out, it would mean a lot to him. If not, maybe you could ask about his games when you call him." This is good information for the noncustodial parent. "Stephanie has said several times that you are going to buy her a car when she turns sixteen. I'm not asking you to do it, but I thought you'd like to know what she's been saying." On the other hand, sharing the teen's desires with the noncustodial parent is sometimes best done by the teenager, especially if the parents are in an adversarial relationship. To say to the teenager, "Maybe you should share that with your father," might be the encouragement the teenager needs.

It will be extremely difficult for some parents, who are pessimistic by nature, to do what I have just suggested. By nature, they see the glass half empty, and they spill this pessimism on their teenager. If this happens to be a part of your personality, I urge you to go for personal counseling and seek to turn your own spirit in a more optimistic direction. Dreams, even impossible dreams, are a part of what makes life bearable on the dark days, and who knows what is impossible? Even the Bible says: "Where there is no vision, the people perish."[1]

If the teen's desires are unrealistic, that will eventually become obvious. But as the teen shares desires, he is sharing information that the parent would not otherwise know. Often many of these desires are in keeping with the teenager's primary love language. Chances are the teen that is wishing his father would come to his games has the primary love language of quality time, and the teenager who is asking for a car may be exhibiting the language of gifts. A teenager may have desires that fall outside his or her primary love language, but if you catalog the desires, you will find that the majority of them fall within the parameters of the teen's primary love language.

For Noncustodial Parents

Now let me share some words with noncustodial parents. I hope you do not feel that I have been unfair to you in the earlier portion of this chapter. The fact is you can play a significant and important role in the life of your teenager. *Your teenager needs you.* Many noncustodial parents acknowledge that they need help in knowing how to parent their teenagers. Some noncustodial parents see the teenager on a regular basis, such as every other weekend or one weekend a month. Others live hundreds of miles from their teenagers and visits are sporadic, interlaced with phone calls and e-mails. How do you make the most of what you have? Let me deal with a couple of pitfalls and then share some positive ideas.

Avoid the Pitfalls

One common pitfall is what is sometimes called the "Disneyland Daddy" syndrome. This is where the time with your teenager is spent in taking your teen to ball games, on shopping excursions, to the movies, and other amusement centers. Your attention is focused on activities rather than the teenager himself. Because of the limited amount of time these parents have with their teenagers, they tend to plan each meeting in advance and try to have fun with their teenager. The teenager and parent come to the end of the visit exhausted. Don't misunderstand me. There is nothing wrong with having fun with your teenager and most teenagers enjoy activities. But let's face it—life is not always fun and games. Your teenager needs to see you in more normal settings. Since you are excluded from the everyday routines of your teenager during the week, you may have little idea of what is going on in the mind and heart of your teenager. This requires open dialogue in a relaxed and sometimes not so relaxed atmosphere. The parent cannot meet the emotional needs of the teenager until he first discovers those needs.

It is not uncommon that fathers and teenagers have different views about the visitation relationship. Research indicates that the father often thinks he has fulfilled his responsibility, whereas the teenager feels something is missing. The father thinks he has loved well, but the teenager feels rejected. One study indicated that whereas most fathers thought they had fulfilled their obligations, three out of four teenagers had the impression that they did not mean very much to their fathers. "They thought that their fathers were physically, but not emotionally, present."[2] It seems apparent that the Disneyland Daddy syndrome is not the most positive approach for parenting your teenager.

Another pitfall is taking advantage of your teenager's time and/or willingness to help. One fifteen-year-old girl tells of arriving at her father's house for the weekend and being told that he had to leave because of an appointment and being asked to babysit two younger half brothers until he and his wife returned. He and his wife returned the following evening well after midnight. Obviously, this teenager did not find her visit to be very satisfying. When her next regularly scheduled visitation rolled around, she refused to go.

I am not implying that the teenager cannot do work during the visit. In fact, involving your teen in the normal flow of your life can be a very positive experience. Simple things like going to the grocery store or bank together can be meaningful to your teenager. But the teen knows when she is being taken advantage of. When your interests center on yourself, rather than the teenager, the teen will quickly resent such behavior.

The third pitfall is to assume that your teenager is emotionally stable if he is not talking about problems. Teens are often reluctant to share their emotional struggles with the noncustodial parent. There are many reasons for this. Some fear that if they are honest about their feelings, their fathers will reject them even further and that visits will cease. Some who remember their father's violent outbursts from younger years fear the wrath of fathers if they share their honest thoughts and feelings. Others fail to share because they don't want to "rock the boat." They may think that it is better to have a calm surface relationship than to get into an argument and make things worse. The bottom line is that silence does not indicate health.

Most teenagers whose parents live apart have the kind of feelings and thoughts discussed earlier in this chapter. They desperately need to share those thoughts and emotions with you. The wise parent will create an atmosphere where this can be done without fear of retaliation. In most cases, the parent will need to take the initiative by saying something like, "I know that my not living with your mother has probably caused a lot of hurt and struggle in your life. If you'd like to talk about it, I want you to know that I am willing to listen. If I continue to do things or fail to do things that disappoint or hurt you, I hope you will tell me. I want to be a better father, and I'm open to your suggestions." Your teenager may not immediately respond to such an invitation, but if he becomes convinced that you are sincere, sooner or later you will hear his struggles.

Deal with Your Personal Issues

If you are a noncustodial parent and have little contact with your teenager because of your own personal problems—emotional struggles, financial problems, drug addiction, etc.—let me encourage you to take steps to deal with your problems. After more than thirty years of marriage and family counseling, I can say with some certainty that the day will come when you will regret your lack of involvement in your teenager's life. You can avoid those regrets by taking positive action now to face your problems head-on and get the help you need.

Find a counselor, pastor, or trusted friend, and be honest about your own needs. Let someone guide you in finding the necessary help in turning your life toward a more positive direction. When you take these steps, your teenager will begin to respect you and you are one step closer to a meaningful relationship with your teenager.

Be Involved and Speak Your Teen's Love Language

On the other hand, if you are having regular contact with your teenager, let me encourage you to make the most of your visits, phone calls, and e-mails. Share your life with your teenager—both successes and failures. Be honest and real with your teenager. The teenager is looking for authenticity. Take time to ask questions that will probe your teenager's thoughts, feelings, and desires. You need not have all the answers. In fact, it's better if you don't have all the answers. The teenager needs to learn to think for himself. Seek to get in touch with the teenager's emotions. Don't limit your time to surface talk. Ask your ex-spouse for ideas that might enhance your contacts with the teenager.

In addition, don't criticize the custodial parent when you are with your teenager. If the teenager is critical about the other parent, listen to what the teen is saying. Then ask his advice on how you might help. Be sympathetic with the teenager's criticisms, but don't join in by adding your own.

Along with being involved, it is imperative that you learn how to speak the five love languages. Discover your teenager's primary love language and speak it often. Your greatest contribution to the well-being of your teenager is to let her know that you care about her well-being, and you love her. Don't assume that she feels your love. Many parents are speaking their own love language and assuming that the teenager feels loved. Thousands of teenagers do not. There is no substitute for speaking your teenager's primary love language.

No matter what your relationship with your teenager has been like through the years—it is never too late to make it better. An honest confession about past failures and requesting the teenager's forgiveness could be the first step on a long road of renewing a warm, loving relationship between you and your teenager. The journey may be painful for both of you, but I can assure you it is a journey worth taking.

Important Guidelines

As we conclude this chapter, I'd like to offer several important guidelines, to both custodial and noncustodial parents, for showing love to your teenagers.

1. *Listen to your teenager.* You cannot adequately raise teenagers without listening to what they are saying. Parents who ignore the statements of teenagers will almost certainly fail to meet the teens' emotional needs and they will be unable to guide them in a positive direction. Guidance starts where the teenager is. Without listening, the parent will be unable to take the first step. In listening to the teenager, you are speaking quality time; you are giving your teen undivided attention. You are communicating that the teen is a person worth knowing, and you are giving a portion of your life to the teenager.

2. *Teach your teenager to handle anger in a positive way.* The first step here may be working on your own patterns of anger management. Most single parents have had their own share of anger. Some of them have learned to handle it constructively, others are holding it inside, and some others are constantly exploding with angry words and behavior. Your teenager is not likely to be open to your help until they see you taking steps to manage your own anger. If you or your teenager needs improvement in this key element of personal relationships, I encourage you to read the previous chapters on *Love and Anger* one more time.

3. *Kindly but firmly keep the boundaries in place.* The teenager needs the security of knowing that parents care enough to say "no" to those things they believe to be detrimental to the teenager. It obviously works best if

both parents can talk about boundaries and have the same list of rules and consequences. This communicates to the teenager that both parents care equally about his well-being.

4. *Above all else, give your teenager unconditional love.* Good or bad, right or wrong, the teenager needs to feel that someone cares and that someone genuinely loves him. The people he would most like to love him are his parents. If possible, each of you should join in the common goal of keeping your teen's love tank full.

5. *Consider joining a single parent study group.* These are available in most communities—often sponsored by civic groups, churches, and colleges. Such groups typically form a two-way street. Someone will have walked your road and have practical ideas for you. Others have recently entered the world of single parenting, and you will be able to encourage them. Such groups can be very helpful in the difficult task of being a successful single parent.

6. *Enlist the help of extended family, friends, and churches.* If your extended family lives nearby, and you think they would be a positive influence on your teenager—don't hesitate to ask for their help. A grandfather, uncle, or older cousin can often supply much of what an absent father has failed to do. Grandmothers have been lifesavers for many troubled teenagers. If family members do not live nearby, or you believe they would be a negative influence on your teenager, then look for friends who can help you.

Along with civic groups and colleges, I have mentioned considering churches as a single parent resource. Churches can be not only the source of spiritual encouragement but also a place for building wholesome friendships. Many churches provide weekly classes for single adults while providing exciting activities for teenagers. Make it a family thing and discuss what you've learned together. In the context of the church and family, many single parents have found individuals who have played significantly positive roles in the development of their teenagers. You need not walk alone; there are people in your community who care. Keep searching until you find them.

Sooner or later your teenager will reach adulthood. They will be immeasurably blessed if they can honestly say, "I know my mother loved me. I know my father loved me." It is my sincere hope that this chapter will help you toward one day hearing that blessing.

CHAPTER 15

The Blended Family, Teenagers, and the Love Languages

One July week a few years ago, I served as the counselor at a youth camp in the beautiful Blue Ridge Mountains of North Carolina. Michael had asked for an appointment, and I invited him to hike to the lookout tower while we talked. (I've found that teenagers talk more freely while walking.) We had been on the trail about fifteen minutes, making small talk, when I asked about Michael's family. He said, "That's what I wanted to talk with you about. I don't like having a stepfather.

"Before Mom married Rod, things were great," Michael continued. "Mom and I got along well. I felt like she respected me. Now I feel like I am a child again. She and Rod have come up with all these stupid rules. I know it was Rod's idea because Mom is not strict like that. But now Mom is siding with Rod and they are making my life miserable. I wish I could go live with my dad."

What Michael said to me that day has been heard countless times in counselor's offices across this country. Most teenagers find life in the blended family extremely difficult. In Michael's case, he had made an adjustment to one particular arrangement years ago, and now he was upset by an all-new family arrangement. After his father left them six years ago, he learned to cope with living with just his mother and younger sister. He had worked through the trauma of feeling rejected by his father. He and his mom had many long conversations in the months after his father left. Michael knew about his mother's sacrifice and her role; she had worked hard in order to meet the needs of the family. "Mom depended upon me to look after my sister in the afternoon after school until she got home," he said with both pride and confidence. "I also helped out with the laundry, and she counted on me to keep the car clean. Mom was treating me like an adult."

But all of that had changed since Rod entered the family. Rod wanted to wash the car with Michael, and he was telling Michael things about how to wash the car that Michael already knew. "Does he think I'm stupid?" Michael asked.

As I listened to Michael, I was relatively sure that his stepfather was sincere and was trying to bond with Michael by doing things together. But I also knew that if Michael's stepdad didn't wake up to the reality that Michael was a teenager whose independence was being threatened—he would eventually find himself rejected by Michael. I also knew that while Michael's mother was currently siding with her new husband, it was only a matter of time until her concern for Michael would cause conflicts between her and Rod. Research has discovered that the number one cause for divorce in second marriages is conflicts over child rearing,[1] and the divorce rate in second marriages is substantially higher than in first marriages.

The blended family is established in a very different way from the original biological family. For the original family, the couple had a period of time together before the child came. The child entered the world as an infant, and the couple learned the skills of parenting over time. The blended family, on the other hand, seldom gives the couple an extended period to be alone. The children are a part of the family from the start. Often the children are now teenagers who are developing their own independence and self-identity. All the normal struggles in this process are intensified for the teenager who wakes up to find himself a part of a blended family.

The Teen's Perceptions and the Parent's Fears

Often the teenager perceives that his own developmental process is being thwarted for the sake of his parents' happiness. If this resentment is not processed, it will soon become bitterness, and the bitterness will lead to rebellion. Meanwhile, parents often enter a second marriage with three overwhelming fears: fear of losing their teenager's love, fear of rebellion, and fear of ruining their teenager's lives.

One mother said, "I have ruined my daughter's life, first by my divorce and then by remarrying. How could I have been so stupid?" These fears often lead the biological parent to forget the basic concepts of discipline and anger management we have discussed earlier in this book. The parent placates the teenager and ends up ostracizing the new spouse.

Numerous other challenges may face the blended family: fighting between stepchildren, sexual abuse between step-siblings or between the teenager and the new spouse, conflicts between biological parent and the stepparent over the definition of "appropriate family guidelines," conflicts between the blended family and the other family over what is best for the teenager. The list of potential challenges extends on and on.

It is not my purpose to paint a bleak picture. It is my purpose to be realistic and to offer hope. I believe that understanding the five love languages and applying them in the blended family will do much to create a climate where blended families can succeed. Since the basic emotional need for all of us is the need to feel loved and since love is the oil that greases the wheels of family relationships, then if we can learn to effectively communicate love, we can create a healthy environment for the blended family. Genuine love creates an atmosphere where conflicts can be resolved, the teenager can continue a healthy process toward independence, and parents can enjoy a growing marital relationship. However, when the emotional need for love is not met, then the family often shifts into an adversarial mode.

Let me encourage you to take seriously the concepts we have shared in the earlier chapters of this book. Practice speaking the love languages to each other, talk about various dialects you might use in expressing love to the teenager, and determine the teen's primary love language (as well as your own). Read a book on the dynamics of blended family relationships.

Realize that teenagers will not always be open to your expressions of love. Don't take it personally. Try a different approach the next day. Learn from your mistakes.

Now let's look at some of the common challenges of loving teenagers in a blended family.

Feelings of Rejection and Jealousy

Often the teenager will be slow in responding to the love of a stepparent. There are many reasons for this. First, the teen may fear rejection by the stepparent. As the stepparent, you may have difficulty understanding why the teenager draws away. After all, you have decided to love the teenager; you have made honest efforts at reaching out and expressing love. What you must understand is that the teenager has already suffered the trauma of parental rejection as he watched his parents go through a divorce. Perhaps this happened when he was a child, but the trauma is a painful memory for the teenager, one he does not want to see repeated. He doesn't want to go through new hurts.

Second, the teenager may also be jealous of the stepparent's relationship with his biological parent. He could see you as a threat to his relationship with that parent. Since you came along, he may be receiving less attention from the biological parent. The teen may also be jealous of the affection you show toward your biological children. Another common struggle for teenagers in blended families is the feeling of being disloyal to his mother if he responds to the love of his stepmother or disloyal to his father if he responds to the love of his stepfather.

An additional reason teenagers may not easily respond to the love of a stepparent is that they see the stepparent as a threat to their independence. This is part of what Michael, whom we met at the beginning of this chapter, was feeling toward his stepfather Rod.

Dealing with the Teen's Feelings

What can a stepparent do to overcome some of these barriers? *The first step is to give the teenager freedom to be who he is.* The emotions and fears we have just discussed are real to the teenager even if they are not expressed. Don't try to talk the teenager out of his thoughts and feelings. If the teen chooses to talk, listen carefully and affirm his emotions. "That makes a lot of sense. I can understand how you would feel that way." These are statements of affirmation.

In contrast, lofty proclamations will ring empty with the teenager. "You don't have to worry about me. I'm never going to leave. And I'm certainly not going to take your mother away from you." The teenager will respond far more positively to your actions than they will to your promises.

Like any adolescent, the teenager growing up in the blended family will express rebellion in his or her search for self-identity and independence. It is also important to understand that in a blended family, hurt, grief, and depression often underlie the teen's rebellious behavior. You will misjudge the teenager if you judge the behavior without reflection upon the emotions. Remember that, and you will show compassion and mercy.

Second, *don't try to take the place of the biological parent of the same sex as yourself*. Encourage the teenager to love and relate to their biological parent whenever that is possible. Don't verbally deprecate the biological parent in front of the teenager.

Dealing with Your Own Thoughts and Feelings

Recognize Your Various Feelings and Fears

Next, be honest with yourself about your own thoughts and feelings. If your marriage is shaky, you too may be pulling back from the teenager because of your fear of another divorce. You don't want to get too close to the teenager because you don't want to hurt him again. You may also feel guilty because you do not have a close relationship with your own biological children. It may seem unfair to build a close relationship with stepchildren when there is so much distance between you and your own children. And there is also the possibility that you may withdraw from the teenager because you are jealous of the time and attention he gets from your spouse. There is also a bit of selfishness in all of us. It is difficult to get outside our own wants, wishes, and desires. Self-centeredness, however, will ultimately destroy any relationship.

How do you deal with these thoughts and emotions that can be barriers to building a love relationship with your teenage stepchild? I suggest that you begin by talking to yourself. Admit the thoughts and emotions. They will not go away by trying to ignore them. But be sure to tell yourself the truth. Selfishness leads to isolation and loneliness. The happiest people in the world are those who give—not those who grab.

Love Your Children and Your Stepchildren

You can love your wife, your biological children, and your stepchildren, and have love left over for others. Your spouse can love her biological children, and you, and still have love left over for your biological children.

The reality is you cannot love your spouse and fail to love her/his children. The parental relationship will not allow the two to be separated. Remember, you always reap what you sow. Love, and eventually you will be loved. Give, and it will be given to you. Success in the blended family is not found in "dealing with the children." It is found in loving the children toward maturity.

Patience is a necessity for stepparents who are committed to loving stepchildren. Teenagers, unlike younger children, do not just sit there and soak in the love you offer. The teen has thoughts, past experiences, and behavior patterns. Research has shown that it typically takes a minimum of eighteen months to two years for the teenager and stepparent to form a loving relationship.[2]

How do you know when the teenager is bonding with you? The signs include the following: The teenager will begin to show spontaneous affection and willingness to receive your love, he will initiate conversations and activities with you, and he will express awareness of your needs and will ask your opinion. When this happens, you are reaping the sweet fruit of unconditional love. Building a strong loving relationship with your teenage stepchild is one of the best things you can do for your marriage. Parents love their biological children and when they see a spouse making consistent efforts to relate positively to their teen, their love for the spouse is enhanced.

Discipline in the Blended Family

Discipline typically becomes a major area of struggle for blended families. Most biological parents do not agree on all the details surrounding the discipline of children. In a blended family, the differences are magnified because one of you is the biological parent and the other is a stepparent, and because each of you had a history in another family before you became a part of a blended family.

The purpose of discipline is to help our teenagers grow into mature and responsible adults. The process may be more difficult in the blended family than in the original family, but it is not impossible. Let me encourage the two of you to read again the material in chapter 12 on love and responsibility. This will help you get the basic concepts of discipline clearly in mind.

About Changes in Family Rules and Discipline

The teenager knows that things are going to be different now that the stepparent has arrived. Some things will have to change. For example, if the stepparent also brings teenagers to the marriage, there may have to be new guidelines about how the teen dresses and undresses in the house. Don't try to be a lone ranger in determining what these guidelines will be. As parents, you have the final word, but teenagers need to be a part of the process in deciding the rules and the consequences when rules are broken. It is highly possible that you and your spouse will have major disagreements over what the rules or consequences should be. My rule of thumb is that in the first year of the blended family, the stepparent should defer to the biological parent's wishes. As emotional relationships are enhanced, these can be revisited in the future if the stepparent feels the guidelines are not adequate.

Minimal changes make for maximum acceptance in the early stages of the blended family. If you establish the idea of a family forum early on, with the understanding that any family member can call a forum anytime he or she feels that something about family life needs to be changed, you will establish a vehicle for processing emotions and ideas. If, in these forums, you take seriously the thoughts and feelings of the teenager as well as younger children while maintaining the right to have the final word, you will create an atmosphere in which family conflicts can be resolved.

It will be much easier to create such a climate if members of the family feel loved by each other. Thus speaking each other's primary love language remains vital to healthy relationships among family members.

About Enforcement and Consistency

During the first year of the blended family, when consequences must be enforced, it's better for the biological parent to be the enforcing parent. Later, when there has been more bonding between stepparent and teenager, either parent can enforce the consequences, especially if the consequences have been determined beforehand and are clearly understood by all. Speaking the teenager's love language before and after enforcing the consequences enhances the likelihood that the teenager will receive the consequences as fair.

Consistency in enforcing consequences is extremely important, particularly in a blended family. In Sam and Yvonne's blended family, the rule was that bicycles were to be placed in the garage before 8 p.m. The consequence for failing to do so was losing the privilege of riding the bicycle the next day. Everyone agreed that this was a fair rule and in the summer when the days were longer, the time was extended to 9 p.m. The rule was tested three weeks later when Yvonne's thirteen-year-old, Erica, left her bicycle in the neighbor's yard. At 9:10 p.m., the neighbor's son knocked on the door with Erica's bicycle in tow.

Yvonne thanked the neighbor's son, put the bicycle in the garage, and calmly informed Erica of what had happened, reminding her that she could not ride the bicycle the next day.

The next afternoon, Erica came to her mother wearing her most winsome smile and said, "I have a favor to ask. I know I left my bike out last night, but this afternoon all the girls in the neighborhood are riding over to the park. Mom, if you will let me go, I won't ride my bicycle for the next two days. Two days for one. That's fair, isn't it, Mom?"

Yvonne wanted to say yes. It would be much easier and Erica's offer did sound fair, but Yvonne knew that if she complied, it would give Erica the wrong message. So she said, "I'm sorry, Erica. But you know the rule and you know the consequences. You don't get to ride the bicycle the next day after you leave it out."

Seeing that her winsome smile and pleasant approach wasn't going to work, Erica switched to the whining mode. "Oh, Mom. Please, Mom. It's fair, it's fair. Two days for one. Two days for one. It's fair, Mom."

"I'm sorry," Yvonne said, "but you know the rule."

Then Erica turned on the pressure. "How could you do this to me? All the girls are going. I don't like all of these new rules. It wasn't this way before Sam came. You used to be understanding and kind. Now you're all hung up on enforcing the rules. It's not fair. I don't like living in this house."

Yvonne wanted to strike back and to tell Erica to leave Sam out of this, that it had nothing to do with him, but wisely she kept those thoughts to herself and said, "Baby, I know you want to go riding with the girls. I wish I could say yes, but that's simply not the way life is. When we do wrong, we have to suffer the consequences. Sometimes those consequences are very painful. I understand how you could be upset. And I understand that sometimes you wish Sam wasn't here, that maybe you think I might give in if Sam wasn't here. I hope that's not true. I loved you before Sam was here and I love you now. I'm enforcing the rule because I know it's best for you."

"Don't give me that *best for you* stuff," Erica muttered as she walked out of the room. Yvonne breathed a sigh of relief and secretly asked herself, *Am I doing the right thing?* In her mind, she knew she was right, but in her heart she wondered. Erica sulked and stayed in her room the rest of the afternoon and evening and the next morning silently left for school. However, that afternoon she was back to her normal cheerful self and never mentioned it again. (This story happened several years ago, and Yvonne reports that Erica has never left her bicycle out of the garage again.) Teenagers learn responsibility when consequences are enforced.

About five weeks later, Sam's fifteen-year old-son, Shawn, also left his bicycle out past the appointed hour. Sam discovered it when he came home from a meeting that evening. He put the bicycle in the garage and informed Shawn that he would not be able to ride his bicycle the next day. "Okay," Shawn said. "I understand. I just forgot." Imagine Yvonne's consternation when the next afternoon she heard Sam say to Shawn, "How about taking your bicycle and going to the store and getting some bread? I need to mow the lawn."

Yvonne said quietly, "Sam, I thought Shawn wasn't supposed to ride his bicycle today"— to which Sam responded, "We need some bread and I need to mow the grass. He's helping me. It's okay."

Shawn rode off to the store, but Yvonne went inside, feeling betrayed. *I can't believe he did that*, she said to herself. *When Erica finds out, I will never hear the end of it.*

Sam has violated one of the cardinal principles of good parental discipline: consistency. Unless he confesses his wrongdoing to Yvonne and Erica, the emotional barrier he has erected by his actions will impede his efforts to build a loving relationship with his wife and stepdaughter. Shawn is also hurt here because of his father's inconsistency. Few things are more important in the blended family than the parents being committed to consistency in enforcing the consequences.

Other Areas of Conflict

Attitudes and Behaviors of the Other Parent

Often the teenager has another family—the other biological parent and maybe his or her spouse. This can create relational challenges. Parents may have unresolved feelings from the previous marriage. One or both parents may still harbor anger, bitterness, or hatred for the ex-spouse. Some also still have feelings of love for the former spouse that can be particularly troublesome to the new partner.

In addition, behavior patterns that led to the divorce may still persist and be troublesome. For example, the workaholic husband who never came home when he promised may now be late in picking up the teenager for the visitation weekend. This may irritate the teenager's mother just as it did when she was married to his father. The whining, "pick at the details" mother may still irritate the ex-husband as he tries to work out the logistics of spending time with his teenager. Many of these conflicts center on "the visitation" because this is the arena in which the ex-spouses most often have contact.

Furthermore, the biological parents will blame each other for any emotional or behavioral problems the teenager may exhibit. Sometimes the other biological parent may make negative comments about you and your spouse to the teenager. These comments are then repeated to you by the teenager—typically when he is angry. Sixteen-year-old Kyle spouted out to his mother, "Dad said that he couldn't buy me a car because he had to spend all of his money paying for everything over here." Seventeen-year-old Lisa was in a fray with her stepmother when she said, "My mom said that you are just a horrible person because you took my father away from us. I'll never forgive you for that."

Different Sets of Values

Sometimes the values of the other household are vastly different from your own. This may be one of the factors that led to the divorce. The greatest struggle between families is often in the area of moral values. The presence of pornographic material, the use of strong profanities, or the use of alcohol and drugs may no longer exist at home, but they remain when the teenager visits his noncustodial parent. The types of movies, videos, or television programs the teen can watch during such visitations may differ from yours. So may the religious beliefs. All of these may become sources of conflict. However, unless these activities are illegal, the custodial parent cannot regulate what takes place when the teenager is with the other parent.

This is where your own positive program of love and discipline is so important. If the teenager is learning from you that every choice has consequences, and if you are giving the teenager choices and making sure he suffers the consequences when he makes poor choices, the teen is more likely to carry this truth with him when he visits the other family. He may be exposed to thoughts and behaviors that you would prefer he not hear or see, but he is more likely to make wise decisions because of the solid love and discipline he has experienced with you.

Keeping the teenager's love tank full is also a deterrent to wrongdoing. The teenager is naturally drawn to the parent from whom she feels genuine love. If the teenager knows you have her best interest in mind and feels deeply loved by you, she is less likely to be pulled into negative behaviors by the other parent. For one thing, she doesn't want to hurt you, and second, she knows that the other parent is not looking out for her well-being or that parent would not expose her to such destructive practices.

In responding to these conflicts with the other family, never fight fire with fire. Do not seek to combat a former spouse's negative behavior by "giving them a dose of their own medicine." Kindly but firmly respond to their behavior in what seems to be an appropriate manner. Do not let their behavior intimidate you and do not seek to intimidate them. The objective is not to defeat your ex-spouse (or the other biological parent you cannot truly replace). The objective is to keep your own marriage growing and to work toward helping your teenager develop into a responsible young adult. Open communication between you, your spouse, and the teenager about the difficulties you are experiencing with the other family and discussing possible ways to handle the conflict can be a learning experience for your teenager.

A Recipe for a Strong Blended Family

In summary, let me emphasize four basic ingredients that lead to a healthy blended family. You can enhance the power of these four ingredients by teaching the family to speak each other's primary love language.

First and foremost, there is unconditional love. Parents must take the lead in unconditionally loving each other and unconditionally loving all the children in the family. The message your teenager and younger children need to hear is "We love you no matter what." Do not say or imply by your actions, "We love you if you will be kind to each other; we love you if you do what we say; we love you if you will love us." Anything less than unconditional love is not true love at all. Love is a choice. It is choosing to look out for the other person's interests. It is seeking to meet their needs. Every teenager needs to know that there is someone who cares deeply about him, and who believes that he is important.

Giving the teen gifts, appropriate affectionate touches, acts of service, quality time, and words of affirmation are the five fundamental ways of expressing unconditional love. Your teenager needs to hear you speak all five languages, but he/she needs heavy doses of their primary love language.

Second is fairness. Please remember that fairness is not sameness. Each of your children is different, even if they are your biological children. Sometimes in efforts to be fair, parents treat each child alike. In fact, this is very unfair. Because children are different, what makes one child feel loved will not necessarily make another feel loved. If one teenager's love language is gifts and the other's is quality time and you give each of them a gift of equal value, one received far more than the other emotionally. Fairness means seeking to equally meet the unique needs of each child or teenager.

Third is attentiveness. Express interest in your teenager's world: go to activities where adults are permitted, show interest in her school and social life, listen to her ideas, desires, and feelings. In short, get into her world and stay there. Research shows that most teenagers want more time with their parents, not less.[3]

Fourth is discipline. Teenagers desperately need boundaries. Parents who take the attitude, "You are a teenager. Do what you want to do" are setting the teenager up for failure. Life without boundaries soon becomes a meaningless life. Parents who love well will set boundaries to protect the teenager from danger and to guide the teenager toward responsible self-control.

When parents in the blended family commit themselves to these fundamentals, they can beat the odds and create healthy family relationships.

Epilogue

Two winds are blowing across the horizon of contemporary teenage culture. One carries the heartfelt cries of thousands of teenagers yearning for community, structure, guidelines, and purpose. The second is a swirling wind of confusion that threatens the first wind.

For many teenagers, the world does not make sense and life hardly seems worth the effort. These teens, caught in that swirling, confusing wind, often spend much of their lives in depression and sometimes end it all in acts of self-destruction—sometimes even taking others down with them.

I deeply believe that the most important influence on the teenager's mood and choices is parental love. Without a sense of parental love, teenagers are more prone to being swept along by that wind of confusion. In contrast, teenagers who genuinely feel loved by their parents are far more likely to respond to the deep longings for community, to welcome structure, to respond positively to guidelines, and to find purpose and meaning in life. Nothing holds more potential for positively changing culture than parental love.

My purpose in writing this book has been to give practical help to sincere parents who genuinely want their teenagers to feel loved. It has been my observation, after thirty years of marriage and family counseling, that most parents love their teenagers. But it has also been my observation that thousands of these teenagers do not feel loved by their parents. *Sincerity is not enough.* If we are to effectively communicate love to a teenager, we must learn the teen's primary love language and speak it regularly. We must also learn the dialects, within the primary love language, which speak most deeply to the soul of the teenager. When we are doing this effectively, we can sprinkle in the other four love languages and they will enhance our efforts.

However, if we do not speak the primary love language of the teenager, our efforts to speak the other four love languages will not fill the love tank of our teenager.

I have tried to be honest in communicating that effectively loving a teenager is not as easy as it may seem, and certainly not as easy as loving them when they were children. In many ways, our teenagers are "moving targets." Not only are they actively involved in pursuing many interests, they also experience radical mood swings. Both of these make it difficult for parents to know which language or dialect to speak on a given day. The teen's emerging independence and developing self-identity also compound the whole process. As parents we cannot minimize these factors if we wish to effectively communicate love to our teenagers.

Although I have written primarily to parents, it is my desire that grandparents, schoolteachers, church youth leaders, counselors, and other adults who care about teenagers will become more effective at loving the teens in their life by reading and practicing the principles found in this book. Teenagers need to feel love from their parents, and they also need the love of other significant adults in their lives. Every encounter leaves the teenager feeling loved or unloved. When the teenager feels loved by the adult, the teenager is open to instruction and influence by that adult. When a teenager does not feel loved, the words of adults will fall on deaf ears. The teenager desperately needs the wisdom of older, more mature adults. But without love, the transfer of wisdom will be ineffective.

The principles laid out in this book should be practiced daily. As surely as the body of the teenager needs food daily, so the soul of the teenager craves love. I wish I could place this book into the hands of all parents of teenagers and say, "I wrote this for you. I know that you love your teenager. But I'm not certain that your teenager feels your love. Don't assume that all is well. Learn the primary love language of your teenager and speak it regularly. It is not easy. I know. I've been there. But it's worth the effort. Your teenager will be the benefactor, and so will you."

Nothing is more important to future generations than effectively loving the teenagers of this generation.

For a free online study guide, other helpful resources,
and further reading materials please visit:

www.fivelovelanguages.com

The study guide takes the concepts from *The Five Love Languages of Teenagers* book and teaches you how to apply them to your life in a practical way. It is ideal for group studies and discussion groups.

Appendix 1
How Teenagers Got Their Name

Before there were teenagers, there were teenagers . . . but they did not go by that name. It wasn't until the early 1940s that adolescents were known as much more than growing kids, but social and industrial changes— propelled by a world war—would transform all that. The "teenager" would appear, a distinct culture in a distinct age group—no longer boys and girls, but not men or women, either. They were in transition, moving toward adulthood, testing and changing in their search for identity and independence. Here's how teenagers got their name.

A decade before World War II, most children aged thirteen through nineteen had worked for a living on farms, in factories, or at home—whatever their families required of them. They helped their parents provide for the younger children in the family. They had little choice in the matter and continued in this working mode until they themselves were married.[1] There was no separate teenage culture through which they passed from childhood to adulthood. There were no teenage movies, music, or fashions because there were no teenagers.

The Great Depression of the 1930s changed all of that. With the collapse of the economy, jobs evaporated. The few jobs that were available went to fathers, and these adolescent workers were left standing idle. Feeling that they were a drain on their families, thousands of them took to the road in search of work. They took freight trains to distant cities or walked to the neighboring villages, but most of them were disappointed. Sleeping in public parks or back alleys, often begging for food, these young people posed a major social problem. As sociologist Grace Palladino wrote, "Adolescent runaways or transient youth, as they were called, forced adult society to focus on teenage problems."[2]

This social dilemma led to President Franklin Roosevelt's National Youth Administration (NYA), designed to provide training and job opportunities for America's disillusioned youth. This, in turn, led to a national emphasis on the public high school. Until this time, attending high school was not even an option for most American youth. For example, in 1900 only 6 percent of the nation's seventeen-year-olds earned diplomas from high school. In contrast by 1939, close to 75 percent of fourteen- to seventeen-year-olds were high school students.[3] The idea was that high school would provide a vocational training program in a disciplined, wholesome environment. In this setting, youth would discover their talents, develop goals, establish good work habits, and, upon graduation, become productive citizens.

This movement of vast numbers of young people from the workforce (or the unemployment lines) to public high schools created the social setting for developing a separate "teenage culture." As Palladino noted, "At the very same time that educators and NYA counselors were focusing on teenage futures, adolescents themselves were discovering a much more immediate, exciting world—a world of radio music, dancing, and fun. As the economy began to recover in the late 1930s (largely due to the outbreak of war in Europe), high school students were developing a public identity that had nothing to do with family life or adult responsibilities."[4]

Advertisers for the retail market began to see potential in these carefree high school students whose main concern in life was to have a good time and dance. They dubbed the term "teeners," later "teensters," and in 1941, "teenagers."[5] These teenagers were identified with the high school student's world of dating, driving, dancing, music, and fun. *Life* magazine offered this picture of the teenager. "They live in a jolly world of gangs, games . . . movies . . . and music. . . . They speak a curious lingo . . . adore chocolate milkshakes . . . wear moccasins everywhere . . . and drive like bats out of hell."[6]

Appendix 2
A Family Forum in Action

Holding a family forum to establish rules is a great strategy for setting boundaries and teaching responsible behavior to your teenager. Chapter 12 offers guidelines for setting rules, but how do you conduct a family forum, and what do you say?

Sometime before your child turns thirteen, call for a family forum with just the teen and his parents. Find an evening when no one has time restraints or is under undue stress. This is how one parent initiated such a family forum.

"Mom and I have called this family forum because we are aware that next week we will have a teenager in this house. We have never had one before but we are looking forward to it with great anticipation." Then turning to his son he said, "Tony, Mom and I have been talking. Over the past twelve years, we have tried to be good parents. I know that we have not been perfect and sometimes we have made mistakes. When we did, we tried to acknowledge them. We have enjoyed these twelve years with you. You have brought much joy into our lives. We are happy about your many accomplishments.

"We know that over the next eight years you are going to experience many changes," Dad continued. "Your world is going to greatly expand. There will be many changes: changes in your body, in your mind, in the world around you. You will make new friends and explore new interests. We are excited for you. We want to continue to be good parents.

"Two things are especially important to us. First, we know that over the next few years, you will become more and more independent. You will want to do your own thinking and make your own decisions. We are glad about that because when you are an adult, you will need to make all your own decisions. We want you to learn how to make good decisions while you are a teenager. Secondly, we know that you want not only more independence but you will want more responsibility. As an adult, you will be responsible for your own family and your own children. We believe that much can be learned about responsibility while you are a teenager. We want to encourage both your independence and your responsibility. Therefore, Mom and I felt we should call a family conference where we could examine our family rules together and decide which ones we should keep and which ones may need to be changed."

Mom, who had been nodding during this beautiful speech, felt compelled to say: "This doesn't mean that we are going to throw our rules away and start over. What we want to do is examine them and see what changes need to be made. We wanted your input because we know that it is your life and we want to consider what you think and how you feel. Of course, we are your parents and we will have the final word. But we think we can do a better job of being parents if we know your thoughts and feelings."

I can assure you that Tony's parents have his full attention. He was ready for this conversation, maybe even a little frightened at the prospect of becoming a teenager. But certainly, he was eager for the journey.

Your opening speech at a family forum, of course, may be different. It could be shorter; you may mention things you've noticed that show you your teen is ready to participate, showing the beginning signs of wise decision-making but also the tendency to make decisions independent of the family. Encourage your teen that this is his opportunity to be heard, and that these rules will benefit him primarily, and the family secondarily. Once you have done this, it's time to enter a dialogue and, with your teenager, to set some rules. Return to chapter 12 to learn how to set up those rules.

Appendix 3
For Further Reading

Expressing Love to Teens and Your Spouse

Ross Campbell. *How to Really Love Your Teen*. Colorado Springs: Cook, 2004.

Gary Chapman. *The Five Love Languages*. Chicago: Northfield, 2010.

Chap Clark. *Hurt: Inside the World of Today's Teenager*. Grand Rapids: Baker, 2004.

Foster W. Cline and Jim Fay. *Parenting Teens with Love and Logic*. Colorado Springs: NavPress, 2006.

James Dobson. *Preparing for Adolescence: How to Survive the Coming Years of Change*. Ventura, CA: Regal, 2005.

Dennis Rainey and Barbara Rainey with Bruce Nygren. *Parenting Today's Adolescent*. Nashville: Nelson, 2002.

Walter Wangerin Jr. *As for Me and My House*. Nashville: Nelson, 2001.

Expressing Love in the Single Parent Family

Sandra P. Aldrich. *From One Single Mother to Another: Advice and Encouragement from Someone Who's Been There*. Ventura, CA: Regal, 2005.

William L. Coleman. *What Children Need to Know When Parents Get Divorced: A Book to Read with Children Going Through the Trauma of Divorce*. Minneapolis: Bethany, 1998.

Archibald D. Hart. *Helping Children Survive Divorce*. Nashville: W Publishing, 1997.

Lynda Hunter. *Parenting on Your Own*. Grand Rapids: Zondervan, 1997.

Gary Richmond. *Successful Single Parenting: Bringing Out the Best in Your Kids*. Eugene, OR: Harvest House, 1998.

Expressing Love in the Blended Family

Ron L. Deal. *The Smart Step-Family: Seven Steps to a Healthy Family*. Grand Rapids: Bethany, 2006.

Dick Dunn. *New Faces in the Frame: A Guide to Marriage and Parenting in the Blended Family*. Nashville: LifeWay, 1994.

James D. Eckler. *Step by Step-Parenting: A Guide to Successful Living with a Blended Family*. Cincinnati: Betterway, 1993.

Tom Frydenger and Adrienne Frydenger. *The Blended Family*. Grand Rapids: Revell, 1985.

Maxine Marsolini. *Blended Families*. Chicago: Moody, 2000.

The Five Love Languages Test
for Teenagers

Instructions:

Your parents have read *The Five Love Languages for Teenagers* and are wondering if they are speaking your love language. If they haven't already explained it to you, your primary "love language" is basically one of the following: words, touch, quality time, gifts, or service. You know your parents love you because they most often express their love to you through one of these "love languages."

You're going to see thirty pairs of things that your parents might do or say to show love to you. All you have to do is pick one item in each pair that you like better. For some of them, you might like both options—but just pick one. When you're finished picking one from all thirty pairs of items, you'll be able to count your score. That'll tell you and your parents what your main love language is.

You might be thinking, "Great, my parents are trying to 'get to know me better.' They've been reading again." But give them a break! They just want to make sure that you know they love you. It's pretty bad when a parent thinks that he or she is showing you love, and then one day you say something like "I never knew if my mom or dad loved me." So take this test! You'll learn something new about yourself, and it'll help your parents love you better!

(Please Note: We've included two copies of the same test below—in case there are multiple teenagers in your family.)

The Five Love Languages Test for Teenagers

Remember, you're going to see thirty pairs of things that parents do or say to show love to their kids. They may be things your parents do or say or that you wish your parents would do or say. Pick only the ONE item in each box that you like the best, and circle the letter that goes with that item. When you finish looking at all thirty pairs, count how many times you circled each letter and transfer that letter to the appropriate blank at the end of the test.

| 1 | Asks me what I think | A |
| | Puts his/her arm around my shoulder | E |

| 2 | Goes to my ball games, recitals, etc. | B |
| | Does my laundry | D |

| 3 | Buys me clothes | C |
| | Watches TV or movies with me | B |

| 4 | Helps me with school projects | D |
| | Hugs me | E |

| 5 | Kisses me on the cheek | E |
| | Gives me money for things I need | C |

| 6 | Takes time off of work to do stuff with me | B |
| | Rubs my shoulders or back | E |

| 7 | Gives me cool things for my birthday | C |
| | Reassures me when I fail or mess up | A |

| 8 | Gives me a high five | E |
| | Respects my opinions | A |

9 Goes out to eat or shops with me — B
Lets me use his/her stuff — C

10 Tells me I'm the best son/daughter in the world — A
Drives me to places I need to go — D

11 Eats at least one meal with me most every day — B
Listens to me and helps me work through problems — A

12 Doesn't invade my privacy — D
Holds or shakes my hand — E

13 Leaves me encouraging notes — A
Knows what my favorite store is — C

14 Hangs out with me sometimes — B
Sits next to me on the couch — E

15 Tells me how proud he/she is of me — A
Cooks meals for me — D

16 Straightens my collar, necklace, etc. — E
Shows interest in stuff that I'm interested in — B

17 Allows my friends to hang out at our house — D
Pays for me to go on school or church trips — C

18 Tells me I look good — A
Listens to me without judging me — B

19 Touches or rubs my head — E
Sometimes lets me pick out where we go on family trips — D

20
Takes me to the doctor, dentist, etc. — D
Trusts me to be at home alone — C

21
Takes me on trips with him/her — B
Takes me and my friends to movies, ball games, etc. — D

22
Gives me stuff that I really like — C
Notices when I do something good — A

23
Gives me extra spending money — C
Asks me if I need help — D

24
Doesn't interrupt me when I'm talking — B
Likes the gifts I buy for him/her — C

25
Lets me sleep in late sometimes — D
Seems to really enjoy spending time with me — B

26
Pats me on the back — E
Buys me stuff and surprises me with it — C

27
Tells me he/she believes in me — A
Can ride in the car with me without lecturing me — B

28
Picks up stuff that I need from various stores — C
Sometimes holds or touches my face — E

29
Gives me some space when I'm feeling upset or angry — D
Tells me that I'm talented or special — A

30
Hugs or kisses me at least once every day — E
Says he/she is thankful that I'm his/her child — A

Your Score:

A = Words of Affirmation

B = Quality Time

C = Receiving Gifts

D = Acts of Service

E = Physical Touch

The letter or love language that receives the most points is your primary love language. If you score the same score for two love languages, then you are bilingual. If you score high on one love language and have a close second, that second highest score is your secondary love language!

The Five Love Languages Test for Teenagers

Remember, you're going to see thirty pairs of things that parents do or say to show love to their kids. They may be things your parents do or say or that you wish your parents would do or say. Pick only the ONE item in each box that you like the best, and circle the letter that goes with that item. When you finish looking at all thirty pairs, count how many times you circled each letter and transfer that letter to the appropriate blank at the end of the test.

| 1 | Asks me what I think | A |
| | Puts his/her arm around my shoulder | E |

| 2 | Goes to my ball games, recitals, etc. | B |
| | Does my laundry | D |

| 3 | Buys me clothes | C |
| | Watches TV or movies with me | B |

| 4 | Helps me with school projects | D |
| | Hugs me | E |

| 5 | Kisses me on the cheek | E |
| | Gives me money for things I need | C |

| 6 | Takes time off of work to do stuff with me | B |
| | Rubs my shoulders or back | E |

| 7 | Gives me cool things for my birthday | C |
| | Reassures me when I fail or mess up | A |

| 8 | Gives me a high five | E |
| | Respects my opinions | A |

9
Goes out to eat or shops with me — B
Lets me use his/her stuff — C

10
Tells me I'm the best son/daughter in the world — A
Drives me to places I need to go — D

11
Eats at least one meal with me most every day — B
Listens to me and helps me work through problems — A

12
Doesn't invade my privacy — D
Holds or shakes my hand — E

13
Leaves me encouraging notes — A
Knows what my favorite store is — C

14
Hangs out with me sometimes — B
Sits next to me on the couch — E

15
Tells me how proud he/she is of me — A
Cooks meals for me — D

16
Straightens my collar, necklace, etc. — E
Shows interest in stuff that I'm interested in — B

17
Allows my friends to hang out at our house — D
Pays for me to go on school or church trips — C

18
Tells me I look good — A
Listens to me without judging me — B

19
Touches or rubs my head — E
Sometimes lets me pick out where we go on family trips — D

| 20 | Takes me to the doctor, dentist, etc. | D |
| | Trusts me to be at home alone | C |

| 21 | Takes me on trips with him/her | B |
| | Takes me and my friends to movies, ball games, etc. | D |

| 22 | Gives me stuff that I really like | C |
| | Notices when I do something good | A |

| 23 | Gives me extra spending money | C |
| | Asks me if I need help | D |

| 24 | Doesn't interrupt me when I'm talking | B |
| | Likes the gifts I buy for him/her | C |

| 25 | Lets me sleep in late sometimes | D |
| | Seems to really enjoy spending time with me | B |

| 26 | Pats me on the back | E |
| | Buys me stuff and surprises me with it | C |

| 27 | Tells me he/she believes in me | A |
| | Can ride in the car with me without lecturing me | B |

| 28 | Picks up stuff that I need from various stores | C |
| | Sometimes holds or touches my face | E |

| 29 | Gives me some space when I'm feeling upset or angry | D |
| | Tells me that I'm talented or special | A |

| 30 | Hugs or kisses me at least once every day | E |
| | Says he/she is thankful that I'm his/her child | A |

Your Score:

A = Words of Affirmation

B = Quality Time

C = Receiving Gifts

D = Acts of Service

E = Physical Touch

The letter or love language that receives the most points is your primary love language. If you score the same score for two love languages, then you are bilingual. If you score high on one love language and have a close second, that second highest score is your secondary love language!

Notes

Chapter 1: Understanding Today's Teenagers

1. YOUTHviews 6, no. 8 (April 1997): 3; published by the George H. Gallup International Institute, Princeton, NJ.
2. 1 Samuel 3:10.
3. YOUTHviews 6, no. 7 (March 1999): 3.
4. James Garbarino, *Lost Boys: Why Our Sons Turn Violent and How We Can Save Them* (New York: Free Press, 1999), 6–7.
5. YOUTHviews 5, no. 9 (May 1998): 2.
6. Jerrold K. Footlick, "What Happened to the American Family?" *Newsweek* (Special Edition), Winter/Spring, 1990, 15.
7. Eric Miller with Mary Porter, *In the Shadow of the Baby Boom* (Brooklyn, NY: EPM Communications, 1994), 5.
8. Richard Louv, *Childhood's Future* (New York: Anchor, 1990), 6.
9. Christian Smith and Melinda Lundquist Denton, *Soul Searching: The Religious and Spiritual Lives of American Teenagers* (New York: Oxford University Press, 2005), 40.
10. Ibid., 31, 40, 45.
11. Ibid., 37.
12. YOUTHviews 5, no. 1 (September 1997): 1.

Chapter 2: The Key: Love from Parents

1. YOUTHviews 5, no. 8 (April 1998): 1; published by the George H. Gallup International Institute, Princeton, NJ.
2. YOUTHviews 5, no. 9 (May 1998): 2.
3. YOUTHviews 6, no. 8 (April 1999): 3.
4. YOUTHviews 5, no. 7 (March 1998): 2.
5. YOUTHviews 5, no. 6 (February 1998): 5.
6. Lawrence Steinberg and Ann Levine, *You and Your Adolescent* (New York: Harper, 1997), 2.
7. YOUTHviews 5, no. 2 (October 1997): 1, 4.

279

8. James Garbarino, *Lost Boys: Why Our Sons Turn Violent and How We Can Save Them* (New York: Free Press, 1999), 50.

9. Ibid., 51.

10. Ephesians 1:6, NKJV.

11. Ken Canfield, *The Heart of a Father* (Chicago: Northfield, 2006), 225.

12. Garbarino, *Lost Boys*, 158.

13. Those who struggle with unresolved anger may profit from reading Gary Chapman, *Anger: Handling a Powerful Emotion in a Healthy Way* (Chicago: Northfield, 2007).

14. Garbarino, *Lost Boys*, 138.

15. Daniel Goleman, *Emotional Intelligence* (New York: Bantam, 2006), 20–30.

16. David Popenoe, *Life Without Father* (New York: Free Press, 1996), 191; Henry Cloud and John Townsend, *Boundaries with Kids* (Grand Rapids: Zondervan, 1998), 46; and Garbarino, *Lost Boys*, 154.

17. Matthew 22:35–40.

18. Garbarino, *Lost Boys*, 168.

19. Ibid., 132.

Chapter 3: Love Language #1: Words of Affirmation

1. Proverbs 18:21, NKJV.

2. Anne Cassidy, "Fifteen Ways to Say 'I Love You,'" *Woman's Day*, 18 February 1997, 24.

Chapter 4: Love Language #2: Physical Touch

1. Ecclesiastes 3:1, 5.

2. For practical help on anger management, see Gary Chapman, *Anger: Handling a Powerful Emotion in a Healthy Way* (Chicago: Northfield, 2007).

3. YOUTHviews 6, no. 8 (April 1999): 1; published by the George H. Gallup International Institute, Princeton, NJ.

Chapter 5: Love Language #3: Quality Time

1. Ross Campbell, *How to Really Love Your Teen* (Colorado Springs, CO: Cook, 2004), 33.

2. Gary Smalley and Greg Smalley, *Bound by Honor* (Wheaton, IL: Tyndale, 1998), 98.

3. Eastwood Atwater, *Adolescence* (Englewood Cliffs, NJ: Prentice Hall, 1996), 198.

4. Ibid., 201–202.

5. Smalley and Smalley, *Bound by Honor*, 107.

6. Lawrence Steinberg and Ann Levine, *You and Your Adolescent* (New York: Harper, 1997), 13.

Chapter 6: Love Language #4: Acts of Service

1. Matthew 20:28.

2. Matthew 20:26.

Chapter 9: Love and Anger—PART ONE: Breaking Destructive Patterns

1. Counting to one hundred, five hundred, or even one thousand can be an effective means of restraining an immediate and uncontrolled anger response. For suggestions on how this can work, see Gary Chapman, *Anger: Handling a Powerful Emotion in a Healthy Way* (Chicago: Moody, 2007), 36.

Chapter 11: Love and the Desire for Independence

1. Lawrence Steinberg and Ann Levine, *You and Your Adolescent* (New York: Harper, 1997), 150.
2. George Sweeting, *Who Said That?* (Chicago: Moody, 1995), 302.
3. Ibid., 370.
4. Lawrence Kutner, *Making Sense of Your Teenager* (New York: William Morrow, 1997), 44.

Chapter 12: Love and the Need for Responsibility

1. Lawrence Steinberg and Ann Levine, *You and Your Adolescent* (New York: Harper, 1997), 16.
2. Ibid.
3. Ibid., 16–17.
4. Ibid., 16.
5. See Exodus 20.
6. The two commandments Jesus said were the greatest were to love God with a whole heart and to love your neighbor as you love yourself; see Mark 12:30–31.
7. Lawrence Kutner, *Making Sense of Your Teenager* (New York: William Morrow, 1997), 141.
8. Steinberg and Levine, *You and Your Adolescent*, 187.

Chapter 13: Loving When Your Teen Fails

1. John Rosemond, *Teen-Proofing: A Revolutionary Approach to Fostering Responsible Decision Making in Your Teenager* (Kansas City, MO: Andrews McMeel Publishing, 1998), 170.
2. To find a local chapter of Al-Anon, visit their website at: www.al-anon.org.

Chapter 14: The Single Parent Family, Teenagers, and the Love Languages

1. Proverbs 29:18, KJV.
2. Shmuel Shulman and Inge Seiffge-Krenke, *Fathers and Adolescents* (New York: Routledge, 1997), 97.

Chapter 15: The Blended Family, Teenagers, and the Love Languages

1. Tom and Adrienne Frydenger, *The Blended Family* (Old Tappan, NJ: Revell, 1984), 19.
2. Shmuel Shulman and Inge Seiffge-Krenke, *Fathers and Adolescents* (New York: Routledge, 1997), 123; Frydenger, *The Blended Family*, 120.
3. Lawrence Steinberg and Ann Levine, *You and Your Adolescent* (New York: Harper, 1997), 13.

Appendix 1: How Teenagers Got Their Name

1. Joseph F. Kett, *Rites of Passage: Adolescence in America, 1790 to the Present* (New York: Basic Books, 1977), 169.
2. Grace Palladino, *Teenagers: An American History* (New York: Basic Books, 1997), 37.
3. U.S. Bureau of the Census, Historical Statistics of the United States, Colonial Times to 1970, Bicentennial Edition, Part I (Washington, D.C.: Government Printing Office, 1975), 380, 379.
4. Palladino, *Teenagers*, 45–46.
5. The Oxford English Dictionary credits *Popular Science* (April 1941) with the first use of the term "teenager."
6. "Sub-Debs—They Live in a Jolly World of Gangs, Games, Gadding, Movies, Malteds, and Music," *Life*, 27 January 1941, 75.

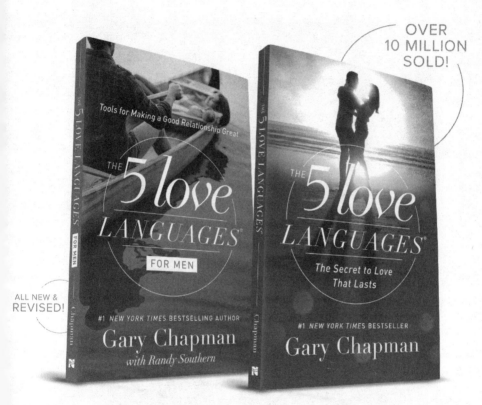

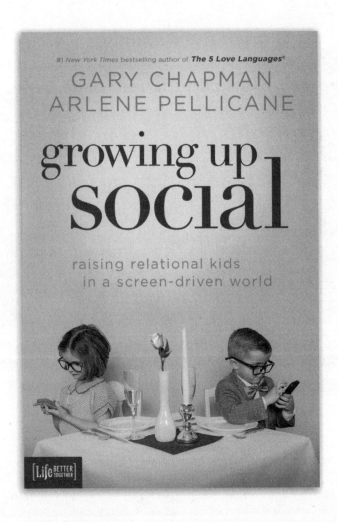

STAY CLOSE.
STAY CONNECTED.

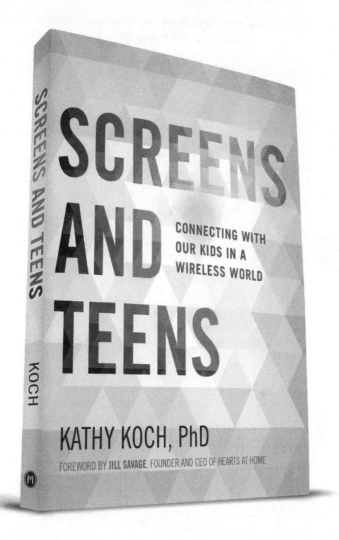

In *Screens and Teens*, Dr. Kathy helps you make sense of all this and empowers you to respond. She exposes the lies that technology can teach your teen, guides you in countering them with biblical truths and helpful practices, and shares success stories of families who have cut back on technology and prioritized each other. Kathy's research, experience, and relatability all come together for an inspiring book, sure to help you be closer with your kids.

WWW.CELEBRATEKIDS.COM

LEARNING TO LOVE OUR KIDS FOR *WHO THEY ARE.*

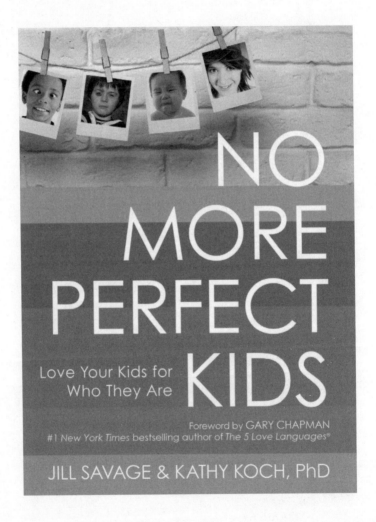